# Learn, Teach...
# Succeed...

With **REA's TExES™ Generalist 4-8 (111)** test prep, you'll be in a class all your own.

MW01049773

# TExES™ GENERALIST 4-8 (111)

TEXAS EXAMINATIONS OF EDUCATOR STANDARDS™

**Authors and Co-Editors:**

**Peggy Semingson, Ph.D.**
Assistant Professor
University of Texas at Arlington
Arlington, TX

**Ann M.L. Cavallo, Ph.D.**
Associate Dean
University of Texas at Arlington
Arlington, TX

**Contributing Authors:**

**Brooke Blevins, Ph.D.**
Assistant Professor
Baylor University
Waco, TX

**Christina Gawlik, Ph.D.**
Assistant Professor
Texas Women's University
Houston, TX

**Emily Summers, Ph.D.**
Associate Professor
Texas State University–San Marcos
San Marcos, TX

**Kevin J. White, Ph.D.**
Assistant Professor
University of Texas at Arlington
Arlington, TX

*Research & Education Association*

**Research & Education Association**
61 Ethel Road West
Piscataway, New Jersey 08854
E-mail: info@rea.com

**TExES™ Generalist 4-8 (111)
with Online Practice Exams**

**Published 2015**

Copyright © 2013 by Research & Education Association, Inc.
All rights reserved. No part of this book may be reproduced
in any form without permission of the publisher.

Printed in the United States of America

Library of Congress Control Number 2012943641

ISBN-13: 978-0-7386-1035-1
ISBN-10: 0-7386-1035-6

The competencies presented in this book were created and implemented by the Texas
Education Agency (TEA) and Educational Testing Service (ETS®). Texas Examinations of
Educator Standards and TExES are trademarks of the Texas Education Agency. For all
references in this book, TEA is a trademark of the Texas Education Agency. In addition,
ETS® is a registered trademark of Educational Testing Service.

All other trademarks cited in this publication are the property of their respective owners.

Cover image: JGI/Blend Images/Getty Images

 REA® is a registered trademark of
Research & Education Association, Inc.

# About Our Authors and Co-Editors

**Dr. Peggy Semingson** is an assistant professor of Literacy Studies at The University of Texas at Arlington. She holds degrees from The University of Texas at Austin, Texas State University, San Marcos, and the University of California, Santa Barbara. She taught bilingual students for eight years in both Southern California and Texas. She has taught fifth grade, third grade, and was a bilingual reading specialist. Dr. Semingson has published in national and state journals. Her research interests include social contexts of literacy learning, digital pedagogies, and students who face challenges in reading. She is also interested in the historical contexts of literacy learning and the politics of reading particularly as it related to phonics. She was awarded the Jeanne S. Chall Research Grant from Harvard University to use the Chall Collection to pursue research on ways to assist upper-grade students in reading instruction.

**Dr. Ann Cavallo** earned a B.S. from Niagara University, and two M.S. degrees in Science Education/Biology and a Ph.D. in Science Education from Syracuse University. She holds teaching certification in Biology, Chemistry, Earth Science, and General Science, and taught middle and high school science prior to earning her graduate degrees. She has held university faculty appointments at The University of Oklahoma, The University of California-Davis, and Wayne State University, and is currently Associate Dean for Teacher Education and Professor of Science Education at The University of Texas at Arlington. Dr. Cavallo's research investigates students' science learning approaches, reasoning, and acquisition of conceptual understandings in the context of inquiry-based teaching and learning. Dr. Cavallo has over 35 publications in internationally and nationally refereed journals, a book, and several book chapters, and has secured more than $5 million in grants from various funding agencies to support her work. She has made more than 60 presentations at professional conferences, and is active in professional organizations in science and in teacher education.

# Contributing Authors

**Dr. Brooke Blevins** is an assistant professor of Curriculum and Instruction, with an emphasis in Social Studies Education at Baylor University in Waco. She holds her Ph.D. from The University of Texas at Austin, and her Bachelor's and Master's degrees from Trinity University in San Antonio, Texas. Prior to earning her graduate degrees, Dr. Blevins taught high school in Texas. Her research interests include historical thinking as a tool for critical civic engagement, pre-service teacher preparation, inquiry-based learning, and citizenship education. Dr. Blevins' research has been presented at state and national conferences as well as in journal articles.

**Dr. Christina Gawlik** is an assistant professor of Mathematics Education in the Department of Mathematics & Computer Science at Texas Woman's University. She earned her B.S.Ed. in Middle and Secondary Mathematics Education, and her M.S.Ed. in Curriculum & Instruction from The University of Kansas. She attended Kansas State University where she earned her Ph.D. in Curriculum & Instruction with an emphasis in K-16 Mathematics Education. Dr. Gawlik taught high school mathematics before she entered into higher education where she has taught mathematics and education courses at junior colleges and universities. Dr. Gawlik actively presents at national and regional conferences about mathematics education and has collaborative projects with local K-12 teachers.

**Dr. Emily Summers** is an associate professor of Curriculum and Instruction at Texas State University–San Marcos. Her scholarship emphasizes issues of equity in education including children and youth cultures, as well as the intersections of formal and informal cultures in constructing educative experiences. Her social studies education work includes numerous peer-reviewed publications in national and international journals, professional evaluation, grants, and conference papers. Dr. Summers works in geographically and/or linguistically marginalized school districts classified as urban, rural, or with 50% or more of students maintaining home languages other than English. She has taught in both English and Spanish in K-12 public school classrooms in Texas and in Guatemala.

**Dr. Kevin J. White** is an assistant professor of Science Education at The University of Texas at Arlington. He holds degrees from Washington State University and the Illinois Institute of Technology. He taught middle and high school science prior to earning his graduate degrees. He has published internationally in the area of science education and has presented numerous times at conferences for the National Science Teachers Association, Association for Science Teacher Education, the National Association for Research in Science Teaching and the European Science Education Research Association. His research interests include the nature of science, model-based learning and conceptual change theory.

## About Research & Education Association

Founded in 1959, Research & Education Association is dedicated to publishing the finest and most effective educational materials—including study guides and test preps—for students in middle school, high school, college, graduate school, and beyond. Today, REA's wide-ranging catalog is a leading resource for teachers, students, and professionals.

## Acknowledgments

In addition to our authors, we would like to thank REA's Larry B. Kling, Vice President, Editorial, for supervising development; Pam Weston, Publisher, for setting the quality standards for production integrity and managing the publication to completion; John Paul Cording, Vice President, Technology, for coordinating the design and development of the REA Study Center; Kathleen Casey, Senior Editor, for project management and editorial preflight review; Alice Leonard, Senior Editor, and Diane Goldschmidt, Managing Editor, for post-production quality assurance; Christine Saul, Senior Graphic Artist, for cover design; and Kathy Caratozzolo of Caragraphics for typesetting.

# CONTENTS

# CHAPTER 4
# DOMAIN III: SOCIAL STUDIES

# CHAPTER 5
# DOMAIN IV: SCIENCE

# Introduction

## Passing the TExES Generalist 4–8 (111)

Congratulations! By taking the TExES Generalist 4–8 (111) exam, you're on your way to a rewarding career teaching upper-elementary or middle school students in Texas. Our book and the online tools that come with it give you everything you need to succeed on this important exam, bringing you one step closer to being certified to teach in Texas public schools. Our TExES test prep package includes:

- A complete overview of the TExES Generalist 4–8 (111) exam

- A comprehensive review of every domain

- Two full-length practice tests with online diagnostic tools to help you personalize your prep

There are many different ways to prepare for the TExES Generalist 4–8 (111) exam. What's best for you depends on how much time you have to study and how comfortable you are with the subject matter. To score your highest, you need a study system that can be customized to fit you: your schedule, your learning style, and your current level of knowledge. Let our experts help put you on the path to success and get you ready for the TExES exam.

## How to Use This Book

### About the Review

The review chapters in this book are designed to help you sharpen the basic skills you need to approach the TExES Generalist 4–8 (111) exam. The exam is composed of four domains and 58 competencies. Each of the domains and its corresponding competencies are examined in separate chapters. The skills required for all four domains are extensively discussed to optimize your understanding of what the test covers.

Keep in mind that your schooling has taught you most of what you need to know to answer the questions on the test. The education classes you took should have provided you with the know-how to make important decisions about situations you will face as a teacher. Our review is designed to help you fit the information you have acquired into specific competency components. Reviewing your class notes and textbooks together with our competency sections will give you an excellent foundation for passing the exam.

## About the REA Study Center

The best way to personalize your study plan is to get feedback on what you know and what you don't know. At the online REA Study Center, we give you two full-length practice tests with detailed score reports that pinpoint your strengths and weaknesses.

Before you review with the book, go to the REA Study Center and take Practice Test 1 as a diagnostic test. Armed with your score report, you can personalize your study plan. Review the parts of the book where you're weakest and focus your study on the areas where you need the most review.

After reviewing with the book, take Practice Test 2 at the REA Study Center to ensure that you have mastered the material and are ready for test day.

If you are studying and don't have Internet access, you can take the printed tests in the book. These are the same practice tests offered at the REA Study Center, but without the added benefits of timed testing conditions and diagnostic score reports.

# An Overview of the Test

## What's on the TExES Generalist 4-8 (111)?

The TExES Generalist 4–8 (111) exam is composed of four domains and 58 competencies. Below are the domains used as the basis for the TExES Generalist 4–8 (111) examination, as well as the percentage of the total test that each domain covers. These domains and the competencies rooted in them represent the knowledge that teams of teachers, subject area specialists, and district-level educators have determined to be important for beginning teachers.

| Domain | Approx. # of Scorable Questions | Percentage |
|---|---|---|
| English Language Arts and Reading | 37 | 31% |
| Mathematics | 28 | 23% |
| Social Studies | 28 | 23% |
| Science | 27 | 23% |

## Format of the TExES Generalist 4-8 (111)

The TExES Generalist 4–8 (111) exam is available in both paper-based and computer-based formats. You may take up to five hours to complete it. The exam includes 120 scorable multiple-choice items and approximately 10 non-scorable items used for field-testing. Your final scaled score will be based only on scorable items. Since you are not penalized for guessing, do not leave any item unanswered. All multiple-choice questions are designed to assess your knowledge of the domains and related skills mentioned above and reviewed in this book. In general, the multiple-choice questions are intended to make you think logically. You are expected in most cases to demonstrate more than an ability to recall factual information; you may be asked to think critically about the information, analyze it, consider it carefully, compare it with knowledge you have, or make a judgment about it.

Answering the multiple-choice questions is straightforward. You will have four choices labeled A, B, C, and D. You must mark your choice on a separate answer sheet or, if you are taking the computer-based version, directly below each test item. You should have plenty of time in which to complete the test, so speed is not important. However, be aware of the amount of time you are spending on each question; maintaining a steady pace when answering the questions will ensure that you complete the whole test. Using our timed online practice tests will help you pace yourself.

## When Should the TExES Generalist 4-8 (111) Be Taken?

Traditionally, teacher preparation programs determine when their candidates take the various tests required for teacher certification. These programs will also clear you to take the examinations and make final recommendations for certification to the State Board for Educator Certification (SBEC). For those seeking elementary or middle school certification right out of an undergraduate program, the test is generally taken just before graduation.

The TExES Generalist 4–8 (111) paper-based exam is usually administered five times a year at locations throughout Texas. The usual testing day is Saturday, but the test may be taken on an alternate day if a conflict, such as a religious obligation, exists. The computer-based examination is also available several times a year at specific locations.

The TExES Registration Bulletin offers information about test dates and locations, as well as registration information and instructions on how to arrange testing accommodations for those with special needs. The registration bulletin is available at *http://texes.ets.org/registrationbulletin/*.

Registration bulletins are also available at the education departments of Texas colleges and universities. To address issues that cannot be solved at the teacher preparation program level, you can contact the offices of SBEC at (512) 936-8400. You can also find information about the test and registration on the Educational Testing Service website at *http://texes.ets.org*.

## Is There a Registration Fee?

Yes, you must pay a registration fee to take the TExES Generalist 4–8 (111) exam. If you are using the registration form, all fees must be paid in full by personal check, cashier's check, or money order payable to ETS. All payments must be made in U.S. dollars. Cash will not be accepted. If you are registering via the Internet or phone during the emergency registration period, payment must be made by VISA or MasterCard.

## Scoring the Exam

The passing score for the TExES Generalist 4–8 (111) exam is generally deter-mined after the first administration of the test. At this writing, it has not been set yet; however, be aware that the cut score is generally set between 70% and 80%. There are 120 scorable multiple-choice questions on each of the practice tests. You must get 84 of those questions correct to score a 70% and 96 questions to score an 80%.

### When and How Will I Receive My Score Report and What Will It Look Like?

The testing agency no longer sends test results via regular mail. As part of the regis-tration process to take TExES examinations, students set up an account with the testing agency (ETS) in which they are assigned a username and password. You will use this information to log in to view the results of the test.

Results of the paper-based examination are generally available within four weeks of the administration, and the results of the computer-based examination can be viewed within a week of the test.

The report you will receive will indicate whether you have passed the test. This report will also give you the following information:

- A total test scaled score that is reported on a scale of 100 to 300 and a minimum passing score. This score represents the minimum level of competency required to be an entry-level educator in this field in Texas public schools.

- Your performance in the major content domains of the test and in the specific competencies of the test.

- Information to help you interpret your results.

## Can I Retake the Test?

If you don't do well on the TExES Generalist 4–8 (111) exam, don't panic! You can take it again, and in fact many candidates do. You can register to retake it at any sub-sequent test administration. To retake a test, submit a new registration along with the correct payment. It is recommended that you wait for your scores before reregistering. If you choose to register for the same test before receiving your scores from a previous administration, you assume responsibility for test fees and any applicable late or emergency registration fees for both test dates.

## 6-Week Study Plan

Although our study plan is designed to be used in the six weeks before the exam, it can be condensed or expanded to suit your schedule. Be sure to set aside enough time (at least two hours each day) to study. The more time you spend studying, the more prepared and confident you will be on the day of the test.

| Week | Activity |
|:---:|---|
| 1 | At the REA Study Center, take Practice Test 1 as a diagnostic exam. Your detailed score report will identify topics where you need the most review. |
| 2 - 3 | Study the review chapters. Use your score report from Practice Test 1 to focus your study. Useful study techniques include highlighting key terms and information, taking notes as you review the book's sections, and putting new terms and information on note cards to help retain the information. |
| 4 | Reread all your note cards, refresh your understanding of the exam's competencies and skills, review your college textbooks and class notes. This is also the time to consider any other supplementary materials (see note below) that your advisor or the Texas Education Agency suggests. Review the agency's website at *www.tea.state.tx.us/*. |
| 5 | Condense your notes and findings. A structured list of important facts and concepts, based on your note cards and this book's competencies, will help you thoroughly review for the test. Review the answers and explanations for all missed questions. |
| 6 | Take Practice Test 2 at the REA Study Center to see how much your score has improved. If you still got a few questions wrong, go back to the review and study any topics you missed. |

**Note:** Since the TExES Generalist 4–8 (111) exam covers content areas in grades 4 through 8, you should review the state curricula for these grades (Texas Knowledge and Skills; or TEKS) available at *www.tea.state.tx.us*. It is also important to review the released examinations that students in grades 4 through 8 take to demonstrate mastery of the state curriculum standards. These tests are released after each administration and can be used to review the content for the TExES examination. Released tests are available at *www.tea.state.tx.us*. Note that the state of Texas has transitioned to a new K-12 testing program. Check the Texas Education Agency website for updates on the new STAAR test.

## Test-Taking Tips

Although you may not be familiar with tests like the TExES Generalist 4–8 (111), this book will acquaint you with this type of exam and help alleviate your test-taking anxieties. Listed below are ways to help you become accustomed to this TExES exam.

**Tip 1. Become comfortable with the format of the test.** When you are practicing, stay calm and pace yourself. After simulating the test only once, you will boost your chances of doing well, and you will be able to sit down for the actual TExES with much more confidence.

**Tip 2. Familiarize yourself with the directions on the test.** This will not only save time but will also help you avoid anxiety (and the mistakes anxiety causes).

**Tip 3. Read all of the possible answers.** Just because you think you have found the correct response, do not automatically assume that it is the best answer. Read through each choice to be sure that you are not making a mistake by jumping to conclusions.

**Tip 4. Use the process of elimination.** Go through each answer choice and eliminate as many as possible. If you can eliminate two answer choices, you will give yourself a better chance of getting the item correct since there will only be two choices left from which to make your guess. Do not leave an answer blank; it is better to guess than to not answer a question on the TExES as there is no penalty for incorrect answers.

**Tip 5. Place a question mark in your answer booklet** next to answers you guessed, and recheck them later if you have time.

**Tip 6. Work at a steady pace and avoid focusing on any one question too long.** Taking the timed practice tests online at the REA Study Center will help you learn to budget your time.

**Tip 7. If you are taking the paper-and-pencil exam, be sure that the answer circle you are marking corresponds to the number of the question in the test booklet.** The test is graded automatically, and marking one answer in the wrong space can throw off your answer key and your score. Be careful to mark your answers in accurate sequence.

**Tip 8. If you are taking the computer-based exam, be sure that your answer registers before you go to the next item.** Look at the screen to see that your mouse-click causes the pointer to darken the proper oval. If your answer doesn't register, you won't get credit for that question.

## The Day of the Test

On the day of the test, make sure to dress comfortably so that you are not distracted by being too hot or too cold while taking the test. Plan to arrive at the test center early. This will allow you to collect your thoughts and relax, and will also spare you the anguish that comes with being late.

Check your TExES registration information to find out what time to arrive at the testing center. Also, 24 hours before the test, return to your testing account and review your admission ticket for any changes. If there is a change, you will have to print out a new ticket.

Before you leave for the test center, make sure that you have your admission ticket and two forms of identification, one of which must contain a recent and recognizable photograph, your name, and your signature (e.g., a driver's license). All documents must be originals (no copies). You will not be admitted to the test center and you will forfeit your test fees if you do not have proper identification.

If you are taking the paper-and-pencil test, you must bring several sharpened No. 2 pencils with erasers, as none will be provided at the test center. Dictionaries, textbooks, notebooks, calculators, briefcases, or packages will not be permitted. Do not bring cell phones, smart phones, PDAs, and other electronic or photographic devices into the test center. Drinking, smoking, and eating are prohibited.

Good luck on the TExES Generalist exam!

# CHAPTER 2

# English Language Arts

## Competency 001 (Oral Language)

*The teacher understands the importance of oral language, knows the developmental processes of oral language, and provides a variety of instructional opportunities for students to develop listening and speaking skills.*

Language acquisition results from the combination of innate ability, imitation of what is said and heard, and multiple environmental influences. Children are born with innate abilities and mechanisms to develop language. Noam Chomsky called this mechanism a Language Acquisition Device (LAD). According to Chomsky, humans possess an "internal grammar" or set of linguistic principles that are activated for all languages. Interestingly, the LAD is considered universal, as the LAD adapts depending on the language being learned. However, it should be noted that linguists have argued that language only emerges if this internal mechanism is triggered by stimuli from people in the child's environment.

**Imitation** is a learning strategy that young children frequently use to replicate someone's behaviors, actions, phrases, etc. In language acquisition, imitation provides young learners with the opportunity to begin producing language by observing and replicating their caregiver's phrases and words. Imitation decreases in effectiveness, however, as language learning becomes more complex.

After age two, imitation alone cannot meet the communication needs of children. It is at this point when they become creative rule makers. Toddlers begin testing language rules on their own as a way of trying to figure out how language operates. For example, imitation alone cannot explain idiosyncratic statements such as "I goed out yesterday." These nonstandard utterances show that the child is field-testing language rules. In this case, the child is testing the rule for the formation of the regular past tense and has applied it to an irregular verb. This type of overgeneralization characterizes the process of first language acquisition during most of the early childhood years. Direct language correction will not generally help in this case. Instead, parents and those around the child will present the standard version of the word, and the child will seem to ignore it until he or she is ready to internalize it. Parents and teachers should always be encouraged to address the communication needs of the child while modeling the standard version of the language. Moreover, appropriate modeling of the target language is a necessary task for teachers, especially when working with students for whom English is not their native language.

## Language Is Learned in Social Settings

Participation in conversation provides children with the vocabulary and the format of conversations they need to begin developing oral language (Stewig and Jett-Simpson, 1995). Interestingly, parents do not always engage in direct language teaching; instead, parents assist in their children's language acquisition by communicating with the child and using the adult version of the language. As a result of this linguistic support, most children come to school with a strong vocabulary and language background. Conversely, some ethnic and linguistic groups might not follow the same pattern of linguistic interaction with their children.

Children quickly understand that the main purpose of language is communication. Children begin to understand that language is used to generally have their needs met.

## Language Components

All teacher candidates need to have a clear understanding of the basic components of any given language. The six components, which are interlocking pieces in a puzzle, are phonology, morphology, syntax, lexicon, semantics, and pragmatics. **Phonology** is the study of the sound system of a language. The basic units of sound are called **phonemes**. Graphemes or individual letters represent phonemes. For example, the word *through* has seven graphemes (i.e., letters) that represent only three sounds /th/ /r/ /u/. Teacher candidates should be able not only to differentiate these two terms, but they should also make their students aware of the difference between letters in a word and the sounds that the letters represent. **Morphology** is the study of the structure of words and word formations. **Morphemes** are the smallest representation of meaning. For example, the word *cars* is made up of two morphemes: the basic word or root word *car* and the plural morpheme *s*. Having an understanding of the morphology of a language will help students when they are required to decode printed information. **Syntax** entails the ways in which words are organized and arranged in a language. English has specific basic sentence structures that are referred to as *kernel sentences*. Examples of the four most common sentence structures in English can be found in Table 2.1.

**Table 2.1**
**Types of Kernel Sentences**

| Noun | Intransitive Verb | Predicate Nominative |
|---|---|---|
| Katrina | was | a hurricane. |
| Katrina | was | destructive. |
| "Bear Mountain" | won | an Academy Award. |
| Mark Cuban | gave | the Mavericks incentive. |

**Lexicon** refers to the vocabulary of a language. Because the meanings of words change based on context and its historical framework, vocabulary is said to be one of the most variable and rich components of a language. For example, the word *hot* can have several different meanings. Some of these include high temperature, fashionable, and lucky. In a few years, any of these more recent meanings might change or actually become obsolete.

**Semantics** refers to the way that meaning is conveyed in a language through the use of its vocabulary. The meaning of words is also based on culture as well as the context of the conversation taking place. Connotation and denotation are used in a language to convey meaning.

On the one hand, **connotation** refers to the implied meaning of words and ideas; therefore, speakers must have knowledge of the culture to understand an expression's implied meaning. Idiomatic expressions are one example of how its use implies meaning as a communication tool. Having this prior knowledge often presents a challenge to English language learners (ELLs) because they generally lack the familiarity with the American culture that native speakers have acquired. For instance, the common idiom "It's raining cats and dogs" may confuse ELLs who do not have such cultural knowledge and are therefore unfamiliar with this idiom. Thus, teachers need to teach idioms in a contextualized situation to provide the background knowledge that students may lack. Teachers must also provide a description of the idiom, especially in regards to their intended meaning to allow students to fully understand their use.

**Denotation** refers to the literal meaning of words and ideas. For instance, a sign that reads "Dog Bites" might seem obvious because all dogs have the capability to bite. However, pragmatically, this phrase directs that people surpass the literal meaning of the phrase and understand that whoever posted such a sign meant that the dog is aggressive and might attack.

The *Amelia Bedelia* series written by Peggy Parish is one example of how the main character understands everything only literally (i.e., denotation). Her limited understanding creates many communication problems and comedic situations.

**Pragmatics** describes how context can affect the interpretation of communication. Pragmatics are the hidden rules of communications understood by native speakers of the same language. Native speakers often call these rules "commonsense rules." However, these rules often make sense only to native speakers. These rules are not immediately evident to ELLs. Thus, teachers should once again introduce these rules within context. Take, for example, a greeting exchange. In English, a person greets another person with a routine statement such as "How are you?" Pragmatically, the receiver in the conversation is expected to answer with a generic statement such as "Not bad," "I am OK," or "Fine." Once such an exchange of words is completed, the conversation is expected to end. However, ELLs and people who are new to the culture might misinterpret the routine question as a literal inquiry and try to answer it directly or provide more information than what the original person intended to hear.

## Stages of Language Development

The process of first-language acquisition is characterized by stages of development and maturation. Also, these stages are highly influenced by the learner's level and quality of exposure to the native language. Therefore, assigning a definite age for each of the language development stages is not possible. Linguistic milestones, however, can provide pointers to identify these stages and develop a working framework for readers. A description of these stages follows.

### Ages Six and Seven

Six to seven-year-olds have a speaking vocabulary of about 2,100 words and a comprehension vocabulary of more than 20,000 words. Children use well-constructed sentences using all parts of speech. They still might have problems with certain words and structures, but their speech is fluent and clear. However, speakers at this age might still have problems with words containing sounds like /v/, /th/, /ch/, and /sh/. Some children will use the sound of the /w/ in place of the required /r/ and /l/ sounds. They are able to separate words into syllables and begin decoding written language. They are beginning to understand and address questions that call for reasons for an action. For example, they can explain their actions and answer questions such as "Why did you pick number five as the answer?" After age six, children continue to polish their language skills and add new and more sophisticated vocabulary.

### Ages Eight to Twelve

The speaking repertoire of eight to twelve-year-olds continues to grow and improve, as their communication needs change from using language to have their needs met, to becoming language makers in academic settings. Eight-year-olds begin using relative pronoun clauses (i.e., The boy *that* you met yesterday is my friend). They also begin to use subordinated clauses that begin with *when, if,* and *because* (i.e., *If* you bother me, I am going to tell the teacher). At age nine, the use of the gerund has become common for speakers of this age (i.e., *Cheating* is bad). Children begin using more complex sentences, vocabulary, and verb construction. Their speech is more coherent through the use of connectors like *first, during, after,* and *finally.* At ages ten through twelve, students are able to make use of roots, prefixes, and suffixes to understand new words in the language. Also, their sentence structure is more complex.

## Assessing Speaking Ability

### Intelligibility

A child's speaking ability is generally assessed informally in class as part of daily activities and conversations. First, teachers have to determine if the speech of the child is **intelligible** and can be understood by native speakers with minimum effort. Developmental issues, the use of dialectical variations, and speech disorders can cause communication or intelligibility problems in native speakers. To assess the speech of the child, teachers need an understanding of the developmental patterns in the process of language mastery, and use these patterns as a foundation for assessing a child's performance. Teachers should also develop an understanding of features from dialects spoken in the community to avoid confusion with features that contrast with Standard English. For example, speakers of **Ebonics**, a language variant used by some African-American children, and speakers of the **Boston dialect** drop the /r/ after a vowel. One example of this is in the statement ". . . park the car in Harvard yard" [Pahk the kah in Hahvud yahd]. In this case, the omission of postvocalic /r/ cannot be identified as a pronunciation problem.

Because of this, teachers need a working knowledge of the dialects used in the community in order to make accurate assessments of the children's speech.

## Speaking Checklist

Students' speaking abilities can also be assessed in the classroom with a structured checklist identifying specific features that teachers want to observe. Lapp et al. (2001) developed an instrument to assess speaking ability called the Speaking Checklist. A summary of key elements is presented below.

### The Speaking Checklist

1. Sticks to the topic

2. Builds support for the subject

3. Speaks clearly

4. Takes turn and waits to talk

5. Talks so others in the group can hear

6. Speaks smoothly

7. Uses courteous language

8. Presents in an organized and interesting way

9. Supports the topical thesis

10. Answers questions effectively

11. Is comfortable speaking publicly

12. Maintains listeners' interest

13. Volunteers to answer in class

The Texas Education Agency (TEA) has developed an instrument in compliance with the No Child Left Behind (NCLB) state accountability system called the Texas Observation Protocol (TOP) to assess language proficiency of ELLs in Texas. This instrument is administered by teachers in the bilingual or ESL classroom and contains a speaking component that assesses the speaking ability, using a holistic scoring system, based on four levels of proficiency: beginning, intermediate, advanced, and advanced-high (TEA, 2011).

### Listening and Speaking

In any given language, meaning is created through socially shared conventions. During the first months of life, babies are active listeners. Long before they can respond orally, however, they communicate nonverbally by waving their arms, smiling, or wiggling. They are also capable of communicating their needs and wants through nonverbal communication, including body language and crying. Through listening, they develop the receptive language needed to begin communicating orally. Although listening is used extensively in communication, it does not receive much attention at school.

Listening and reading both require the use of skills in phonology, syntax, semantics, and knowledge of the structure of text, and both language skills seem to be controlled by the same set of cognitive processes. Teachers can guide students' listening activities by setting a purpose for listening, providing questions before and after the listening activity, and encouraging children to forge links between the new information that was just heard and the knowledge already in place. In addition, children need to be coached in the use of appropriate volume and speed when they speak, and in the rules to participate in discussions. Students also need to follow the culturally defined rules for maintaining a polite conversation. In the American culture, such rules include staying on a topic and taking turns without interrupting speakers.

A communication disorder occurs when a person's speech interferes with his/her ability to convey messages during interactions with community members. The four classifications of language disorders include disorders in voice, fluency, articulation, and language processing (Piper, 2006).

### Voice Disorders

Voice disorders are considered any type of distortion of the pitch, timbre, or volume of spoken communication. There are two types of voice disorders: phonation and resonance. **Phonation** disorder describes any kind of abnormality in the vibration of the vocal fold. For example, *hoarseness* or extreme breathiness can interfere with comprehension. **Resonance** disorder describes abnormalities created when sound passes through the vocal tract. The most typical example of resonance disorder occurs when the sound passing through the nasal cavity changes oral sounds to nasal. This is called *hypernasality*. This type of disorder should not be confused with the nasal quality of Southern dialects like the Texas twang.

### Fluency Disorders

Fluency disorders refer to any kind of condition that affects the child's ability to produce coherent and fluent communication. *Stuttering* and *cluttering* cause the most common types of fluency disorders. **Stuttering** is characterized by multiple false starts or the inability to produce the intended sounds. **Cluttering** occurs when children try to communicate in an excessively fast mode that makes comprehension difficult. Teachers have to be cautious when assessing ELLs who might experience temporary fluency dysfunction, such as hesitations, false starts, and repetition, which can be attributed to anxiety or confusion with the two languages. For instance, ELLs may stutter because they cannot find or might not know the appropriate word in English. Allowing students to (a) code switch from English to their first language and (b) providing them more wait time can both be used as temporary remedies to stuttering. Additionally, children new to the language often use the intonation pattern and the speed of delivery of their native language. Thus, the delivery might become incomprehensible and be mistaken as a cluttering.

### Articulation Problems

The most common articulation disorder is *lisping*. **Lisping** is a term used when children (or adults) produce the sound /s/, /sh/, /z/, and /ch/ with their tongue between the upper and lower teeth. Some other sounds that can present challenges to children are the /w/, /l/, and /r/ sounds. Children may have problems with specific sounds that can cause unintelligibility and the production of aesthetically displeasing sounds. Some of these problems might be developmental and will eventually be eliminated, while others might require speech therapy.

## Activities to Promote Oral Communication

The best way to promote oral communication is to guide students into using language in meaningful situations. In classroom situations, teachers can organize activities to resemble real-life situations in order to promote communication among students. Some of these activities are described below.

### Role-Play

Role-play or dramatic enactment allows students to recreate a variety of scenarios across the curriculum. Using scripts or reader's theater is an ideal activity to develop communication. In role-play, students are given open opportunities to role-play by acting in real-life situations. Students may be given either a specific role to play, or they can improvise roles. For instance, fifth grade students in a history class could reenact the Boston Tea Party.

Students can also play the role of a talk show host and "interview" classmates who can pretend to be characters from a novel or famous historical figures from a specific time era.

### Language Play

Language play involves the use of language in rhyme, alliteration, songs, and repeating patterns to amuse children. Tongue twisters are commonly used to practice pronunciation and language patterns. Through these activities, children acquire language knowledge in a relaxed and fun environment. Teachers can also use content related songs, poems, and stories that contain rhyme to introduce these language features.

### Sharing

In sharing, children bring artifacts and personal items to class. Children show the object and are expected to describe its features to the class. In addition to the obvious benefit of oral communication, this kind of activity can be used to promote both home and cultural pride as well as multicultural awareness in one's classroom. Older students can prepare presentations that describe and detail information for a specific audience.

### Pair Interview

Pair interview is an additional strategy that can be used to promote oral communication. In this strategy, children are paired to learn information from each other and then report their findings to the larger group. Depending on the children's age, the responses gathered during the pair interview can also be recorded in writing to be used later in the children's presentation. This strategy can be used throughout the year and for different classroom activities. The pair interview is also a recommended instructional strategy that can be used for the first day of class when students need to get to know each other.

### Presentations

Preparing children to communicate what they think and know is common practice in classrooms. Elementary and middle school students are expected not only to use correct language when speaking, but to have accurate information when creating a presentation. To this end, students are expected to also find reliable information and sources when investigating a topic of interest or one assigned.

Elementary and middle school students also learn that a topic of a presentation can be delivered to multiple and different audiences. In other words, students will need to be given opportunities to understand how one presentation can be modified to meet the needs of their audience. For example, children can be led to prepare a short presentation to inform other children at their school why recycling is important to the environment, and to ask them to start a recycling project in their classrooms. Then, these same students could be asked to revise their presentation to deliver it to community leaders so that they can receive the resources needed to start recycling projects in their communities. Regardless of the audience, students should be expected to create and deliver presentations in groups and individually.

## Explicit, Systematic Oral Language Instruction

Key principles of oral language development can help both native speakers and English Language Learners in their oral language development. Some key ideas, based on work by Gersten, Baker, Shanahan, Linan-Thompson, Collins, and Scarcella (2007) include the following:

- Increase academic vocabulary and multiple encounters with words.

- Students should be provided with lots of opportunities to engage in dialogue.

- Vocabulary can be enhanced by combining oral language with visual supports (e.g., increase visual aides).

- The teacher can focus on comprehension through strategic reading and think-aloud practice.

### Connecting Oral Language to Reading Instruction

Students can be encouraged to connect oral language to reading instruction through the use of discussions and questioning. Both small group and large-group discussions can facilitate comprehension by encouraging students to integrate reading, listening, and speaking. Teachers should ask all levels of questions to students including literal questions, inferential (higher-level), and application (real-world) questions. Additionally, teachers should consider whether the questions posed orally genuinely invite dialogue and response for all students. To foster discussion, the questions should not be retrieval or yes/no questions. Teachers should also allow sufficient wait-time for student response. Asking follow-up questions such as "Why do you think so?" or "What evidence in the text told you that?" can help to foster both critical thinking and a deeper level of dialogue.

Additionally, through read-aloud and shared reading, the teacher can increase exposure to higher-level academic vocabulary of both narrative and expository text. Students can participate in dialogue with support and modeling from the teacher and their peers. Other benefits of shared reading to enhance oral language development include the following (Herrell & Jordan, 2007).

Shared reading supports fluency as well as vocabulary and comprehension development. English is an *intonation* language; meaning and understanding are created through expression, pitch, and tone in reading.

Understanding of text can be aided through hearing the story as the teacher models expressive reading and active reading of the text.

### Spoken and Written English

The productive skills of language—speaking and writing—are interconnected. A strong oral development can facilitate the development of written communication. However, because spoken language is generally more informal than written language, teachers need to be sure that students use formal language when writing.

English favors the use of active voice as opposed to passive voice in both oral and written communication. For example, the sentence *Katrina devastated the city of New Orleans* is stronger and more effective than a sentence using the passive voice such as *The city of New Orleans was devastated by Katrina*. To provide support in this area, guide students to work with a partner in converting passive sentences to active sentences; then guide them to discuss how these changes affect the tone and meaning of the sentences. If a student is having problems connecting sounds to written text, teachers can provide phonics instruction. Guiding students to "sound out" or "stretch out" words as a foundation for spelling can improve written performance.

### Using Technology to Develop Oral Language

There are many technological resources available to develop students' oral language. For listening skills, students can view multimedia presentations to hear stories, news events, and other types of formal, academic language. Students can listen to or view podcasts, video clips, and CDs on a variety of topics. To increase speaking opportunities, students can design and create their own podcasts, videos, and other multimedia texts to share with other students and families. Increasingly, students are expected to be skilled in using and creating such digital media.

## Competency 002 (Early Literacy Development)

*The teacher understands the foundations of early literacy development.*

### Balanced Reading Program

Today, many classrooms are places where young children enjoy learning to read and write in a balanced reading instructional program. Research into best practices strongly suggests that the teaching of reading requires solid skill instruction, including several techniques for decoding unknown words. These techniques include but are not limited to, phonics instruction embedded in interesting and engaging reading and writing experiences with whole and **authentic literature-based** texts to facilitate the construction of meaning. In other words, this approach to instruction combines the best skill instruction and the whole language approach in order to teach both skills and meaning as well as to meet the reading needs of individual children. Some of the reading strategies used in a balanced literacy program include:

- Teacher-directed reading to students (read-aloud)

- Shared reading, guided reading, and reading workshops

- Student directed reading and independent reading

- Teacher directed writing, writing to/for students as part of the classroom routines, and process writing

- Shared writing as in language experience/interactive writing, writing workshops

- Student directed writing and independent writing activities

### Importance of Phonological and Phonemic Awareness for Reading and Writing

Phonological and phonemic awareness constitute the foundation for the development of the metalinguistic awareness that children need to become successful language learners and effective readers. **Phonemic awareness** refers to a child's ability to understand that words have smaller components called sounds, and that these sounds together create syllables and words. Phonemic awareness is the basic linguistic principle required to develop an understanding of oral and written communication. Once children understand this principle, they begin discovering more sophisticated linguistic principles like phonological awareness. Children who have developed phonemic awareness are able to dissect a word into each phoneme, and put it back to recreate the word. The ability to manipulate spoken words has been linked to successful reading development.

## Phonological Awareness

Phonological awareness is the ability to recognize and manipulate components of the sound system of a language. It includes the ability to segment words into smaller units like syllables and phonemes (sounds). Phonological awareness also encompasses the ability to identify and separate words within a sentence, identify stress in individual words, and identify the intonation pattern used in sentences.

## Syllabication

Syllabication is an important component of phonological awareness. It refers to the ability to conceptualize and separate words into their basic pronunciation components, which are syllables. Syllables can be as simple as one vowel, or can be a combination of vowels and consonants. For example, the word *elegant* contains three syllables (el/e/gant), one of which is a vowel alone. Phonemes are the basic unit of a syllable, and syllables constitute the basic units for the pronunciation of the English language. Consequently, syllables influence the rhythm of the language, poetic meter, and word stress. Syllabication can be taught using the appropriate voice intonation in order to indicate the beginning and ending of a syllable. Teachers often use clapping to indicate syllable boundaries.

## Phonemic Stress

**Phonemic stress** can be taught through the use of nursery rhymes, short poems, or stories like the traditional Humpty Dumpty character of Mother Goose nursery rhymes. The use of these rhythmic patterns in an enjoyable and relaxed environment introduces children to the sounds and music of language. Eventually, children will notice the ending of the words and how specific sounds relate to each other. Moreover, rhymes are particularly beneficial to ELLs as they begin to develop phonemic awareness and phonemic stress. They can also learn chunks of language that they can use to participate in classroom conversations and communicate with peers and their teacher in the classroom.

## Alliteration

**Alliteration** is a technique used to emphasize phonemes by using successive words that begin with the same consonant sound or letter. Tongue twisters are the best-known form of alliteration. Children can repeat tongue twisters for fun, and, at the same time, develop an awareness of the sound symbol correspondence. In the following example, the /p/ sound is emphasized:

**P**eter **P**iper **p**icked a **p**eck of **p**ickled **p**eppers.

## Word Stress

English has at least four levels of word stress but, for practical purposes, we only need to be concerned with the first two: main stress and secondary stress. Word stress can affect the ability to understand words and can also alter meaning. For example, the word *present* can have two meanings depending on how it is pronounced. With the stress on the first syllable (*present*), it becomes a noun; but if the stress is placed on the last syllable (*present*), it becomes a verb.

## Intonation Patterns

The intonation pattern describes the pitch contour of a phrase or a sentence that is used to change the meaning of the sentence. In English, there are utterances that might appear to be identical but convey a different meaning. In the question below, the rising point at the verb *are* makes the utterance a question, while a slight change of intonation to the pronoun *you* changes the utterance to a reply to the question.

Question: How **are** you? Reply: How are **you**?

## Teaching Phonemic and Phonological Awareness

Teachers can promote phonemic and phonological knowledge through a variety of strategies. A list of these strategies follows:

- Teach the child to isolate phonemes. To follow a pattern from the simplest to the most difficult, begin with initial and final sounds first, and then add phonemes in the middle. Ask questions such as "What is the first sound of the word *boy*?"

- Guide children to blend sounds and come up with rhymes. Ask the child, "What word can you create when you blend the sounds *l* and *ake,* or *t* and *ake.*"

- Introduce blending by guiding children to identify the word created when the following sounds are blended: /b/, /a/, and /t/.

- Guide children to identify a word like *tape* and then remove the onset and ask the child: "What word is left when we remove the first sound, *t*?" (Answer: *ape*.) Then ask students, "Is this a word?"

- Teach word segmentation by saying a word, and then guiding children to identify the sounds that they hear. Teachers can begin with simple monosyllabic words like *car* and then expand to more sophisticated words.

- Use onsets and rimes to teach the sound symbol relationship. Guide children to create new words by substituting the first letter of monosyllabic words. For example, using the word *ring*, the child can replace the initial sounds to create additional words like *sing*, *king*, and *spring*. An activity like this can emphasize phonemic awareness and also teach how word families can support vocabulary development.

- Teachers should lead children to segment or separate the sounds in words. Begin with words with consistent sound symbol correspondence, like *bag* and *lag*, and later expand to words that contain clusters/blends as in the word *splash* and diagraphs as in the word *church*.

- Introduce minimal pairs, which are sets of words that differ in only one phoneme like *pail* and *bail*, to guide students to notice the difference. Teachers should pronounce both words and ask students if the words are the same or different. Initially, contrast words with initial consonant sounds as in *pat* and *bat*, and later expand to include more sophisticated contrasting pairs as in *bit* and *beet*.

- Say words and guide children to identify the number of sounds that they hear. Initially, avoid "stop" sounds because children might have difficulties perceiving the brief sound represented by these sounds.

The **alphabetic principle** has been described as the ability to connect letters with sounds, and to create words based on these associations. Children learning to read also must develop an understanding that letters and letter patterns represent the sounds of spoken English (TEA, 2002). Understanding the ways in which these sound symbol relationships are created allows them to conceptualize that there are predictable connections between phonemes and graphemes.

### How Is the Alphabetic Principle Learned?

Traditionally, children go through specific stages in the process of learning new words and mastering the alphabetic principle (Ehri, 1998). Preschoolers are exposed to components of the alphabetic principle through their environment. They can identify the logo of stores like Wal-Mart or Burger King by their design instead of by the specific letters contained in the logo. But because they are not connecting the letters and the sounds of the logo, this stage is generally considered a **pre-alphabetic phase.**

At home, children might also get exposed to the alphabet song, which most of them learn in a subconscious manner. Eventually, children engage in a **partial alphabetic phase** as they get exposed to alphabet block playing and concrete letter objects that are typical in early childhood programs. They begin connecting the shape of the letters with the sound that they represent. Children are also often exposed to children's literature and books in which the sound symbol correspondence is carefully controlled. Children also begin connecting initial letters with the sound of the names of peers, like the **N** of Nancy and **A** of Alex.

A third phase of learning new words is identified as the **full alphabetic stage**. At this stage, children begin making connections between the letters, the sounds that they represent, and the actual meaning of the word. Children get very excited during this stage because they are beginning to "crack" the written code of the language. In the fourth and last stage of development, called the **consolidated alphabetic stage**, children begin conceptualizing that they can use components of words that they know to decode new words. They begin discovering how they can create new words with the use of onsets, rhymes, and other letter sequences. One of the main purposes of phonics instruction at this stage is to guide children into understanding the connection between the grapheme and phoneme and the sequence that they create to form words and sentences. This knowledge allows students the opportunity to expand the number of words that they recognize instantly (sight words), which prepares them for literacy.

### Teaching the Grapheme-Phoneme Correspondence

The introduction of the grapheme-phoneme correspondence can be presented through games, songs, and other engaging activities; but eventually, the correspondence should be presented explicitly. Teachers have to bring the skills to the surface level and make students aware of the concepts and skills that they need to learn in order to become effective readers. Teachers should take into account the complexity of the language and the maturity level of the children when introducing children to the alphabetic principle. A list of considerations and strategies for teaching the grapheme-phoneme connection follows.

- The introduction of the letter-sound correspondence should be guided by the potential support of the children's efforts to become readers. That is, introduce the spelling of the letters that the child is most likely to encounter in text. For example the letters *m, a, t, s, p,* and *h* are used more frequently in writing than letters like *x, q,* or consonant diagraphs like *ght* or *gn*.

- It is also important to begin instruction in the grapho-phonemic relationship using sounds that present the least possible distortion or confusion with other sounds. Some of the sounds that are easier to perceive are the nasals /m/, /n/, the fricatives /f/, the sibilant /s/, and the English retroflex /r/.

- Teachers should postpone the introduction of less clear phonemes like the nasal /ng/, the distinction between the sibilants /s/ and /z/, the troublesome sounds in English like the voiced *th* in the word *them*, and the voiceless counterpart in words like *think*.

- Introduce words with one or two consonants and one short vowel sound such as in the words *on* and *car*. Later, long vowel sounds can be introduced.

- Next, add consonant blends like *try*, followed by digraphs like *th*, *sh*, and *ch* in words like *thanks*, *show*, and *chop*. Digraphs can lead students to recognize common words such as *this*, *she*, and *chair*. Introduce single consonants and consonant blends or clusters in separate lessons to avoid confusion.

- Avoid voiceless stop sounds (/t/, /p/, /k/) at the beginning or middle of words because the short duration of these phonemes makes them difficult to perceive. Teachers should postpone the introduction of conflicting letter–sound correspondence of phonemes like the /b/ and /v/ or /i/ and /e/, or visually confusing graphemes like the *b* and *d* or *p* and *g*.

## Types of Writing Systems

Several classifications exist for writing systems. Three of the most commonly known writing systems are pictographic, syllabic, and alphabetic writing. In a **pictographic writing system**, words, ideas, and concepts are represented with a visual or image. Pictographic writing was the first type of written language developed in the history of civilizations. In **syllabic writing systems**, syllables are depicted through the use of unique symbols. The **alphabetic writing system** uses the sounds of the language as a basic unit for writing. English uses an alphabetic writing system that is based upon phonetic signs. Theoretically, each symbol represents one unit of sound in this system. However, this principle works better with languages with consistent sound–symbol relationships. Many alphabetic languages like Spanish are more phonetically consistent than English. An analysis of the grapheme–phoneme correspondence of English follows.

## The Grapheme–Phoneme Correspondence of English

The connection between graphemes and phonemes in English is not always consistent. English has 26 graphemes to represent 44 phonemes. The consonant system is more consistent than the vowel system. English has five letters to represent 12 vowel sounds, which makes decoding and pronunciation more challenging. This inconsistency is partially caused by the evolution of the English language and the influence of multiple languages in the development of modern English. Teachers need to be proactive by identifying these troublesome areas and organizing instruction to address these issues. Some of the potential areas of concern are explained below:

Graphemes can represent multiple phonemes. For example, the grapheme *s* can represent multiple phonemes: car**s**/z/, call**s**/z/, **s**ugar/sh/, mi**ss**ion/sh/, and walk**s**/s/. This grapheme-phoneme inconsistency represents a challenge when attempting to use a phonic approach to teach reading.

English has graphemes that represent a sound in some words and remain silent in other words. For example, the graphemes *s* and *l* become silent in the following examples without giving readers a reliable clue for this change: *island*, *calm*, and *palm*. (Some speakers will make an attempt to pronounce the /s/ and /l/ in these words.)

English has multiple consonant diagraphs, which are two or more letters representing one sound. These consonant diagraphs are voiceless. This inconsistency presents a challenge to native English speakers as well as ELLs.

**Table 2.2**
**Consonant Diagraphs**

| Diagraphs | Examples |
|-----------|----------|
| ch | chair |
| gh | ghost |
| gn | gnat |
| kn | know |
| ght | thought |
| pn | pneumonia |
| ps | psychology |
| rh | rhythm |
| wr | write |
| sc | scene |

English speakers use multiple contractions in daily communication. These can create listening comprehension problems for students and especially for ELLs. Teachers should introduce contractions together with the long version of the words to avoid confusion. Table 2.3 presents a few examples of the type of confusion that contractions can cause.

**Table 2.3**
**Contractions in English**

| Contractions | Regular Form | Possible Confusion |
|---|---|---|
| they're | they are | there and their |
| he's | he is | his |
| he'll | he will | hill, heel, heal |
| you're | you are | your |

English has multiple initial consonant clusters, which require students to be able to blend the sounds and at the same time recognize the sounds of individual phonemes. These sounds also represent a challenge for native Spanish speakers because Spanish does not have words that begin with particular letter sequences that exist in English. These types of clusters occur in medial positions and they are always preceded by the vowel *e*, such as in the words *espero*, *escapar*, and *estar*. Based on this feature, Latino children will place an *e* in front of English words containing the following clusters: *sp* (as in speak), *sc* (school), *st* (street), *spr* (spring), *scr* (scream), *str* (stream), *sm* (small), *sn* (snow), and *sl* (slate).

Several words in English end in consonant clusters (e.g., *rant*, *cord*, *first*, and *card*). Both young native English-speaking children and ELLs may have difficulties blending clusters at the end of the words. For native Spanish speakers, these clusters represent a unique challenge because Spanish does not have words that end in consonant clusters. Based on this feature, Spanish speaking children, and possibly most children in early childhood, may tend to simplify a final consonant cluster in English. For example, the word *board* might become *boar*.

## Stages of Reading Development

A vast amount of research has been conducted on the stages of reading development. Three widely used labels for these stages include emergent readers, early readers, and fluent readers. It is important to note that researchers have concluded that these stages are considered to be cumulative (Chall, 1983); that is, children need to develop the skills and knowledge in each of these stages to be used in subsequent ones.

### Emergent Readers

Emergent readers understand that print contains meaningful information. They imitate the reading process and display basic reading readiness skills like directionality movement (i.e., eye movement from top to bottom and from left to right). Emergent readers can participate in shared reading activities and are able to follow and match words with their pronunciation when teachers point to the words as they are read. Additionally, children at this stage:

- Use illustrations embedded in the texts to support comprehension.

- Listen and follow a story attentively and can easily develop an awareness of the story structure.

- Represent the main idea of a story through drawings and can retell major events in the story with or without illustrations.

- Use illustrations and prior experiences to make predictions and to support comprehension.

- Possess some degree of phonemic awareness.

- Are able to connect the initial letter of words with its representing phoneme.

### Early Readers

Early readers have mastered reading readiness skills and are beginning to read simple text with some degree of success. They are also developing an internal list of high frequency words in print. Their reliance on picture clues has decreased now that they can get more information from print. Children at this stage also:

- Begin using the cuing system to confirm information in the text.

- Rely on grapho-phonemic information to sound out words as a decoding strategy.

- Show preference for certain stories.

- Begin noticing features from language and text like punctuation and capitalization, as well as the use of bold print and variation in format.

- Retell stories read to them with detail and accuracy.

- Engage in discussion of stories read and identify the main idea and story characters.

- Engage in self-correction when text does not make sense to them.

### Newly Fluent Readers

Newly fluent readers can read with relative fluency and comprehension. They are able to use several cuing systems to obtain meaning from print (i.e., semantic, structural, visual, and grapho-phonemic cuing systems). They self-monitor their reading, and can identify and correct simple errors with minimum external support. They ask clarification questions to develop an understanding of the content. Newly fluent readers can also:

- Summarize the part of the story that they have read, and make inferences about the content.

- Handle more challenging vocabulary through the use of context clues.

- Begin using literary terms and grammar concepts.

- Enjoy reading from a variety of genres for information and for pleasure.

Children at this stage are not totally independent readers, but with practice and support from teachers, they soon become fluent and independent readers.

## Knowledge and Use of Literacy Assessment

There are two main types of assessment: formal and informal. Both have a place in the classroom, particularly in the literacy classroom. The effective teacher understands the importance of ongoing assessment as an instructional tool and uses both informal and formal assessment measures to understand students' learning in his/her classroom. There is never an occasion to group children permanently on the basis of one assessment, either formal or informal. Any grouping of students should come about after the consideration of several assessments, and the grouping should be flexible enough to consider individual differences among the students in each group.

### Informal Assessments

Teachers can learn valuable information by simply observing their students at work. Many school districts use a type of inventory/report card to inform adults at home about the progress that children are making. Experienced teachers usually develop, through trial and error, their own means of assessing the skills of students in their classes. Almost every book on teaching reading and writing contains its own informal tests. Teachers can also develop their own informal reading assessment. The purpose of these assessments is to collect meaningful information about what students can and cannot do. A **running record** (Clay, 2002) is a way to assess students' word identification skills, accuracy, and fluency in oral reading. In a running record, the teacher uses a copy of the page to mark each word the child mispronounces as the teacher listens to a student read a text. The teacher writes the incorrect word over the printed word, draws a line through each word the child skips, and draws an arrow under repeated words. Through informal observations and through the use of inventories (formal and informal), teachers should be able to determine the **learning styles** of their students. Student learning styles play an important role in determining classroom structure.

## Formal Assessments

Formal measures may include teacher-made tests, district exams, and standardized tests. Both formative and summative evaluations are part of effective instruction. **Formative evaluation** occurs during the process of learning when the teacher or the students monitor progress while it is still possible to modify instruction. **Summative evaluation** occurs at the end of a specific time or course of study. Usually, a summative evaluation applies a single grade or score to represent a student's performance.

The effective teacher uses a variety of formal assessment techniques. Teacher-made instruments are ideally developed at the same time as the planning of goals and outcomes, rather than at the last minute after the completion of the lessons. Carefully planned objectives and assessment instruments serve as lesson development guides for the teacher. Paper-and-pencil tests are the most common method for evaluating student progress.

## Criterion-Referenced Tests

In **criterion-referenced tests (CRTs)**, the teacher attempts to measure each student against uniform objectives or criteria. CRTs allow for the possibility that all students can score 100 percent on the test if they understand the concepts being tested. Teacher-made tests should be criterion-referenced because the teacher should develop them to measure the achievement of predetermined outcomes for the course. If teachers have properly prepared lessons based on the outcomes and, if students have mastered the outcomes, then scores on CRTs should be high. In this type of test, students are not in competition with each other for a high score, and there is no limit to the number of students who can score well. Some commercially developed tests are criterion-referenced; however, most are norm-referenced.

## Norm-Referenced Tests

The purpose of a norm-referenced test (NRT) is to compare the performance of groups of students. This type of test is competitive because a limited number of students can score well. A plot of NRT scores resembles a bell-shaped curve, with most scores clustering around the center, and a few scores at each end. The midpoint is the average of test data; and, therefore, half of the population will score above average and half below average. The bell-shaped curve is a mathematical description of the results of tossing coins. As such, it represents the chance or normal distribution of skills, knowledge, or events across the general population. A percentile score (not to be confused with a percentage) is a way of reporting a student's NRT score. The percentile score indicates the percentage of the population whose scores fall at or below the student's score. For example, a group score at the eightieth percentile means that the group scored as well as or better than 80 percent of the students who took the test. A student with a score at the fiftieth percentile has an average score. Percentile scores rank students from highest to lowest. By themselves, percentile scores do not indicate how well the student has mastered the content objectives. Raw scores indicate how many questions the student answered correctly and are, therefore, useful in computing a percentage score. The Texas Education Agency (TEA) has a comprehensive list of approved norm-referenced tests that districts can choose from to assess achievement of students in the state.

## Performance-Based Assessment

Some states and districts are moving toward performance-based tests, which assess students on how well they perform certain tasks. Students must use higher-level thinking skills to apply, analyze, synthesize, and evaluate ideas and data. For example, a content-based performance based assessment might require students to read a problem, design and carry out a laboratory experiment, and then write summaries of their findings. The performance-based assessment would evaluate both the processes students used and the output they produced. An English performance-based test might ask students to first read a selection of literature and then write a critical analysis. Performance-based assessments allow students to be creative in solutions to problems or questions, and it requires them to use higher-level skills. During these assessments, students work on content-related problems and use skills that are useful in various contexts. There are weaknesses in this approach, however. This type of assessment can be time consuming. Performance-based assessments often require multiple resources, which can be expensive. Teachers must receive training in applying the test. Nonetheless, many schools consider performance-based testing to be a more authentic measure of student achievement than traditional tests.

## Classroom Tests

Teachers must consider fundamental professional and technical factors when constructing effective classroom tests. One of the first factors to recognize is that test construction is as creative, challenging, and important as any aspect of teaching. The planning and background that contribute to effective teaching are incomplete unless evaluation of student performance provides accurate feedback to the teacher and the student about the learning process.

Good tests are the product of careful planning, creative thinking, hard work, and technical knowledge about the various methods of measuring student knowledge and performance. Classroom tests that accomplish their purpose are the result of the development of a pool of items and refinement of those items based on feedback and constant revision. It is through this process that evaluation of students becomes valid and reliable. Tests serve as a valuable instructional aid because they help determine student progress and also provide feedback to teachers regarding their own effectiveness. Student misunderstandings and problems that the tests reveal can help the teacher understand areas of special concern in providing instruction. This information also becomes the basis for the remediation of students and the revision of teaching procedures. Consequently, the construction, administration, and proper scoring of classroom tests are among the most important activities in teaching.

## Authentic Assessments

Paper-and-pencil tests and essay tests are not the only methods of assessment. Other assessments include projects, observations, checklists, anecdotal records, portfolios, self-assessments, and peer assessments. Although these types of assessments often take more time and effort to plan and administer, they can often provide a more authentic measurement of student progress.

## Essay Tests

There are advantages and disadvantages to essay tests. Advantages of essay questions include the possibility for students to be creative in their answers, the opportunity for students to explain their responses, and the potential to test for higher-level thinking skills. Disadvantages of essay questions include the time students need to formulate meaningful responses, and the time teachers need to evaluate the essays. In addition, language difficulties can make essay tests extremely difficult for some students, including ELLs. Consistency in evaluating essays can also be a problem for some teachers, but an outline of the acceptable answers—a scoring rubric—can help a teacher avoid inconsistency.

Teachers who write specific questions and know what they are looking for are more likely to be consistent in grading. Also, if there are several essay questions, the effective teacher grades all student responses to the first question, then moves on to all responses to the second, and so on.

## Using Rubrics for Assessment

A **rubric** is a checklist with assigned point values. To construct a rubric, a teacher uses the lesson objectives. Students should receive an explanation of the rubric *before* starting to work on their writing assignment, and they can use the rubric as a guideline while they are preparing their writing assignment. The teacher can use the rubric to evaluate the completed assignment. Then teachers can provide clear, well-planned instructions and guidelines for activities; they can significantly decrease student frustration. Rubrics can provide this valuable guidance. When teachers model what they expect and state clear objectives or goals for each assignment, students perform better. Accordingly, there should be a clear and obvious link between the assignment's goals and the students' achievement.

### Ongoing Assessment

Ongoing assessment provides teachers with updated information about the progress and challenges that children are facing in writing. This information can then be easily incorporated in daily instruction.

## Monitoring Reading Comprehension with Retellings

**Story retelling** is a strategy used with children to assess listening and reading comprehension. This strategy can also assess sentence structure knowledge, vocabulary, speaking ability, and knowledge about the structure of stories. An informal or more structured checklist can be used to assess a student's comprehension, sentence structure knowledge, and vocabulary development as they retell a story. Any checklist for listening comprehension should assess the ability of the child to (Lapp et al., 2001):

1. Retell the story with details

2. Show evidence of comprehension of the story line and plot, including the characters, setting, author's intention, and literal and implied meaning

3. Show evidence that the child understood major ideas and the ideas that support it

4. Bring background information to the selection

5. Analyze and make judgments based on facts

6. Retell the selection in sentences that make grammatical sense

7. Retell the story using sentences that include standard usage of verbs, adjectives, conjunctions, and compound sentences

8. Use a rich and meaningful vocabulary with minimal use of slang and colloquial expressions

9. Adapt spoken language for various audiences, purposes, and occasions

10. Listen for various purposes including critical listening to evaluate a speaker's message, and listening to enjoy and appreciate spoken language

## Competency 003 (Word Identification Skills and Reading Fluency)

*The teacher understands the importance of word identification skills (including decoding, blending, structural analysis and sight word vocabulary) and reading fluency and provides many opportunities for students to practice and improve word identification skills and reading fluency.*

Word analysis refers to the way that children approach a written word in order to decode and obtain meaning from it. Vocabulary building is a skill that needs to be practiced daily in the classroom. One of the goals of this is to assist children in becoming skillful in rapid word recognition. Research suggests that fluent word identification needs to be accomplished before a child can readily comprehend text. If a child needs to painstakingly analyze many words in a text, the memory and attention needed for comprehension are absorbed by word analysis, and the pleasure in a good story is lost. Typically, children who are beginning readers decode each word as they read it. Through repeated exposure to the same words, instant recognition vocabulary grows. It is particularly important that developing readers learn to recognize those words that occur very frequently in print. These words are called sight words.

### Sequence of Word Analysis Instruction

**Phonics** is a method of teaching beginners to read and pronounce words by teaching them the phonetic value of letters, letter groups, and syllables. Because English has an alphabetic writing system, an understanding of the letter–sound relationship may prove helpful to the beginning reader. However, this view of reading instruction is that these relationships should be taught in isolation, in a highly sequenced manner, followed by reading words that represent the regularities of English in print. The children are asked to read decodable texts by sounding out words. Typically, this approach uses reading programs that offer stories with controlled vocabulary that are made up of letter-sound relationships and words with which children are already familiar.

Teaching children to use phonics is different from teaching them about phonics. In summary, the skills-based approach begins reading instruction with a study of single letters, letter sounds, blends and digraphs, blends and digraph sounds, and vowels and vowel sounds in isolation, and in a highly sequenced manner. The children read and write decodable words, with a great emphasis on reading each word accurately, as opposed to reading to comprehend the text as a whole. More information about the TEKS that relate to word study and spelling can be found in the TEKS document located on the Texas Education Agency website.

### Dolch Words

In 1948 Edward W. Dolch identified 220 of the most frequently used words in the English language. He believed that if children were exposed to these words and learned to recognize them as sight words, they would become fluent readers. Some examples of Dolch words are *a*, *an*, *am*, *at*, *can*, *had*, *has*, *ran*, *the*, *after*, *but*, *got*, and *away*. The introduction of these sight words can expedite the decoding process and develop fluency among early readers.

### Decoding Clues

In addition to working on placing sight words into readily available memory, there is sound research suggesting that students can use **context clues** to help identify unknown words. This body of research further suggests that instruction can help improve students' use of context clues. There are three main kinds of context clues: **semantic, syntactic, and structural**.

### Semantic Clues

Semantic clues require a child to think about the meanings of words and what is already known about the topic being read. For example, when reading a story about hawks, teachers can help children to activate prior knowledge about the bird, and to develop an expectation that the selection may contain words associated with hawks, such as *predator*, *carnivorous*, *food chain*, and *wingspan*. This discussion might help a child gain a sense of what might be reasonable in a sentence. For ELLs who might not be familiar with the hawk, teachers need to identify equivalent species from their geographical area.

## Syntactic Clues

The word order in a sentence might also provide clues to readers. For example, in the sentence, "Hawks are," the order of the words in the sentence indicates that the missing word must be an adjective. This open-ended sentence can lead students to words such as *carnivorous*, *predators*, or other descriptors for the bird. Furthermore, the illustrations in the book can often help with the identification of a word. A picture of a hawk eating prey can lead students to the words *predator* or *carnivorous*. Still, context clues are often not specific enough to allow students to predict the exact word. However, when context clues are combined with other clues such as phonics and structural clues, accurate word identification is usually possible.

## Structural Clues

Another strategy to provide clues to readers is to pay attention to letter groups because there are many groups of letters that frequently occur within words, which are called morphemes. These specific clusters of letters can be taught. Common **derivational morphemes** in the form of prefixes, suffixes, and **inflectional endings** should be pointed out to students. An analysis of derivational and inflectional endings follows.

Most of the **derivational morphemes** come from foreign languages like Greek and Latin, and they represent relatively consistent meanings. For example, the meaning of the prefixes *pre*, *anti*, and *sub* is very consistent in English and in other languages; namely *pre* = before, *anti* = against, and *sub* = under. A large number of English prefixes are common to multiple Western languages such as Spanish, French, and German. See Table 2.4 for examples in English and Spanish. Derivational morphemes can change the syntactic classification of the word. That is, by adding a morpheme to a word, it can be changed from a verb to a noun or from an adjective to an adverb. Children who are guided to recognize derivational morphemes will have a definite advantage when decoding words.

**Table 2.4**
**Examples of Common Prefixes in English and Spanish**

| Roots | Meaning | Words in English | Words in Spanish |
|---|---|---|---|
| bio | life | symbiosis | simbiosis |
| phobia (fobia) | fear of | xenophobia | xenofobia |
| phono (fono) | sound | phonetics | fonética |
| photo (foto) | light | photography | fotografía |
| geo | land, earth | geology | geología |

**Inflectional morphemes** do not change the syntactic classification and typically follow derivational morphemes in a word. These are native of English and always function as suffixes. English has eight inflectional endings.

Short Plural **-s**, e.g., two *cars*, three *pens*

Long plural **-s**. Use long plurals after *ch*, *sh*, *s*, *z*, and *x*, e.g., *churches*, *washes*, *cases*, and *boxes*

Third person singular **s**, e.g., Mary *walks* quickly.

Possessive **-'s,** e.g., *Martha's* boy

Progressive **-ing**, e.g., She is *walking*. The gerund is not included in this group, i.e., **Walking** is good for your health.

Regular past tense **-ed**, e.g., He *worked* very hard.

Past participle **-en** or **-ed**, e.g., She has *beaten* the system, or It has been *ruined*.

Comparative and superlative **-er** (**better**) and **-est** (**best**), e.g., "Alex Rodríguez is **better** than Derek Jeter," or "He is the rich**est** player in the major leagues." Understanding the meaning of these morphemes can definitely enhance students' decoding and comprehension skills. The ability to rapidly and accurately associate sounds with a cluster of letters leads to more rapid and efficient word identification. As young readers build an increasing repertoire of words that they can recognize with little effort, they can use the words they know to help them recognize other, possibly related, words that are unfamiliar. The best practice for helping students gain skill in word-recognition is real reading and writing activities.

As children read and reread texts of their own choice, they have many opportunities to successfully decode a word, and realize that each time a letter combination such as *cat* is found in the selection, it's read as *cat*. With each exposure to that word, the child reads the word more easily. A child who writes a sentence with that word is developing a greater sensitivity to meaning or context clues. The child attempting to spell that word is reviewing and applying what he knows about letter sound associations.

### Words That Can Create Comprehension Problems

There are words that children can decode but they might have problems identifying the intended meaning. Some of these difficult words include homonyms and homophones. **Homonyms** are words that have the same sound and the same spelling but differ in meaning. Homonyms are common in the content areas and can create comprehension problems. The context will determine the meaning of the words. Examples of homonyms are presented in Table 2.5.

### Table 2.5
### Examples of Homonyms

| Word | Meaning 1 | Meaning 2 |
| --- | --- | --- |
| Club | A place to socialize | A wooden stick |
| Fine | To imply good or okay | A penalty |
| Bank | A place where money is stored | Margins of a river |
| Rock | A stone | Type of music |

**Homophones** are words that sound the same but are spelled differently and have different meanings. Examples of homophones are *blew* and *blue*, *cents* and *sense*, *heir* and *air*, *wait* and *weight*, *hear* and *here*, *eight* and *ate*, *to*, *two*, and *too*, *there* and *their*, *deer* and *dear*, and *hair* and *hare*. **Homographs** are words that are spelled the same way but have more than one pronunciation and different meanings. For example, the word *bow* has two pronunciations, the first referring to the front part of a ship or the way that people bend to salute; the second referring to the decorative knot used in clothing. Consider the use of the word in the following sentence: The Japanese ambassador wore a red **bow**, stood on the **bow** of the ship and graciously **bowed** to the audience.

**Compound words** are created when two independent words are joined to create a new word. Often, knowing the meaning of the two words will guide students to understand the meaning of the compound word. For example, the compound word *birdhouse* is composed of the words *bird* and *house*. With this information, children can understand that the new word refers to a refuge or a house for birds. However, there are some examples of compound words in which the two words can create confusion among children. Examples of these deceptive compound words are *butterfly*, *nightmare*, and *brainstorm*.

## Assessing Word Identification

### Miscue Analysis

Miscue analysis is an assessment procedure to assess oral reading (Clay, 2002). Miscues refer to any deviation from text made during oral reading. Here is the procedure for its implementation:

- Select reading material a little bit above the current reading level of the child. The complete story should be about 500 words in length.

- Provide a copy of the selection to the child.

- Get a copy of the selection that is triple spaced to allow room to write comments.

- Record the reading.

- Provide instructions to the child, and tell the student that you cannot help him/her during the reading.

- Ask questions about the story.

- Let the reader listen to the recording and then analyze it.

- Look for consistent miscues and pay special attention to initial and final clusters/blends and digraphs.

## Correcting a Student's Miscues During Oral Reading

Teachers can provide feedback and assistance to students as they read aloud orally. If the student makes a meaning changing error, wait to see if she will self correct it. If she or he finishes the sentence or paragraph without self-correcting, try one of these **scaffolding tools:**

- Ask, "Does that make sense?"

- Help her or him to recognize visual and phonetic cues. Ask, "Do you see any word parts/chunks that you recognize?"

- Give nonverbal cues. For example, scaffold with gestures by pointing to the word or first letter.

- Suggest starting the sentence again. Say, "Try that again."

- Quickly supply the word to keep the flow going, if needed.

## Other Factors that Affect Word Analysis and Spelling

Various factors affect students' ability to identify words. Home factors can affect oral language vocabulary, receptive vocabulary, and other factors related to word identification.

The classic study by Hart and Risley (1995) suggests there are discrepancies in vocabulary across different socioeconomic classes. To compound this gap in language and vocabulary, the phenomenon of the Matthew Effect impacts students' reading achievement (Stanovich, 1986). According to Stanovich, good readers, already fluent and skilled at reading text, become better readers, while poor readers become worse. According to Chall and colleagues (1990), this slump in achievement in reading after 4th grade can be largely attributed to this gap in vocabulary and limited skill in fluently reading text. The school therefore becomes a crucial site of learning for academic vocabulary; this is especially the case for students in poverty (Chall, Jacobs & Baldwin, 1990).

## Reading Fluency

**Reading fluency** is the ability to decode words quickly and accurately in order to read text with the appropriate word stress, pitch, and intonation pattern (or prosody). Reading fluency requires automaticity of word recognition and reading with prosody to facilitate comprehension. **Automaticity** is the quick and accurate recognition of letters, words, and language conventions. Automaticity is achieved through continuous practice using texts written at the reading level of the child.

### Fluency and Comprehension

Fluency is a prerequisite for language comprehension. Children struggling with fluency devote their time to mastering their language skills, which is an effort that takes away from the concentration that they should be placing on reading comprehension. When students read aloud in class, the main purpose of the activity is to develop fluency. If after reading aloud, teachers ask the child comprehension questions, the child will most likely have to read the same passage silently to be able to respond to the questions. Thus, teachers should separate these two activities—read silently for comprehension and read aloud to promote fluency.

### What Is the Expectation?

The typical child in first grade should be able to read about 60 words correct per minute (wcpm) and the rate should increase by 10 words in each grade, i.e., second grade (70 wcpm), third grade (80 wcpm), and fourth grade (90 wcpm). To determine the number of words correct per minute read, a simple formula is used; namely, words read in a minute, minus errors, equals words per minute. The expectation is that children in the first to fourth grade will be able to read independently with minimum difficulty, i.e., finding no more than 1 in 20 words difficult. Students in middle school should be reading at about 120-150 wcpm (Denton, Bryan, Wexler, Reed & Vaughn, 2007).

## How Do We Teach Fluency?

Teachers can use several strategies to promote reading fluency. Descriptions of these strategies follow.

### Guided Oral Repeated Reading

Teachers can promote opportunities for **guided oral repeated reading** using text at the reading level of the child. Teachers, parents, and peers can provide support and feedback for these students. Allow the child to read the same story repeatedly to develop fluency.

### Choral Reading

Reading "in group" is another activity used to promote reading fluency. This activity is ideal for ELLs and struggling readers because pronunciation and fluency problems will not be publicly noticed and they can use the model provided by fluent readers.

### Pairing Students

Pairing proficient readers with ELLs or struggling readers can benefit both groups— the proficient child receives additional practice reading, and the ELLs and struggling readers are able to listen to fluent readers. ELLs and struggling readers can also read to their partners and receive input.

### Interactive Computer Programs

Using interactive reading programs can provide individualized reading support for children. These computer programs often contain colorful pictures and interesting stories. The child should have the option of clicking on the words or pictures in order to have the selected word read aloud or to get animation of the word's meaning. The program can also read a story at normal speed while the child follows the highlighted words in a printed text.

### Silent Sustained Reading (SSR)

While the primary goal of SSR is to boost reading comprehension, guiding the child to read silently and continuously for about 20 minutes a day can definitely improve reading fluency. Students might need assistance in learning how to select a book that is appropriate for them and that they will find interesting. Books should be appropriately challenging.

## Readers' Theater

This activity has been used successfully to emphasize reading fluency. In this activity, a story is modified so that students are reading a scripted play. Students rehearse their reading part and then create a theater format to present the reading. Children enjoy this new approach and it improves reading fluency.

## Developing Reading Fluency

Pointing to words while reading helps students see the letter–sound correspondence; however, this practice can also affect the development of reading fluency. Second graders should be guided to discontinue this practice. Continuous monitoring of reading fluency is required to insure children develop and maintain reading fluency when they are exposed to more challenging text. To be sure that students maintain reading fluency, teachers can conduct individual assessment using teacher-developed checklists or timed readings.

## Assessing Reading Fluency

A running record is an assessment strategy designed by Marie Clay (2002) to assess students' word identification skills and fluency in oral reading. As the teacher listens to a student read a page, the teacher uses a copy of the page or a blank page to mark each word the child miscues on while reading. The teacher writes the incorrect word over the printed word, draws a line through each word the child skips, and draws an arrow under repeated words. In this activity teachers can identify the type of miscues made and can then provide additional support to individual learners.

## Timed Readings

Because there are three key components of fluency instruction: rate, accuracy, and expression (prosody), each aspect can be evaluated. Typically, students are assessed for fluency through timed one-minute readings. Students should generally be reading at or above grade-level norms for wcpm (words correct per minute). Any words read incorrectly are subtracted from the number of words read aloud accurately in one minute. Students can graph their fluency rates as a visual sign of progress. To assess expression in reading, teachers can informally observe and monitor student's use of expression or prosody in their oral reading.

Two other ways to support oral reading include **echo reading** and **choral reading**. In echo reading, the teacher models the page or sentence of text at the student's instructional reading level and then asks the student(s) to echo or repeat the reading of the same text.

These continue until the students can build fluency and are able to read the text independently (Rasinksi, 2003). In choral reading, students read together at the same time in unison. This is best done in small groups. Other research-based ways to **build fluency** include independent reading and assisted reading (having students listen to a book on tape, CD, or audio book).

**Independent reading** is a crucial component of a balanced literacy program. Students can read alone or with partners for extra support.

To review, the key components of balanced reading include:

- Read Aloud
- Shared Reading
- Guided Reading
- Independent Reading

This means teachers are reading **TO children** to model the reading process, **WITH children** to provide support in the reading process, and children are reading **BY themselves** to practice and develop fluency and automaticity. Matching students to the right text is essential for independent reading.

## Competency 004 (Reading Comprehension and Assessment)

*The teacher understands the importance of reading for understanding, knows components and processes of reading comprehension and teaches students strategies for improving their comprehension.*

Helping students read for understanding is the central goal of reading instruction. Comprehension is a complex process involving the text, the reader, the situation, and the purpose for reading. There are a number of factors that come into play as a child attempts to comprehend a passage. First, students cannot understand texts if they cannot read the words. Thus, a teacher who is interested in improving students' comprehension skills needs to teach them to decode well. In addition, children need time during the school day to read texts that are easy for them to read, and also have time to discuss what has been read. Children need to read and reread easy texts often enough that decoding becomes rapid, easy, and accurate. It has been noted frequently in the literature that children who comprehend well have bigger vocabularies than children who struggle with reading. In part, this is true because their knowledge of vocabulary develops through contact with new words as they read text that is rich in new words. However, it has also been suggested that simply teaching vocabulary in isolation does not automatically enhance comprehension.

## Continuum of Reading Comprehension Skills

You will need to browse the actual TEKS documents to look for comprehension TEKS for each of the grade levels covered in this test domain (4-8). Specific grade-level TEKS that relate to comprehension can be found in the TEKS documents. The Language Arts TEKS for all levels can be located here for further review: *www.tea.state.tx.us*. Many TEKS continue across grade levels while others introduced in later grades are at a more sophisticated level. You are responsible for learning the TEKS covered by your grade levels.

## Background Knowledge

Reading comprehension can be affected by **prior knowledge**, and readers who possess rich prior knowledge about the topic of a reading often understand the reading better than classmates with less prior knowledge. A discrepancy between the schema intended by the author and the schema that the reader brings to the reading process can create confusion and comprehension problems. When students lack the background knowledge related to the topic(s) in a text, the teacher will need to build background knowledge and schema prior to reading the text.

## Guided Practice and Independent Practice

Through a gradual release of responsibility (Pearson & Gallagher, 1983) and careful and strategic scaffolding, teachers can guide students to practice and apply specific reading strategies in their independent reading. In guided practice, teachers provide various types of support and resources. Scaffolding learners with guided support means working within their zone of proximal development, or what the students can do with the assistance of a peer or adult (Vygotsky, 1978). In independent practice, students have opportunities to practice and apply the skills and strategies they learned during modeling and guided practice. Students, through independent practice, practice reading skills with text that is at their instructional and independent reading level. Teachers should reinforce reading strategies and skills on an ongoing basis through both guided and independent practice.

## Pre-Reading Activities

Prior knowledge affects students' interest in what they read and what they want to read about. Generally, students like to read about topics that are familiar to them. This is an area in which the skill of the teacher can play a significant role. Teachers should identify interests in children and find appropriate stories to match their interests. A teacher can also make a previously unfamiliar topic seem familiar through **pre-reading activities** during which prior knowledge is activated, new prior knowledge is formed, and interest is stirred up. Teachers of ELLs often have to spend more time in pre-reading activities than the actual time devoted to reading the stories as they need to review unknown vocabulary, assess students' understanding of terminology and then build on this newly formed knowledge to increase students' interest in what is about to be read.

## Setting the Purpose for Reading

Effective teachers clearly set up a purpose for reading and ask the students to predict what the purpose of the text being read is. By doing so, both the teacher and the students can obtain and draw on students' prior knowledge about the topic. Making predictions about the upcoming text and then reading based on their predictions allows them to identify key points they need to pay attention to while reading. Children should be encouraged to generate questions about ideas in the text while reading. Successful teachers encourage children to also construct mental images representing ideas in the text, or to construct actual images from texts that lend themselves to this kind of activity.

### Linking Prior Knowledge to New Knowledge

A successful teacher will help readers to process text containing new factual information through reading strategies, and to relate the new information to their prior knowledge. Questioning techniques is a simple but powerful mechanism to guide children to link current knowledge to new knowledge. Through questioning, teachers guide children to question the facts, the intent of the author, and also to check the answers through text verification. It is through conversation that children are able to compare their predictions and expectations about the content. It is also through these conversations that children see the need to revise their prior knowledge when compelling new ideas are encountered that conflict with prior knowledge. As part of these ongoing conversations, teachers will become alert to students who are applying the incorrect schema as they read, and will be able to encourage use of more appropriate knowledge. These conversations help children figure out the meanings of unfamiliar vocabulary words based on context clues, the opinions of others, and sometimes through the use of appropriate source materials such as glossaries, dictionaries, or an appropriate selection in another text. After reading activities, able teachers encourage children to revisit the text—to reread and make notes and paraphrase—in order to remember important points, interpret the text, evaluate its quality, and review important points. Children should also be encouraged to think about how ideas encountered in the text might be used in the future. As children gain competence, they enjoy showing what they know.

**Integrating Reading, Writing, Listening, and Speaking**

Conversation is a crucial component of integrating reading, writing, listening, and speaking towards the goal of developing comprehension. One research-based method to facilitate this with students in grades 4-8 is by implementing **reciprocal teaching** (Palincsar & Brown, 1984).

**Reciprocal Teaching**

Reciprocal teaching is a research-based method that develops comprehension (Palincsar & Brown, 1984). In small groups of four, students take on roles and practice four key comprehension strategies. The four strategies are:

- summarizing

- questioning

- clarifying

- predicting

The procedure is as follows:

- Students should be taught the four key roles prior to implementation in a small-group setting.

- With a shared text, and in small groups, students read to a pre-designated stopping point (usually a few paragraphs or a few sentences, depending on the grade and reading level of the students).

Students take turns doing the following activities, according to their designated role. Roles vary each time the students engage in reciprocal teaching. Reciprocal teaching can be used across the content areas anytime there is a shared text to be read.

- The summarizer highlights and synthesizes a few key ideas from the selected text.

- The questioner poses a higher-level or literal question or set of questions the group.

- The clarifier tries to clarify any confusing or unusual ideas in the text.

- The predictor makes a hypothesis about what will happen next. If it's non-fiction text, the predictor can guess what the author will write about next in the selection.

## Monitoring Comprehension

Children need to be taught to monitor their own comprehension and to decide when they need to exert more effort, or to apply a strategy to make sense of a text. The goal of comprehension instruction is for the child to reach a level at which the application of strategies becomes automatic. In summary, comprehension is maximized when readers are fluent in all the processes of skilled reading—from the decoding of words to the articulation and easy application of the comprehension strategies used by good readers. Therefore, teachers need to teach predicting, questioning, seeking clarification, relating to background knowledge, constructing mental images, and summarizing. The teaching of comprehension strategies has to be conceived as a long-term developmental process, and the teaching of all reading strategies is more successful if they are taught and used by all of the teachers on a staff. In addition, teachers need to allow time for in-school reading, and recognize that good texts are comprehended on a deep level only through rereading and meaningful discussions.

## Assessing Comprehension

A frequent device for assessing comprehension is the use of oral or written questions. A question may be **convergent**, which indicates that only one answer is correct, or **divergent**, which indicates that more than one answer is correct. Most tests, however, include a combination of question types. Questioning, whether done formally, or informally, can be done to check for students' understanding of reading and listening comprehension.

## Levels of Questioning

Generally, there are three levels of questions: literal, inferential, and applied. The state standardized test will cover the first two areas: literal and inferential types of questions. These three types of questions can be describes as follows:

**Literal** questions: Questions that are easily answered and can be easily located within the text.

**Inferential** questions: Students must draw conclusions, e.g., about a feeling, a new idea; "reading between the lines."

**Applied** questions: creative questions that extend beyond the text, e.g., "So what does this mean for us?" or "What would you have done if you were _____?" Additionally, teachers can use *Bloom's Revised Taxonomy* (Bloom, 1956; Anderson and Krathwohl, 2001) to make sure they are asking questions from across the taxonomy.

Another device for checking on comprehension is a **cloze test**, or a passage with omitted words the test-taker must supply. The test-maker must decide whether to require the test-taker to supply the exact word or to accept synonyms. Passing scores reflect which type of answer is acceptable. If assessing an understanding of meaning is the intent of the exercise, the teacher might accept synonyms and not demand the surface-level constructs, or the exact word.

The **speed** at which a student reads helps in determining the level of comprehension, up to a point. The faster that a student reads, the better that student comprehends, with some limitations. In general, the slow reader who must analyze each word does not comprehend as well as the fast reader. It is possible, however, to read too fast. Most students have had the experience of having to reread materials. For example, a student reading a chapter in preparation for a test might read more slowly than when reading a short story for pleasure or reading to get the main idea of a story.

**Semantic mapping** (Nagy, 1988) can also be used as a strategy to make direct connections between the vocabulary or words they are learning in the classroom and those that they may have seen, heard or learned. The strategy generally works as follows:

1.  The teacher puts a word or phrase representing the story in the middle of the board/paper/transparency. The teacher can have preselected categories related to the central word (3–5 categories).

2.  The teacher asks students to brainstorm related words in each category. The teacher also introduces words related to the text.

3.  Students can also look through the text to locate more words that may fit with the key word or phrase. Related words that may appear in future readings can be included also.

4.  In discussing the words, students can also talk about their personal connections with the book.

5.  Have some categories ready to add to the organizer. Preselect key words from the text and/or related to the concept to introduce to the semantic map.

## Reading Levels

Reading specialists have identified three reading proficiency levels—independent, instructional, and frustration. If the student reads 95% of the words correctly, the book is at the child's **independent level**. If the student reads 90% to 94% of the words correctly, the book is at the child's **instructional level**, which means the child can perform satisfactorily with help from the teacher. If the student reads 89% or fewer words correctly, the book is probably at the child's **frustration level**. These reading levels are determined based on the ability of children to answer comprehension questions after reading passages, typically done with an informal reading inventory. Reading levels are generally assessed through reading informal reading inventories. Reading levels help the teacher to know whether the student is appropriately matched with the level of text he or she is reading. The ongoing assessments a teacher can conduct in the classroom such as comprehension questions, teacher-designed quizzes, informal reading inventories, and other informal assessments can help the teacher to determine whether a student is meeting the objectives of the state content and performance standards. If students are not meeting the objectives, materials can be retaught more explicitly.

### Informal Reading Inventories

Informal reading inventories are informal assessment instruments designed to identify the reading levels of children. Most basal reader books contain some type of informal reading inventory. These are graded (by reading levels) passages that include **comprehension questions**. Teachers begin with a passage at the reading level of the child and continue increasing the complexity until the child is not able to respond to the comprehension questions.

Asking a child to **retell a story** is another type of informal assessment. The ability to retell a story is an informal type of assessment that is useful to the teacher, parent, and eventually, the child. Informal assessment measures can also include observations, journals, written drafts, and conversations. The teacher can then use this information to determine individual student's strengths and challenges in the area of comprehension. This data can be used in forming guided reading groups or in forming additional intervention groups beyond the regular classroom instruction.

The teacher may also make **observations** during individual or group work. Usually, the teacher makes a **checklist** of competencies, skills, or requirements, and then uses the list to check off the ones a student or group displays. A teacher wishing to emphasize interviewing skills could devise a checklist that includes personal appearance, mannerisms, confidence, and addressing the questions asked. A teacher who wants to emphasize careful listening might observe a discussion with a checklist that includes paying attention, not interrupting, summarizing the ideas of other members of the group, and asking questions about others.

Checklists give teachers the potential for capturing behaviors that cannot be accurately measured with a paper-and-pencil test, such as following the correct sequence of steps in a science experiment, or including all-important elements of a speech in class. One characteristic of a checklist that is both an advantage and a disadvantage is its structure, which provides consistency but inflexibility. However, an open-ended comment section at the end of a checklist can help overcome this disadvantage.

**Anecdotal records** are helpful in some instances, such as capturing the process a group of students' uses to solve a problem. These anecdotal records can be useful when giving feedback to the group. Students can also be taught to write explanations of the procedures they use for their projects or science experiments. One advantage of an anecdotal record is that it can include all relevant information. Disadvantages include the amount of time necessary to complete the record and the difficulty in assigning a grade. If the anecdotal record is used solely for feedback, no grade is necessary.

### Developing Comprehension with Writing Journals

Teachers should provide students with many opportunities to read, write, and discuss what they have read. Drawing on ideas from reader-response theory (Rosenblatt, 1993), students can respond to literature in open-ended and interpretive ways by recording their thinking about the text in written response journals. Students can write in response to the text heard (through read-aloud) or a text the student reads in guided reading or independent reading. The teacher can use the student's journal writing as an informal assessment to gain insight into the student's meaning making and understanding of the text. Students can do the following with written response journals that align with the Texas state standards:

- Write about their understanding

- Make inferences

- Predict

- Give reasons for the inferences they make

- Write about the author's use of craft and style

- Make connections to self, other text(s), and the world

### Criterion-Referenced Tests: STAAR™

The **State of Texas Assessments of Academic Readiness** (STAAR) is a basic skills test for children in grades 3 to 12. This criterion-referenced test assesses the implementation and the mastery of the Texas Essential Knowledge and Skills (TEKS)—the Texas state curriculum. The test contains both literary and informational types of texts, so teachers should expose students to a broad array of text genre in the classroom. More information about the STAAR reading test can be located at the Texas Education Agency website: *www.tea.state.tx.us* under the *Testing/Accountability* link.

## Assessing English Language Learners

The Texas English Language Proficiency Assessment System (TELPAS) was designed to comply with the accountability system required in the No Child Left Behind (NCLB) Act (TEA, 2011). The legislation requires that ELLs are assessed yearly in all language skills—listening, speaking, reading, and writing. The multiple-choice online reading test is an assessment that measures reading skills of ELLs.

The TELPAS is broken down into four levels: beginning, intermediate, advanced, and advanced high. To assess the writing component for ELLs in grades 2 through 12, writing samples are collected and assessed holistically to comply with the four language levels mentioned earlier—beginning, intermediate, advanced, or advanced high level. More information on the TELPAS assessment can be located *www.tea.state.tx.us* under the *Testing/Accountability* and *TELPAS* link.

## Interventions for Students Who Face Challenges

Students who face challenges in reading need more intensive support and intervention. Based on the data from the comprehension section of informal reading inventories and other formative and ongoing classroom assessment data, the teacher can develop, or work with the reading specialist or other educational support person, to develop targeted interventions in the area of comprehension for students below grade level. The following techniques can offer assistance to students who need additional support in this area. Many of these techniques are beneficial for all students:

- Teachers can identify crucial concepts to be covered in the reading and activate prior knowledge about the topic (Caldwell & Leslie, 2005).

- Build background knowledge through visual scaffolds (video clips, Internet, pictures, real objects). (Caldwell & Leslie, 2005).

- Implement vocabulary instruction throughout the reading process. (Caldwell & Leslie, 2005)

- Engage students in oral retellings. Model this technique to students using graphic organizers or other aides to support retellings. (Caldwell & Leslie, 2005)

By using these techniques, in addition to forming smaller intervention groups that meet regularly with the teacher and/or reading specialist for more intensive intervention, students can learn successful strategies for developing comprehension.

## Competency 005 (Reading Applications)

*The teacher understands reading skills and strategies appropriate for various types of texts and contexts and teaches students to apply these skills and strategies to enhance their reading proficiency.*

### Transition from "Learning to Read" to "Reading to Learn"

Children from pre-K to second grade spend much of the language arts portion of their day trying to decode and make sense of written language. The main purpose of this stage is to read for pleasure. Traditionally, short stories with pictures that have a specific structure and predictable story line are used to guide the child in the process of "learning to read." However, in the upper elementary grades, the needs of the children go beyond decoding and reading for pleasure, and "reading to learn" becomes the main task. The "reading to learn" stage require students to decode written language, understand the content, and obtain vital information from the content. One important component of the process of "reading to learn" is to understand how text is organized in the content areas. Children need to identify key components of the organizational format and identify the type of information offered. Teachers have to guide children to notice and study the structure of text, including the table of contents, titles, subtitles, and headings.

### Structure of Text

Students need to look closely at the structure of the text in order to comprehend it and understand the different purposes for reading. For instance, when reading narrative text, readers need to understand the components of narrative text and how they differ from the components and structures of expository text. To accomplish this task, skillful teachers guide the students through a picture, table, and graphic walk-through of the text while asking questions and pointing out useful text features to the students. Most texts have titles, subtitles, headings, glossaries, and bolded words. What techniques were used to make them stand out? Figuring out the structure of a text helps readers to read more efficiently. Children can anticipate what information will be revealed in a selection when they understand textual structure. Understanding the pattern of the text helps students organize ideas. Authors have a fairly short list of organizational patterns to choose from. The following are the most common patterns:

- Chronological order relates events in a temporal sequence from beginning to end

- Cause-and-effect relationships between described events, with the causal factors identified or implied

- Problem description, followed by solutions

- Comparisons and/or contrasts to describe ideas to readers

- Sequential materials, presented as a series of directions to be followed in a prescribed order

Once children understand how information in the content areas is organized, they can become more efficient readers.

### Content Area Literacy

Students in fourth through eighth grades are "reading to learn" (Chall, 1983). Even if the teacher specializes in a content area, literacy skills need to be continued to be taught to students so they can be successful in reading expository text. Additionally, students should know how to use resources such as dictionaries, glossaries, and other tools to help them as they encounter unknown or lesser-known words. In addition, the Internet provides resources such as visual dictionaries and other multi-modal representations of words that can help students' develop conceptual understandings of technical content area vocabulary (e.g., in science, social studies, math, health, and other areas). The teaching and practice of academic vocabulary is especially important for ELLs.

The teacher should also help students to understand how to comprehend information that is in a representational format (e.g., maps, tables, graphs). Teachers can model and have students practice locating these types of resources in both text and digital resources (e.g., the Internet). With increased use of digital literacies and technologies, many examples of these types of informational representations should be demonstrated to students. One way to point out these items of information in text to students is by doing shared reading where the teacher is reading the text aloud and pointing out text features, text structure, and format along the way.

### Fluent Readers

Students in upper-grades and middle-school (6th-8th grades) are reading across the content areas and encounter technical vocabulary in the types of texts they encounter in school. In this stage, students are:

- Developing an academic vocabulary

- Reading broadly across both expository and narrative texts

- Making inferences about more abstract concepts

**Becoming More Efficient Readers**

Students with strong comprehension skills and decoding ability are now ready to become more efficient readers by practicing the techniques of scanning and skimming to get content information. In **scanning**, children are guided to look for specific information in text. Children are taught to use headings, indices, boldface and italics to guide them.

## Reading Strategies

Identifying strategies used by proficient readers can help teachers make skillful choices of activities that will maximize student learning. Anne Goudvis and Stephanie Harvey (2000) offer the following suggestions for useful activities.

### Activating Prior Knowledge

Readers pay more attention when they can relate to the text. Readers naturally bring their prior knowledge and experience to reading, but they comprehend better when they think about the connections they make between the text, their lives, and the larger world. This strategy is especially important when teaching children from diverse cultural and linguistic backgrounds. Teachers need to explore the schemata necessary for children to understand the story and the background knowledge that children bring to the reading process. One of the strategies used to explore a child's background is the KWL chart. This is a chart that asks students to describe what they **K**now, **W**ant to know, **L**earned and still want to learn, or areas that the students did not understand that well. Because this is a class activity, children can benefit from what others already know, what others want to learn, and what areas were difficult for others.

### Predicting or Asking Questions

Questioning is the strategy that keeps readers engaged. When readers ask questions, even before they read, they clarify understanding and forge ahead to make meaning. Asking questions is also at the heart of active reading. A variation of this strategy is to give students a true or false question about the content to be read. Once the students complete the questions, they then read to corroborate the answers.

### Visualizing

Active readers create visual images based on the words they read in the text. These created pictures, in turn, enhance readers' understanding.

### Drawing Inferences

Inferring is when the readers take what they know, garner clues from the text, and think ahead to make a judgment, discern a theme, or speculate about what is to come.

### Determining Important Ideas

Thoughtful readers grasp essential ideas and important information when reading. Readers must differentiate between less important ideas and the key ideas that are central to the meaning of the text.

### Synthesizing Information

Synthesizing information involves combining new information with existing knowledge to form an original idea or interpretation. Reviewing, sorting, and sifting important information can lead to new insights that change the way readers think.

### Repairing Understanding

If confusion disrupts meaning, readers need to stop and clarify their understanding. Readers may use a variety of strategies to "fix" comprehension when meaning goes awry.

### Confirming Predictions

As students read and after they have finished reading, they should confirm the predictions they originally made. One can confirm negatively or positively. Determining if a prediction is correct is a goal. A good strategy to practice this is to make a two-column "T-chart" where students can list predictions about the text prior to reading. Then, during reading, students can check off in the second column whether their confirmations were correct or incorrect.

### Using Parts of a Book

Students should use the various parts of a book such as the charts, diagrams, indexes, and table of contents to improve their understanding of the reading content.

### Reflecting

An important strategy is for students to think about, or reflect on, what they have just read. Reflection can be just thinking, or it can be more formal, such as a discussion or writing in a journal. While providing instruction in a subject area, the teacher needs to determine if the reading material is at the students' level of reading mastery. If not, the teacher needs to make accommodations either in the material itself or in the manner of presentation to specific words or content. In **skimming**, students read major headings, table of contents, bold letters, graphic materials, and summary paragraphs to get the main idea of the content.

## Children's Literature

**Genre** is a particular type of literature that can be classified in multiple categories. Some of the most common genres used in elementary schools are science fiction, biography, and traditional literature, which encompass folktales, fables, myths, epics, and legends. Classifications of genre are largely arbitrary and are based on conventions that apply a basic category to an author's writing. Classifications give the reader a general expectation of what sort of book is being chosen. Teachers today are expected to share a wide range of texts with children. The most common type of books for younger children is picture books. **Picture books** are books in which the illustrations and the text work together to communicate the story. It is a very good idea to share picture books with children in several different formats. Sometimes, teachers simply read the book to the child without showing any of the pictures. The story is then discussed, and the children are asked if they would like the book to be reread, this time with the pictures being shared. Typically, this technique sparks a lively conversation about why the book with its illustrations is better than hearing the words alone. Picture books can also be used with upper-grade and even middle-school students for specific teaching purposes.

**Traditional literature** comprises the stories that have their roots in the oral tradition of storytelling and have been handed down from generation to generation. This genre also includes the modern versions of these old stories. Teachers can read and share multiple versions of old stories, and then compare and contrast each version. It is also interesting to read a number of folktales and keep track of the elements that these old stories have in common and to guide children towards noticing where these old stories show up in their day-to-day lives. Children enjoy sharing what they notice. Some examples of folk literature are:

- **Animal tales** in which the characters are animals exhibiting human characteristics, e.g., *Anansi the Spider*.

- **Fables** in which the main characters are also animals and these present a moral, e.g., *The Tortoise and the Hare*.

- *The Pourquois Tales* comprise stories from around the world that explain how things were created. Every culture may have a different version of the way things were created, e.g., *How the Sea Was Created* and *The Legend of the Bluebonnet*.

- **Wonder tales** describe stories of enchantment in faraway lands. Traditionally, it presents the themes of good vs. evil, e.g., *Snow White*.

- **Noodle head tales** are stories of lovable fools. These stories include individuals that are not very bright, but manage to survive and often succeed, e.g., *Puss in Boots*.

- **Cumulative tales** represent stories in which the information is presented in a sequence and all the events in the sequence are repeated, e.g., *The Gingerbread Man* and *The Three Little Pigs*.

- **Tall tales** describe the story of legendary people or fictitious characters that manage to accomplish great things in life, e.g., *Paul Bunyan*, *John Henry*, and *Pecos Bill*.

- **Ghost stories** have traditionally been used to regulate the behavior of children. For example, the "Boogie Man" has been used in multiple cultures to scare children and encourage them to behave properly. In the Mexican culture, the "Boogie Man" is called "El Cucuy"; in the Puerto Rican culture, "El Cuco" or "El Coco."

**Multicultural literature** is a term used to describe literature other than traditional European stories. Traditionally, these are stories from countries throughout the world that are written by people from those countries. Original works of people from other countries are regularly used in American public schools. The term **authentic multicultural** has been used to describe literature written by members of a particular cultural group to represent their own historical development and culture. Some examples of literature that reflect the Latino experience are *The Gold Coin* by Alma Flor Ada, *Chato's Kitchen* by Gary Soto, *Hairs-Pelitos* by Sandra Cisneros, *Friends from the Other Side* by Gloria Anzaldua, *When I Was Puerto Rican* by Esmeralda Santiago, and *Tomas and the Library Lady* by Pat Mora.

**Modern fantasy** is a genre that presents make-believe stories that are the product of the author's imagination. Often, they are so beyond the realm of everyday life that the stories can't possibly be true. Extraordinary events take place within the covers of these books. Fantasy allows a child to move beyond the normal life in the classroom and speculate about a life that never was, and may never be. Fantasy is a genre that typically sparks intense discussions and provides ample opportunities to illuminate the author's craft for the child. The popular *Harry Potter* series by J. K. Rowling is a perfect example of both the genre and the debate generated by this type of fiction.

**Historical fiction** is fiction that is set in the past. This type of fiction allows children to live vicariously in times and places they cannot experience in any other way. This type of fiction often has real people and real events depicted, with fiction laced around them. Historical fiction informs the study of social studies. Examples include *Don't You Know*

*There's a War On?* by James Stevenson (WWII), *Klara's New World* by Jeanette Winter (Swedish immigrant family), *A Horse Called Starfire* by Betty Boegehold (Native Americans' first encounter with the horse), and *Wagon Wheels* by Barbara Brenner (an African-American boy and family in 1870 Kansas).

**Nonfiction** books have the real world as their point of origin. These books help to expand the knowledge of children when they are studying a topic; however, these books need to be evaluated for accuracy, authenticity, and inclusion of the salient facts. Nonfiction books can be used to support the teaching of content and to promote higher-level comprehension skills.

**Biography** is a genre that deals with the lives of real people. Autobiography is a genre that deals with the life of the author. These books invigorate the study of social studies because, through careful research, they often include information that transforms a name in a textbook into a person that one may like to get to know better.

**Poetry** is a genre that is difficult to define for children, except as "not prose." Poetry is the use of words to capture something: a sight, a feeling, or perhaps a sound. Poetry needs to be chosen carefully for a child, as poetry ought to elicit a response from the child—one that connects with the experience of the poem. All children need poetry in their lives. Poetry should be celebrated and enjoyed as part of the classroom experience, and a literacy-rich classroom will always include a collection of poetry to read, reread, savor, and enjoy. *The Owl and the Pussycat* by Edward Lear, Mother Goose rhymes, limericks, and haiku are all poems or types of poems that appeal to young children.

In summary, today there is an overwhelming variety of children's literature from which to choose. When selecting books for use in a classroom, a teacher has a number of issues to consider: Are the facts presented in the book accurate? Is the book aesthetically pleasing? Is the book engaging? Bear in mind that all children deserve to see positive images of children like themselves in the books they read, as illustrations can have a powerful influence on their perceptions of the world. Children also need to see positive images of children who are not like themselves, as who is or is not depicted in books can have a powerful influence on children's perception of the world. Teachers ought to provide children with literature that depicts an affirming, multicultural view, and the selection of books available should show many different kinds of protagonists. Both boys and girls, for example, should be depicted as able and strong.

Teachers can introduce most of the terminology to study literature by using words to which students can relate. Once students understand the concept, teachers can introduce standard terminology to describe literature. Some of the concepts and terminology to describe literature follow:

- *Information* about the story including the author and illustrators, the publishing company, and even the International Standard Book Number (ISBN)

- Terminology to describe the characters of the story (the protagonist, the antagonist or villain, animals, humans)

- For older students, introduce the *point of view* of the author. A story's point of view can be first person (the author is one of the characters of the story and the narrator), the omniscient point of view (the narrator is an outsider who knows what the characters are thinking or feeling), or the *limited point of view*, or subjective consciousness (the narrator is not a character in the story). In the limited point of view, the narrator guides readers to see the story from a point of view of one of the characters.

- The *narrator* also conveys information that might seem unnatural coming from a character in the story.

- The *setting* refers to the geographical location and the general environment and historical circumstances of the story.

- The **plot** tells us what happens and the theme tells us why it happens.

Some examples of **themes** are: problems of growing up and maturing, linguistic and cultural adjustment, love and friendship, family issues, and achieving one's identity.

**Literary style**, which includes descriptions of the following:

| | |
|---|---|
| *Exposition*: | It is usually used to introduce the background information and to understand or introduce characters |
| *Dialogue*: | Communication among the characters |
| *Vocabulary*: | Word choice, use of concrete vs. abstract terminology (i.e., Is the vocabulary appropriate for the intended audience?) |
| *Imagery*: | The use of words to create sensory impressions. It conveys sights, sounds, textures, smells, and tastes. Imagery includes the collection of images used to create an emotional response in the reader. |
| *Tone*: | The author's mood and manner of expression. It might be humorous, serious, satirical, passionate, sensitive, childlike, zealous, indifferent, poignant, or warm. |
| *Analysis of the story*: | It might be multicultural or traditional, or include possible stereotypes, sexism, religious issues, controversial elements, or words or ideas that might create controversy. |

## Story Grammar

Children should be encouraged to analyze stories using the story-grammar components of setting, characters, problems encountered by characters, attempts at a solution to the problem, successful solution, and ending. Teachers can use graphic organizers to present a visual clue of these components. Story frames can be modified to introduce various components of literature, as well as an assessment tool to check for comprehension.

As children's comprehension grows more sophisticated, they move from merely attempting to comprehend what is in the text to reading more critically. This means that they grow in an understanding that comprehension can go beyond the denotative components of the facts portrayed in text. With skillful instruction, children come to read not only what a text says, but also how the text portrays the subject matter. Students recognize the various ways in which every text is the unique creation of a unique author, and they also learn to compare and contrast the treatment of the same subject matter in a number of texts. For example, teachers can introduce the multiple versions of stories like *Cinderella* in order to discuss how stories can represent similar themes using unique settings and situations. To see different versions of the Cinderella story, visit *The Children's Literature Web Guide* (Brown, 1997). Examples of variations on Cinderella are *Mufaro's Beautiful Daughters: An African Tale*, by John Steptoe; *Yeh-Shen, a Cinderella Tale from China*, by Ai-Ling Louie; and *The Egyptian Cinderella*, by Shirley Climo. Teachers can help students grow in comprehension through stages. In the beginning, teachers are usually happy if children are able to demonstrate their comprehension of what a text says in some authentic way.

The next stage is to have the children ponder what a text does—to describe an author's purpose, to recognize the elements of the text, and how the text was assembled. Finally, some children can attain the skill set needed to successfully engage in text interpretation, to be able to detect and articulate tone and persuasive elements, to discuss point of view, and to recognize bias. Over time, and with good instruction, children learn to infer unstated meanings based on social conventions, shared knowledge, shared experience, or shared values. They make sense of text by recognizing implications and drawing conclusions, and they move past the point of believing the content of a selection simply because it was in print.

## Reflecting Reading—Bias in Traditional Stories

Certain traditional children's stories are filled with episodes of violence, sexism, and stereotypes. Fairy tales like *Cinderella* and *Snow White* portray women as weak creatures in need of support and rescuing. They also present old people as ugly and often as evil, e.g., the evil witch. Killing is also rampant in stories such as *Hansel and Gretel* where the main characters are left to die in the woods, and then are imprisoned by an "ugly and old witch" whom they eventually kill. Thievery and killing are also promoted in the story of *Jack and the Beanstalk*. In the original story the main character, Jack, steals from the "ugly" giant and kills him. Teachers should not ignore violence and bias in literature, and they should use these stories as a foundation to guide children to discuss and challenge bias and stereotypes.

Teachers can use traditional stories to examine controversial events in the stories. Teachers can lead children to discuss the actions of characters like Jack in *Jack and the Beanstalk* who steals the golden goose from the giant. Teachers can also introduce new stories and modern versions of traditional stories in which stereotypes and violence are challenged. In the *Paper Bag Princess*, the protagonist presents the idea that women do not always need to be saved by men or to marry a man who will protect them. In this story, the princess saves the prince from the dragon and eventually she decides not to marry him. Guiding children to examine themes and bias in literature can make them better readers and, more importantly, they can become reflective learners.

### Reading Application: Authors as Mentors

A well-stocked and well-chosen classroom library should be full of books by exemplary authors who can become mentors and exemplars for students' writing. Students can choose an author or genre they are familiar with from books, which they have read or which have been read aloud in class. They can look for other books by this author and then read all they can by and about that author. Additionally, through read-aloud and thinking-aloud, the teacher can feature and highlight aspects of craft, style, and structure about the author's writing to students in order to encourage them to model their own writing after the author's sense of craft and style.

### Reading Workshop to Foster Independent Reading

Not all students and districts in Texas use guided reading groups. The reading workshop model uses a different design and rationale for reading instruction. In reading workshop, students read on their own while applying reading strategies that were modeled by the teacher during a mini-lesson. The reading workshop model fosters skills in independent reading while building fluency and vocabulary.

Independent and oral reading builds reading fluency (Worthy, Broaddus & Ivey, 2001). Additionally, it is important to have a well-stocked classroom library so that students can select texts they will be motivated to read during independent reading (Worthy, Moorman & Turner, 1999).

Through independent reading, students can be exposed to a wide variety of texts and genre. Students should be encouraged to interact with their classmates to discuss their reading. These methods can encourage students to become lifelong learners and readers. Students can also be taught to select their own independent reading texts, based on both their personal preferences in reading as well as their independent and instructional reading levels. However, in helping students select independent reading materials, the teacher should also be aware of the student's background knowledge as this will impact understanding of the text.

### Technology: Reading Applications

A wide range of technologies can be used to enhance reading applications in the classroom. More often, students are reading and writing using computers, mobile technologies, and laptop computers. Storybooks and textbooks are increasingly available in digital formats. Indeed, many public libraries have books available as digital downloads for students to access. With the teacher's guidance, students can read books online and also discuss books online (e.g., on blogs or other types of moderated forums). Care should be taken to ensure online "netiquette," student privacy, and appropriate content filters are in place. Additionally, students should be taught to think critically and evaluate the credibility of online information.

## Competency 006 (Written Language—Writing Conventions)

*The teacher understands the conventions of writing in English and provides instruction that helps students develop proficiency in applying writing conventions.*

The transition from oral language development to written communication requires students to develop an awareness of the following concepts (Peregoy, Boyle & Cadiero-Kapplan, 2008):

1. Print carries meaning and it conveys a message.

2. Spoken words can be written and preserved.

3. English reading and writing follows a specific direction; that is, from left to right, and top to bottom.

4. Spoken language is composed of phonemes, and these sounds can be represented by specific letters of the alphabet (alphabetic principle).

5. As an alphabetic language, English has a sound–symbol correspondence but often it is inconsistent.

6. Spoken language can be used as a foundation for spelling (phonics).

## Spelling Stages

As children begin to name letters and read print, they also begin to write letters and words. Writing development seems to occur at about the same time as reading development—not afterward, as traditional reading readiness assumed. Holistic approaches seek to integrate the language arts rather than sequencing them. Just as change has marked educators' beliefs about reading instruction and the way that reading develops, change has also marked the methods and philosophies behind the teaching of writing in schools.

Drawing is the beginning of children's attempt to convey a message in written form. Teachers can use this interest to introduce writing skills by guiding them to add words to drawings to supplement the information. Initially, the children can dictate the story to teachers until they feel comfortable enough to write it on their own. The development of written communication generally follows a predictable sequence beginning with scribbling, then developing pseudo letters and invented words until conventional spelling is achieved. An analysis of the stages of spelling follows.

### Scribbling

In this phase, children pretend that they are writing. Eventually, they develop letter-like symbols. This stage represents an awareness of the difference between writing and drawing to communicate. Scribbling is different from drawing because in scribbling, the child purposely scribbles from left to right and often also follows the top to bottom progression.

### Pseudo-Letters

In this phase, children attempt to create forms that resemble letters, but these forms cannot always be identified as such. They become aware that the alphabet contains characters of different shapes and attempt to reproduce these in a random way resulting in some form of invented spelling.

### Random Letters

In this phase, children create individual letters from the alphabet in an attempt to create words. The letters are randomly selected with no clear connection with the phonemes that they are to represent. That is, children are not producing phonetic spelling at this stage. They write letter strings and often leave a space between strings, which suggest that they are beginning to understand word boundaries.

## Invented Spelling

At this stage, children try to connect the sounds (phonemes) and the letters (graphemes) to create words resulting in nonstandard writing. A single letter or a series of letters, which represent the phonemes contained in the intended word, often represent this phonetic spelling. A child can write an *m* to represent the word mother and often they can point to the word. They can also use strings of letters, mostly consonants, to represent a word. For example, a kindergartner wrote the word *park* as *prk*, producing the three consonants and omitting the vowel. Because the phoneme–grapheme correspondence of vowels is not consistent, children generally have problems writing them.

## Transitional Spelling

Eventually, children discontinue over-reliance on phonetic spelling and begin noticing visual clues and developing a knowledge of word structure. Sight word training becomes very important at this stage. Students begin producing more standard spelling and attempt self-correction. Writing samples might become difficult to read because students erase continuously in an attempt to self-correct. Some inflectional endings (plurals, comparative, superlative, past tense, and present progressive) may appear in writing samples. Students may continue having problems with words with double vowels, like *book* and *feed*, and words containing consonant diagraphs like ***through*** or *eight*.

## Conventional Spelling

At this stage, children spell most words using conventional spelling. They still may have problems with consonant digraphs, homonyms, contractions, compound words, as well as prefixes, suffixes, and more difficult letter combinations.

## Writing Expectations

Children in fourth through eighth grade are expected to progress through the stages of writing and develop conventional spelling and coherent compositions. The fourth-grade and seventh-grade STAAR examinations require students to develop a coherent piece of writing free of major errors. It is also expected that children produce and refine compositions for general and specific audiences. Children are required to edit their work and the work of others based on clarity of ideas, coherence, and the conventions of writing.

## Strategies for Using Writing Conventions

The main objective of writing is to put ideas in writing in a logical pattern. Once this is accomplished, students have to check for writing conventions—grammar, punctuation, and capitalization. Some of the strategies to introduce writing conventions are listed below.

## Modeling

Modeling is one of the best tools to introduce effective writing. To model effective writing, teachers can introduce writing samples in which conventions are used appropriately. A variant of this activity is to present a writing sample to the whole class that contains typical errors in English conventions and to ask them to provide corrective feedback.

## Sentence Builders

One of the typical problems found in the writing samples produced by children is the use of sentence fragments. To guide children to produce complete sentences, teachers can use a technique called "sentence builders." With this technique, the teacher provides students with a list of words by syntactic categories (articles, adjectives, nouns, verbs, and conjunctions) and guides children to produce sentences using each component. As a follow-up activity, children are asked to identify the subject and the predicate, and specifically the verb. They are also asked to read the sentence to see if it contains a complete idea.

## Punctuation Exercises

To teach the importance of punctuation, teachers can use sentences in which commas or periods are necessary to deliver the intended ideas and guide students to use punctuation to clarify the intended message. For example, in the sentence *Mary, a student from Italy, requested bread, coffee and olive oil for breakfast*, it is not clear if Mary wants coffee mixed with olive oil or just coffee and also olive oil. In this case a comma is needed for clarification.

## Identifying Common Grammar Problems

Assess students' writing to identify common problems across the group, and design lessons to address the identified problems. For example, if students are producing words like *bred* and *sale boat* in place of *bread* and *sailboat*, provide training in vowel digraph and compound words. A vowel digraph occurs when two vowels produce one sound, e.g., *ea* in beach. A consonant digraph is more than one consonant that produces only one sound, e.g., *th* in thought.

## Connecting Discourse

Connecting discourse can be a challenge to some students. Children can produce choppy sentences without transition words or phrases to connect ideas or paragraphs. Most of these connectors are not used in daily speech unless students have had some speech training or an academic preparation in the area; thus, teachers need to teach connectors directly. When writing a composition, teachers can provide a list of possible sentence connectors to guide students to use them. Some of these include phrases such as "on the one hand," "moreover," and "furthermore," among others.

## Dependent and Independent Clauses

Another way to minimize the use of choppy sentences in compositions is by guiding children to combine sentences in one of the following ways:

1. Use conjunctions such as *and, but, or, nor, or yet*. For example, *My car is beautiful, but it is getting old*. Notice that in the sentence, there are two independent clauses joined by a coordinate conjunction, *but*. A comma is required before the conjunction.

2. Join two complete sentences with a semicolon. For example, the sentence *Maricela is a highly intelligent student; she was the Valedictorian of the 2009 class*. Notice that lowercase is used after the semicolon.

3. Use dependent and independent clauses. For example, the sentence *Although Dora is my friend, she did not vote for me*. Notice that in this case, the use of a dependent linking word *although* at the beginning clause made the second clause necessary to complete the whole idea. The last statement makes sense by itself, but it becomes a more complete sentence when used together.

## Assessing Writing Conventions

Teachers can provide ongoing assessment of writing conventions using multiple measures. Some of these measures include editing checklists, revision checklists, student self-assessment, peer editing, and use of technology (such as spelling and grammar check) to help support correct use of conventions in writing. These tools can be used on a daily and weekly basis as students work through the writing process. Typically, editing is done after students have composed, drafted, and revised their original work.

Teachers can also provide daily or weekly "quizzes" where students make corrections to sentences or paragraphs that contain multiple types of convention errors. These activities should be discussed in class so students understand the rules and rationale for the conventions. Teachers can also design their own rubrics for students to use during the composing process. Students in grades 4-8 should be encouraged to do self-editing of their own written work, in addition to seeking editing help from the teacher, peers, or resources. Editing rubrics can be created with the help of websites such as Rubistar: *http://rubistar.4teachers.org/*

## Interventions for Students Below Grade Level

Through ongoing assessment, the teacher can determine which students need additional support in the classroom. Students can work with the teacher in small groups and also be paired with other students to get additional help. Editing checklists can help students to monitor their own work. Other resources and tools that will help students in the area of writing conventions include the following:

- Word bank lists with sight words and other high-frequency words to help with spelling.

- Spelling tools (spell-check, electronic spelling tools, etc.)

- Editing checklists

- Examples of model papers

- Direct instruction in conventions (spelling, punctuation, grammar, etc.)

- Modeling and demonstration of the editing process

- Mini-lessons, as described below.

## Mini-Lessons on Conventions

Another way to use informal, ongoing assessment in the classroom to teach conventions is for the teacher to periodically (e.g., weekly) read through students' writing to look for patterns of errors with conventions. The teacher can then design a mini-lesson (from 5 to 20 minutes) surrounding one or more writing conventions. The rule and examples of the rule can be discussed and demonstrated for the class, followed by student practice with the convention. Teachers can also use classroom data on individual students to tailor instruction towards helping students who are working below grade level in the area of writing instruction.

# Competency 007 (Written Language—Composition)

*The teacher understands that writing to communicate is a developmental process and provides instruction that promotes students' competence in written communication.*

Writing is a developmental process that requires students to go through a series of steps to complete a written product. Some of these steps include brainstorming, semantic mapping, outlining, reading, and researching. Students must also know that they need to write for various audiences and purposes (e.g., expressive, informative, persuasive), and that they will be required to use their knowledge of text genres, structures (e.g., letter, poem, story, play), and strategies (e.g., peer conferences) for completing a written piece. Some of the steps that students must go through include drafting, editing, revising, proofreading, and publishing. Students should be aware, however, that writing is a recursive and iterative process; that is, there are always opportunities to continue improving what they are writing.

Children also need knowledge of English grammar and mechanics to revise their writing. It includes revising given texts in terms of sentence construction like revising run-on sentences and misplaced modifiers; revising subject-verb and pronoun-antecedent agreement; revising verb forms, pronouns, adverbs, adjectives, and plural and possessive nouns; and revising capitalization, punctuation, and spelling. Students also need to analyze and revise written work in relation to style, clarity, organization, intended audience, and purpose. This includes revising text prepared for a given audience or purpose, and improving organization and unity. Adding transition words and phrases, reordering sentences or paragraphs, deleting unnecessary information, and adding a topic sentence are other ways students can revise their work. Another strategy is to increase text clarity, precision, and effectiveness through word choices.

Many students struggle with writing instruction in grades 4-8. Graham and Perin (2007) report on the strong need for professional development for teachers based on data that suggest that students in K-12 settings in the United States are generally performing poorly on standardized tests in writing. The National Writing Commission highlights the significance of effective writing instruction and calls it the "neglected 'R'" (National Commission on Writing, 2003).

Dr. Donald Graves, a professor of education at the University of New Hampshire, developed an approach to writing instruction called **process writing** (2003). His notion was simple—teach children to write the way real writers write. What do writers do? They tend to write about what they want to write about. Then they may read about the subject, talk about the subject, take notes, or generally play with the topic before they compose. Then they may write a draft, knowing up-front that they are not done at this point. Writers may share the draft with others and end up writing all over it. They may also go over every sentence, thinking about word choice and looking for vague spots, or spots where the piece falls off the subject. Writers may then revise the draft again, share it again, revise it again, and so on, until they are satisfied with the product. Then they publish it. Often, writers receive feedback before and after the piece is published, which may lead to a new writing effort. Some writers save scraps of writing in a journal. They may save a turn of phrase, a comment overheard on a bus, a new word, good quotes, or an interesting topic.

Another aspect of process writing is celebration. Children are invited to share their work with the class. After young authors read their piece, classmates ought to offer affirmations and suggestions. Teachers should have children save each piece of paper generated in the writing process, and store them in a personal portfolio for review.

## Writing Stages

In addition to the traditional spelling stages, students also go through specific stages of writing. Lapp et al. (2001) divided the process into three stages: emerging writers, early writers, and newly fluent writers. A summary of these stages follows (Lapp et al., 2001).

### Characteristics of Emerging Writers

Students at the emerging stage of writing development are generally able to:

- Dictate an idea or a complete story

- Use initial sounds in their writing

- Use pictures, scribbles, symbols, letters, and/or known words to communicate a message

- Understand that writing symbolizes speech

### Educational Implications

Read stories to children and ask them to retell the story while you record it. Then, read the story back to the child to emphasize the connection between speech and print. When children begin writing words or pseudo words, ask them to read it to you, and if necessary, provide conventional spelling as an alternative. Use the *Language Experience Approach* to guide children to connect spoken words with their written representations. That is, guide children to dictate words and sentences while you record them on the board. Read the words while pointing to them. Then, ask students to copy the sentences. The next day, review the sentences written and use them for additional language development. Introduce writing for functional tasks like labeling objects and places in the classroom, writing the plan of the day, taking notes, and listing names or things to remember.

## Characteristics of Early Writers

Typically, children at the early stage of writing exhibit the following behaviors:

- Understand that a written message remains the same each time it is read

- Utilize their knowledge of sounds and letters as they progress through the stages of spelling development

- With modeling and assistance, incorporate feedback in revising and editing their own writing

- Begin to use conventional grammar, spelling, capitalization, and punctuation

### Educational Implications

Guide children to read and reread the same information to establish a connection between letters and sounds. Identify specific words and divide them into syllables to establish a connection between the sounds within a syllable. Take expressions that are commonly used in children's literature and oral communication and guide them to hear word boundaries. For example, children at this stage might write the statement "Once upon a time" as "Oncesoponditim," which represents the way the expression is produced orally without appropriate word boundaries. Model the writing process using a LCD projection system or the traditional chalkboard. Think aloud while you are writing and ask for guidance from students, e.g., Do we need a comma here or a final period? Do we need a capital *A* in the word "american"? In the writing samples of children, use peer input for editing and guide students to conduct self-corrections. Instead of making direct error corrections, ask questions leading children to examine the grammaticality of the sentences and to make their own corrections.

## Characteristics of Newly Fluent Writers

Newly fluent writers are generally able to:

- Use prewriting strategies to achieve their purposes

- Address a topic or write to a prompt creatively and independently

- Organize writing to include a beginning, a middle, and an end

- Consistently use conventional grammar, spelling, capitalization, and punctuation

- Revise and edit written work independently and/or collectively

- Produce many genres of writing

## Educational Implications

Use prewriting activities to plan for writing using an outline that indicates the sequence of ideas. This activity is especially important for children whose native language does not require the use of the linear progression required in English writing. The outline will guide children to comply with this linear rhetorical pattern. Provide interesting writing prompts to children to guide their writing. You may use the prompt given on the STAAR released tests available online. Traditionally, the Texas Education Agency releases the tests used in its yearly examinations. For information on released STAAR tests, see the Texas Education Agency, Student Assessment Division, at *www.tea.state.tx.us* under *Student Assessment/STAAR*.

Continue using peer editing and encourage self-corrections. Guide students to produce different kinds of writing such as response to literature, journal writing, and persuasive writing (writing to convince someone or to argue a point).

## Characteristics of Fluent Writers

Students in the upper elementary and middle-school grades are generally able to:

- Have an improved sense of audience

- Can write from different points of view

- Have more skills in revising and editing their own and other's work

- Show a wide range of skill in writing

- Like to experiment with voice and new forms of writing

## Educational Implications

Teachers can expose students to a wide variety of genre and format. Students should be able to write for a sense of audience and teachers can model this through "mentor text" lessons by focusing on the author's use of style to write for a certain audience. Students should be encouraged to write with increasing complexity in sentence length and fluency. Students should be encouraged to use a writing notebook in which to experiment with different forms and styles of writing. Pieces from the writing notebook can be drafted, revised and edited to become complete pieces that students take through different iterations of the writing process. Students should be expected to peer edit one another's work, with modeling and guidance from the teacher.

## New Trends in Writing

In addition to process writing, there is a new trend emphasizing specific elements of the writing process. The best-known system is called the 6+1 Trait® Writing. This system, which was developed by the Northwest Regional Educational Laboratory (NREL), emphasizes seven elements of the writing process (2012). These elements are described below.

1. **Organization**—the internal structure of the sample

2. **Ideas**—how ideas are presented in the sample

3. **Voice**—the uniqueness of the author and how ideas are projected

4. **Word Choice**—the vocabulary used to convey meaning

5. **Sentence Fluency**—the flow of ideas and the use of connectors

6. **Conventions**—the use of capitalization, punctuation, and spelling

7. **Presentation**—how the final product looks in print

The Texas Education Agency developed a similar writing program emphasizing similar components for scoring student writing. Expository and narrative writing rubrics for both fourth and seventh grade STAAR writing test focus on the following on their scoring rubrics:

- Organization/Progression

- Development of Ideas

- Use of Language/Conventions

Both the 6+1 Trait Writing and the STAAR writing program guide children to demonstrate knowledge of writing traits. To assess their performance, both programs develop a four-point rubric for each of the writing traits.

## Identifying the Characteristics of Modes of Writing

Writing serves many different functions. The main functions are to narrate, to describe, to explain, and to persuade. Students need to be aware of each of these functions. In any event, these four categories are neither exhaustive nor mutually exclusive. The **narrative** is a story or an account. It may recount an incident or a series of incidents.

The account may be autobiographical to make a point. The narrative may be fiction or nonfiction.

The purpose of **descriptive** writing is to provide information about a person, place, or thing. Descriptive writing can be fiction or nonfiction. Description is a powerful tool in advertisement. Advertisements describe items using factual information, but the way the information is presented can become a persuasive type of writing for prospective buyers.

The purpose of **expository** writing is to explain and clarify ideas. Students are probably most familiar with this type of writing. While the expository essay may have narrative elements, the storytelling or recounting aspect is minor and subservient to the explanation element. Expository writing is typically found in many textbooks; for instance, a textbook on the history of Texas would likely be expository in nature.

The purpose of **persuasive** writing is to convince the reader of something. Persuasive writing fills current magazines and newspapers, and permeates the World Wide Web. The writer may be trying to push a political candidate, to convince someone to vote for a zoning ordinance, or even to promote a diet plan. Persuasive writing usually presents a point, provides evidence, which may be factual or anecdotal, and supports the point. The structure may be very formal, with counter positions and counterarguments. Whatever the organizational pattern, the writer's intent is to persuade readers of the validity of some claim. Nearly all essays have some element of persuasion. Authors choose their form of writing not necessarily just to tell a story but also to present an idea. Whether writers choose the narrative, descriptive, expository, or persuasive format, they have something on their minds that they want to convey to their readers.

### Writing for a Variety of Audiences, Occasions, and Purposes

The writer must consider the audience, the occasion, and the purpose when choosing the writing mode. The writer's responsibility is to write clearly, honestly, and cleanly for the reader's sake and so the **audience** is very important. The teacher can designate an audience for students' writing. Knowing who will read their work, students can modify their writing to suit the intended readers. For instance, a fourth-grade teacher might suggest that the class take their compositions about a favorite animal to second graders and allow the younger children to read it. The writers soon will realize that they need to use manuscript and not cursive writing, to employ simple vocabulary, and to omit complex sentences when they write for their young audience.

The **occasion** also helps to determine the elements of writing. The language should fit the occasion. Students should keep in mind that particular words may have certain effects, such as evoking sympathy or raising questions about an opposing point of view. The students and teacher might try to determine the likely effect on an audience of a writer's choice of a particular word or words.

The **purpose** helps to determine the format (narrative, expository, descriptive, or persuasive) and the language of the writer. The students, for instance, might consider the appropriateness of written material for a specific purpose such as a business letter, a communication with residents of a retirement center, or a thank-you note to parents. The teacher and students might try to identify persuasive techniques used by a writer in a passage.

In selecting the mode of writing and the content, the writer might ask the following:

1. What would the audience need to know to believe you or to accept your position? Imagine someone you know (visualize her or him) listening to you declare your position or opinion and then saying, "Oh yeah? Prove it!" What evidence do you need to prove your idea to this skeptic?

2. With what might the audience disagree?

3. What common knowledge does the audience share with you?

4. What information do you need to share with the audience?

The teacher might wish to have the students practice selecting the mode and the language by adapting forms, organizational strategies, and styles for different audiences and purposes.

## Types of Writing

Teachers need to encourage children to write for meaningful purposes. Meaningful writing can be easily incorporated as part of daily classroom activities and can enhance not only writing skills, but also content area mastery. Some of the types of writing that can be incorporated are functional writing and journal writing.

### Functional Writing

Functional writing describes activities in which writing is used to achieve a specific purpose. For example, labeling areas and objects in the classroom is a meaningful and useful activity for all students, especially ELLs. Note taking or developing a grocery list or list of holiday gifts becomes a meaningful activity and will motivate children to write.

### Journal Writing

- Various types of journals can be used in elementary grades. Some of these include:

- **Personal journals** are used to record personal information and to encourage self-analysis of their experiences. This is a personal document and it is up to the child to make it available to others.

- **Dialogue journals** promote written communication among students and between the teacher and students. The main purpose is to communicate, not to teach writing skills. Teachers can model writing when they reply to children.

- **Reflective journals** are used to respond in writing to specific situations or problems. It is often shared with the teacher for input.

- **Learning logs** are commonly used in the content areas to record elements discussed in class. In these logs, students describe what they have learned and elements in which they have difficulties. Teachers read the document and act on the request for assistance.

## Strategies to Promote Written Communication

Reading to students can provide multiple benefits to children. It develops print awareness and understanding of the intonation pattern of the language. A discussion on the content of the story allows students opportunities to enhance comprehension and practice speaking. It also provides a model of fluent reading together with the appropriate intonation pattern of the language. Reading together can be enjoyable. Students laugh and talk about the story and the characters. Children can also be exposed to different kinds of writing (genre) like fiction, biography, and short stories. Finally, they are exposed to the story framework, which is the setting, characters, plot, climax, and resolution.

### Interactive Journals

As it was discussed earlier in the chapter, writing in journals provides students with opportunities to use language authentically in literary contexts. Teachers and students can have a designated time for journal writing to communicate on a daily basis. This gives students the freedom to use their own mechanics and invented spellings. Because the purpose of written journals is to communicate, teachers should not correct children's journal writing, but should write comments on content and provide encouragement and reassurance. Some of the key advantages of interactive journals for children and teachers are located in Table 2.5.

## Table 2.5
## Advantages of Interactive Journal Writing for Students and Teachers

| Advantages for Students | Advantages for Teachers |
|---|---|
| • Students learn that written language communicates.<br><br>• Students experience making choices about topics and develop a sense of ownership of the written product.<br><br>• Students develop their writing within meaningful context.<br><br>• Students develop a personal interaction with the teacher and with peers.<br><br>• Students can use this safe environment to experiment with language. | • Teachers learn about each child's interest, ideas, and everyday concerns.<br><br>• Teachers interact and communicate on an individual basis with each child.<br><br>• Teachers model standard convention or writing in the context of authentic communication. |

## Technology and Writing Instruction

A wide variety of technology can be incorporated into writing instruction and the writing process for students in grades 4–8. In addition to word processing and publishing, students can participate in more interactive types of writing such as creating and participating in a blog (weblog). In this way, students can write for a real audience of peers or even students in other classes. Additional types of technology-based writing include:

- PowerPoint Presentations

- Brochures

- Newsletters

- Websites

## Mentor Texts: Connecting Reading and Writing

There are many ways teachers can combine reading, writing, listening, and speaking in the writing composition experience. One way is to incorporate mentor text lessons (e.g., see Dorfman & Cappelli, 2007) into writing composition instruction for students in grades 4–8.

### Connecting Reading and Writing with Mentor Texts

With mentor texts, teachers model good writing by a certain author or genre by sharing exemplar texts that are representative of that author or genre with students. An example of a mentor text writing lesson to teach the writing of historical fiction is using *Minty: A Story of Young Harriet Tubman* by Alan Schroeder and Jerry Pinkney. An overarching goal of this mentor text writing lesson might be the following: Through listening to a touchstone text during a teacher read-aloud, the students will begin to develop their understanding of the characteristics of the genre of historical fiction. By the end of the unit, they will be able to articulate and explain what historical fiction is. Through a read-aloud experience, the teacher can think aloud about how the author uses dialogue and details to portray a realistic and authentic account of what a glimpse into the life of a historical figure, Harriet Tubman, might have been like. The teacher can say something like, "As I read, I want you to keep noticing what kind of person Harriet Tubman is. What words and details does the author use to let us know she was a strong person?" Mentor texts can be used for both fiction and nonfiction writing.

## Assessing Writing Composition

Informal assessment can be very useful in giving students feedback on their writing. It can be based on observations, conferring (conversations with students), and collection of student work in a systematic way (portfolios). Each is described below.

### Informal, Ongoing Assessment: Conferring with Students

Conferring (Graves, 2003) with students offers teachers a chance to discuss student's written work informally. Teachers can meet with students individually on a weekly basis to check-in and ask informal questions about what each student is composing and offer assistance to students. Teachers can record observations in the form of anecdotal notes and records to keep track of a student's strengths, needs, and overall progress.

### Informal, Ongoing Assessment: Revising Checklists and Self-Assessment

Teachers can provide revision checklists to students so that they can self-monitor their own compositions. These checklists can help students to consider their audience as they write. Students can also focus on clarity, coherence, and other traits of quality writing. Teachers can design their own revision checklists or find ready-made ones online. Students need to be taught the purpose of these checklists and how to use them. The best way to model the use of a revision checklist is by the teacher demonstrating how to use a revision checklist with her or his own writing.

### Informal, Ongoing Assessment: Portfolios

**Portfolios** are collections of students' best work. They can be used in any subject area in which the teacher wants students to take more responsibility for planning, carrying out, and organizing their own learning. Like a portfolio created by an artist, model, or performer, a student portfolio provides a succinct picture of the child's achievements over a certain period. Portfolios may contain essays or articles written on paper, videos, multimedia presentations on computer disks, or a combination of these. Language arts teachers often use portfolios as a means of collecting the best samples of student writing over an entire year. An important consideration when working with portfolios is that teachers should provide, or assist students in developing, guidelines for what materials should go in their portfolios because it would be unrealistic to include every piece of work in one portfolio. Using portfolios requires that the students devise a means of evaluating their own work. A portfolio should not be a scrapbook for collecting handouts or work done by other individuals, but it can certainly include work by a group in which the student was a participant.

Some advantages that portfolios have over testing are that they provide a clear picture of students' progress, they are not affected by one inferior test grade, and they help develop students' self-assessment skills. One disadvantage of portfolios is the amount of time required to teach students how to develop meaningful portfolios. However, the time is well spent if students learn valuable skills. Another concern is the amount of time teachers must spend to assess portfolios. However, as students become more proficient at self-assessment, the teacher can spend more time in coaching and advising students throughout the development of their portfolios. Another concern is that parents may not understand how the teacher will grade the portfolios. The effective teacher devises a system that the students and parents understand before work on the portfolios begins.

## Scoring Compositions

Holistic scoring is used to evaluate the composition and writing performance of students in Texas. The whole writing sample is scored based on a pre-established criterion contained in a rubric.

## Criterion-Referenced Writing Assessment

As of this writing, the State of Texas is now implementing the STAAR (State of Texas Assessments of Academic Readiness). For the purposes of this test prep manual, you will need to know how writing is assessed on the STAAR test for students in grades 4 and 7.

Browse and try part or all of a STAAR writing test for fourth or seventh grade found on the TEA website under *Student Assessment/STAAR* under *Writing*.

Especially note the writing prompts. Students are now expected to write *two* essays for the STAAR writing test in 4th and also in 7th grade. Rubrics for this test can be located on the Texas Education Agency website.

# Competency 008 (Viewing and Representing)

*The teacher understands skills for interpreting, analyzing, evaluating and producing visual images and messages in various media and provides students with opportunities to develop in this area.*

According to the TEKS (2009a; 2009b), students in grades 4-8 need to develop the necessary skills to create and understand images and messages in a variety of media. The skills required by the students increase in complexity as they move from lower elementary grades to upper elementary. For instance, students in grades 1–3 are required to produce visual representations of the information they are learning in school or the tasks they are involved in (e.g., creating an image summarizing a story read). Students are also required to know how to discuss the visual representations they have created. In grades 4–8, students need to be able to understand, interpret, analyze, critique, and produce these visual representations as well as discuss their meaning or significance through the use of multiple media, including newsletters, charts, and electronic presentations, among others. Students are also required to understand the author's purpose and choice of various elements that were used by him/her to get their message across through the use of multiple media. The characteristics and functions of the various different types of media are explained below. More information on the TEKS that relate to viewing and representing for students in grades 4-8 can be located in the TEKS documents on the Texas Education Agency website.

## Types and Characteristics of Media

Media is considered to be any means used to convey information to others. There are at least three main types of media available. These include print, visual, and electronic media. **Print media** is what is used to disseminate information in print form such as that found in newspapers, magazines, and direct mail. Print media is static; that is, once it is published, the information cannot be changed. **Visual media** incorporates the use of visual imagery to either complement or supplement the message being carried. Visual media can also stand by itself. For example, photographs and paintings can convey meaning without the need of including text. Moreover, visual media is also an integral part of print media to illustrate messages. As such, visual media can take many forms, including photography, film, and even cartoons. Visual media can be either static (e.g., still photograph) or dynamic as seen in movies or videos. In addition to incorporating print and visual imagery, **electronic media** requires the use of an external device such as a television, computer, or personal assistant device to display the information and images being presented. Electronic media is used in many different fields including journalism, fine arts, commerce, education, and communications. A primary type of electronic media that encompasses different electronic tools is the Internet, where one can find blogs, email, Web sites, etc.

Technology changes at a rapid pace, and teachers must keep this in mind when working with students. In fact, many of the tools that are used for presenting information are improved and refined every day. For instance, the process for creating photographs has evolved from creating these on plates and then film to now being created digitally.

In this information era, beginning teachers should also understand that there is a vast array of possibilities to create and display information by making use of existing types of media. In fact, as the need for using and sharing massive amounts of information with others becomes necessary, some of these types of media will take precedence over others. Take, for instance, the use of electronic media such as the use of online sources. The use of online information has become so pervasive in today's society that static types of media such as print media is now being channeled electronically (e.g., newspapers). Also, the use of online resources and Web sites has become a staple activity. As such, students expect those around them to know how to use the tools and to use them appropriately. Students are also looking to have opportunities for using and producing different types of products through the use of various types of media.

## Representing Messages and Meanings through Media

Charts, tables, graphs, pictures, and print and non-print media are examples of materials used to solely present or summarize information and/or to complement the message being conveyed. For instance, a chart can be used to summarize large amounts of information without the need to use extensive written explanations. Students should understand that visual representations are important and that the purpose for using them is to present information and to facilitate the communication of the message. Visual images should also be used to make information more understandable. A graphic can expand a concept, serve as an illustration, support points, summarize data, organize facts, add a dimension to the content (such as a cartoon adding humor), compare information, demonstrate change over time, or furnish additional information. Through graphics, the reader can interpret, predict, and even apply information with some careful observation. Actively questioning students as they create visual images (e.g., asking them what they are trying to convey or how they think someone will interpret their image) as well as providing ongoing feedback may allow students to specifically focus on and clarify the information that is being presented and that can be derived in such graphic formats.

## Understanding How Students May Interpret and Evaluate Visual Images

It is important for teachers to realize that even a graphic that appears uncomplicated may challenge a reader's interpretive skills. Many inferences may be necessary for even the simplest visual aid or graphic. Many students may initially skip over graphics, or may just notice their presence without interpreting them. Likewise, students may only focus on the graphic aspects being presented in such visual media but not focus on the complementary or written explanations. Even students who have some training in the use of graphic information may not be able to transfer that knowledge to other content areas, or may have trouble going from print to graphic and then back to print. In either case, students may not have been taught how to use multiple representations of information. Teachers can help students use multiple representations of information by using open-book and guided reading. A teacher can also demonstrate how to use a chart or graph through the use of electronic tools including overhead projectors and interactive whiteboards. Examples of presentations and steps toward creating an effective presentation can be shared with the students. Resources and software that would be useful as "mentor texts" (Dorfman & Cappelli, 2007) can give students representative examples of how to best select images to use in parallel with the text (e.g., consideration of how the image parallels or complements the text).

Visual design can be thought of as containing its own grammar (Kress & van Leeuwen, 2001). Teachers can help students to understand and apply the elements of such visual grammar by teaching its component parts (Wysocki, Johnson-Eilola, Selfe & Sirc, 2004):

- **Visual impact:** the ways in which the overall visual design appeals to the reader (e.g., through detail, layout, use of color).

- **Visual coherence:** the ways in which the design of the piece creates a sense of unity and wholeness (e.g., by use of shapes, line, imagery).

- **Visual salience:** using design features to generate a certain effect (e.g., through varying size, colors, clip art, etc.).

- **Organization:** the layout of the page to create a unique pattern, especially one that is understandable to the reader (e.g., through consideration of how the different aspects of the layout might be arranged).

Of course, these features of visual literacy overlap and can be used flexibly to guide students towards creating an awareness of the visual literacy that parallel and differ from the features of print literacy.

Teachers should model how to read, complement, and interpret visual images whenever students are required to create visual images as part of their work in the classroom. Pictures and other graphics can arouse interest and stimulate thinking. Additionally, graphics can add clarity, prevent misunderstandings, show step-by-step developments, exhibit the status of things, events, and processes, and demonstrate comparisons and contrasts (Vacca and Vacca, 1989).

## Integrating Technology for Producing Communications

Teachers should provide students with opportunities to use state-of-the-art technology and tools to not only motivate children to read, write, and monitor their writing, but to create various kinds of communications products with a variety of media. For instance, one could assume that the goal for using **word-processor** software is to simply record written information. Interestingly, with the advances in technology, such software has improved their features to even offer writers assistance with the actual editing of their documents. Other uses for this type of software include creating semantic maps, tables, charts, and graphs. Writing-related elements like spell check, definitions of terms, thesaurus, and even suggestions for sentence constructions are commonly available in programs like Microsoft Word. The real function of a spell checker is not only to identify misspelled words, but also to free students from the pressure of getting spelling right, at least at the drafting stage. Students should be encouraged to put their ideas in writing without stopping to check for spelling. Once they finish the content of the writing, they can take care of other important elements like spelling. Students should, however, be aware that there may be cases in which the spell checker may be ineffective. Therefore, children should be guided to pay attention to corrections and to learn from them.

Teachers have to teach children how to use and take advantage of programs available for communicating and creating electronic products in their classrooms. Some of these products include creating a classroom newsletter, a multimedia presentation, and a video response to a group project. Students should be aware that they must keep their audience and purpose for creating such products in mind whenever they are creating their pieces. Students should also make sure that the language being used is appropriate and understandable for their audience.

# Competency 009 (Study and Inquiry Skills)

*The teacher understands the importance of study and inquiry skills as tools for learning in the content areas and promotes students' development in study and inquiry skills.*

## Study Skills

Students need to know how to study the information that has been presented to them in texts and other media. Graphic organizers help students to review material, and help them to see the relationships between one bit of information and another. For example, a Venn diagram helps students identify how things are alike and different. A Venn diagram can also be used to help students recognize how a single topic is treated in two readings, or how two books, animals, or ecosystems are alike and different. The student labels the two overlapping circles and lists items that are unique to each one in each respective circle. In the area in the center where there is an overlap, the student records the elements that the two items have in common.

Another skill students need to master is **note-taking**. Unless a teacher wants to read passages directly out of an encyclopedia or other source material, he or she should take the time to actively teach note-taking techniques. Teachers should also think of an authentic task that requires students to accomplish higher-level manipulation of the given information. First, help the children to formulate a researchable question. Second, have them highlight the words that might be used as key words in searching for information. Third, have students brainstorm in groups of other words to be used as key words. Next, ask then to list appropriate sources. Finally, as they skim articles, they can fill in the chart with little chunks of information.

Other examples of using study and inquiry skills in the classroom include having students take notes, incorporate test-taking strategies, using metacognitive strategies such as organizing information, creating summaries of information, and reading graphic information. Teachers can incorporate demonstration and practice of these skills across the content areas. Additionally, teachers need to be able to use formative assessment and knowledge of the state standards (TEKS) to support students in their acquisition of study skills. At times, intervention will be needed to support students who would benefit from additional instruction in the area of study skills.

## Graphic Organizers

Graphic organizers help students improve organizational skills and provide a visual representation of facts and concepts and their relationships within an organized framework.

The ability to organize information and ideas is fundamental to effective thinking. To increase reading comprehension among ELLs, allow students to share information about the story or passage. Through this activity, students can help each other using peer scaffolding and oral language interaction. Semantic mapping can be used before and after readings to organize materials in new ways by highlighting connections among ideas.

**Think-Aloud**

Think-alouds allow the teacher and students to problem solve together. The teacher poses a question to students and then, the teacher, group of students, or entire class responds at the same time. This strategy can be easily used to increase reading comprehension in the content areas. In modeling a think-aloud, the following steps are used (Wilhelm, 2001).

1. The teacher explains *what* the strategy is and what it is used for.

2. The teacher explains *why* the strategy is important for improving reading comprehension.

3. The teacher explains in what context to use the strategy: *when* to use the strategy.

4. The teacher models *how* to use the strategy using an authentic text. Modeling continues until the students begin to use prompts and strategies aloud.

5. The teacher guides student practice using *authentic* text. The teacher gradually releases responsibility for doing the think-aloud to students.

6. Students practice the strategy in pairs or independently. The teacher asks that students do a think-aloud in which they explain and articulate their thought processes for using the strategy.

**Summarizing and Organizing Content**

When children are guided to summarize and organize content, they are using basic reading comprehension and taking this content to a higher level of thinking including evaluation, analysis, and synthesis. By guiding children to go beyond the literal meaning and to reorganize content requires students to develop a deeper understanding of content. Guide students to reorganize content (study skills) by creating their own tables, charts, and graphs. For example, students can develop a chart containing the longest rivers of the world organized by regions and countries. When children are required to process and present information using a new structure, comprehension and knowledge of the content area increases and memory retention is enhanced.

## Study Plans

To increase content comprehension, teachers might acquaint students with several study plans to help them read content materials. Many of these plans are well known and easily accessed, and the teacher and the students can simply select the plan(s) that works best for them within various subjects. Students may use **mnemonic devices**, or memory-related devices, to help them remember the steps in reading a chapter effectively.

## SQ4R

Students often use plans like **SQ4R** when reading text in content areas. The acronym stands for **survey, question, read, reflect, recite, and review** (Tomas & Robinson, 1972). An explanation of the different components of the SQ4R follows:

- **Survey:** During the **survey (S)** part, readers examine the headings, illustrations, bold letters, and major components of the text in order to develop predictions and generate **questions (Q)** about the topic.

- **Question:** The student may wish to devise some questions that the chapter will probably answer. Through these questions, students establish the purpose for reading and the questions serve as a reading guide. If the chapter has questions at the end, the student can also study these before reading the chapter.

- **Read (1R):** During the next stage, students read while looking for answers to the questions previously generated and/or those questions written by the publishers, which are usually located at the end of the section.

- **Write (2R):** Students monitor their comprehension as they write a summary of the story or text. Creating a summary allows students opportunities to internalize and make their own interpretation of the content.

- **Recite (3R):** The student attempts to answer orally, or in writing, the student-developed questions or the questions at the end of the chapter.

- **Review (4R):** Finally, students review the text to evaluate the accuracy of their answers and to show how much they learned about the content.

Reciprocal teaching is an instructional activity designed for struggling readers in which the teacher engages students in a dialogue about specific portions of a text (Palinscar & Brown, 1984). The main purpose of this activity is to guide children to construct meaning and to monitor reading comprehension. The dialogue is structured to elicit four components:

1. Summarizing the content of a passage

2. Asking a question about the main idea

3. Clarifying difficult parts of the content

4. Predicting what will come next

## DRTA

The acronym **DRTA** stands for Directed Reading/Thinking Activity. This teacher-directed strategy helps students to establish a purpose for reading a story or reading expository writing from a content book (Reutzel & Cooter, 1992). The teacher models the process of creating and correcting predictions as the story progresses to strengthen comprehension. DRTA has three main steps:

1. Sample the text to develop background: Children are guided to read the title, look at pictures or any kind of visual representations, and read some sample lines from the text to develop hypothesis about the content of the text.

2. Make predictions: Students make predictions based on a sample of the text.

3. Confirm or correct predictions: Children read the text and engage in follow-up activities to corroborate if the predictions were correct.

## Reading Comprehension in the Content Areas

To assist children and especially ELLs in reading material that may be beyond their reading level, teachers can incorporate the following strategies.

- Record selected passages that students can listen to while reading along with the text. Teachers can use adult volunteers and fluent readers in the group to read to children unable to read it for themselves.

- Pair children off into a tutor/tutee arrangement or in a small group reading format. Teachers should pair children of different linguistic levels and degree of achievement to create a peer-support system.

- Introduce the technical vocabulary of the content areas prior to reading. Introduce elements such as connotation (implied meaning), denotation (literal meaning), and idioms in the way they are used in text. For example, the word *right* can have multiple meanings depending on the content area or the activity. In mathematics, *right* is an angle of 90 degrees, but in social studies *right* can be used to provide directions or to declare correctness.

- Teach content vocabulary through direct, concrete experiences as opposed to definitions. Definitions can lead to misinterpretations since additional words are required to define the term. Teaching vocabulary in a contextualized situation is particularly important for ELLs because they often rely on translations that do not always represent the intended concept. For example, in English, the word *bayou* is used extensively in Texas and Louisiana. However, *bayou* is very difficult to define for someone who has never seen one. What is the difference between a bayou, a creek, a swamp, or a marshland? How big is a bayou? If an adult has difficulty answering these questions, imagine how young children may struggle!

- Introduce instructional strategies for self-monitoring reading comprehension. In this kind of strategy, students read aloud a passage and then pause to question themselves about the meaning of the passage.

### Strategies for Developing Critical-Thinking Skills

Critical-thinking skills include analysis, synthesis, and evaluation. Benjamin Bloom (1956) created taxonomy for categorizing levels of thinking processes typical in school children. The taxonomy presents a structure to categorize the levels of thinking required in order to ask and answer questions. These questions have traditionally been used to guide children from the basic recalling of information (**knowledge**) and understanding information (**comprehension**) to using higher order thinking skills such as analysis, synthesis, and evaluation. Recalling and understanding are important parts of reading comprehension; however, it is a teacher's responsibility to help children move from literal comprehension and explicit ideas to a more figurative comprehension and implicit ideas. Teachers have to guide children to analyze (**analysis**) the ideas presented in text and then to make inferences (**analysis**), to assess their inferences (**evaluation**), to draw conclusions about the ideas (**synthesis**), and perhaps to apply the ideas to new situations (**application**). Children who are able to go beyond the literal and explicit information in text develop a deeper understand of the content areas and are able to manipulate the content at higher levels of thinking.

### Linguistic Accommodation Testing for ELLs and Special Education Students

The state of Texas provides for linguistic accommodation for ELLs and special education children taking the content portion of the STAAR examination in grades 3–8 and 10 in order to ensure that reading comprehension does not interfere in assessing content mastery. Based on specific recommendations from the Admission, Review, and Dismissal (ARD) and/or the Language Proficiency Assessment Committee (LPAC), districts can allow linguistic accommodations for special education and ELL students when taking the basic skills test (STAAR).

## References

Anderson, L. W., and Krathwohl, D. R. (Eds.). 2001. A taxonomy for learning, teaching and assessing: A revision of Bloom's Taxonomy of educational objectives: Complete edition, New York: Longman.

Bloom, B. S. 1956. Taxonomy of educational objectives: The classification of educational goals: Handbook I, cognitive domain. New York: Toronto: Longmans, Green.

Caldwell, J.S. and L. Leslie. 2005. Intervention strategies To Follow, Informal Reading Inventory Assessment: So what do I do now? Boston: Pearson Education, Inc.

Chall, J. S. 1983. Stages of reading development, New York: McGraw-Hill.

Chall, J. S., Jacobs, V. A., and L.E. Baldwin. 1990. The reading crisis: Why poor children fall behind. Cambridge, Mass.: Harvard University Press.

Clay, M. M. 2002. An observation survey of early literacy achievement. 2nd ed. Portsmouth, NH: Heinemann.

Denton, C., Bryan, D., Wexler, J., Reed, D., and S. Vaughn. 2007. Effective instruction for middle school students with reading difficulties: The reading teacher's sourcebook. Austin, TX: Vaughn Gross Center for Reading and Language Arts at The University of Texas at Austin.

Dorfman, L. R., and R. Cappelli. 2007. Mentor texts: Teaching writing through children's literature, K–6. Portland, ME: Stenhouse Publishers.

Ehri, L. 1998. Grapheme-phoneme knowledge is essential for learning to read words in English. In Word Recognition in Beginning Literacy, eds. J. Metsala and L. Ehri, 3–40. Mahwah, NJ: Erlbaum.

Gersten, R., Baker, S.K., Shanahan, T., Linan-Thompson, S., Collins, P., and R. Scarcella. 2007. Effective literacy and English language instruction for English Learners in the elementary grades: A practice guide. Washington, DC: National Center for Education Evaluation and Regional Assistance, Institute of Education Sciences, U.S. Department of Education.

Goudvis, A. and S. Harvey. 2000. Strategies that work. Portland, ME: Stenhouse Publishers.

Graham, S., and D. Perin. 2007. Writing next: Effective strategies to improve writing of adolescents in middle and high schools – A report to Carnegie Corporation of New York. Washington, DC: Alliance for Excellent Education.

Graves, D. 2003. Writing: Teachers and children at work, 20th Anniversary Ed. Portsmouth, NH: Heinemann.

Hart, B., and R.T. Risley. 1995. Meaningful differences in the everyday experience of young American children. Baltimore: Paul H. Brookes.

Herrell, A. and M. Jordan. 2007. Fifty strategies for teaching English language learners. 2nd ed. New York: Pearson.

Kress, G. and T. J. Van Leeuwen. 2001. Multimodal Discourse: The modes and media of contemporary communication. London, England: Oxford University Press.

Lapp, D., D. Fisher, J. Flood, and A. Cabello. 2001. An integrated approach to the teaching and assessment of language arts. In Literacy assessment of second language learners. eds. S. Rollins Hurley and J. Villamil Tinajero. 1–24. Boston, MA: Allyn and Bacon.

Nagy, W.E. 1988. Teaching vocabulary to improve reading comprehension. Newark, DE: International Reading Association.

The National Commission on Writing in America's Schools and Colleges. 2003. The neglected "R:" The need for a writing revolution. Washington, DC: College Entrance Examination Board.

Northwest Regional Education Laboratory. 2012. 6+1 Trait Writing.

Palinscar, A. S. & Brown, A. L. 1984. Reciprocal teaching of comprehension-fostering and comprehension-monitoring activities. Cognition and Instruction (1): 117–175.

Pearson, P.D., and M.C. Gallagher. 1983. The instruction of reading comprehension. Contemporary Educational Psychology, 8, 317-344.

Peregoy, S. F., O. F. Boyle, and K. Cadiero-Kapplan. 2008. Reading, Writing and Learning in ESL: A Resource Book for K-12 Teachers. 5th. ed. New York: Pearson.

Piper, T. 2006. Language and learning: The home school year. 4th ed. Columbus, Ohio: Merrill Prentice Hall.

Rasinski, T. V. 2003. The fluent reader: Oral reading strategies for building word recognition, fluency, and comprehension. New York: Scholastic.

Reutzel, R. D., and R. Cooter. 1992. Teaching children to read: From basals to books. New York: Macmillan Publishing Co.

Rosenblatt, L. 1993. Literature as exploration. New York: Modern Language Association of America

Stanovich, K.E. 1986. Matthew Effects in Reading: Some Consequences of Individual Differences in the Acquisition of Literacy. Reading Research Quarterly. 21(4), 360–407.

Stewig, J. W. and Jett-Simpson. 1995. Language arts in the early childhood classroom. Belmont, CA: Wadsworth.

TEKS. 2009a. Chapter 110. English Language arts and reading. Subchapter A. Elementary. Texas Education Code, §28.002.

TEKS. 2009b. Chapter 110. English Language arts and reading. Subchapter B. Elementary. Texas Education Code, §28.002.

TEA. 2011. Texas English Language Proficiency Assessment System (TELPAS).

Tomas, E., and H. Robinson. 1972. Improving reading in every class: A source book for teachers. Boston: Allyn and Bacon.

Vacca, R. T., and J. A. Vacca. 1989. Content area reading. Glenview, IL: Scott Foresman.

Vygotsky L. 1978 Mind in society Cambridge Mass: Harvard University Press

Worthy, J., Broaddus, K., and G. Ivey. 2001. Pathways to independence: Reading, writing, and learning in grades 3-8. New York: Guilford.

Worthy, J., Moorman, M., and M. Turner. 1999. What Johnny likes to read is hard to find in school. Reading Research Quarterly, 34(1), 12-27.

Wysocki, A. F., J. Johnson-Eilola, C. L. Selfe, and G. Sirc. 2004. Writing new media: Theory and applications for expanding the teaching of composition. Logan, UT: Utah State University Press.

# Mathematics

*The teacher understands the structure of number systems, the development of a sense of quantity, and the relationship between quantity and symbolic representations.*

## Place Value

Place value is based on powers of 10. It assigns a value to a digit depending on its placement in a numeral.

| Millions | Hundred thousands | Ten thousands | Thousands | Hundreds | Tens | Ones | . | Tenths | Hundredths | Thousandths | Ten thousandths | Hundred thousandths |
|---|---|---|---|---|---|---|---|---|---|---|---|---|
| | | | 7 | 3 | 2 | 5 | . | 4 | | | | |

## Expanded Form

Any number can be written in expanded form, which shows place value by multiplying each digit in a number by the appropriate power of 10.

*Example*     $7{,}325.4 = 7 \times 1{,}000 + 3 \times 100 + 2 \times 10 + 5 \times 1 + 4 \times \dfrac{1}{10}$

or

$$7 \times 10^3 + 3 \times 10^2 + 2 \times 10^1 + 5 \times 10^0 + 4 \times 10^{-1}$$

## Natural Numbers

Natural numbers are also called counting numbers and they include $\{1, 2, 3, 4, \ldots, \infty\}$.

## Whole Numbers

Whole numbers are the set of natural numbers including zero.

## Integers

The set of integers includes positive and negative whole numbers. The set of integers include: $\{-\infty, \ldots, -4, -3, -2, -1, 0, 1, 2, 3, 4, \ldots, \infty\}$. Integers are often represented on a number line that extends in both directions from zero.

## Rational Numbers

A rational number can be expressed as a ratio or quotient of two non-zero integers. Rational numbers are commonly expressed as fractions or decimals, such as $\dfrac{3}{10} = 0.3$, or $\dfrac{2}{3} = 0.\overline{666}$. Rational numbers when represented in decimal form terminate or repeat. Nonrepeating decimals cannot be expressed in this way and are called irrational numbers.

## Irrational Numbers

Irrational numbers are not rational, meaning they cannot be represented as fractions, and when in decimal form they do not terminate or repeat. Common examples of irrational numbers are $\pi$, $e$, or $\sqrt{2}$.

## Real Numbers

Real numbers consist of rational and irrational numbers. The figure below is an illustration of the real numbers.

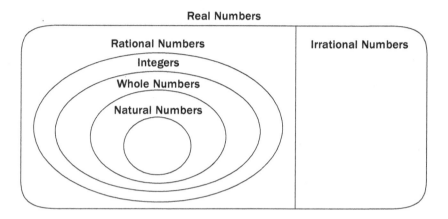

## Scientific Notation

Scientific notation is a form of writing a number as the product of a power of 10 and a decimal number between 1 and 10.

> *Example 1*      $4,040,700,000 = 4.0407 \times 10^9$
>
> *Example 2*      $0.005806 = 5.806 \times 10^{-3}$

## Absolute Value

The absolute value of a number is the distance of that number from zero on a number line.

> *Example*      $|-3| = 3$ since the position of $-3$ on a number line is 3 steps away from zero.

# Competency 011

*The teacher understands number operations and computational algorithms.*

## Operations and Algorithms

Several of the rules of properties of numbers will be helpful as you develop understanding of this competency.

## Properties of Numbers

### Closure Property of Addition

If $a$ and $b$ are real numbers, then $a + b$ is a real number.

### Commutative Property of Addition

The order of the addends does not change the sum.

$$a + b = b + a$$

### Associative Property of Addition

The order of the addends does not change the sum.

$$(a + b) + c = a + (b + c)$$

### Identity Property of Addition

The sum of a number and zero is the number itself.

$$a + 0 = a = 0 + a$$

### Closure Property of Multiplication

If $a$ and $b$ are real numbers, $a \times b$ is a unique real number.

### Commutative Property of Multiplication

The order of the factors does not change the product.

$$a \times b = b \times a$$

### Associative Property of Multiplication

The order of the factors does not change the product.

$$(a \times b) \times c = a \times (b \times c)$$

### Identity Property of Multiplication

The product of a number and 1 is the number itself.

$$a \times 1 = a = 1 \times a$$

### Zero Multiplication Property

The product of a number and zero is zero.

$$a \times 0 = 0 = 0 \times a$$

### Distributive Property

The order of the addends does not change the sum.

For all numbers $a$, $b$, and $c$, $a(b + c) = ab + ac$

### Order of Operations

Often students learn the distributive property when they investigate problems requiring the order of operations. When presented with the task of evaluating $2(7 + 3)$, two possible approaches will produce the same correct result. One approach is to add first, then multiply: $2(10) = 20$, whereas another approach is to multiply first, then add: $14 + 6 = 20$. Obtaining the same answer using two different strategies may be cumbersome for some students.

Providing more examples of a different nature is needed for students to understand that the order of calculating mathematical problems will impact the outcome. Consider the problems $3 + 4 \times 8$ and $4 \times 8 + 3$. Work both problems from left to right and notice two different results.

*Example 1*     $3 + 4 \times 8 = 7 \times 8 = 56$

*Example 2*     $4 \times 8 + 3 = 32 + 3 = 35$

Notice that the numbers in both expressions are the same but the order of the mathematical operations is different. In the first example, the addition sign comes before the multiplication, and the second example is the reverse. The second example actually shows the process that should be completed for the first example. Although the addition symbol is the first symbol one encounters in the problem when reading from left to right, addition is one of the last operations when evaluating expressions.

**Please Excuse My Dear Aunt Sally** or **PEMDAS** is the common phrase and acronym students learn to remember the order of operations. The words in the phrase or the letters of PEMDAS stand for *Parentheses, Exponents, Multiplication, Division, Addition,* and *Subtraction.* More important is the understanding of what each word means in regard to evaluating problems. Presenting the order of operations vertically can be helpful to explain the order of the calculations.

**Parentheses:** First, compute within any grouping symbols, which may include parentheses ( ), brackets [ ], absolute value | □ |, or square root $\sqrt{\phantom{□}}$ symbols.

**Exponents:** Next, calculate any exponential terms.

**Multiplication/Division:** Read the problem from left to right and top to bottom. If a division symbol comes before a multiplication symbol, perform the division first. If a multiplication symbol occurs before a division symbol, perform the multiplication first.

**Addition/Subtraction:** The process is similar to the rule for multiplication and division. Subtraction will occur before addition if the subtraction symbol comes before the addition symbol, whereas addition will precede subtraction if an addition symbol occurs before a subtraction symbol.

## Computations with Fractions

A fraction is a number that represents part of a set, part of a whole, or a quotient in the form $\frac{a}{b}$, which can be read as $a$ divided by $b$. Computations with fractions include finding equivalent fractions and simplifying; converting improper fractions to mixed numbers; and addition, subtraction, multiplication, and division.

### Equivalent Fractions and Simplifying

Although the fractions $\frac{1}{4}$ and $\frac{2}{8}$ do not look alike, they represent the same rational number and are called equivalent or equal fractions; hence $\frac{1}{4} = \frac{2}{8}$.

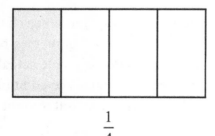
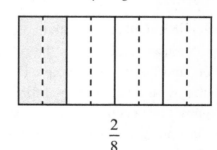

$$\frac{1}{4} \qquad\qquad\qquad \frac{2}{8}$$

Simplifying fractions requires identifying common factors among the numerator and denominator of a fraction. For example, to simplify we can recognize that both 60 and 140 are divisible by 10.

$$\frac{60}{140} = \frac{6 \cdot 10}{14 \cdot 10} = \frac{6}{14}$$

Also,

$$\frac{6}{14} = \frac{3 \cdot 2}{7 \cdot 2} = \frac{3}{7}$$

It was shown that $\frac{60}{140}$ was simplified to $\frac{6}{14}$ by factoring out the common factor of 10; then $\frac{6}{14}$ was simplified to $\frac{3}{7}$ by factoring out a common factor of 2. This means that $\frac{60}{140} = \frac{3}{7}$. Since the simplification process identified two common factors of 10 and 2, the **greatest common factor** (GCF) or **divisor** (GCD) of 60 and 140 is 20. This means the simplification process could have been completed in one step instead of two by factoring out the greatest common factor of both numbers.

$$\frac{60}{140} = \frac{3 \cdot 20}{7 \cdot 20} = \frac{3}{7}$$

The greatest common factor of $a$ and $b$ is the greatest number that divides both $a$ and $b$ evenly.

### Converting Improper Fractions to Mixed Numbers

To convert an improper fraction like $\frac{7}{2}$, divide the numerator by the denominator. Many problems like this can be computed mentally by asking yourself, "How many times does 2 go into 7 evenly?" The answer is 3 times. "How much is left over?" One. The remainder is the numerator of the fractional portion of the mixed number and the denominator stays the same. So, $\frac{7}{2} = 3\frac{1}{2}$.

## Addition and Subtraction of Fractions

There are two different cases to consider when adding or subtracting fractions: fractions with like denominators (homogeneous fractions) and fractions with unlike denominators. To add or subtract fractions with like, or the same, denominators, combine numerators and the denominator stays the same. For example, $\frac{2}{7}+\frac{4}{7}=\frac{6}{7}$ and $\frac{3}{5}-\frac{1}{5}=\frac{2}{5}$.

When denominators are unlike, first determine a common denominator, create equivalent fractions with that common denominator, and then combine numerators as above. For example, find the sum of $\frac{2}{7}+\frac{1}{3}$. To determine a common denominator, find the **least common multiple** of 7 and 3, which is 21. Next, change both fractions into equivalent fractions with 21 as the denominator. Finally, combine numerators.

$$\frac{2}{7}+\frac{1}{3}=\frac{2\cdot 3}{7\cdot 3}+\frac{1\cdot 7}{3\cdot 7}=\frac{6}{21}+\frac{7}{21}=\frac{13}{21}$$

## Multiplication of Fractions

If $\frac{a}{b}$ and $\frac{c}{d}$ are any rational numbers, then $\frac{a}{b}\cdot\frac{c}{d}=\frac{a\cdot c}{b\cdot d}$. In short, find the product of the numerators and the product of the denominators, and simplify if possible.

$$\frac{5}{6}\times\frac{3}{4}=\frac{15}{24}$$

$$\frac{15}{24}=\frac{5\cdot 3}{8\cdot 3}=\frac{5}{8}$$

## Division of Fractions

If $\frac{a}{b}$ and $\frac{c}{d}$ are any rational numbers and $\frac{c}{d}\neq 0$, then $\frac{a}{b}\div\frac{c}{d}=\frac{a}{b}\cdot\frac{d}{c}=\frac{a\cdot d}{b\cdot c}$. To divide fractions, multiply the first fraction by the reciprocal of the second fraction, and simplify if possible. A common phrase to recall is *invert and multiply*.

$$\frac{1}{6}\div\frac{2}{3}=\frac{1}{6}\cdot\frac{3}{2}=\frac{3}{12}$$

$$\frac{3}{12}=\frac{1\cdot 3}{4\cdot 3}=\frac{1}{4}$$

## Computations with Decimals

Rational numbers can be expressed in the form of decimals, which are fractional numbers written using base 10. A mixed decimal number has a whole number part, too. For example, 2.8 is a mixed decimal number, whereas 0.75 is a decimal number.

### Addition and Subtraction of Decimals

Decimal numbers can be written as fractions whose denominators are powers of 10 (i.e., 10, 100, 1,000, etc.). For example, 0.125 written in word form is one hundred twenty-five thousandths and is equivalent to the fraction $\frac{125}{1,000}$. When adding or subtracting fractions, we created equivalent fractions that had common denominators, then combined numerators. Similarly, with decimal addition or subtraction, we will combine digits of the same place value. Using the standard algorithm to add or subtract two decimal numbers, arrange the decimal numbers vertically, aligning the decimal points, and then combine the digits in the same place values.

> ***Example***    Find the sum of 25.07 and 14.326.
>
> $$\begin{array}{r} 25.07 \\ +14.326 \\ \hline 39.396 \end{array}$$

### Multiplication of Decimals

Multiplication of decimals does not require aligning decimal points. Like addition/subtraction, the numbers can be arranged vertically but with right justification. The numbers can be multiplied as if they were whole numbers and the number of digits to the right of the decimal point in the product should be equal to the total number of decimal places within the two factors.

> ***Example***    Find the product of 3.25 and 0.3.
>
> $$\begin{array}{r} 3.25 \\ \times 0.3 \\ \hline 0.975 \end{array}$$

## Division of Decimals

Division of decimals can be calculated in the same way as division of traditional whole numbers. When the divisor is a whole number, the division can be handled as with whole numbers and the decimal point placed directly over the decimal point in the dividend. When the divisor is not a whole number, as in $1.44 \div 0.2$, we can obtain a whole-number divisor by treating the quotient as a fraction and multiplying both numerator and denominator by a power of 10.

$$
\begin{array}{r}
7.2 \\
2\overline{)14.4} \\
-14\phantom{.4} \\
\hline
0\,4 \\
-4 \\
\hline
0
\end{array}
$$

## Laws of Exponents

### First Law of Exponents

$$a^n \bullet a^m = a^{n+m} \qquad\qquad 5^2 \bullet 5^1 = 5^{2+1} = 5^3 = 125$$

### Second Law of Exponents

$$(ab)^n = a^n \bullet b^n \qquad\qquad (3 \bullet 2)^2 = 3^2 \bullet 2^2 = 9 \bullet 4 = 36$$

### Power of a Power

$$\left(a^n\right)^m = a^{nm} \qquad\qquad \left(4^3\right)^2 = 4^{3 \circ 2} = 4^6 = 4,096$$

### Power of a Quotient

$$\left(\frac{a}{b}\right)^n = \frac{a^n}{b^n} \qquad\qquad \left(\frac{1}{3}\right)^4 = \frac{1^4}{3^4} = \frac{1}{81}$$

### Fractional Exponents

$$a^{1/n} = \sqrt[n]{a} \qquad\qquad 27^{1/3} = \sqrt[3]{27} = 3$$

### Negative Exponents

$$a^{-n} = \frac{1}{a^n} \qquad\qquad 6^{-2} = \frac{1}{6^2} = \frac{1}{36}$$

## Complex Numbers

Complex numbers, also known as imaginary numbers, are not a part of the real number system, but they exist in their own number system. Similar rules or properties for computation exist in the complex number system. Standard form for complex numbers is $a + bi$, where $a$ and $b$ are real numbers.

The imaginary number $i$ is defined as

$$i = \sqrt{-1}$$

Also,

$$i^2 = \left(\sqrt{-1}\right)^2 = -1$$

A pattern can be developed for investigating the powers of $i$.

$$i = i$$
$$i^2 = -1$$
$$i^3 = -i$$
$$i^4 = 1$$
$$i^5 = i$$
$$i^6 = i^2 = -1$$
$$i^7 = i^3 = -i$$
$$i^8 = i^4 = 1$$

### Computations with Complex Numbers

Computations with complex numbers are similar to those of variable expressions—combining like terms. However, if an $i^2$ appears in the problem, we use $-1$ in its place.

**Example 1**    Evaluate $5 + 7i - 3i + 9$.

Combine the constants and the imaginary terms.

$14 + 4i$

***Example 2***    Evaluate $3i(-2 + 5i)$.

Begin by distributing the $3i$ through the parentheses.

$-6i + 15i^2$

Next, substitute $i^2 = -1$ and multiply 15 by $-1$.

$-6i + 15(-1) = -6i - 15$

Then write the expression in standard form, $a + bi$.

$-15 - 6i$

***Example 3***    Evaluate $(7 + 2i)(3 - 4i)$.

**FOIL** is a common mathematical process used to multiply two binomials. It is similar to the distributive property. Take the first term in the first set of parentheses and distribute through the second set of parentheses. Continue the process with the second term in the first set of parentheses. FOIL stands for

**First**: multiply the first terms in the parentheses        $7(3) = 21$

**Outer**: multiply the outside terms of the problem        $7(-4i) = -28i$

**Inner**: multiply the inside two terms of the problem        $2i(3) = 6i$

**Last**: multiply the last two terms in the parentheses        $2i(-4i) = -8i^2$

After calculating each product, combine like terms, change any $i^2 = -1$, and write the expression in standard form, $a + bi$.

$(7 + 2i)(3 - 4i)$

$21 + (-28i) + 6i + (-8i^2)$

$21 - 22i - 8(-1)$

$21 - 22i + 8$

$29 - 22i$

**Rationalize the Denominator**

To rationalize a quantity literally means to make the quantity rational. A rational number is one that can be expressed as the ratio or quotient of two non-zero integers. Rational numbers are commonly expressed as fractions or decimals, such as $\frac{3}{10} = 0.3$, or $\frac{2}{3} = 0.\overline{666}$. So, to rationalize the denominator of a fraction, we will create an equivalent fraction with a rational denominator.

Consider the example $\frac{6+i}{3i}$. The denominator, $3i$, is imaginary and not a rational number. However, we will use the fact that $i^2 = -1$ to rationalize the denominator. Multiply $\frac{6+i}{3i}$ by the factor of one, $\frac{i}{i}$.

$$\frac{6+i}{3i} \cdot \frac{i}{i} = \frac{6i+i^2}{3i^2}$$

Next, substitute $-1$ for $i^2$, and simplify.

$$\frac{6i+(-1)}{3(-1)} = \frac{-1+6i}{-3} = \frac{1-6i}{3}$$

The new denominator, 3, is a rational number; therefore, the denominator is now rational. In addition, we can say $\frac{6+i}{3i}$ is equivalent to $\frac{1-6i}{3}$, or $\frac{6+i}{3i} = \frac{1-6i}{3}$.

If the denominator to be rationalized is a binomial, multiply by a factor of 1, changing the sign within the binomial. For example, consider $\frac{5i}{3-2i}$. To rationalize this denominator, we multiply by $\frac{3+2i}{3+2i}$.

$$\frac{5i}{3-2i} \cdot \frac{3+2i}{3+2i} = \frac{15i+10i^2}{9+6i-6i-4i^2}$$

Substitute $-1$ for $i^2$, and simplify.

$$\frac{15i+10(-1)}{9-4(-1)} = \frac{-10+15i}{9+4} = \frac{-10+15i}{13}$$

# Competency 012

*The teacher understands ideas of number theory and uses numbers to model and solve problems within and outside of mathematics.*

## Composite Number

A composite number is number that is divisible by at least one other number besides 1 and itself. For example: 12 is a composite number because it has more than two factors: 1, 2, 3, 4, 6, 12.

## Prime Numbers

A prime number is a number that is divisible by only 1 and itself, meaning it has only two factors. For example, 11 is a prime number since the only factors are 1 and 11.

## Prime Factorization

Exponents can be used to write the prime factorization of a number; that is, every number can be written as a product of prime numbers. When a factor is repeated in a prime factorization, express the repeated factor in exponential form. Most often, students use a factor tree to find the prime factorization of a composite number. To begin factorizing, choose two factors of the number and continue factoring each number until you have all prime numbers.

> ***Example***      What is the prime factorization of 36?

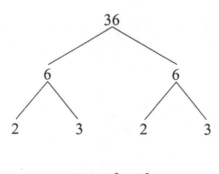

$$36 = 2^2 \times 3^2$$

## Divisibility Rules

Sometimes it is handy to know if one number is divisible by another just by looking at a number or by performing a simple test.

| Divisibility Rule for | Rule |
|---|---|
| 2 | Any integer is divisible by 2 if it is an even number. |
| 3 | Any integer is divisible by 3 if the sum of its digits is divisible by 3. |
| 4 | Any integer is divisible by 4 if the last two digits of the integer represent a number divisible by 4. |
| 5 | Any integer is divisible by 5 if it ends in 0 or 5. |
| 6 | Any integer is divisible by 6 if it is divisible by both 2 and 3. |
| 8 | Any integer is divisible by 8 if the last three digits of the integer represent a number divisible by 8. |
| 9 | Any integer is divisible by 9 if the sum of the digits is divisible by 9. |
| 10 | Any integer is divisible by 10 if it ends in 0. |

## Common Multiple

A common multiple is a whole number that is a multiple of two or more given numbers. For example, the common multiples of 2, 3, and 4 are 12, 24, 36, 48, . . . .

Some students might claim 6 and/or 8 are common multiples of 2, 3, and 4, but this is incorrect. Six is a common multiple only among the numbers 2 and 3, but not 4. Likewise, 8 is a common multiple among the numbers 2 and 4, but not 3.

## Greatest Common Divisor

The greatest common divisor (GCD) of two or more non-zero integers is the largest positive integer that divides into the numbers without producing a remainder. The GCD is useful for simplifying fractions into lowest terms, which was explored earlier in this chapter. The term *greatest common factor* (GCF) is often used when simplifying fractions.

*Example:* Find the greatest common divisor of 40 and 56. To identify the GCD, make a list of all the factors of each number. Then, identify the largest common factor between the two sets of numbers.

$$\begin{cases} 40 : 1, 2, 4, 5, 8, 10, 20, 40 \\ 56 : 1, 2, 4, 7, 8, 14, 28, 56 \end{cases}$$

The largest or greatest common factor of each list is 8. Therefore, the GCD of 40 and 56 is 8.

## Using Dollars, Dimes, and Pennies

Money is familiar to students and an apt manipulative for classroom use. Since 10 dimes are worth a dollar and 100 pennies are also worth a dollar, fractional concepts and decimal computations can easily be taught. Since a dollar is worth 1 or one whole, a dime represents $\frac{1}{10}$ and a penny represents $\frac{1}{100}$. A natural progression of this is to represent decimal numbers in the form of money. For example, the number 24.78 can be modeled with two \$10 bills, four \$1 bills, seven dimes, and eight pennies. Expanded notation easily follows as

$$2 \cdot 10 + 4 \cdot 1 + 7 \cdot \frac{1}{10} + 8 \cdot \frac{1}{100}.$$

## Decimal Representations with Base-10 Blocks

Base-10 blocks are handy manipulatives for fractional and decimal representations and computations. Graph paper or 10-by-10 grids can be used to transform the concrete use of base-10 blocks into pictorial form. The number 1.45 is represented in the figure below.

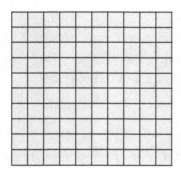 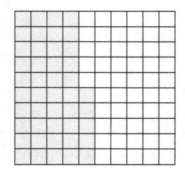

The first shaded 10-by-10 grid shows $\frac{100}{100} = 1$, and the second grid has 45 of the 100 cells shaded; therefore, it models $\frac{45}{100} = 0.45$. The pictorial representation is also an area model, meaning the visual representation shows the amount of space taken up by the shaded region. By modeling multiple decimal numbers in this form, students can more easily order a set of numbers from least to greatest.

## Mental Mathematics and Estimation

The ability to make accurate estimates is important in today's society. Always look for **easy combinations** or **compatible numbers** when doing mental calculations. Consider the two examples below:

***Example 1***     Evaluate $25 \times 8$.

Compute $25 \times 4 = 100$ and then $100 \times 2 = 200$. Ultimately, the number 8 was broken down to its factors of $4 \times 2$ to rearrange the problem to be $25 \times 4 \times 2$.

***Example 2***     Evaluate $25 + 17 + 15$.

First combine $25 + 15 = 40$, and then find $40 + 17 = 57$. The numbers 25 and 15 are good compatible numbers since they both have 5 in the ones place-value; 40 is a nice round even number to add any other value to, hence we add 17 last.

**Rounding** is often a common task in mathematics. The **5-up rule** is the standard method used when rounding numbers to a certain place value. First, determine which position you are rounding. If the digit to the right of this position is 5 or more, add 1 to the digit in the position to which you are rounding and replace zeros for all of the digits to the right of the position to which you are rounding. If the digit to the right of the position to be rounded is less than 5, leave the digit unchanged and drop all of the digits to the right of the position. For example, round 37,250 to the nearest (a) hundred and (b) thousand.

(a) The digit 2 is in the hundreds position with the digit 5 to its right. Since the digit to the right is 5, round 2 to 3 to get 37,300.

(b) The digit 7 is in the thousands place, and 2 is the digit to the right. Since 2 is less than 5, we will leave the 7 as is and replace all numbers to its right with zeros. Rounding the given number to the nearest thousand produces 37,000.

## Permutations of Unlike Objects

A permutation of a set of objects is all possible arrangements in which the order of the items makes a difference. For example, find all the different ways three books can be placed on a shelf. Label the books *A*, *B*, and *C*. Create a **sample space** to show all the possible outcomes of this experiment.

A, B, C

A, C, B

B, C, A

B, A, C

C, A, B

C, B, A

There are six ways to arrange three books on a shelf. The number of permutations of *n* distinct objects is *n*!, read as "*n* factorial."

$$n! = n \times (n-1) \times (n-2) \times \ldots \times 2 \times 1$$

***Example 1***   Suppose we wanted to arrange all the letters in the word *MATH*. How many choices would we have? The problem we want to investigate is $4! = 4 \times 3 \times 2 \times 1 = 24$ arrangements.

## Permutations of Like Objects

In the above examples, each object to be counted was distinct. Suppose we wanted to arrange the letters in the word *POOR*. Since the letter *O* appears twice in the word, we need to determine how to remove the duplication in arrangements. To eliminate the duplication, we divide the number of arrangements shown by the number of ways the two *O*'s can be rearranged, which is 2!. Therefore, there are $\frac{4!}{2!} = \frac{4 \times 3 \times 2 \times 1}{2 \times 1} = 12$ ways of arranging the letters in *POOR*.

## Combinations

A combination is a way of selecting several objects out of a larger group, where order does not matter. For example, suppose there are four members of a club {Allison, Ben, Chris, Dave}, and they need to elect a two-person committee with no chair. In this case, order is not important; an Allison-Ben choice is the same as a Ben-Allison choice. The number of combinations of *n* objects taken *r* at a time is denoted and computed as follows:

$$_nC_r = \frac{n!}{r!(n-r)!}$$

In our problem, choosing a two-member committee from four people, $n = 4$ and $r = 2$. So,

$$\frac{4!}{2!(4-2)!} = \frac{4!}{2!2!} = \frac{4 \times 3 \times 2 \times 1}{2 \times 1 \times 2 \times 1} = 6$$

# Competency 013

*The teacher understands and uses mathematical reasoning to identify, extend, and analyze patterns, and understands the relationships among variables, expressions, equations, inequalities, relations, and functions.*

## Patterns

There are two types of patterns explored in grades 4 through 8: repeating patterns and growing patterns. An important concept in working with repeating patterns is identifying the core of the pattern, or the string of elements that repeats. Consider the musical pattern created by clapping and stomping: *stomp, stomp, clap, stomp, stomp, clap, stomp, stomp, clap, . . . .* The core of the pattern is *stomp, stomp, clap* and can be written in the form of *AAB*. Number patterns can be used to predict numbers down the line. For example, consider 3, 5, 7, . . . . The number pattern is odd numbers beginning with 3. Add 2 each time. The next three numbers in the pattern would be 9, 11, and 13.

Growing patterns involve a progression from step to step. Students should not only extend these patterns but also look for a generalization or an algebraic relationship to create a function that represents the pattern. Investigate the three steps below and generalize the growing pattern.

A table can be constructed to record the number of objects per step and identify the pattern.

| Step | 1 | 2 | 3 | 4 | . . . | $n$ |
|---|---|---|---|---|---|---|
| Number of Objects | 1 | 3 | 5 | | . . . | |

The pattern is increasing by 2 on each step, so on the fourth step there will be 7 objects, and on the $n$th step there will be $2n - 1$ objects. Moreover, we can graph this relationship or function:

$$f(n) = 2n - 1$$

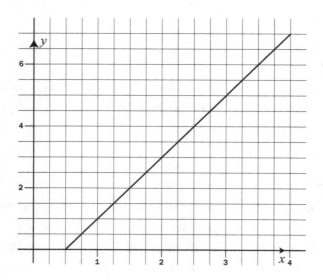

The function $f(n) = 2n - 1$ represents the number of objects is one less than twice the step. This problem illustrates the concept of a function using models, tables, graphs, and symbolic and verbal representations, which are important concepts within mathematics.

## Variables

Variables can express relationships. Consider the following statement and question: Jose was born on his three-year-old sister Kendra's birthday. How are their ages related? Three different relationships can be represented:

- Jose is three years younger than Kendra.                    $J = K - 3$

- Kendra is three years older than Jose.                      $K = J + 3$

- The difference in age between Kendra and her               $K - J = 3$
  younger brother Jose is three years.

# Competency 014

*The teacher understands and uses linear functions to model and solve problems.*

## Linear Functions and Slope

Linear functions are commonly written in the form of $y = mx + b$, where $m$ is the slope of the function and $b$ is the $y$-intercept, $(0, b)$, or the point at which the line crosses the $y$-axis. When the slope of a line is positive, $m > 0$, the line goes up from left to right (increases); if the slope is negative, $m < 0$, the line goes down from left to right (decreases).

***Example 1*** The function $y = x$ has a positive slope of $m = 1$ and a $y$-intercept of $(0, 0)$.

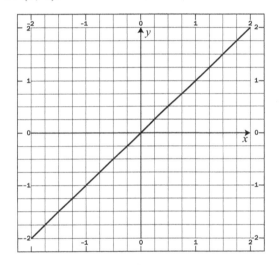

***Example 2*** The function $y = -x$ has a negative slope of $m = -1$ and a $y$-intercept of $(0, 0)$.

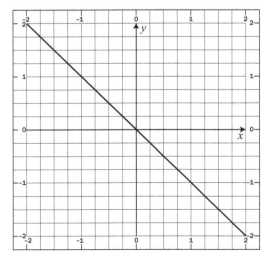

A line is defined by two points or coordinates. To find the equation of a line passing through two points, $(x_1, y_1)$ and $(x_2, y_2)$, we will calculate the **slope** and use the **point-slope formula**.

$$\text{slope} = m = \frac{y_2 - y_1}{x_2 - x_1} \qquad \text{point-slope formula: } y - y_1 = m(x - x_1)$$

***Example***     Find the equation of a line passing through the points $(-1, -3)$ and $(2, 2)$.

Begin by calculating the slope between the two points.

$$m = \frac{2 - (-3)}{2 - (-1)} = \frac{2 + 3}{2 + 1} = \frac{5}{3}$$

Next, choose one point and the slope to evaluate the point-slope formula.

$$y - (-3) = \frac{5}{3}[x - (-1)]$$

$$y + 3 = \frac{5}{3}(x + 1)$$

$$y + 3 = \frac{5}{3}x + \frac{5}{3}$$

$$y + 3 - 3 = \frac{5}{3}x + \frac{5}{3} - 3$$

$$y = \frac{5}{3}x - \frac{4}{3}$$

The equation of the line passing through points $(-1, -3)$ and $(2, 2)$ is $y = \frac{5}{3}x - \frac{4}{3}$, where $m = \frac{5}{3}$ and the *y*-intercept is $(0, -\frac{4}{3})$. The graph of the line is shown below.

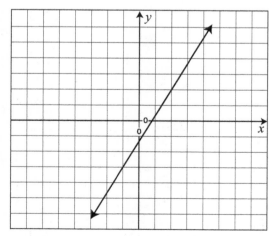

Linear equations can also be written in **standard form**, $Ax + By = C$, where $A$, $B$, and $C$ are integers and $A \neq 0$ and $B \neq 0$. Let's take the equation from above, $y = \dfrac{5}{3}x - \dfrac{4}{3}$, and write it in standard form. First, all coefficients need to be integers. Since the slope is in fractional form, we can multiply both sides of the equation by 3 (the denominator) to clear the fractional portion of the equation, making all coefficients integers:

$$3(y) = 3\left(\dfrac{5}{3}x - \dfrac{4}{3}\right)$$
$$3y = 5x - 4$$

Then, subtract $5x$ from both sides to isolate the constant from the variable terms.

$$-5x + 3y = -4$$

## Modeling Linear Functions to Solve Problems

Applications, or word problems, are popular and frequently used to help students understand linear functions and modeling problems. They can prepare students for situations they might encounter later in life. The scenario below requires students to perform multiple mathematical tasks such as creating a table, drawing a graph, and evaluating problems within the posed scenario.

*Scenario:*

A survey of car owners shows that the monthly cost (in dollars) to own and drive a car is given by the function $f(x) = 0.41x + 225$. Here, $x$ represents the number of miles driven throughout the month and 225 represents the monthly expenses that come with ownership of a vehicle, such as insurance, vehicle license fees, and so on, which are independent of the miles driven.

(a) Make a table that shows the cost of having a car that is driven 0, 100, 200, . . . , 500 miles per month.

(b) Use the table to draw a graph that shows the cost of driving a car for up to 500 miles in a month.

(c) Use your graph to estimate the corresponding limit on the number of miles driven in a month if your monthly budget is limited to $400.

(d) What is the approximate number of miles driven throughout the month if the expenditures are $350?

*Solution:*

(a)  To create a table we must first identify the variables: $x$ is the miles driven, and $y$ is the cost of owning and driving the car. We will evaluate the function $f(x) = 0.41x + 225$ when $x$ is 0, 100, 200, 300, 400, and 500. The outputs represent the cost of owning and driving the car based on those numbers of miles driven in the month.

| Miles, $x$ | 0 | 100 | 200 | 300 | 400 | 500 |
|---|---|---|---|---|---|---|
| Cost, $y$ | 225 | 266 | 307 | 348 | 389 | 430 |

(b)  To use the table to create a graph, plot the coordinates from the table. For example, (0, 225) is the $y$-intercept of the graph.

**Cost of Owning and Operating a Car**

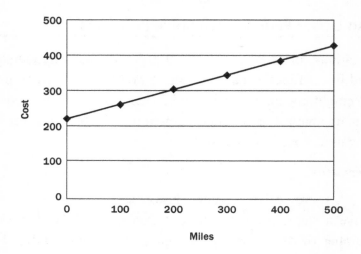

(c)  To use the graph to determine how many miles can be driven if there is a budget of $400, place your finger where 400 is on the $y$-axis and then slide your finger to the right until it meets the function. The $x$-value below this intersection tells how many miles can be driven if the budget is $400. Based on the graph above, one could drive about 425 miles for the cost of $400.

(d)  To determine the approximate amount of miles driven if the expenditures are $350, we will evaluate the function when $f(x) = 350$. Therefore, our equation to solve is

$$350 = 0.41x + 225$$
$$-225 \qquad\qquad -225$$
$$\frac{125}{0.41} = x$$

$$x \approx 304.88 \text{ miles driven}$$

# Competency 015

*The teacher understands and uses nonlinear functions and relations to model and solve problems.*

### Quadratic Functions

A function defined by $f(x) = ax^2 + bx + c$, where $a$, $b$, and $c$ are constants with $a \neq 0$, is called a quadratic function. The most elementary quadratic function is $f(x) = x^2$, whose graph is called a **parabola** (see figure below).

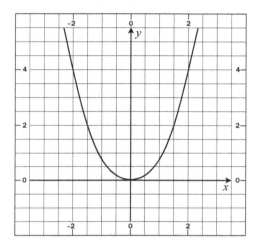

The parabola is a symmetrical function, meaning it has a **line of symmetry** through the **vertex**. In the figure above, the vertex is at (0, 0), or the bottom point on the graph, also called the **minimum**. This graph of $f(x) = x^2$ opens upward, but a similar quadratic function of $f(x) = -x^2$ opens downward (see graph below). The vertex on a parabola that opens downward is the topmost point of the function, called the **maximum**.

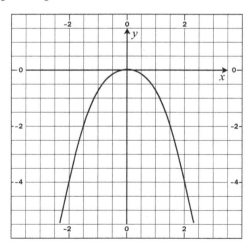

The value of the leading coefficient $a$ determines if the graph of a quadratic function will open up or down. If $a > 0$, the parabola opens up, as in the function $f(x) = x^2$, where $a = 1$. If $a < 0$, the parabola opens down, as in the similar function $f(x) = -x^2$, where $a = -1$.

## Transformations

We often call the function $f(x) = x^2$ the parent function for quadratics, and any manipulation to this function performs a transformation of the graph. As shown above, the graph of $f(x) = -x^2$ opens downward, whereas the parent function opens upward. The graph of the function when $a = -1$ was reflected across the $x$-axis. To reflect the graph across the $y$-axis, let $f(x) = f(-x)$ or in our case $f(x) = (-x)^2$. Below is a table of transformations that may occur on any type of function.

### Transformations of Functions

| Rule | Result | Example |
|---|---|---|
| $f(x) = -f(x)$ | Reflects the graph across the $x$-axis | $f(x) = -x^2$ |
| $f(x) = f(-x)$ | Reflects the graph across the $y$-axis | $f(x) = (-x)^2$ |
| $f(x) = f(x) + c$ | Vertical shift upward by $c$ units | $f(x) = x^2 + 2$ |
| $f(x) = f(x) - c$ | Vertical shift downward by $c$ units | $f(x) = x^2 - 2$ |
| $f(x) = f(x + c)$ | Horizontal shift left by $c$ units | $f(x) = (x + 2)^2$ |
| $f(x) = f(x - c)$ | Horizontal shift right by $c$ units | $f(x) = (x - 2)^2$ |
| $f(x) = af(x)$ | If $a > 1$, vertical stretch by a factor of $a$ units<br><br>If $0 < a < 1$ (a proper fraction), vertical compression by a factor of $a$ units | $f(x) = 2x^2$<br><br>$f(x) = \dfrac{1}{2}x^2$ |
| $f(x) = f(ax)$ | If $a > 1$, horizontal compression by a factor of $a$ units<br><br>If $0 < a < 1$ (a proper fraction), horizontal stretch by a factor of $\dfrac{1}{a}$ units | $f(x) = (2x)^2$<br><br>$f(x) = \left(\dfrac{1}{2}x\right)^2$ |

**Vertex and Line of Symmetry**

The vertex of a parabola occurs at the point $\left(\dfrac{-b}{2a}, f\left(\dfrac{-b}{2a}\right)\right)$, where the values for $a$ and $b$ are found in the function $f(x) = ax^2 + bx + c$. As mentioned before, parabolas are symmetrical about a line of symmetry. Such a line is $x = \dfrac{-b}{2a}$, a vertical line through the vertex.

Identify the vertex and line of symmetry in the function $f(x) = -16x^2 + 32x - 10$. To find the $x$ coordinate of the vertex, we compute $\dfrac{-b}{2a} = \dfrac{-32}{2(-16)} = \dfrac{-32}{-32} = 1$. Next find, $f(1) = -16(1)^2 + 32(1) - 10 = 6$. Therefore, the vertex or maximum is located at $(1, 6)$ and the line of symmetry is at $x = 1$. Below is the graph of $f(x) = -16x^2 + 32x - 10$.

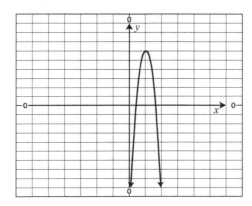

## Solving Quadratic Equations

The solutions to a quadratic equation are called ***zeros*** or ***roots***. Graphically, the solutions are $x$-intercepts, or where the graph crosses or touches the $x$-axis. We determine the value(s) when $y = 0$, which are the $x$-intercepts.

If the graph crosses the $x$-axis in two places, there are two solutions to the equation when $f(x) = 0$. The function above, $f(x) = -16x^2 + 32x - 10$, crosses the $x$-axis at two places when $x$ is positive. Therefore, the two answers for $x$ are both positive. The function $f(x) = x^2$ does not cross the $x$-axis, but it touches it at the point $(0, 0)$. Quadratic functions that touch but do not cross the $x$-axis have only one solution when $f(x) = 0$: the $x$-value of the coordinate at which it touches the axis. The one solution to $f(x) = 0 = x^2$ is $x = 0$.

Some quadratic equations do not touch or cross the $x$-axis. Instead, they are suspended above or below the $x$-axis, and their solutions are complex or imaginary. The function $f(x) = x^2 + 2$ lies above the $x$-axis and has two complex solutions when $f(x) = 0$ (see graph on next page).

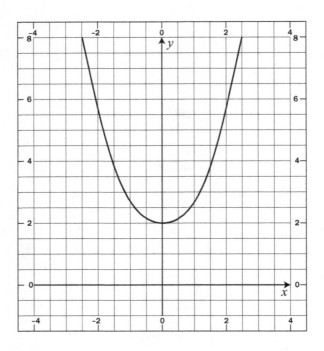

The solutions for $f(x) = 0$: can be found by evaluating the **quadratic formula**: $x = \dfrac{-b \pm \sqrt{b^2 - 4ac}}{2a}$, where $a$, $b$, and $c$ are the coefficients in the function $ax^2 + bx + c = 0$. Determine the values for $a$, $b$, and $c$, and then substitute them into the quadratic formula. For the function $f(x) = x^2 + 2$, the $x$-intercepts can be calculated as:

$$a = 1, b = 0, c = 2$$

$$x = \frac{0 \pm \sqrt{0^2 - 4(1)(2)}}{2(1)} = \frac{\pm\sqrt{-8}}{2} = \frac{\pm\sqrt{-4(2)}}{2} = \frac{\pm 2i\sqrt{2}}{2} = \pm\sqrt{2}\,i$$

The $\pm$ symbol means there are two answers for $x$: $\sqrt{2}\,i$ and $-\sqrt{2}\,i$.

To determine the type (real or complex) and number of solutions (one or two), calculate the **discriminant**, $b^2 - 4ac$, and follow these rules:

If $b^2 - 4ac > 0$, there are two real solutions.

If $b^2 - 4ac = 0$, there is one real solution.

If $b^2 - 4ac < 0$, there are two complex solutions.

*Example* Determine the type and number of solutions to the function $f(x) = 0 = x^2 - 7x + 12$, then find the solutions. First, determine the values for $a$, $b$, and $c$ and use them to find the discriminant.

$a = 1, b = -7, c = 12$

$(-7)^2 - 4(1)(12) = 49 - 48 = 1$

Since $1 > 0$, there are two real solutions. Next, compute the quadratic formula to find these two real solutions.

$$x = \frac{-(-7) \pm \sqrt{(-7)^2 - 4(1)(12)}}{2(1)} = \frac{7 \pm \sqrt{49 - 48}}{2} = \frac{7 \pm 1}{2}$$

$$x = \frac{7 + 1}{2} = \frac{8}{2} = 4 \text{ and } x = \frac{7 - 1}{2} = \frac{6}{2} = 3$$

Therefore, $x = 3$ and $4$, or the $x$-intercepts are $(3, 0)$ and $(4, 0)$.

Factoring can be a helpful and quick method for solving some quadratic equations. Consider the example we just solved using the quadratic formula: $x^2 - 7x + 12 = 0$. When the leading coefficient, $a$, equals 1, as is the case here, the first step is to determine the factors of $c$ that when added together equal $b$. In this example, the factors of 12 whose sum is $-7$ are $-3$ and $-4$. Next, use these factors to factor the quadratic into $(x - 3)(x - 4) = 0$. To solve the factored quadratic, set each binomial equal to zero and solve for $x$.

$$x - 3 = 0 \quad \text{and} \quad x - 4 = 0$$
$$x = 3 \qquad\qquad x = 4$$

As seen on the graph below, the $x$-intercepts are $(3, 0)$ and $(4, 0)$.

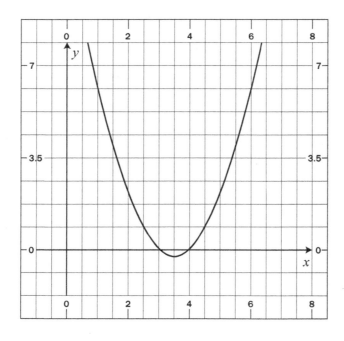

## Additional Nonlinear Functions

| Function | Equation | Graph |
|---|---|---|
| Cubic | $y = x^3$ | |
| Exponential | $y = e^x$ | |
| Logarithmic | $y = \log x$ | |
| Absolute value | $y = |x|$ | |

# Competency 016

*The teacher uses and understands the conceptual foundations of calculus related to topics in middle school mathematics.*

Foundations of calculus are built on expanding understanding of functions through other mathematical experiences. Students use functions, equations, and limits as useful tools for expressing generalizations and as a means for analyzing and understanding a broad range of mathematical relationships.

## Limits of a Sequence

A sequence can be denoted as $\{a_n\}$. We say that the sequence $\{a_n\}$ **converges** or has a limit $L$, written $\lim_{n\to\infty} a_n = L$, if the terms of the sequence can be made as close to $L$ by making $n$ sufficiently large. If a sequence is not convergent, it is **divergent**. Determine whether each of the following infinite sequences converges or diverges:

*Example 1*  $\left\{\dfrac{1}{n}\right\}$

The terms of the sequence are $1, \dfrac{1}{2}, \dfrac{1}{3}, \dfrac{1}{4}, \ldots, \dfrac{1}{n}, \ldots$. As the denominator increases, the terms of the sequence approach or converge to zero. Therefore, $\lim_{n\to\infty}\dfrac{1}{n}=0$.

*Example 2*  $\left\{\sqrt{n}\right\}$

The terms in this sequence are $\sqrt{1}, \sqrt{2}, \sqrt{3}, \ldots, \sqrt{n}, \ldots$; they become larger and larger as $n$ increases. Therefore, this sequence diverges.

## Secant and Tangent Lines

A secant line passes through two points of a function, $(a, f(a))$ and $(x, f(x))$. The **average rate of change** of $f(x)$ or **slope of the secant line** is $\dfrac{f(x)-f(a)}{x-a}$. The **slope of the tangent line** to the graph $f(x)$ at the point $P(x, f(x))$ is given by $\lim_{h\to 0}\dfrac{f(x+h)-f(x)}{h}$, if it exists.

Below is a graph of some function $f(x)$. The secant line passes through $f(x)$ at two points, whereas the tangent line touches $f(x)$ at a point. In this case, the slopes of both lines are positive.

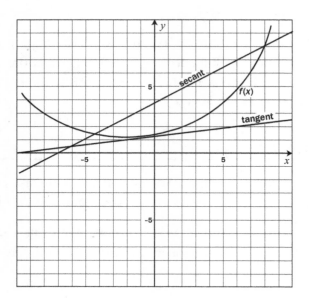

## Area Under a Curve

The top of a doorway is to have a window in the shape of an arc. We need to supply glass to close in the archway. To find the amount of glass needed we need to know the area under the curve. There are two methods to find the area under the curve: (1) using approximation by finding areas of rectangles, and (2) using integration. The first method will be explored below.

Let's assume the curve is the function $y = 1 - x^2$. The height of each rectangle is found by calculating the function values, say $x = c$. Below is the graph of the function and four rectangles between $x = 0$ and $x = 1$. The width of each rectangle is $\frac{1}{4}$.

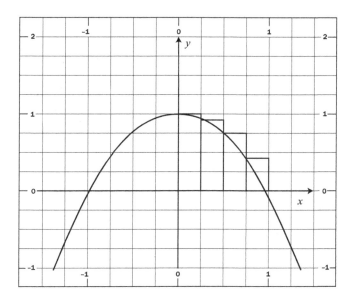

To find the area of the first rectangle, we need to compute the height at $f(0)$.

$$f(0) = 1 - (0)^2 = 1 - 0 = 1$$

The area for the first rectangle is $\frac{1}{4}(1) = \frac{1}{4} = 0.25$. The heights and areas of the additional rectangles are as follows:

Rectangle 2:  height  $f\left(\frac{1}{4}\right) = 1 - \left(\frac{1}{4}\right)^2 = 1 - \frac{1}{16} = \frac{15}{16}$

area  $\frac{1}{4}\left(\frac{15}{16}\right) = \frac{15}{64} = 0.234375$

Rectangle 3:  height  $f\left(\frac{1}{2}\right) = 1 - \left(\frac{1}{2}\right)^2 = 1 - \frac{1}{4} = \frac{3}{4}$

area  $\frac{1}{4}\left(\frac{3}{4}\right) = \frac{3}{16} = 0.1875$

Rectangle 4:  height  $f\left(\frac{3}{4}\right) = 1 - \left(\frac{3}{4}\right)^2 = 1 - \frac{9}{16} = \frac{7}{16}$

area  $\frac{1}{4}\left(\frac{7}{16}\right) = \frac{7}{64} = 0.109375$

Next, find the sum of the rectangular areas: $0.25 + 0.234375 + 0.1875 + 0.109375 = 0.78125$. Since this is half of the area under the curve, we double it to find the total area under the curve, or $1.5625$.

This approximation is greater than the actual area under the curve since we found the area of the "outer" rectangles. The same process can be repeated to find the area of the "inner" rectangles, and then average the two results. The graph of the inner rectangles is as follows:

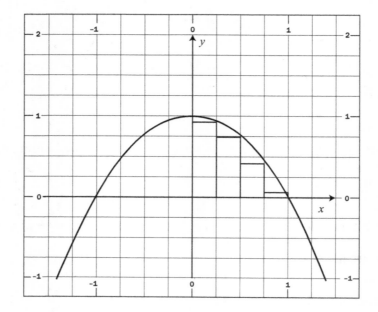

Another way of solving this problem would be to find the "midpoint" rectangles.

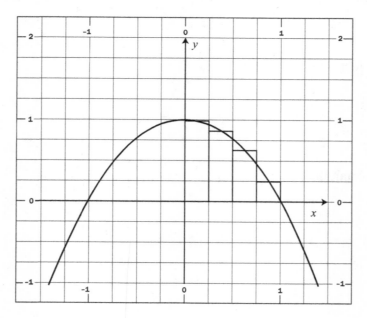

## Competency 017

*The teacher understands measurement as a process.*

Measurement is an area of mathematics used by many on a daily basis, whether it be calculating the area of a garden, estimating time to complete a project, or calculating distance of travel from point *A* to *B*. Often we are posed with converting units of measure. Below are charts of the U.S. and metric units of measure. Note that U.S. units are sometimes called U.S. customary units, standard units, or English units.

**Units of Measure**

| U.S. | |
|---|---|
| 12 inches | 1 foot |
| 3 feet | 1 yard |
| 5,280 feet | 1 mile |
| **Metric** | |
| 10 millimeters | 1 centimeter |
| 1000 millimeters | 1 meter |
| 100 centimeters | 1 meter |
| 10 centimeters | 1 decimeter |
| 10 decimeters | 1 meter |
| 10 meters | 1 decameter |
| 1,000 meters | 1 kilometer |

*Example*    Sasha walked $\frac{1}{4}$ mile from home to her friend Nick's house. Together they walked 30 yards to the public pool. How many feet did Sasha walk altogether?

We use the fact that 1 mile = 5,280 feet and 1 yard = 3 feet to answer this question. First, we need to convert $\frac{1}{4}$ of a mile into feet: $\frac{1}{4}$(1 mile) = $\frac{1}{4}$(5,280 feet) = 1,320 feet. Next, we convert 30 yards into feet: 30(3 feet) = 90 feet. Finally, find the sum of the two distances: 1,320 + 90 = 1,410 feet. Sasha walked a total of 1,410 feet.

## Units of Mass

| U.S. | |
|---|---|
| 16 ounces | 1 pound |
| 2,000 pounds | 1 ton |
| **Metric** | |
| 1,000 grams | 1 kilogram |
| 1,000 kilograms | 1 metric ton |

*Example*

Jesse sells heavy furniture. For shipping purposes, he must inform the movers of the weight of each shipment in metric tons. Jesse will be shipping an order of furniture that weights 750 kilograms. How many metric tons will he be shipping?

Creating a proportion can be handy when converting units.

$$\frac{1 \text{ metric ton}}{1,000 \text{ kilograms}} = \frac{x \text{ metric tons}}{750 \text{ kilograms}}$$
$$750 = 1,000x$$
$$x = \frac{750}{1,000} = 0.75 \text{ metric tons}$$

Jesse will be shipping 0.75 metric tons of furniture.

## Units of Capacity

| U.S. | |
|---|---|
| 3 teaspoons | 1 tablespoon |
| 2 tablespoons | 1 fluid ounce |
| 8 fluid ounces | 1 cup |
| 16 fluid ounces | 1 pint |
| 2 cups | 1 pint |
| 2 pints | 1 quart |
| 4 quarts | 1 gallon |
| **Metric** | |
| 10 milliliters | 1 centiliter |
| 10 centiliters | 1 deciliter |
| 1,000 milliliters | 1 liter |
| 10 deciliters | 1 liter |
| 1,000 liters | 1 kiloliter |

*Example*    A recipe for lemonade spritzer requires 1 pint of fresh lemon juice, 1 cup of sugar, 2 quarts of club soda, and 2 limes sliced very thin for garnishing. How much liquid, in cups, is needed for this recipe?

First, we need to know which ingredients are liquid: 1 pint of lemon juice and 2 quarts of club soda. Next, we need to convert pints and quarts into cups. We know 1 pint = 2 cups. We know 1 quart = 2 pints, so 2 quarts = 4 pints. Since 1 pint = 2 cups, then 4 pints = 8 cups. Altogether, we need 2 cups of lemon juice and 8 cups of club soda for a total of 10 cups of liquid for the recipe.

**Units of Time**

| 60 seconds | 1 minute |
|---|---|
| 60 minutes | 1 hour |
| 24 hours | 1 day |
| 7 days | 1 week |
| 52 weeks | 1 year |
| 12 months | 1 year |

*Example*    Mercedes determined she worked on her science project for a total of 1 day, 7 hours, and 24 minutes. How many total hours did she spend on her project?

First, let's start by converting the 24 minutes into a portion of an hour. We know 60 minutes = 1 hour, so 24 minutes = $\frac{24}{60}$ = 0.4 hours. Also, 1 day = 24 hours. Mercedes spent 24 + 7 + 0.4 = 31.4 hours working on her science project.

## Temperature

A thermometer measures temperature in **Fahrenheit** and/or **Celsius**. Conversion formulas can be used to convert temperatures from Fahrenheit to Celsius and vice versa.

$$F = C \cdot \frac{9}{5} + 32$$

$$C = \frac{5}{9}(F - 32)$$

## Error of Measurement

Often, measuring physical objects with tools such as rulers and protractors can result in a slight error of measurement. For example, most textbooks are rectangular in shape and have four right angles. If using a protractor to measure the angle of a book corner results in finding the angle to be 88.5 degrees instead of 90 degrees, there is a 1.5 degree error of measure. To determine the percent of error, divide the amount of error by the original amount that should be present. For example, $\frac{1.5}{90} = 0.01\overline{66}$ or $1.\overline{66}\%$ of error.

## Right Triangle Trigonometry

The study of right triangles and their measures of sides and angles is right triangle trigonometry.

$$\text{sine } \theta = \sin \theta = \frac{\text{opposite}}{\text{hypotenuse}}$$

$$\text{cosine } \theta = \cos \theta = \frac{\text{adjacent}}{\text{hypotenuse}}$$

$$\text{tangent } \theta = \tan \theta = \frac{\text{opposite}}{\text{adjacent}}$$

*Example*      Using the figure below, find the sine, cosine, and tangent of $\theta$.

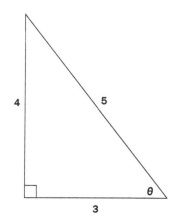

$$\sin\theta = \frac{\text{opposite}}{\text{hypotenuse}} = \frac{4}{5}$$

$$\cos\theta = \frac{\text{adjacent}}{\text{hypotenuse}} = \frac{3}{5}$$

$$\tan\theta = \frac{\text{opposite}}{\text{adjacent}} = \frac{4}{3}$$

## Similar Triangles

Triangles are said to be similar if the triangles have the same angles and their sides are proportional. Consider the figure below of similar triangles $\triangle ABC$ and $\triangle ADE$. Find the measure of $x$ using proportional reasoning.

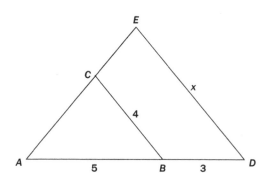

In the figure, we can see $\overline{AB} = 5$, $\overline{AD} = 8$, and $\overline{CB} = 4$. Using this information, we can create a proportion to solve for $\overline{ED} = x$.

$$\frac{AB}{CB} = \frac{AD}{ED}$$

$$\frac{5}{4} = \frac{8}{x}$$

Using cross products or cross multiplication, we find

$$5x = 32$$

$$x = \frac{32}{5} = 6.4$$

## Pythagorean Theorem

The Pythagorean theorem is a relation among the three sides of a right triangle, $a^2 + b^2 = c^2$, where $a$ and $b$ are the **legs** of the right triangle and $c$ is the **hypotenuse**, or side across from the right angle. We use the equation $a^2 + b^2 = c^2$ when given two of the side lengths of a right triangle and we need to find the third.

> **Example**  Diane is going to mount a new 40-inch LCD TV on the wall. The base of the TV is 35 inches. What is the height? Round your answer to the nearest inch.

Before beginning this problem, some background knowledge on televisions is needed. When buying a 40-inch television, the 40 inches refers to the diagonal (see picture below). A television is also a rectangle, not a triangle. However, the diagonal of the rectangle creates two right triangles, allowing the Pythagorean theorem to be a solution strategy.

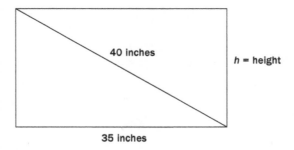

Next, substitute the values into the Pythagorean theorem and solve for $h$.

$$35^2 + h^2 = 40^2$$

$$1,225 + h^2 = 1,600$$

$$h^2 = 375$$

$$\sqrt{h^2} = \sqrt{375} \approx 19.36 \approx 19 \text{ inches}$$

The LCD TV is about 19 inches high and 35 inches wide, with a 40-inch diagonal.

## Competency 018

*The teacher understands the geometric relationships and axiomatic structure of Euclidean geometry.*

The fundamental building blocks of geometry are **points**, **lines**, and **planes**. These terms are called undefined terms, but an intuitive notion of these terms is illustrated in the table below.

| Term and Symbol | Illustration |
|---|---|
| Point $A$<br><br>Point $A$ is a vertex of the triangle.<br><br>Point $A$ is located at $(-7, 0)$. | |

*(continued)*

| Term and Symbol | Illustration |
|---|---|
| **Line ℓ**<br><br>Line ℓ is similar to the center line of a road. The outer lines and the center line are **parallel** lines.<br><br>Lines $x$ and $y$ are **perpendicular** lines.<br><br>Two points are needed to create a line, as they determine the direction or slope of the line. Line $m$ passes through $(-5, 0)$ and $(0, 5)$. | |
| **Ray**<br>A portion of a line which starts at a point and goes off in a particular direction to infinity | |
| **Line segment**<br>A straight line which links two points without extending beyond them | |
| **Plane γ**<br><br>Plane γ is like a tabletop or a flat surface.<br><br><br><br>Plane $ABC$ or plane γ | |

## Angles and Their Measures

When two rays or lines meet at a point, they form an **angle**, measured in **degrees**. Congruent angles are any two or more angles that have the same size or measure, regardless of their orientation or how they are drawn. Descriptions of types of angles are given below.

- **Right angles** measure exactly 90 degrees.

- **Acute angles** measure between 0 and 90 degrees.

- **Obtuse angles** measure greater than 90 degrees but less than 180 degrees.

- **Straight angles** measure 180 degrees and are also called lines.

- **Supplementary angles** are any two angles whose sum is 180 degrees.

- **Complementary angles** are any two angles whose sum is 90 degrees.

- **Vertical angles** are opposite angles formed by two intersecting lines; where vertical angles are congruent.

## Angles Formed by Parallel Lines Cut by a Transversal

Let parallel lines $m$ and $n$ be cut by another line, called a transversal $t$. The following congruent angles are formed by these lines (see figure below):

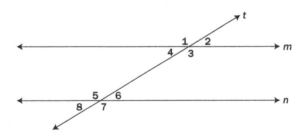

- There are four pairs of congruent **vertical** or **opposite angles**: $\angle 1 \cong \angle 3$, $\angle 2 \cong \angle 4$, $\angle 5 \cong \angle 7$, $\angle 6 \cong \angle 8$.

- There are four pairs of **congruent corresponding angles**: $\angle 1 \cong \angle 5$, $\angle 4 \cong \angle 8$, $\angle 2 \cong \angle 6$, $\angle 3 \cong \angle 7$.

- There are two pairs of congruent **alternate interior angles**: $\angle 4 \cong \angle 6$, $\angle 3 \cong \angle 5$.

- There are two pairs of congruent **alternate exterior angles**: $\angle 1 \cong \angle 7$, $\angle 2 \cong \angle 8$.

- There are two pairs of **same side interior angles** that are supplementary: $\angle 4 + \angle 5 = 180$, $\angle 3 + \angle 6 = 180$.

## Constructions with a Compass and Straight Edge

### Constructing Parallel Lines

Parallel lines never intersect as they have the same slope or incline.

*Example*  Given line $\ell$ and point $P$, we will construct a parallel line to line $\ell$.

To construct a line parallel to a given line follow these four steps:

Step 1:  Choose a point $A$ anywhere on line $\ell$, and draw the line passing through it and point $P$.

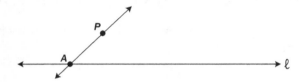

Step 2:  Set the compass to the width of $\overline{AP}$, with the point on point $A$ and the pencil on point $P$. With the pointer still on point $A$, draw an arc that intersects line $\ell$. Where the arc intersects line $\ell$, label this point $X$.

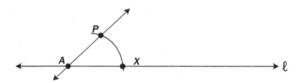

Step 3:  With the same opening of the compass, draw intersecting arcs, first with the pointer at $P$ and then with the pointer at $X$ to create a point $Y$. Point $Y$ is the fourth vertex of the rhombus.

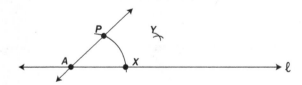

Step 4:  Draw $\overleftrightarrow{PY}$. Line $\overleftrightarrow{PY} \parallel$ line $\ell$.

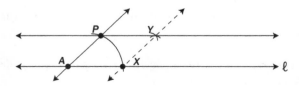

**Constructing an Angle Bisector**

An angle bisector is a ray that divides an angle into two congruent parts. To construct an angle bisector, follow these three steps:

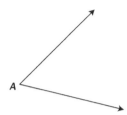

Step 1: With the compass pointer on *A*, the vertex of the angle to be bisected, draw an arc intersecting the angle at points *B* and *C*.

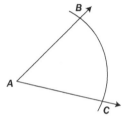

Step 2: Keep the compass set at the same distance as in Step 1. Place the pointer on point *B* and create a small arc near the center of the angle, then place the pointer on point *C* and make an intersecting arc near the center of the angle. Where the two small arcs intersect, label this point *D*.

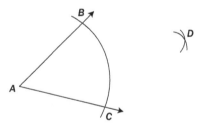

Step 3: Draw $\overline{AD}$, which is the angle bisector of $\angle A$. Therefore, $\angle BAD \cong \angle CAD$.

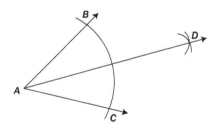

## Constructing Perpendicular Lines

Lines that are perpendicular form right angles. To construct a line perpendicular to line $\ell$ going through point $P$, follow these three steps:

Step 1: Place the compass pointer on $P$ and draw an arc that intersects line $\ell$ at points $A$ and $B$.

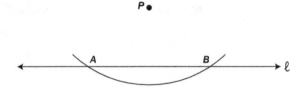

Step 2: With the same compass opening, place the pointer on $A$ and make an arc below line $\ell$, and then place the pointer on $B$ and make an intersecting arc. Call the intersection point $C$.

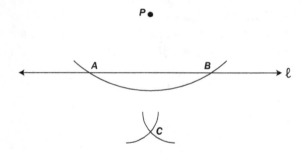

Step 3: Draw a line from point $P$ through $C$, creating a perpendicular line. Line $\overleftrightarrow{PC} \perp$ line $\ell$.

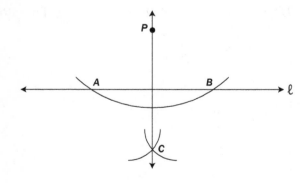

### Constructing a Perpendicular Bisector

A perpendicular bisector is a line that is perpendicular to a given line segment and bisects the line segment into two congruent parts. To construct a perpendicular bisector of segment $\overline{AB}$, follow these two steps:

Step 1: Set the compass pointer on $A$ and the pencil between points $A$ and $B$, but more than halfway between the points. Then, create an arc through the line. Keeping the same compass setting, place the pointer on $B$ and create an arc intersecting the first. Label the points of intersection $C$ and $D$.

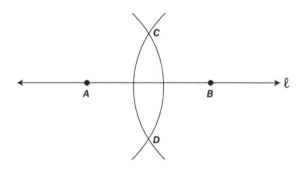

Step 2: Draw a line through points $C$ and $D$. Label point $M$ the point of intersection of $\overleftrightarrow{CD}$ and $\overleftrightarrow{AB}$. Point $M$ is the midpoint of $\overline{AB}$.

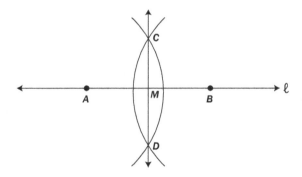

We now know $\overleftrightarrow{CD} \perp \overleftrightarrow{AB}$, $\overleftrightarrow{CD}$ bisects $\overline{AB}$, and $\overline{AM} \cong \overline{MB}$.

## Competency 019

*The teacher analyzes the properties of two- and three-dimensional figures.*

### Area (A) and Perimeter (P) Formulas

| | | Area | Perimeter |
|---|---|---|---|
| Square | | $A = s^2$ | $P = 4s$ |
| Rectangle | | $A = l \times w$ | $P = 2(l + w)$ or $2l + 2w$ |
| Parallelogram | | $A = b \times h$ | $P = 2(a + b)$ or $2a + 2b$ |
| Trapezoid | | $A = \frac{1}{2}(b_1 + b_2)h$ | $P = b_1 + b_2 + a + c$ |
| Triangle | | $A = \frac{1}{2}(b \times h)$ | $P = a + b + c$ |
| Right Triangle | | $A = \frac{1}{2}(b \times h)$ | $P = a + b + c$ |
| Equilateral triangle | | $A = \frac{\sqrt{3}}{4}s^2$ | $P = 3s$ |
| Circle | | $A = \pi r^2$ | $C = \pi r = \pi d$ ($C$ = circumference $d$ = diameter = $2r$) |

## Volume (*V*) and Surface Area (*SA*) Formulas

*B* = area of the base shape
*P* = perimeter of the base shape

|  |  | Volume | Surface Area |
|---|---|---|---|
| Rectangular solid | | $V = l \times w \times h$ | $SA = 2lw + 2wh + 2lh$ |
| Triangular prism | | $V = B \times h$ or (area of triangle) $\times h$ | $SA = 2B + Ph$ |
| Pyramid | *The base shape can change | $V = \frac{1}{3} \times B \times h$ | $SA = B +$ (area of each triangle) |
| Cylinder | | $V = \pi r^2 h$ | $SA = 2\pi rh + 2\pi r^2$ |
| Cone | | $V = \frac{1}{3}\pi r^2 h$ | $SA = \pi r^2 + \pi rs$ |
| Sphere | | $V = \frac{4}{3}\pi r^3$ | $SA = 4\pi r^2$ |

## Nets

A **net** of a three-dimensional solid is what it would look like if it were opened out flat.

| Three-dimensional Solid | Net |
|---|---|
| Cube | |
| Rectangular prism | |
| Triangular prism | |
| Square-based pyramid | |

| Three-dimensional Solid | Net |
|---|---|
| Tetrahedron | |
| Cylinder | |
| Cone | |

## Euler's Formula

A **polyhedron** is a solid object whose surface is made up of polygons. The **vertices** are the points at which the polygons meet. Each polygon is called a **face** of the polyhedron, and an **edge** is the side of the polygon. For any convex polyhedron, the sum of the **vertices** and **faces** is two more than the number of **edges**: $V + F = E + 2$.

| Solid | Vertices | Faces | Edges |
|---|---|---|---|
| Cube | 8 | 6 | 12 |
| Rectangular prism | 8 | 6 | 12 |
| Triangular prism | 6 | 5 | 9 |
| Square-based pyramid | 5 | 5 | 8 |
| Tetrahedron | 4 | 4 | 6 |

## Dimensions and Relationships

**Example 1**  A certain cylinder has height 5 units and radius 3 units. If the height triples, how is the volume affected?

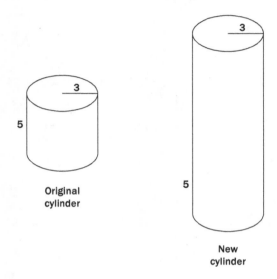

Original
cylinder

New
cylinder

The volume of the original cylinder is $V = \pi r^2 h = \pi(3^2)(5) = 45\pi$.

The volume of the new cylinder with the height tripled is $V = \pi r^2 h = \pi(3^2)(15) = 135\pi$.

The new volume is three times that of the original cylinder.

**Example 2**  A certain cylinder has height 5 units and radius 3 units. If the radius triples, how is the volume affected?

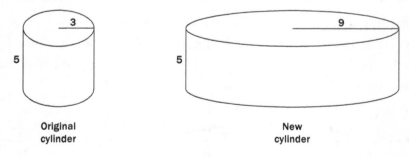

Original
cylinder

New
cylinder

The volume of the original cylinder is $V = \pi r^2 h = \pi(3^2)(5) = 45\pi$.

The volume of the new cylinder with the radius tripled is $V = \pi r^2 h = \pi(9^2)(5) = 405\pi$.

The new volume is nine times that of the original cylinder.

## Competency 020

*The teacher understands transformational geometry and relates algebra to geometry and trigonometry using the Cartesian coordinate system.*

### Translations

A translation is a motion or transformation of a plane that moves every point of the plane a specified distance in a specified direction along a straight line. A **translation in a coordinate plane** is a function that slides a point $(x, y)$ to the corresponding point $(x + a, y + b)$, where $a$ and $b$ are real numbers.

### Reflections

A reflection about a line $\ell$ is a transformation of the plane that pairs each point $P$ of the plane with a point $P'$ in such a way that line $\ell$ is the perpendicular bisector of $\overline{PP'}$, as long as $P$ is not on line $\ell$. If $P$ is on line $\ell$, then $P = P'$.

The coordinates of a **reflection in a coordinate plane** about the $x$- or $y$-axis can be quite easy to find, given the coordinates of the original point. A reflection across the $x$-axis takes a point $(x, y)$ to the corresponding point $(x, -y)$. A reflection across the $y$-axis takes a point $(x, y)$ to the corresponding point $(-x, y)$. A reflection about the line $y = x$ interchanges the coordinates of the point. For example, if we reflect the point $(1, 3)$ across the line $y = x$, the new point is $(3, 1)$.

### Rotations

A rotation is a transformation of the plane determined by holding one point, the center, fixed, and rotating the plane about this point by a certain amount (degrees) in a certain direction (clockwise or counterclockwise).

### Glide Reflections

Another basic transformation is called a glide reflection. A glide reflection is a transformation consisting of a translation followed by a reflection in a line parallel to the slide direction.

## Dilation

A dilation is also referred to as a **size transformation** that assigns some point $A$ to a collinear point $A'$. To dilate a point or figure we use a scale factor $r$ and multiply both the $x$- and $y$-coordinates by $r$. When dilating a figure, if $r > 0$, the figure is enlarged by a factor of $r$; if $0 < r < 1$, the figure is contracted or made smaller by a factor of $r$.

For example, suppose we have a triangle with vertices at $A(1, 2)$, $B(3, 5)$, and $C(5, 3)$ and we want to dilate the figure by a scale factor of 3. The transformed points are $A'(3, 6)$, $B'(9, 15)$, and $C'(15, 9)$. The triangles are similar and the side lengths are proportional by a scale factor of 3.

## Lines of Symmetry

Figures may have lines of symmetry, which can be thought of as imaginary folding lines that produce two congruent mirror-image figures. In the figures below, we can see a square has four lines of symmetry and a circle has an infinite number of lines of symmetry.

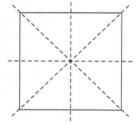 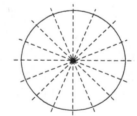

## Tessellations

A tessellation is a pattern formed by repeating a single unit or shape that when repeated fills the plane with no gaps and no overlaps. Brick patterns or a cross section of a beehive are common tessellations found in the real world.

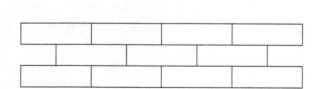 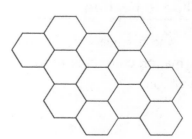

## Competency 021

*The teacher understands how to use graphical and numerical techniques to explore data, characterize patterns, and describe departures from patterns.*

A number of graphs can be used to organize and describe data. Categorical data represent characteristics of objects of individuals in groups or categories. Numerical data are collected on numerical variables (distance, time, scores, etc.).

### Pictographs

A picture graph, or *pictograph*, represents tallies or frequencies of categories. A picture, or symbol, represents a quantity of items and is denoted in a legend. In the following example, a class of students was surveyed about the types of animals they have at home. The frequencies are displayed in the table below, followed by a pictograph representing the data.

| Type of Animal | Frequency |
|---|---|
| Dog | 7 |
| Cat | 4 |
| Snake | 2 |
| Fish | 10 |

| Type of Animal | ☺ = 2 Animals |
|---|---|
| Dog | ☺ ☺ ☺ ☺ |
| Cat | ☺ ☺ |
| Snake | ☺ |
| Fish | ☺ ☺ ☺ ☺ ☺ |

## Bar Graphs

A bar graph is used to depict frequencies of categorical data. The following bar graph represents the same data as the pictograph just shown.

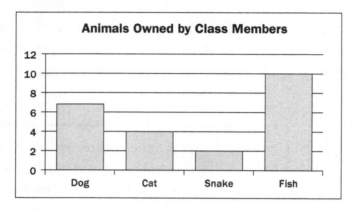

## Circle Graphs or Pie Charts

A circle graph, also called a pie chart, is used to depict frequencies of categorical data. The data from the pictograph and bar graph produces the circle graph below.

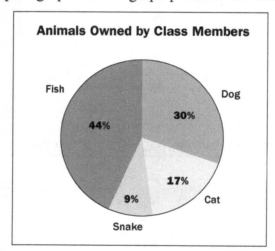

## Line or Dot Plots

A line or dot plot provides a quick way of organizing numerical data when there are less than 50 values. Suppose there is a set of test scores: 70, 72, 83, 75, 88, 81, 94, 94, 80, 85, 93. A line plot for the set of test scores consists of a horizontal number line on which each score is denoted by an X or a dot.

## Stem and Leaf Plots

The stem and leaf plot is akin to the line plot, but the number line is typically vertical and digits are used to represent data rather than dots or X's. The numbers on the left side of the vertical segment are called the **stem**. The **leaves** are the numbers on the right side.

**Temperatures in Dallas, Texas, in October**

```
8 │ 0, 1, 2
7 │ 0, 1, 2, 3, 3, 4, 7, 8, 8, 8
6 │ 5, 7, 9
```

Legend: 6│5 = 65

## Histograms

Histograms look similar to bar graphs, but they display grouped numerical data and have adjoining bars. Below is a stem and leaf plot showing ages of presidents at death with its accompanying histogram.

```
4 │ 6, 9
5 │ 3, 6, 7, 7, 8
6 │ 0, 0, 3, 3, 4, 5, 6, 7, 7, 7, 8
7 │ 0, 1, 1, 2, 3, 4, 7, 8, 8, 9
8 │ 0, 1, 1, 2, 3, 5, 8
9 │ 0, 0, 3, 3
```

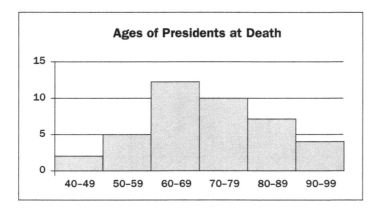

## Line Graph

A line graph shows the trend of a variable over time. Typically, time is marked on the horizontal axis, with the other variable marked on the vertical axis. Below is a line graph showing Anna's average weight per month for a year.

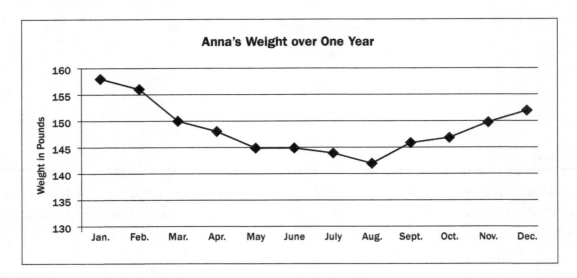

## Scatterplots

Scatterplots show relationships between two variables. Below, the scatterplot depicts the relationship between hours studied and homework scores.

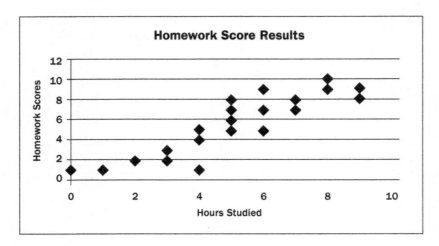

Since the data points are somewhat clustered in an upward direction, we say there is a **positive relationship** between the number of hours studied and homework scores. If the data points were moving downward to the right, we would say there is a **negative relationship** between the number of hours studied and homework scores. If the data points were more scattered across the graph and were not grouped in any direction, we'd say there is **no relationship** between the number of hours studied and homework scores.

A **trend line**, or **line of best fit**, closely fits the data and can be used to describe the data. The closer the data points are to the line, the better the fit.

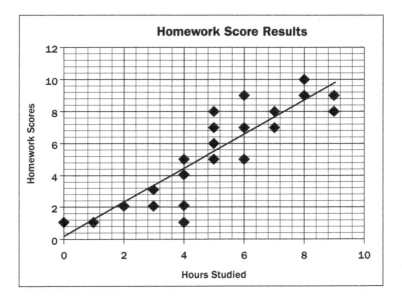

## Measures of Central Tendency

Two important aspects of data are its **center** and its **spread**. The mean and median are measures of central tendency and describe the center of the data. The spread of data is explained by the range, interquartile range, variance, and standard deviation.

- The **mean** of a set of data is the **average** of the data values. To find the mean, calculate the sum of all data values and then divide this sum by the number of values in the set.

- The **median** of a set of data is the middle value of all the numbers. To find the median, order the data values from least to greatest and then cross out one value on each end of the list until you reach the middle number. If there are two values in the middle, find the middle value or average of those two data values.

- The **mode** of a set of data is the value (or values) that appear in the set more frequently than any other value. If all the values in a set of data appear once, the set does not have a mode. If there are two values that appear the same number of times and are the most frequent, then the data set is **bimodal**.

## Box-and-Whisker Plots

A box-and-whisker plot, or box plot, is a way to represent the **five-number summary** of the data. The five numbers are the minimum, first quartile, median (or second quartile), third quartile, and maximum (or fourth quartile). A box plot can be either horizontal or vertical. We draw lines at the first, second, and third quartiles, which will form the box, and place dots or short lines at the minimum and maximum values; draw segments from each end of the box to these extreme values to create the whiskers.

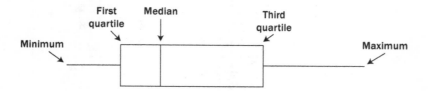

The quartiles of a data set divide the data into four regions with the same number of data values in each. The first quartile has 25% of the data values below it, the second quartile has 50% of the data values below it, the third quartile has 75% of the data values below it, and the fourth quartile has 100% of the data values below it. If there are 12 data points in the set, the third quartile includes the first 9 data values when in order from least to greatest.

Notice, the lengths of the whiskers and portions within the box are not the same. Many students confuse this to mean there are more data values represented between the median to the third quartile, but this is untrue. Box-and-whisker plots divide the data set into four regions with the same amount of data values in each region. The lengths differ based on the ranges of each area. The **interquartile range** is the range between the values at the third and first quartiles.

## Outliers

An outlier is a value that is widely separated from the rest of the data. An outlier is any value that is more than 1.5 times the interquartile range above the upper quartile (third quartile) or below the lower quartile (first quartile).

## Variance and Standard Deviation

The variance and standard deviation measure how far the data values are from the mean. To find how far each value is from the mean, we subtract each data value from the mean to obtain the deviation. Some may be positive and others negative. Since the mean is a balance point, the total of the deviations above the mean is the same as the total of the deviations below the mean. Squaring the deviations makes them all positive, and the mean of the squared deviations is called the **variance**. Taking the square root of the variance produces the **standard deviation**.

## Normal Distributions

A normal curve is a smooth, bell-shaped curve that depicts frequency values distributed symmetrically about the mean. The mean, median, and mode all have the same values in a normal curve. On a normal curve, about 68% of the values lie within 1 standard deviation of the mean, about 95% of the data values lie within 2 standard deviations of the mean, and about 99.7% lie within 3 standard deviations.

# Competency 022

*The teacher understands the theory of probability.*

Describing how likely a particular outcome will occur is the notion of **probability**. A random event occurs when a selection is made without looking or making direct observation. To describe the results of a probability experiment, fractions can be used, where the numerator is the number of favorable outcomes for the experiment and the denominator is the number of total possible outcomes for the experiment.

*Example*    Gaston is randomly selecting a marble from a bag that contains one red, one blue, and one yellow marble. What is the probability he will choose a yellow marble on a single pull?

Since there is only one yellow marble out of a total of three marbles in the bag, the probability of selecting the yellow marble is $\frac{1}{3}$.

$$P(\text{Yellow}) = \frac{\text{Number of favorable outcomes}}{\text{Total number of possible outcomes}} = \frac{1}{3}$$

The probability of Gaston choosing a marble other than yellow is $\frac{2}{3}$ since there are two other colored marbles to select from.

## Theoretical and Experimental Probability

A **sample space** is the set of all possible outcomes of an experiment. For example, if you roll a die, it will land on either 1, 2, 3, 4, 5, or 6. The **theoretical probability** of rolling a certain outcome is the same as described above: it is the number of favorable outcomes out of the total number of possible outcomes. For example, the theoretical probability of rolling an even number is $\frac{3}{6} = \frac{1}{2}$, since there are three even numbers out of six numbers on a die. However, **experimental probability** is the probability of a certain outcome occurring after an experiment was performed. If we rolled a die six times and the outcomes were 3, 4, 2, 1, 5, and 1, the experimental probability of rolling an even number is $\frac{2}{6} = \frac{1}{3}$ because only two even numbers were rolled out of the six total rolls.

## Constructing Sample Spaces

A tree diagram can be helpful for representing compound events. For example, if we toss a coin and roll a die, there are 12 possible outcomes.

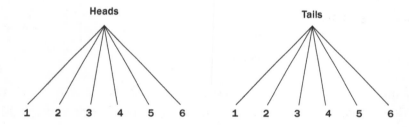

## Geometric Probability

Geometric probability typically refers to finding a ratio of two areas. For example, find the probability of throwing a dart at the shaded region in a square with side length $s$.

The probability of throwing a dart at the shaded region is the area of the shaded region divided by the area of the total region or square. We know the area of a square with side length $s$ is $s^2$. The shaded region is truly half of the square. One might draw a line through the middle of the triangle to see that there are four congruent triangles that make up the whole square (see figure below).

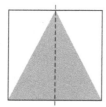

The area of half of the square is $\frac{1}{2}s^2$. Therefore, the probability of throwing a dart in the shaded region is $\frac{\frac{1}{2}s^2}{s^2} = \frac{1}{2}$.

## Competency 023

*The teacher understands the relationship among probability theory, sampling, and statistical inference and how statistical inference is used in making and evaluating predictions.*

Scatterplots are useful for detecting and examining relationships between two characteristics of a population. Students might explore the relationship between the length and width of their own hands and create a class data set. The graph below depicts six students' hand measures, comparing their length (wrist to tip of middle digit) to width. The graph clearly shows a strong positive linear relationship.

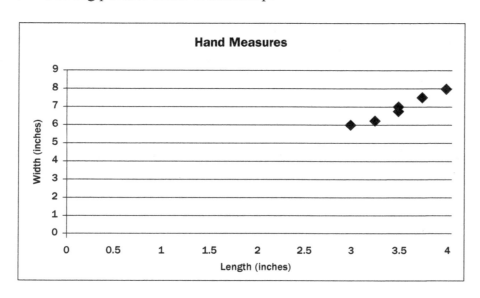

The **correlation coefficient**, $r$, measures the strength and direction of a linear relationship between two variables. This coefficient is also referred to as the Pearson product moment correlation coefficient, in honor of Karl Pearson, the developer. The value of $r$ will be between $-1$ and $+1$. The closer $r$ is to $-1$ or $+1$, the stronger the correlation among the values of the two variables. If $r$ is close to 0, there is little or no correlation between the two variables. If $r$ is negative, then the slope of the line of best fit will be negative, and as one variable increases the other decreases. If $r$ is positive, the slope of the line of best fit is positive, and as one variable increases so does the other. A perfect correlation between the two variables would be $r = \pm 1$.

## Sample Statistics, Random Samples, and Confidence Intervals

Often, it is not possible to study an entire population, as it would be very expensive or time consuming. In such a case, a sample is a part of a population that is to be observed or investigated. A **random sample**, also known as **probability sampling**, is a random selection of people from a larger target population about whom we hope to generalize through a study. For example, for investigating differences between males and females who work in a particular company, the population could be all employees at this company. However, a random sample would be a subset of male and female employees, and not all of them.

The **confidence interval** is related to a **margin of error**. It tells how sure you can be about how often the true percentage of the population lies within the confidence interval. A confidence interval gives an estimated range of values that is likely to include an unknown population parameter, the estimated range being calculated from a given set of sampled data. The selection of a **confidence level** for an interval determines the probability that the confidence interval produced will contain the true parameter value. Common choices for the confidence level are 0.90, 0.95, or 0.99. These levels correspond to percentages of the area of the normal curve. For example, a 95% confidence interval covers 95% of the normal curve; the probability of observing a value outside of this area is 5% or 0.05.

The **binomial distribution** gives the discrete probability distribution of obtaining exactly $n$ successes of observations. The binomial distribution is used when a researcher is interested in the occurrence of an event, not in its magnitude. For example, in a clinical trial, a patient may get sick or be healthy. The researcher studies the number of sick patients—not how long they are sick.

## Binomial Experiments

A binomial experiment is an experiment that satisfies four conditions:

1. There must be a fixed number of trials. Denote this number by $n$.

2. There must be exactly two possible mutually exclusive outcomes for each trial. Call them *success* and *failure*.

3. The trials must be independent. That is, the outcome of a particular trial is not affected by the outcome of any other trial.

4. The probabilities of success and failure must remain constant for each trial.

## Binomial Distribution Theorem

Let $X$ be a random variable for the number of successes in $n$ independent and identical repetitions of an experiment with two possible outcomes, success and failure. If $p$ is the probability of success, then $P(X = k) = \left( \dfrac{n}{k} \right) p^k (1-p)^{n-k}$, where $k = 0, 1, \ldots, n$.

***Example*** A manufacturer makes electrical outlets. Suppose three items are chosen at random from a day's production and are classified as defective (F) or nondefective (S). We are interested in the number of successes (here, nondefective items) obtained. Suppose that an item has a probability of 0.2 of being defective, and therefore a probability of 0.8 of being nondefective. Let $X =$ the number of successes (or nondefective items) obtained. Calculate the probabilities.

First, create the sample space and the probabilities for each.

| Sample Space | Associated Probabilities |
|:---:|:---|
| 1. FFF | $(0.2)(0.2)(0.2) = (0.2)^3$ |
| 2. FFS | $(0.2)(0.2)(0.8) = (0.8)(0.2)^2$ |
| 3. FSF | $(0.2)(0.8)(0.2) = (0.8)(0.2)^2$ |
| 4. SFF | $(0.8)(0.2)(0.2) = (0.8)(0.2)^2$ |
| 5. FSS | $(0.2)(0.8)(0.8) = (0.8)^2(0.2)$ |
| 6. SFS | $(0.8)(0.2)(0.8) = (0.8)^2(0.2)$ |
| 7. SSF | $(0.8)(0.8)(0.2) = (0.8)^2(0.2)$ |
| 8. SSS | $(0.8)(0.8)(0.8) = (0.8)^3$ |

Using the binomial distribution theorem, we can get the same results below.

$$P(X=0)=\binom{3}{0}(0.8)^0(0.2)^3=1\cdot1\cdot(0.008)=.008$$

$$P(X=1)=\binom{3}{1}(0.8)^1(0.2)^2=3\cdot(0.8)(0.04)=.096$$

$$P(X=2)=\binom{3}{2}(0.8)^2(0.2)^1=3\cdot(0.64)(0.2)=.384$$

$$P(X=3)=\binom{3}{3}(0.8)^3(0.2)^0=1\cdot(0.512)\cdot1=.512$$

## Competency 024

*The teacher understands mathematical reasoning and problem solving.*

Teachers need to create opportunities to motivate children to develop logical thinking skills through exploratory mathematics and problem solving. Such exploration can be done with partners or in learning centers, which are designed to expose students to manipulatives, which are used to teach mathematical concepts in an indirect fashion through student-selected activities.

Problem solving requires frequent opportunities to formulate, grapple with, and solve complex problems. Students are able to acquire ways of thinking, habits of persistence, and curiosity in unfamiliar situations (NCTM, 2000). Solving problems requires more than numerical computations. There are a number of problem-solving strategies. These can include drawing a picture, making a list, acting out a problem, creating a graph, using logical reasoning, looking for a pattern, developing a systematic list, working backward, writing an equation, and using guess-and-check methods.

George Polya wrote a classic book, *How to Solve It* (1994), that outlined four steps for doing mathematics. These steps are widely adopted in textbooks and resource books to help students develop problem-solving skills. The four steps are described briefly in the following list:

1. *Understanding the problem.* In this phase students determine what the problem is about and identify what question or problem is being posed.

2. *Devising a plan.* Students think about how they intend to solve the problem and select a problem-solving strategy.

3. *Carrying out the plan.* Students implement the plan they just devised. If they get stumped, students can reevaluate their plan and try a different approach if needed.

4. *Looking back.* This phase can be the most important as well as the most skipped by students. Once they've arrived at an answer after the first three steps, students should determine whether their answers make sense and check their work if possible.

**Logical reasoning** is thinking about something in a way that makes sense to the student. Thinking about mathematics problems involves logical reasoning. Logical reasoning can be used to find patterns in a set of data, then those patterns can be used to draw conclusions about the data, which can then be used to solve problems. Finding patterns involves identifying characteristics that numbers or objects have in common. A sequence of geometric objects may have some property in common. For example, they may all be quadrilaterals or all have right angles.

Through mathematical reasoning skills, students should investigate mathematical conjectures and develop, as well as evaluate, mathematical arguments and proofs (NCTM, 2000). Strong reasoning skills are needed for building skill sets in all five content standards: Number and Operations, Algebra, Geometry, Measurement, and Data Analysis and Probability.

**Deductive reasoning** requires moving from the assumptions to the conclusion, or from the general to the specific. Deductive reasoning is often used in students' daily lives. For example, if a student sees it is raining outside before leaving home to head to school, she might conclude she needs an umbrella. The student's conclusion is reached through deductive reasoning.

**Inductive reasoning** involves examining particular instances to come to some general assumptions, and should be intuitive. When thinking inductively, students will make hypotheses, extend patterns of thought, use analogies, and make reasonable conclusions from examining what appears to be a body of evidence.

## Competency 025

*The teacher understands mathematical connections within and outside of mathematics and how to communicate mathematical ideas and concepts.*

Mathematics is an integrated field of study. When students connect mathematical ideas, their understanding is deeper and more lasting. Students can come to view mathematics as a coherent whole (NCTM, 2000). One of the challenges teachers face in promoting interest in mathematics is to convince students that mathematics plays an important role in their lives. Based on this assumption, teachers need to introduce mathematics concepts in a problem-solving format using situations that are real to the students' lives. Some examples to connect mathematics to students' lives are explained below.

### Planning Projects

- Have students plan a field trip for the class. As a class or in small groups, students might have to decide where the field trip will take place and estimate the cost of the trip. They will need to determine a means of transportation, number of adult volunteer chaperones, the duration of the field trip including travel time, cost per student, and total cost of the trip. Students can also develop a plan to pay for the field trip, including fund-raising opportunities, and create a field trip permission slip form for parents/guardians to sign. Once all information is collected, they can write a proposal for the field trip and present it to the principal and potentially get approval to take the trip.

- Have students plan a road trip to a vacation spot they would like visit one day. Using an online mapping website, students can obtain the appropriate information to determine distance from one place to the other, and use this distance to calculate travel time and gas expenses based on mileage of driving their family car. Students can also investigate traveling by bus, train, or plane, and then they can compare costs to determine the most cost-effective trip.

- Organize cooking activities using recipes requiring specific units of measurement. These activities should include some that can be completed in school and at home. The recipes should require students to convert units and use proportional reasoning to double recipes or make portions of a recipe.

- Develop a "class store" to help students with concepts of fractions, decimals, and percents, as well as basic computational skills. Using a token or sticker system, students can earn forms of money as tokens or stickers, and use them to purchase items in the class store. Often teachers reward students for good behavior for following directions or having good listening skills. However, students could earn their tokens/stickers by helping students in class mathematically, presenting a problem to the class, posing questions, leading class discussions, or explaining where they used mathematics outside of school and/or bringing proof of such experience.

# Competency 026

*The teacher understands how children learn and develop mathematical skills, procedures, and concepts.*

Contextual factors are important elements that help teachers plan and meet the needs of all students. Understanding students' backgrounds, prior knowledge, and personal experiences can influence what content is taught and how to teach it. Understanding how students differ in their problem-solving approaches can create an effective learning environment.

Students should experience mathematics through the use of manipulatives and technological tools that allow learning to occur at a concrete level. Manipulatives and tools allow students to touch, move, rearrange, and explore mathematics. From these experiences, students can then transfer their knowledge to the pictorial level, where they use pictures to problem solve. They can create and design their own pictorial representations for the given task. Once students master the concrete and pictorial phases, they can then apply the mathematical content in a more abstract form.

The teacher is responsible for motivating and engaging students in challenging and worthwhile mathematics, through individual, small-group, and large-group settings. The five Process Standards defined by the National Council of Teachers of Mathematics (NCTM) are essential for students to successfully learn mathematics. They are problem solving, reasoning and proof, representations, communication, and connections (NCTM, 2000). Rarely are these standards experienced in isolation. Rather, students fluctuate among and within the standards regularly during their mathematical learning experiences.

The NCTM, established in 1920, is one of the most well-known organizations in mathematics education to date. NCTM's goals include the development and improvement of mathematics education through six principles and ten standards that children in kindergarten through grade 12 should master. In 2000, NCTM published the *Principles and Standards for School Mathematics*, a resource intended for all who make decisions that affect mathematics education for K–12 students. This document has influenced states and district curricula development, and specifies the mathematics content students should learn.

## Principles of Mathematics

The NCTM (2000) identified six principles that should guide mathematics instruction. These include equity, curriculum, teaching, learning, assessment, and technology.

- **Equity**: Excellence in mathematics education requires equity: high expectations and strong support for all students.

- **Curriculum**: A curriculum must be coherent, focusing on important mathematics and clearly articulating concepts across grades. Curriculum is more than a collection of activities.

- **Teaching**: Effective mathematics teaching requires understanding what students know and need to learn and then challenging and supporting students to learn it well.

- **Learning**: Students must learn mathematics with understanding, actively building new knowledge from experience and former knowledge.

- **Assessment**: Assessment should support the learning of important mathematics, and furnish useful information to both teachers and students.

- **Technology**: Technology is essential in teaching and learning mathematics; it influences the teaching of mathematics and enhances students' learning.

## Standards of Mathematics

NCTM (2000) has identified five Content Standards and five Process Standards. The Content Standards explicitly describe the mathematical content students should learn, whereas the Process Standards highlight ways of attaining and using content knowledge.

## Texas Mathematics Standards

The State Board of Educator Certification (SBEC) and the State Board of Education (SBOE) approved Texas educator standards that outline what the beginning educator should know and be able to do. These standards are based on the required state curriculum for students, the Texas Essential Knowledge and Skills (TEKS). The Texas Education Agency (TEA, 2009) has defined eight mathematical standards as follows:

### Standard I — Number Concepts

The mathematics teacher understands and uses numbers, number systems and their structure, operations and algorithms, quantitative reasoning, and technology appropriate to teach the statewide curriculum (Texas Essential Knowledge and Skills [TEKS]) in order to prepare students to use mathematics.

## Standard II — Patterns and Algebra

The mathematics teacher understands and uses patterns, relations, functions, algebraic reasoning, analysis, and technology appropriate to teach the statewide curriculum (Texas Essential Knowledge and Skills [TEKS]) in order to prepare students to use mathematics.

## Standard III — Geometry and Measurement

The mathematics teacher understands and uses geometry, spatial reasoning, measurement concepts and principles, and technology appropriate to teach the statewide curriculum (Texas Essential Knowledge and Skills [TEKS]) in order to prepare students to use mathematics.

## Standard IV — Probability and Statistics

The mathematics teacher understands and uses probability and statistics, their applications, and technology appropriate to teach the statewide curriculum (Texas Essential Knowledge and Skills [TEKS]) in order to prepare students to use mathematics.

## Standard V — Mathematical Processes

The mathematics teacher understands and uses mathematical processes to reason mathematically, to solve mathematical problems, to make mathematical connections within and outside of mathematics, and to communicate mathematically.

## Standard VI — Mathematical Perspectives

The mathematics teacher understands the historical development of mathematical ideas, the interrelationship between society and mathematics, the structure of mathematics, and the evolving nature of mathematics and mathematical knowledge.

## Standard VII — Mathematical Learning and Instruction

The mathematics teacher understands how children learn and develop mathematical skills, procedures, and concepts; knows typical errors students make; and uses this knowledge to plan, organize, and implement instruction; to meet curriculum goals; and to teach all students to understand and use mathematics.

### Standard VIII — Mathematical Assessment

The mathematics teacher understands assessment and uses a variety of formal and informal assessment techniques appropriate to the learner on an ongoing basis to monitor and guide instruction and to evaluate and report student progress.

## Mathematics and Cognitive Development

Learning mathematics requires students to create mathematical relationships and develop meanings for abstract ideas. Students need concrete interactions with mathematical ideas that may not be accessible from abstractions and symbols. Jean Piaget, a developmental biologist, observed and recorded the intellectual abilities of infants, children, and adolescents. Piaget developed stages of intellectual development related to brain growth that led him to conclude that thinking and reasoning skills of children were-dominated by preoperational thought, a pattern of thinking that is egocentric, centered, irreversible, and nontransformational (Piaget and Inhelder, 1969). His theory included the growth of intelligence and emergence and acquisition of schemata—schemes of a child using "developmental stages" to explain how children acquire new information. The four main stages are the Sensorimotor stage (birth–2 years), Preoperational stage (years 2–7), Concrete Operational stage (years 7–11), and Formal Operational stage (years 11–adult).

Piaget describes the Preoperational stage of development to include the processes of symbolic functioning, centration, intuitive thought, egocentrism, and inability to conserve. Students in the Concrete Operational stage exhibit the developmental processes of decentering, reversibility, conservation, serialization, classification, and elimination of egocentrism. The Formal Operation stage of Piaget's cognitive development focuses on the ability to use symbols and to think abstractly (Piaget and Inhelder, 1969).

Students in the Preoperational stage experience problems with at least two perceptual concepts: conservation and centration, according to Susan Sperry Smith (2008). Conservation is the understanding that the quantity, length, or number of items is unrelated to the arrangement or appearance of the object or items. Students encountering problems with conservation may have difficulty measuring volume or understanding the value of money. For example, students may think a dime is worth less than a nickel since it is thinner and smaller in diameter. Centration is characterized by a child's focus on one aspect of a situation or problem. For example, take two 8.5-inch-by-11-inch sheets of paper and roll each into a tube, one a long skinny tube, and the other a short wider tube. A young student might judge the capacity of the shorter tube to be less than that of the taller tube based on his perception of short and tall.

Children ages 7 to 11 years old (about second through seventh grades) experience rapid growth during the Concrete Operational stage of cognitive development. At this time students are developing the ability to think logically about concrete objects or relationships. Some of the characteristics of students at this stage are

- **Classification:** The student can identify and name sets of objects according to appearance, size, color, or other characteristics. The student can arrange objects based on characteristics.

- **Conservation:** The student understands that the quantity, length, or number of items is unrelated to the arrangement or appearance of the object. The student can discern that if water is transferred from a glass to a pitcher, the quantity of water will be conserved; that is, the quantity of water in the pitcher will be equal to the quantity that had been in the glass.

- **Decentering:** The student can take into account multiple aspects of a problem to solve it. The student can form conclusions based on reason rather than perception.

- **Elimination of egocentrism:** The student is able to view things from another student's perspective. The student can retell or summarize a story from another child's perspective.

- **Reversibility:** The student understands that objects can be changed and then returned to their original state. The student can determine that four rows of two crayons is the same original quantity as two rows of four crayons.

Piaget's stages of cognitive development were foundational during his time. Contemporary researchers have found Piaget underestimated the abilities of children in preschool and early elementary years. Some students can develop more sophisticated thinking and reasoning skills by as early as second or third grade, especially if they have adequate instruction and support from teachers and peers (Vygotsky, 1986). Students' cognitive development is influenced by their culture and instruction and is related to cognitively guided instruction (CGI) (Carpenter et al., 1999; Kamii, 2000; Santrock, 2003).

## Mathematical Literacy

Literacy skills are essential for students to be successful learners. More than reading and writing, literacy includes purposeful social and cognitive processes that help students discover ideas and create meaning; it requires analysis, synthesis, organization, and evaluation of reading tasks (Jacobs, 2008; Moss, 2005; Tovani, 2000). Mathematical literacy involves the capacity to identify, understand, and engage in mathematics; it includes the ability to make sound judgments about the role mathematics plays in one's present and future life as a constructive, concerned, and reflective citizen (Kramarski and Mizrachi, 2006). NCTM (1989) describes mathematically literate students as having an appreciation of the value and beauty of mathematics and being able, as well as being inclined, to value and use quantitative information.

Successful readers determine what is important. They synthesize information to create new thinking, construct sensory images, and self-monitor their own comprehension. Students struggle when reading if they lack the comprehension strategies needed to unlock meaning, sufficient background knowledge, and the ability to recognize organizational patterns (Tovani, 2000). Gardner (1983, 1993) would describe students with mathematical literacy to have logical-mathematical intelligence, which is the ability to understand and use logical structures including patterns, relationships, statements, and propositions through experimentation, quantification, conceptualization, and classification.

Students may face a number of challenges with the technical vocabulary and literacy skills of mathematics. The mathematics classroom tends to abound in assumptions concerning students' prior knowledge of specialized academic terms such as *numerator*, *denominator*, *product*, *quotient*, *minuend*, *divisor*, *subtrahend*, and other technical concepts and words. The terms that have one meaning in one subject domain can have an entirely different meaning in the vocabulary of mathematics. These terms include *quarter*, *column*, *product*, *rational*, *even*, and *table*. Also, mathematics vocabulary tends to encompass a variety of homophones (words pronounced in the same way but having different meanings). Table 3-1 depicts various mathematics terms and their structures that may be confusing for all students. Table 3-2 lists homophones that may pose challenges for students.

## Table 3-1 Mathematical Terminology and Meanings

| Terminology | Common Meaning | Mathematical Meaning |
|---|---|---|
| Even | Equal amount, same level | Numbers divisible by 2 |
| Face | Front of a human head | Surface of a geometric solid |
| Plane | Aircraft | A two-dimensional surface |
| Mean | Not nice, or to express a particular message | Arithmetic average of a set of data values |
| Right | Correct, proper; or a direction | A 90-degree angle |
| Volume | Loudness of sounds | Capacity or quantity of liquid |

## Table 3-2 Homophones

| Mathematical Term | Everyday Term |
|---|---|
| Sum | Some |
| One | Won |
| Two | To, too |
| Whole | Hole |
| Plane | Plain |
| Hour | Our |
| Chord | Cord |
| Eight | Ate |
| Weigh | Way |
| Real | Reel |

## Contextual Mathematics

Mathematical concepts are integral aspects of daily life. Students should encounter mathematics in real-world contexts that are associated with activities found in their daily lives. For instance, children may often be involved in recreational activities such as baseball or softball. Common mathematics associated with these sports includes players' batting averages, calculated by the number of hits divided by the number of times at bat. Providing students with a mathematical context allows students to develop a deeper meaning to the mathematics, assisting in conceptual versus procedural understanding.

Consider the following examples:

*Example 1*    During the second week of July 2011, the temperatures for Monday through Friday were 98, 102, 99, 99, and 105 degrees. What was the average temperature during this week?

*Example 2*    Find the average of 98, 102, 99, 99, and 105.

Both examples ask for the same mathematical task: compute the average of the data set by calculating the sum of the numbers and dividing by the number of data values—five. However, Example 1 poses the mathematical problem in a context or real-world scenario that students can relate to: temperature. Knowledge of the daily temperature is helpful to determine what a student might wear to school one day. In warm temperatures, as depicted in the problem, students might wear shorts to school, but if the temperatures were in the 30s and 40s, they'd probably choose to wear jeans and a jacket. Example 2 has less connotation or meaning to students, as the problem is not posed in a specific context. Although having the ability to calculate the mean or average of a set of values is important, students should have a balance of problems presented and not presented in real-world contexts.

## Manipulatives in the Mathematics Classroom

Manipulatives are powerful tools to help students explore mathematics in a concrete and hands-on approach. Manipulatives provide a visual representation of a concept that assists in developing deeper understanding, which will help explain and improve the abstract meaning of mathematics. Students need opportunities to work collaboratively, applying numeric and algebraic reasoning; generating and analyzing data; and developing an understanding of ratios, proportions, and rate, as well as of critical thinking and making sound predictions and estimates. The importance of using manipulatives to teach these skills and mathematical concepts is reinforced by Piaget's theories on the cognitive development in children (Dienes and Sriraman, 2008).

## Two-Color Counters

Two-color counters are circles, with one side red and the other white. Sometimes the product is sold in sets of yellow and red. In primary grades, two-color counters are used for building number concepts from 0 to 20 using five-frames and ten-frames. In grades 4 through 8, two-color counters can depict multiplication problems in the form of rectangular arrays. They are great tools for teaching operations with integers, specifically zero pairs and why the product of two negative numbers is positive.

## Fraction Bars

Fraction bars can be constructed from paper using paper-folding techniques, or the product can be purchased. As their name implies, fraction bars are length models of fractions. They model relationships and equivalencies. For example, by the diagram below, we can see two $\frac{1}{4}$ bars is equivalent to one bar the length of $\frac{1}{2}$. So, $\frac{2}{4}=\frac{1}{2}$. Although students learn how to simplify fractions by finding a GCF and removing a factor of 1, the fraction bars approach equivalent fractions by using length to model the equivalencies. In addition to exploring fraction equivalencies, students can use fraction bars to display mixed numbers and to solve addition and subtraction problems.

| 1 | | | | | | | | | | | | | | | |
|---|---|---|---|---|---|---|---|---|---|---|---|---|---|---|---|
| $\frac{1}{2}$ | | | | | | | | $\frac{1}{2}$ | | | | | | | |
| $\frac{1}{4}$ | | | | $\frac{1}{4}$ | | | | $\frac{1}{4}$ | | | | $\frac{1}{4}$ | | | |
| $\frac{1}{8}$ | | $\frac{1}{8}$ | | $\frac{1}{8}$ | | $\frac{1}{8}$ | | $\frac{1}{8}$ | | $\frac{1}{8}$ | | $\frac{1}{8}$ | | $\frac{1}{8}$ | |
| $\frac{1}{16}$ | $\frac{1}{16}$ | $\frac{1}{16}$ | $\frac{1}{16}$ | $\frac{1}{16}$ | $\frac{1}{16}$ | $\frac{1}{16}$ | $\frac{1}{16}$ | $\frac{1}{16}$ | $\frac{1}{16}$ | $\frac{1}{16}$ | $\frac{1}{16}$ | $\frac{1}{16}$ | $\frac{1}{16}$ | $\frac{1}{16}$ | $\frac{1}{16}$ |

## Fraction Circles

Fraction circles are similar to fraction bars. However, this manipulative models fractions in an *area* model. Students can explore equivalent fractions, mixed numbers, and computations with fraction circles.

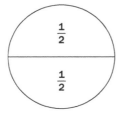 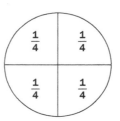

## Pattern Blocks

Pattern blocks consist of six different polygons that are identified by color and shape: orange square, green equilateral triangle, yellow regular hexagon, red isosceles trapezoid, blue rhombus, and brown parallelogram. Pattern blocks can be used to teach number and operation skills of basic fractional concepts and relationships, as well as addition, subtraction, multiplication, and division of fractions. In geometry, they are used for modeling transformations, tessellations, and geometric probability.

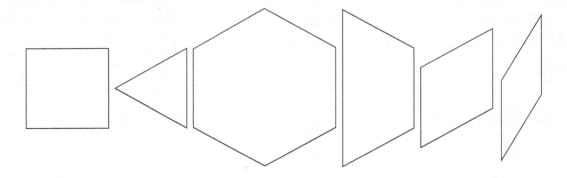

## Cuisenaire Rods

Cuisenaire rods are similar to fraction bars as they depict length models. There are 10 different rods denoted by color and length. The rods are used in primary grades to discuss whole number addition and subtraction. In grades 4 through 8, they are frequently used to explore fractional concepts, equivalencies, and computations.

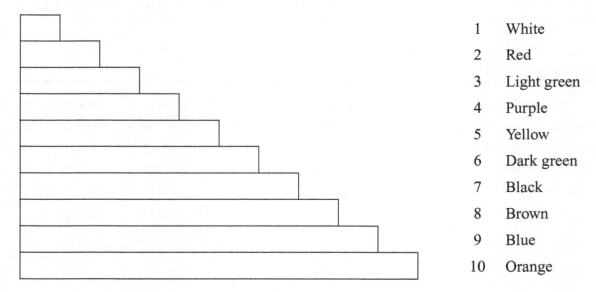

| 1 | White |
| 2 | Red |
| 3 | Light green |
| 4 | Purple |
| 5 | Yellow |
| 6 | Dark green |
| 7 | Black |
| 8 | Brown |
| 9 | Blue |
| 10 | Orange |

## Algebra Tiles

Algebra tiles comprise three different shapes, each with two different-colored sides. They represent variables and constants and are used to solve equations, factor polynomials, expand or multiply polynomials, and investigate zero pairs. A strong foundation of integer operations should be formed prior to using algebra tiles. Specifically, students should understand why the product of two negative numbers is a positive number, most often taught using two-color counters. Then when students apply their knowledge of integer operations to algebra tiles, the approach is less procedural and more conceptual.

The constant and $x$ bar have one side red and the other green. The square has one side red and the other blue. The red side is to represent negative values. The green and blue sides are to represent positive values.

## Double-Sided Geoboard

Double-sided geoboards include a five-by-five pin array on one side and a circular array on the other side. They come with rubber bands to create various shapes used to explore properties, area, and perimeter. The side with the circular array can be used to investigate chords, angle measures and their relationships, sectors, and so on. The circle can represent a clock, too, so students can represent a time and then discuss angle measures and fractions or portions of a circle.

## Competency 027

*The teacher understands how to plan, organize, and implement instruction using knowledge of students, subject matter, and statewide curriculum (Texas Essential Knowledge and Skills [TEKS]) to teach all students to use mathematics.*

Substantial thought to lesson planning is crucial for all teachers regardless of experience. Every class of students is different, so choices of which tasks to use and how they are presented to students must be made daily. Addressing all students' needs for a diverse classroom and including the state and local curriculum objectives are essential components of the lesson-plan process. The following are key components to consider when planning a lesson:

- Determine the mathematics and learning objectives.

- Consider the students' needs.

- Select, design, or adapt a task or activity.

- Identify essential questions.

- Design lesson assessments.

**Differentiated instruction** is a teaching method in which the teacher's plan includes strategies to support the range of different academic backgrounds. Students' interests and their prior knowledge impact instruction. Three elements to consider when differentiating instruction are content (what you want each student to be able to do), process (how you will engage students in that learning), and product (what students will show for what they have learned at the end of the lesson) (Tomlinson, 2001).

The state curriculum, Texas Essential Knowledge and Skills (TEKS), should guide the mathematical content taught in the classroom. How the specific content is taught is up to the classroom teacher but can often be guided by curriculum specialists within school districts.

## Competency 028

*The teacher understands assessment and uses a variety of formal and informal assessment techniques to monitor and guide mathematics instruction and to evaluate student progress.*

One of NCTM's (2000) six principles for school mathematics is assessment, which should support the learning of important mathematics and furnish useful information to both teachers and students. In traditional testing, the focus is on what students do not know, but a shift toward assessing students has led to an emphasis on determining what students do know. This shift resulted in the *Assessment Standards for School Mathematics* published by NCTM in 1995. This document outlines four specific purposes of assessment: (1) monitoring student progress, (2) making instructional design, (3) evaluating student achievement, and (4) evaluating programs. Additional considerations about what should be assessed were identified as concepts and procedures, mathematical processes, and productive dispositions (NCTM, 1995).

Assessments can be formative or summative. **Formative assessments** are regularly planned checkups of students' progress. When implemented well, formative assessments can increase the speed of learning by providing feedback that promotes learning. Formative assessments should also guide instruction, impacting decision making for future steps in the learning progression (NCTM, 1995; Van de Walle et al., 2010). Some formative approaches include performance-based tasks, journals, observations of problem solving, and diagnostic interviews.

**Summative assessments** are cumulative evaluations that often generate a single score, such as a unit exam or standardized test. This type of assessment shows what students know at that particular point in time, whereas formative assessments depict active student thinking and reasoning over time.

## References

Billstein, Rick, Shlomo Libeskind, and Johnny Lott. 2010. *A Problem Solving Approach to Mathematics for Elementary School Teachers*, 10th ed. Boston: Pearson Education, Inc.

Carpenter, T. M., E. Fennema, M. L. Franke, L. Levi, and S. B. Empson. 1999. *Children's Mathematics: Cognitively Guided Instruction*. Portsmouth, NH: Heinemann.

Dienes, Z. P., and B. Sriraman, eds. 2008. *Mathematics Education and the Legacy of Zoltan Paul Dienes*. Charlotte, NC: Information Age Publishing.

Gardner, Howard. 1983. *Frames of Mind*. New York: HarperCollins Publishers, Inc.

Gardner, Howard. 1993. *Multiple Intelligences: The Theory in Practice*. New York: HarperCollins Publishers, Inc.

Jacobs, V. A. 2008. "Adolescent Literacy: Putting the Crisis in Context." *Harvard Educational Review* 78: 7–39.

Kamii, C. 2000. *Young Children Reinvent Arithmetic: Implications of Piaget's Theory*. New York: Teachers College Press.

Kramarski B., and N. Mizrachi. 2006. "Online Discussion and Self-regulated Learning: Effects of Instructional Methods on Mathematical Literacy." *Journal of Educational Research* 99: 218–230.

Long, Calvin T., Duane W. DeTemple, and Richard S. Millman. 2012. *Mathematical Reasoning for Elementary Teachers*, 6th ed. Boston: Pearson, Inc.

Moss, B. 2005. "Making a Case and a Place for Effective Content Area Literacy Instruction in Elementary Grades. *The Reading Teacher* 59: 46–55.

National Council of Teachers of Mathematics (NCTM). 1989. *Curriculum and Evaluation Standards for School Mathematics.* Reston, VA: NCTM.

_____. 1995. Assessment Standards for School Mathematics. Reston, VA: NCTM.

National Council of Teachers of Mathematics (NCTM). 2000. *Principles and Standards for School Mathematics.* Reston, VA: NCTM.

Piaget, J., and B. Inhelder. 1969. *The Psychology of the Child.* New York: Basic Books.

Polya, George. 1994. *How to Solve It.* Princeton, NJ: Princeton University Books.

Santrock, J. W. 2003. *Children*, 7th ed. Boston: McGraw-Hill.

Smith, Karl J. 2007. *The Nature of Mathematics*, 11th ed. Belmont, CA: Brooks/Cole.

Sperry Smith, S. 2008. *Early Childhood Mathematics*, 4th ed. Boston: Allyn and Bacon.

Tan, S. T. 1999. *Applied Calculus*, 4th ed. Pacific Grove, CA: Brooks/Cole.

Texas Education Agency (TEA). 2009. Texas Essential Knowledge and Skills. Texas Administrative Code (TAC), Title 19, Part II, Chapter 111. Texas Essential Knowledge and Skills for Mathematics. Austin: Texas Education Agency.

Texas Education Agency (TEA). 2011. *Texas Examinations of Educator Standards Preparation Manual 111 Generalist 4–8.*

Tomlinson, C. 2001. *How to Differentiate Instruction in Mixed-Ability Differentiated Classrooms*, 2nd ed. Alexandria, VA: Association for Supervision and Curriculum Development.

Tovani, C. 2000. *I Read It, but I Don't Get It: Comprehension Strategies for Adolescent Readers.* Portland, ME: Stenhouse Publishers.

Van de Wall, John A., Karen S. Karp, and Jennifer M. Bay-Williams. 2010. *Elementary and Middle School Mathematics: Teaching Developmentally*, 7th ed. Boston: Allyn and Bacon.

Vancil, C. 1966. *College Algebra: A Graphing Approach*, preliminary ed. Fort Worth, TX: Saunders College Publishing.

Vygotsky, Lev Semyonovich. 1986. *Thought and Language*, new rev. ed. Cambridge, MA: MIT Press.

# Social Studies

## Competency 029: History

*The teacher understands and applies knowledge of significant historical events and developments, multiple historical interpretations and ideas and relationships between the past, the present and the future as defined by the Texas Essential Knowledge and Skills (TEKS).*

### World History

The World History Encyclopedia divides the history of the world into five periods: the Ancient World, the Middle Ages, the Age of Discovery, Revolution and Industry, and the Modern World (Ganeri, Martell, and Williams, 1999). A summary and time line of key events in each period is presented here.

### The Ancient World (4 Million Years Ago to 500 CE)[1]

Study of the ancient world focuses on the development of the first humans, the first farmers, and the first civilizations. It emphasizes the history of the ancient civilizations of Mesopotamia, Sumer, Assyria, Babylon, Egypt, the Indus Valley, megalith Europe, ancient China, Phoenicia, ancient America, ancient Greece, the Celts, the Romans, and empires in Africa and India.

---

[1] The terms "Before the Common Era (BCE)" and "Common Era (CE)" are used here in place of the traditional "Before Christ (BC) and Anno Domini (AD). These designations cover the same historical periods.

### Time Line of the Ancient World

| | |
|---|---|
| 4000 BCE | Homo sapiens appear in various regions in the world |
| 3500 BCE | The Sumerians of Mesopotamia invent writing and the wheel |
| 3100 BCE | Egypt becomes unified |
| 2800 BCE | Building begins in Stonehenge, England |
| 2500 BCE | Indus civilization flourishes in India |
| 1600–1100 BCE | Mycenaean control of Greece |
| 1200–400 BCE | Olmecs civilization flourishes in western Mexico |
| 1000–612 BCE | New Assyrian Empire flourishes |
| 753 BCE | Foundation of Rome |
| 605–562 BCE | King Nebuchadnezzar rebuilds the city Babylon |
| 476–431 BCE | Golden age of Athens |
| 336–323 BCE | Alexander the Great rules the world |
| 27 BCE to 14 CE | Augustus rules as the first Roman emperor |
| 476 CE | Western Roman Empire falls |

## The Middle Ages (500–1400 CE)

This period includes the Byzantine civilization, the rise of Islam, civilizations of the Americas, the Vikings, the feudal system, the Crusades, Genghis Khan and China, the African kingdoms, and the Hundred Years' War

### Time Line for the Middle Ages (CE)

| | |
|---|---|
| 500 | Eastern Roman (Byzantine Empire) at its peak |
| 600 | Teotihuacán civilization flourishes in Mexico |
| 600 | Rise of Islam |
| 700 | Mayan civilization at its height in Central America |
| 700 | Feudal system begins in Europe; peasants serve a lord in exchange for protection |
| 711 | Moors invade Spain |
| 750 | Abbasid dynasty is founded; Arab Empire at its peak |
| 800 | Charlemagne crowned emperor of the Holy Roman Empire |
| 900 | Rise of Toltec civilization in Mexico |

| 1000 | Vikings land in North America |
|------|-------------------------------|
| 1095 | Muslim Turks take Jerusalem and ban Christian pilgrims from the city |
| 1096–1270 | Crusades try to rescue Jerusalem from the Muslims |
| 1215 | Genghis Khan and the Mongols invade China |
| 1271 | Marco Polo travels to China from Italy |
| 1300 | Renaissance begins in Europe |
| 1325 | Aztecs established Tenochtitlán near modern day Mexico City |
| 1368 | Foundation of the Ming dynasty in China |
| 1453 | Fall of the eastern Roman Empire (Constantinople) |
| 1454 | Gutenberg invents the printing press |
| 1500 | Inca Empire at its peak in Peru |

## Age of Discovery (1400–1700)

The Age of Discovery was a period in history starting in the early 15th century and continuing into the early 17th century during which Europeans engaged in intensive exploration and mapping of the world, establishing contact with Africa, the Americas, and Asia. This period in history bridges the distance between the Middle Ages, which was characterized by a rise in Islam, the feudal system, the Crusades, the Hundred Years' war, and the Modern Era. Accounts from exploring distant lands and maps spread with the help of the new printing press, increasing worldly curiosity and ushering in a new age of scientific and intellectual inquiry. European colonization led to the rise of colonial empires, increased and diversified trade routes, a wide transfer of plants, animals, foods, human populations (including slaves), the spread of communicable diseases, and the sharing of culture between the Eastern and Western hemispheres. The Age of Discovery resulted in a new world-view as distant civilizations came into contact with one another.

### Time Line for the Age of Discovery

| 1441 | Portuguese begin slave trade from Africa to Europe |
|------|----------------------------------------------------|
| 1448 | Portuguese explorers reach the southern part of Africa |
| 1492 | Columbus sails from Spain to America |
| 1492 | Spain becomes unified and expels the Moors |
| 1497 | Portuguese reach India |
| 1517 | Martin Luther begins the religious Reformation in Europe |
| 1520 | Suleiman rules the Ottoman Empire |

| 1522 | Magellan travels around the world |
| 1535 | Spain completes the conquest of the Aztecs in Mexico and the Incas in Peru |
| 1543 | Copernicus suggests that the sun is the center of the universe, not the Earth |
| 1571 | Europeans defeat the Muslim Ottomans in the battle of Lepanto |
| 1588 | England defeats the Spanish Armada and becomes the greatest naval power in the world |
| 1607 | England begins the colonization of North America |
| 1609 | Galileo uses a new invention, the telescope, to study the universe |
| 1618 | Thirty Years' War begins |

## Revolution and Industry (1700–1900)

This period includes the Russian Empire, the Manchu dynasty in China, the period of Enlightenment in Europe, the growth of Austria and Prussia, the birth of the United States, the French Revolution, the Napoleonic era, the Industrial Revolution, the British Empire, the American Civil War, and the unification of both Italy and Germany.

### Time Line for the Age of Revolution and Industry

| 1644 | The Manchu overthrow the Ming dynasty of China |
| 1682–1725 | Peter the Great rules Russia |
| 1740 | Frederick the Great becomes king of Prussia—Domination of Europe |
| 1756–63 | Seven Years' War ensues, with France, Austria, and Russia clashing against Prussia and England |
| 1768 | James Cook visits regions in the Pacific |
| 1776 | America declares independence from England |
| 1789 | French Revolution begins with the fall of the Bastille in Paris |
| 1791 | As part of the Enlightenment period, Thomas Paine publishes *The Rights of Man*, his best-seller |
| 1804 | Napoleon declares himself emperor of France, beginning the Napoleonic Era |
| 1808 | Wars for independence begin in Spanish America |
| 1837–1901 | British Empire at its peak under Queen Victoria |
| 1848 | Year of revolution in all of Europe |
| 1861–65 | American Civil War |
| 1869 | Union Pacific Railroad links the East and West coasts of the United States |

## The Modern World (1900–Present)

This period includes the struggle for equal rights for women, World War I, the Russian Revolution, the Great Depression, the rise of fascism, revolution in China, World War II, Israel versus Palestine, the Cold War, the space race, the Korean and Vietnam wars, and globalization.

### Time Line for the Modern World

| | |
|---|---|
| 1914 | World War I begins when Austria declares war on Serbia and Germany on Russia |
| 1917 | Russian Revolution starts when the Bolsheviks, led by Lenin, seize power from Czar Nicholas II |
| 1918 | World War I ends; Europe is in ruins, and Germany is heavily punished |
| 1929 | Great Depression begins in the United States |
| 1933 | Adolf Hitler achieves power in Germany |
| 1936–39 | Spanish Civil War brings Francisco Franco to power |
| 1939 | World War II begins when Germany invaded Poland and Czechoslovakia |
| 1941 | United States enters World War II |
| 1945 | Germany surrenders to the Allied Forces, and Japan surrenders after the United States detonates two atomic bombs in Hiroshima and Nagasaki |
| 1947 | Pakistan and India obtain independence from Great Britain |
| 1948–49 | State of Israel is founded in Palestine, and the Arabs declare war |
| 1949 | Communist Mao Zedong (Tse-tung) gains control of China |
| 1959 | Cuban Revolution |
| 1960 | Many countries in Africa gain independence |
| 1965–72 | America participates in the Vietnam War |
| 1969 | Neil Armstrong lands on the moon |
| 1990 | Germany is reunited |
| 1991 | Soviet Union collapses, and the Cold War ends |
| 1994 | Free elections in South Africa and the end of apartheid |
| 2001 | 9/11 terrorist attacks in New York City and Washington, D.C. |
| 2001 | War in Afghanistan against the Taliban |
| 2003 | War in Iraq |
| 2009 | Barack Obama sworn in as the 44th President of the United States |

For details about these historical periods, go to these websites: Kidipede—History for Kids (*www.historyforkids.org*) and Ancient Mesoamerican Civilizations, created and maintained by Kevin L. Callahan of the University of Minnesota, Department of Anthropology (*www.angelfire.com/ca/humanorigins*).

## The Industrial Revolution and Modern Technology

The Industrial Revolution began in England in the mid-eighteenth century. Inventions that made mining of fossil fuel (charcoal) easier provided the energy needed to expand and promote industrial development. Improvement on the steam engine and industrial machines led to the mass production of goods and a better distribution system. The economic growth motivated people to leave the rural areas and move to the cities. The following time line highlights inventions that supported the industrial revolution and modern life:

### Time Line for Industrial and Technological Development

| | |
|---|---|
| 1769 | Richard Arkwright patents the spinning machine powered by a waterwheel |
| 1810 | A German, Frederick Koenig, invents an improved printing press |
| 1831 | An American, Cyrus H. McCormick, invents the reaper |
| 1836 | Samuel Colt invents the first revolver |
| 1837–1938 | Samuel Morse invents the telegraph and Morse code |
| 1846 | Ascanio Sobrero, an Italian chemist, invents nitroglycerin |
| 1856 | Louis Pasteur invents the process of pasteurization |
| 1858 | Jean Lenoir invents an internal combustion engine |
| 1866 | Albert Nobel invents dynamite |
| 1876 | Alexander Graham Bell patents the telephone |
| 1885 | Gottlieb Daimler invents the first gas engine motorcycle |
| 1900 | Ferdinand Von Zeppelin invents a hot air balloon called the zeppelin |
| 1903 | The Wright brothers invent the first gas-powered airplane |
| 1905 | Albert Einstein publishes the theory of relativity: $E = mc^2$ |
| 1914 | Henry Ford introduces the assembly line to mass produce automobiles |
| 1928 | Biologist Alexander Fleming discovers penicillin |
| 1930 | Vannevar Bush at the Massachusetts Institute of Technology in Boston invents the analog computer |

| 1940 | Peter Goldmark invents modern color television |
| 1945 | The atomic bomb is tested in Alamogordo, New Mexico |
| 1955 | The antibiotic tetracycline is invented |
| 1959 | Jack Kilby and Robert Noyce invent the microchip |
| 1969 | The predecessor of the Internet, called the ARPAnet, is invented |
| 1971 | Ray Tomlinson invents Internet-based e-mail |
| 1985 | Microsoft invents the Windows program |
| 1988 | Digital cellular phones are invented |
| 1990 | Tim Berners-Lee created the Internet protocol HTTP and the World Wide Web language HTML |

## Ancient Civilizations of the Americas

Native Americans lived throughout what we now call the Americas for centuries prior to European colonization. These ancient civilizations each had unique and rich cultural heritage. They made major contributions to the development of the Americas in all aspects of social, political, and cultural life. Their legacies continue to influence modern day history. Unfortunately, many of the ancient civilizations were destroyed as a result of European colonization.

### Mayans

One of the earliest civilizations of Mesoamerica was the Mayan, from regions of Mexico's Yucatán Peninsula, Guatemala, and Honduras. The Mayas developed a highly integrated society with elaborate religious observances for which they built stone and mortar pyramids. The center of the Maya civilization was the city of Chichén Itzá and its religious centers, where human victims were sacrificed. The Mayas developed an elaborate calendar, a system of writing, and the mathematical concept of zero. They also had highly advanced knowledge of astronomy, engineering, and art. By the time the Spanish conquerors arrived, most of the Mayan religious centers had been abandoned and the civilization was in decline.

### Zapotecs, Olmecs, and Toltecs

Farther north in Mexico, three highly sophisticated civilizations emerged: the Olmecs, Zapotecs, Teotihuacán, and Toltecs. Beginning with the Olmecs, who flourished around 1200 BCE and followed by the Toltecs and Zapotecs, these groups developed highly sophisticated civilizations. They had already begun to use a ceremonial calendar and had built stone pyramids on which they performed religious observances. Teotihuacán is the best-known example of religious ceremonial sites built by these civilizations. They developed a partly alphabetic writing system and left codices describing their history, religion, and daily events.

## Aztecs

The Aztec civilization achieved the highest degree of development in Mexico. They had a centralized government headed by a king and supported by a large army. The Aztecs were also skilled builders and engineers, accomplished astronomers, and mathematicians. They built the famous city of Tenochtitlán, with many pyramids, palaces, plazas, and canals. At the peak of their civilization, the Aztecs had a population of about five million.

## Incas—Children of the Sun

The Inca civilization covered the modern countries of Ecuador, Peru, and central Chile. Although they were not as advanced in mathematics and the sciences as the Mayans and Aztecs, the Incas had a well-developed political system. They also built a monumental road system to unify the empire. Their civilization was at its peak when the Spanish conquerors arrived in Cuzco, the capital of the empire.

## Algonquians

This tribe is perhaps the most famous Native American tribe because they were the first to interact with the English settlers at Plymouth. They were skilled hunters, gathers, and trappers who were adept at farming. They wore clothing made from animal skins and lived in wigwams. The Algonquians shared their extensive knowledge of agriculture with the English settlers, a practice that most likely saved the colonists' lives.

## Iroquois

The Iroquois inhabited the area of Ontario, Canada, and Upstate New York for at least 4,500 years before the arrival of Europeans. They hunted and fished, but farming became the main economic activity for the group. The Iroquois had a matrilineal line of descent, with women doing most of the farming to support the community. They developed the Iroquois Confederation to discourage war among the groups and to provide for a common defense.

### Seminoles and Muscogee Creeks

These two tribes lived in the Southeast United States in open bark covered houses called *chickees*. They were excellent hunters and planters. They are best known for their struggle against Spanish and English settlers in the mid 1800s.

### Cherokee

The Cherokee also lived in the Southeast and were one of the most advanced tribes, with their domed houses and deerskin and rabbit fur clothing. Accomplished hunters, farmers, and fisherman, they were known on the continent for their basketry and pottery.

### Pueblo

The Pueblo people lived in Pueblos and wore clothes made of wool and woven cotton. They were able to produce drought-resistant corn and squash, which became the foundation of their diet. The Pueblo Indians managed to survive the Spanish conquest and colonization period.

### Apache

The Apache and their famous leader Geronimo lived in wickiups, which were made of bark, grass, and branches. They wore cotton clothing and were skilled hunters and gathers. The Apache lived in the Southwestern portion of the United States.

### Navajo

The Navajo people lived in the Southwest as well and were excellent weapon makers, weavers, and silversmiths. They lived in Hogans, round homes built of forked sticks, and wore rabbit skin clothes.

## American History

### Colonization

In the early 15th century, Portugal, under the leadership of Prince Henry the Navigator, began sea exploration. Over the next few decades, the Portuguese explored further south along the African coast. In 1498, Vasco de Gama successfully navigated the Cape of Good Hope at the southern tip of Africa, opening a new route to India.

Columbus's voyage to the New World in 1492 also had tremendous impact on both Europe and the New World. By opening the Western Hemisphere to political and economic development by Europeans, Columbus changed the face of the world. Native populations that had existed prior to Columbus were decimated by disease and warfare. As Spanish, French, and English settlers began claiming territories in the Americas as their own, they displaced and killed millions of Native Americans.

In 1565, the Spaniards established the first successful European settlement in North America in St. Augustine, Florida. Following the Spaniards, the English attempted to establish a permanent colony on Roanoke, an island off the coast of North Carolina. This colony eventually disappeared. Further north, the Dutch settled colonies in the region of present-day New York and New Jersey. Following the Dutch, numerous private companies received royal charters, or patents, permitting them to begin the colonization process in North America. Three of the first and most successful companies were the Plymouth Company, the Massachusetts Bay Company, and the London Company. The London Company was the first to exercise this patent.

## The English Colonies

Thirteen colonies were established on the Atlantic coastline. English settlers left England to establish colonies for several reasons. Three types of colonies developed based on three types of charters: corporate colonies, royal colonies, and proprietary colonies. These were divided in three geographical regions: the New England Colonies, the Middle Colonies, and the Southern Colonies. The New England Colonies consisted of: Massachusetts, Connecticut, Rhode Island, and New Hampshire. The economy of the New England colonies was based on farming and very small industries such as fishing, lumber, and crafts. The Middle Colonies consisted of: New York, New Jersey, Delaware, Maryland, and Pennsylvania. The economy of the Middle Colonies was based on farming, shipping, fishing, and trading. The Southern Colonies were: Virginia, North Carolina, South Carolina, and Georgia. The economy of the Southern Colonies was based on the crops of tobacco, rice, indigo, and cotton. Plantations produced agricultural crops in large scale and exploited workers as well as the environment.

### Virginia (1607)

The London Company established the first English colony in Jamestown, Virginia. The leader of the colony was Captain John Smith. Natives of the area captured Smith and sentenced him to death. Pocahontas, daughter of the tribe's chief, intervened and saved his life. Contrary to popular belief, John Smith did not marry Pocahontas; instead, Pocahontas married John Rolfe, a tobacco farmer from the same colony.

### Massachusetts (1620)

The Puritans, who fled England to avoid religious persecution, founded Plymouth. The group obtained a patent from the London Virginia Company. Before arriving at their destination, they wrote the Mayflower Compact, a document containing rules to guide life in the community. This compact established the first type of government in North America.

### New Hampshire (1623)

Two groups founded the colony of New Hampshire. The first group was led by Captain John Mason, who established a fishing village in 1623. In 1638, a group led by John Wheelwright founded a second settlement called *Exeter*. That colony began as a proprietorship but eventually became a royal colony.

### New Jersey (1623)

The Dutch founded the New Jersey colony in 1623. After taking over the Dutch territory between Virginia and New England in 1664, King George II of England gave these possessions to his brother, the Duke of York. The duke then gave the territory as a proprietary grant to Sir George Carteret and Lord Berkeley. In 1702, New Jersey became an English colony.

### New York (1624)

The area of New York was part of New Amsterdam, a possession of the Dutch government. In 1674, the British took control of the territory, and in 1685 New York officially became a royal colony.

### Maryland (1633)

In 1632, King Charles I granted a Maryland Charter to Lord Baltimore (George Calvert). In 1633, the colony was established as a refuge for freemen, especially Catholics.

### Rhode Island (1636)

Roger Williams founded the Rhode Island colony in 1636, and in 1638 Anne Hutchinson settled an additional part of the colony. Both Williams and Hutchinson had been banned from Massachusetts for their religious and political views and were looking for sanctuary. The colony was initially a corporation and eventually became a royal colony.

### Connecticut (1636)

As early as 1633, Dutch traders had established a permanent settlement near Hartford. After the decline of the Dutch influence in the area, Thomas Hooker established the colony of Connecticut. Hooker and his followers were also seeking religious freedom after being expelled from Massachusetts. In 1662, Connecticut obtained a Royal Charter under the leadership of John Winthrop Jr.

### Delaware (1638)

The Dutch and Swedish initially settled this colony. With the decline of the Dutch influence in the area, the English took control. In 1682, Delaware was awarded to William Penn.

### North Carolina (1653)

By 1653, Virginia colonists began moving south and settling in the North Carolina region. In 1691, the region was officially recognized as a colony, and Charles I granted a royal charter in 1729.

### South Carolina (1663)

In 1663, King Charles II created the colony of Carolina by granting the territory, of what is now the region of present-day North Carolina, South Carolina, and Georgia, to loyal supporters. It began as a proprietary colony and became a royal colony in 1719. Sir John Yeamans, a plantation owner from Barbados, founded the city of Charleston in 1670.

### Pennsylvania (1683)

As early as 1647, Swedish, Dutch, and English settlers tried to establish permanent settlements in Delaware. In 1681, a large territory, which included Pennsylvania, was granted to William Penn. Penn was a member of a religious group persecuted in England, the Quakers. He made Pennsylvania a safe haven for Quakers, and a large number of German Quakers settled in the colony. In 1683, the first group of settlers arrived in Pennsylvania and formed Germantown near Philadelphia.

### Georgia (1732)

This colony was founded with two main purposes: to establish a buffer zone from the Spanish settlement south of the colony and to provide a safe haven for poor people.

## Table 4.1 The Thirteen American Colonies

| Colony | Year Established | Colonizer | Historical Features/ Characters |
|---|---|---|---|
| Virginia | 1607 | London Company | Captain John Smith, John Rolfe, and Pocahontas |
| Massachusetts | 1620 | Puritans with a patent from the London Virginia Company | Puritans, Mayflower, Mayflower Compact, John Smith |
| New Hampshire | 1623 | Proprietary colony | Captain John Mason, John Wheelwright |
| New Jersey | 1623 | Dutch possession, then a proprietorship | Duke of York |
| New York | 1624 | Dutch possession, then a proprietorship | Purchase of the island of Manhattan, Duke of York |
| Maryland | 1633 | Proprietorship | George Calvert (Lord Baltimore), the colony served as a refuge for persecuted Catholics |
| Rhode Island | 1636 | Corporate colony | Roger Williams and Anne Hutchinson |
| Connecticut | 1636 | Corporate colony | Thomas Hooker and John Winthrop |
| Delaware | 1638 | Corporate colony | First, under the Dutch, Swedish, and finally under British control. William Penn |
| North Carolina | 1653 | Proprietorship | King Charles II |
| South Carolina | 1663 | Proprietorship, then a charter colony | King Charles II, Sir John Yeamans |
| Pennsylvania | 1682 | Proprietorship | William Penn and Quakers |
| Georgia | 1732 | Charter colony | James Edward Oglethorpe |

## Representative Government in Colonial America

The colonies were founded with the idea that people would have a substantial autonomy and liberty in regards to political and religious life. Colonists brought with them their tradition of hard work, individual freedom, and representative government. When the colonists first arrived in America they were still under British rule. Believing in the right to elect the people who would represent them on issues such as taxation, the colonists felt that they should have representation in the British Parliament. Unfortunately, the colonists (those in America and in other British colonies) were not given a seat in parliament or given the right to vote for any member of parliament. As such the colonists did not have any form of representation in the British political system. This reality would later be a major cause of the American Revolution and formation of a new nation.

The idea of representative government, or the idea that people can vote for their own lawmakers, would become fundamental to the formation of the United States. Along with the ability to elect lawmakers, representative government also includes the notion that concepts and ideas can be deliberated and discussed by both legislators and the people who elected them. This principle would later be reflected in the design of United States Congress.

The Virginia House of Burgesses was the first colonial assembly of elected representatives from the Virginia settlement. It was established in Jamestown to represent the colonists in the state of Virginia in the lawmaking process and met for the first time in July 1619.

The Mayflower Compact was drawn and signed in 1620 by the Pilgrims aboard the Mayflower. They pledged to consult one another to make decisions and to act by the will of the majority. It is one of the earliest agreements to establish a political body and to give that political body the power to act for the good of the colony.

## Indentured Servants

The indentured servant system was used to bring workers to the New World. In practice, the indentured servant would sell him or herself to an agent or ship captain before leaving England. In turn, the contract would be sold to a buyer in the colonies to recover the cost of passage. Criminals and people in debt could also be sold for life or until they paid their debts. In some cases, at the end of the service, servants remained as salaried workers, or in the best situations, the servants were given a piece of land for their services. This system of provisional servitude was not applied to Africans; instead, permanent slavery was instituted.

### The Enlightenment—The Age of Reason

The Enlightenment refers to a period during the seventeenth and eighteenth centuries when people began questioning religious dogmas and emphasizing scientific reasoning and knowledge. As a result of this quest for knowledge, modern chemistry and biology were developed. Additionally, people also began to think critically about the rights, freedoms, and powers of man in relation to political systems. The Enlightenment stirred people to action in fighting the tyranny of religious and political oppression. For example, the quest for freedom led to the American and the French Revolutions. Some of the leading thinkers of this period were Jean-Jacques Rousseau, John Locke, Charles Montesquieu, Voltaire, and Francis Bacon. The ideas of the Enlightenment quickly reached the British colonies. Many of the leaders responsible for the writing of the Constitution were familiar with the leading thinkers of the movement. As such they framed the Constitution around the powerful ideas of these thinkers, including the protection of the natural rights of the individual and limiting the power of the government.

### American Revolution

The main reasons why the British colonists revolted against British control were economic in nature. England, as well as other European nations, had established the mercantilism system to exploit the colonies. This system had three main principles:

1. The wealth of the nation is measured in terms of commodities accrued, especially gold and silver.

2. Economic activities can increase the power and control of the national government.

3. The colonies existed for the benefit of the mother country.

England used the system of mercantilism quite effectively in the thirteen colonies, but after more than a century of British rule, the colonists resented England's economic and political control. Outraged and spurred on by Enlightenment ideas, the colonists were primed for independence, and war with England became inevitable.

Another reason for the rebellion was the cost of the French and Indian War. This war, which was the North American portion of the Seven Years' War, emptied the British coffers, and the British Crown needed a quick way to recover financially. The taxation system that followed the French and Indian War was unbearable for the colonies. The colonies responded with civil disobedience and by boycotting the government of King George. In response to civil disobedience, the British sent troops to Boston, where the groups clashed and several colonists were killed. The event was called the Boston Massacre. One of the best-known boycotts was the Boston Tea Party, in which the colonists dumped tea in the Boston harbor to protest against taxation. "No taxation without representation" became a rallying cry for the colonists. All these events and the repression that followed led to the American Revolution.

## Continental Congress

Following the events in Boston, Massachusetts, representatives of the colonies met in Philadelphia to discuss the political and economic situation in the colonies. No clear solutions were reached at this congress. Once the hostilities started, the Second Continental Congress met to discuss preparations for war. George Washington was elected commander of the American forces, and war was declared against the British. The congress named a committee, led by Thomas Jefferson, to prepare the Declaration of Independence, which was officially signed on July 4, 1776.

## The Declaration of Independence

The Declaration of Independence pronounced the colonies free and independent states. It consists of a preamble, or introduction, followed by three main parts. The first part stresses natural unalienable rights and liberties that belong to all people from birth. The second part consists of a list of specific grievances and injustices committed by Britain. The third part announces the colonies as the United States of America. This document provided the foundation to establish equal rights for all people.

## Revolution

The American Revolution began in Massachusetts in the outskirts of the towns of Concord and Lexington. In 1775, while the colonists were preparing for war, hundreds of British soldiers marched against them. Paul Revere warned the colonists of British troop movements, and minutemen took up arms to face the enemy. At Concord, the British were repelled and forced back to Boston. On their way back, American sharpshooters ambushed and killed hundreds of British soldiers. Following this initial victory for the colonists, the battle of Bunker Hill was fought near Boston. In this battle, the British lost large numbers of soldiers but managed to defeat the colonial troops. Later, in Long Island, the British won another decisive victory over the Americans. The French joined the war in support of the Americans, in retaliation for their defeat at the hands of the British in the Seven Years' War. Eventually, with the support of the French, the American troops defeated the British forces in Yorktown, Virginia, in 1781. The Treaty of Paris, officially signed in 1783, ended the war and gave independence to the new nation. For additional details about the American Revolution, go to *historycentral.com*.

## Articles of Confederation

The Articles of Confederation was an agreement among the 13 founding states that legally established the United States of America as a confederation of sovereign states and served as its first constitution. It was drafted by the Continental Congress in 1776–77, went into use in 1777 and was formally ratified by all 13 states in 1781. The Articles gave legitimacy to the Continental Congress to direct the American Revolutionary war, conduct diplomacy with Europe, and deal with territorial issues and Indian relations. The Articles of Confederation established a new government, with limited power, that was composed of representatives from thirteen independent states. The Congress could not declare war or raise an army. They could ask the states for money or for soldiers, but it was up to the states to agree to provide them. Under this type of government, each state printed its own money and imposed taxes on imports from the other states.

On the positive side, the new government provided for a common citizenship—citizens of the United States. It organized a uniform system of weights and measurements and the postal service. It also became responsible for issues related to Native Americans living within the borders of the new nation. The confederation served as the official government of the young republic until 1789, when the states ratified the Constitution.

## United States Constitution

After six years under the Articles of Confederation, the leaders of the nation realized that the American government needed revision to bolster its strength. To accomplish this goal, a constitutional convention was held in Philadelphia in 1787. The leaders of this initiative were George Washington, James Madison, Benjamin Franklin, and Alexander Hamilton. From this convention, a new form of government emerged. The Constitution was officially ratified in 1788, and in 1789 George Washington was selected to be the first president of the United States. The U.S Constitution allowed for a much stronger national government, with a president, courts, and taxing powers. The republic defined by the Constitution was composed of three branches, the executive, judicial, and legislative, with a system of checks and balances to regulate each branch. To learn more about historical American documents, go to "A Chronology of U.S. Historical Documents," a website created and maintained by the University of Oklahoma Law Center, at *www.law.ou.edu/hist*.

## War of 1812

Twenty-nine years after the end of the American Revolution, conflict between Great Britain and the young United States flared up again. The War of 1812 broke out for a variety of reasons, including Britain's seizure of American ships, impressment of American sailors into the British navy, and restriction of trade between the United States and

France. In June 1812, James Madison became the first U.S. president to ask Congress to declare war. Fought in three theaters, the conflict ended with the Treaty of Ghent in 1815.

## Monroe Doctrine

In 1823, President Monroe made clear to European countries that the United States was not going to permit the establishment of colonies in the Western Hemisphere. Monroe also banned European countries from attacking the new American republics that were just becoming established in the early nineteenth century. The U.S. was not to become involved in European affairs. This concept of "America for Americans" is known as the Monroe Doctrine.

## Westward Expansion (1807–1912)

After the War of 1812 much of America's attention turned to exploration and settlement of its territory to the West, which had been greatly enlarged by the Louisiana Purchase. Pioneer families moved westward and founded new communities throughout what is now the Midwest. Between 1816 and 1821, six new states were admitted to the Union. This westward expansion occurred for a number of reasons, primarily economic.

First, cotton had become an important resource in the southern states. As the effects of the industrial revolution—which began in England—reached the United States, new inventions, for example, Eli Whitney's cotton gin, encouraged faster and more efficient production of goods. With the invention of the cotton gin, the demand for cotton grew and more and more farmers became involved in the production of cotton. Innovations in long-distance transportation, most notably, the railroad, allowed cotton and other goods to be shipped cross-country with more ease. As demand for cotton and prices increased, southern farmers began expanding their farms toward the west where there was fertile soil. As farm sizes increased, so did the demand for a large supply of cheap labor. As a result, the system of slavery expanded both in numbers and in regional movement to the west.

Secondly, expansion westward continued as people moved west to seek their economic fortunes. Miners, trappers, ranchers, merchants, and others went west to find new resources and economic riches. The Lewis and Clark Expedition played a prominent role in promoting westward expansion and in mapping the west. Fur companies recruited "mountain men" to search for fur-bearing animals that would increase the supply of such goods and meet the needs of the East and of Europe. Finally, the California gold rush attracted easterners to push westward in hopes of finding riches.

Thirdly, increased settlement in the West encouraged missionaries to travel west with the fur traders to seek converts among the native peoples. Missionaries sent word back to the east and encouraged more settlers to come to the west. The results of which produced a tremendous influx of westward settlers.

Finally, Manifest Destiny, or the belief that the United States was destined to expand across the country encouraged westward expansion. In 1844, President James K. Polk declared to the world that the United States would eventually become a world power and expand to its natural borders. Some of the borders mentioned were the Pacific to the west and Mexico to the south. Manifest Destiny would ultimate cause huge issues between the U.S. Government and Native Americans, England, Spain, and Mexico. Eventually, Polk's expectations became a reality as a result of the war between Mexico and the United States that lasted from 1846 to 1848.

**Results of Westward Expansion**

A major aspect of the conquest of the West was the removal of the Indians who dwelled there. Under the leadership of President Andrew Jackson, the Indians who remained East of the Mississippi were cruelly and violently driven from their homes and concentrated in reservations in what is now Oklahoma. The U.S. Army crushed any resistance to removal. With the West cleared of this "obstacle," westerners focused on developing new methods of transporting their goods to market. The canal and railroad systems, which grew up in the North, facilitated a much larger volume of trade and manufacturing while greatly reducing costs. Great cities sprang up throughout the North and Northwest, bolstered by the improvement in transportation.

After the Midwest had been substantially developed, the national focus turned toward the far West. The territory of Texas, controlled by the Spanish, was settled by Americans, who eventually undertook the Texas Rebellion in efforts to win independence. When the United States admitted Texas to the Union in 1845, the Mexican government was outraged, and from 1846 to 1848, the two nations squared off in the Mexican War. As a result of this war, the United States gained control of Texas, New Mexico, and California. When the Oregon territory was annexed in 1846, the U.S. stretched all the way to the Pacific Ocean.

As the population of the West soared and the prospects of statehood for western territories appeared clearer and clearer, the nation battled over the future of slavery in the West. This battle was one reason for the Civil War, which slowed the acceleration of expansion. However, the last three decades of the nineteenth century saw the return of accelerated expansion due to the successful struggle to contain the Plains Indians in reservations, and the completion of The Transcontinental Railroad in 1869. By the early twentieth century, the organization of the West was completed, and the United States consisted of 48 contiguous states.

## Slavery in the United States

The Dutch brought the first African slaves to Virginia in 1619 to work on plantations. From 1640 to 1680, large numbers of slaves were brought to the Americas. With the invention of Eli Whitney's cotton gin, cotton became the economic mainstay of the South, and the demand for labor increased the slave trade. From 1798 to 1808, more than 200,000 African slaves were brought to America, mostly to the southern region.

Beginning in 1774, the North began regulating and eventually prohibiting slavery. By 1804, New York and New Jersey had passed gradual emancipation laws. Meanwhile, the slave trade in the South grew to meet the economic needs of the area. Eventually, the issue of slavery, along with other economic and ideological differences between the regions, resulted in the American Civil War. In 1862, Abraham Lincoln issued the Emancipation Proclamation, granting freedom to slaves in the rebellious states. After the war, the Thirteenth Amendment to the Constitution officially abolished slavery. Additionally, in 1866 the Fourteenth Amendment gave African-Americans full citizenship, and the Fifteenth Amendment granted voting rights to black men.

## Compromises

This period in history was marked by a number of compromises between the various regions. Most of the time these compromises were short-lived and broke down quickly. One of the compromises was the ***three-fifths compromise*** proposed at the Constitutional Convention of 1787. This compromise centered on how to count slaves in deciding the number of representatives for the House of Representatives and the amount of taxes to be paid. Residents of the South wanted to count the slaves for the purposes of representation but not taxation. Northerners, on the other hand, wanted the opposite. As a compromise, the two sides agreed to count 3/5 of the slave population for both taxation and representation purposes.

The ***Missouri Compromise*** was an agreement passed in 1820 between the pro-slavery and anti-slavery factions in the United States Congress, involving primarily the regulation of slavery in the western territories. In 1819 the United States had 21 states: 10 slave states and 11 free states. The territory of Missouri allowed slavery and if admitted as a state in the Union, would cause an imbalance in the number of U.S. senators. Alabama had recently been added to the Union, thus balancing the representation of free and slave states at 22 senators each. To resolve the conflict, the first Missouri Compromise allowed Maine to be admitted as a free state to the Union along with Missouri.

Additionally, the compromise prohibited slavery in the former Louisiana Territory north of the parallel 36°30' except within the boundaries of the proposed state of Missouri. Prior to the agreement, the House of Representatives had refused to accept this compromise and a conference committee was appointed. Southern congressmen accepted this proposal since growing cotton on land north of this line was not profitable. One year after the first compromise was passed, tensions heated up again as Missouri's state constitution discriminated against free Blacks. Anti-slavery advocates demanded that Missouri not be admitted to the union. Under the leadership of Henry Clay, known as the great compromiser, it was proposed that the Constitution of the United States guaranteed the protection and privileges of citizens in states and thus Missouri's state constitution could not deny any person these rights. This proposal was accepted in 1820 and Missouri was admitted to the Union.

The *Compromise of 1850* was another compromise crafted by Henry Clay and Stephen Douglas to try and end the continuing struggle between slave and non-slave states. This compromise was comprised of a series of five bills that were intended to stave off sectional strife over slavery. Its goal was to deal with the spread of slavery to territories in order to keep northern and southern interests in balance. The five bills are summarized below:

1. California was entered as a free state.

2. New Mexico and Utah were each allowed using *popular sovereignty* or the idea that people living in territories or states should decide for themselves if slavery should be permitted.

3. The Republic of Texas gave up lands that it claimed in present day New Mexico and received $10 million to pay its debt to Mexico.

4. The slave trade was abolished in the District of Columbia.

5. The *Fugitive Slave Act* made any federal official who did not arrest a runaway slave liable to pay a fine. This was the most controversial part of the Compromise of 1850 and caused many abolitionists to increase their efforts against slavery.

The *Kansas–Nebraska Act* of 1854 created the territories of Kansas and Nebraska, opened new lands that would help settlement in them, repealed the Missouri Compromise of 1820, and allowed settlers in those territories to determine via popular sovereignty if they would allow slavery within their boundaries. Designed by Democratic Senator Stephen Douglas, the Kansas–Nebraska Act created huge controversy because of the popular sovereignty provision. Both pro and anti-slavery supporters flooded into Kansas with the goal of voting slavery up or down. One group of Northern abolitionists, led by

**John Brown**, also flocked to the territory and set up their own government in Lawrence. A band of proslavery men, however, burned Lawrence to the ground in 1856. In revenge, an abolitionist gang killed five men at the **Pottawatomie Massacre**. In 1859, John Brown and his followers also seized the federal arsenal at Harper's Ferry in what is now West Virginia. Their purpose was to steal the guns in the arsenal, give them to slaves nearby, and begin a widespread rebellion. Brown and his men were captured by Colonel Robert E. Lee and found guilty. Brown was later hanged. These two events sparked an internal war so savage that many referred to the territory as **"Bleeding Kansas."**

The decision rendered in the ***Dred Scott v. Sandford*** Supreme Court case served to intensify the debate regarding the issue of slavery in the United States. Dred Scott was a slave whose owner had taken him from Missouri, a slave state, to Illinois and Minnesota, both free states, and back to Missouri. Scott petitioned the Supreme Court (after petitioning two lower courts) for his freedom based on the fact that he had resided in two free states each with state laws that declared that slaves brought into the state were set free. The Supreme Court ruled that Scott and all other slaves were not citizens of any state or or the United States and thus had no rights. A slave was deigned property, not a person nor a citizen. Thus, Scott or other slaves had no right to sue in either state or federal court. Further, the court held that the federal government had no legal right to interfere with the institution of slavery. Slavery advocates were encouraged and began to make plans to expand slavery into all of the western territories and states, thus creating much of the tension that led to the Civil War.

## Civil War

### Political, Economic, Social Differences

As the nation expanded and territories became states, each new state developed its own unique political, social, economic, and cultural identity. Over time, regional identities evolved leading to regionalism or the political division of and loyalty to the interests of particular regions. Each region came to be defined by the economic and social institutions most prevalent in the area. In the North, the industrialized factory system created a division between factory owners who reaped huge profits and factory workers who were subjected to poor working conditions. The industrialized North had a boom in the number of factories and towns while the South remained primarily agricultural where slaves and indentured servants worked on large plantations owned by wealthy whites. The South defended their economy on the basis that states had the right to self-determination with regard to their economic and social institutions. The West was a vast expanse of newly explored and settled land in which ranching became a mainstay. Settlers who traveled to the west were looking for land, wealth, and opportunity. Many were from the South and brought slaves with them.

As such, the identity of each of these regions was distinctly different, especially in the role of children, women, trade, religion, and labor systems. As might be expected, these differences led to conflicts between the inhabitants of each region.

### Slavery and Sectionalism

The issue of slavery became a major issue between the North and South and created deep divisions for the young nation. By the 1800s, slavery had been virtually abolished in the North. The northern states' reasons for turning against slavery were primarily economic: the North had become more urban and industrialized than the South, and northern states received large numbers of immigrants who provided the necessary labor. Southern states remained mostly rural and received few immigrants, making slavery the foundation of their economy. This economic difference coupled with the publication of Harriet Beecher Stowe's book *Uncle Tom's Cabin* and efforts by the national government to control trade between the regions created a huge rift between the North and the South. The disagreement over slavery, specifically over the issue of who was guaranteed the inalienable right to be free, led to sectionalism, or the excessive devotion to local interests and customs. This growing sectionalism would be a primary cause of the Civil War.

The issue of slavery became the main topic of the presidential election of 1860. The candidates were clearly aligned either in favor of or against slavery. The southern Democrats backed a strong proslavery candidate, John C. Breckinridge of Kentucky, while the new Republican Party selected a strong antislavery candidate in the figure of Abraham Lincoln. The election of Abraham Lincoln resulted in the secession of the southern states from the union, the creation of the Confederacy, and the start of the American Civil War. The southern states created the Confederate States of America and selected Jefferson Davis as president.

### Secession

In response to the election of Abraham Lincoln, 11 southern slave states, led first by South Carolina, seceded from the Union and formed the Confederate States of America or the Confederacy. Twenty-five states supported the federal government and remained part of the Union. Both sides began preparations for war. The North had a greater advantage over the South because of a larger population, financial security, industrial resources, increased means of transportation, and natural resources. The South, largely agricultural in nature, did not have the same caliber of resources or infrastructure as the North. The South, however, had some advantage in the vastness of their territory and the experience of their army leaders, many of whom were educated at West Point and had extensive experience in previous wars.

The major aim of the Confederacy's war efforts was to win independence, protect the institution of slavery, and earn the right to govern themselves. The war efforts of the North began to protect the sanctity of the union under the leadership of Lincoln. However, the abolition of slavery became increasingly more important as an issue as the war continued.

### Battle of Gettysburg

Hundreds of battles were fought in this war, but none was as devastating as the Battle of Gettysburg. Fought in 1863, this battle was the most disastrous event of the war; more than 50,000 soldiers from the North and the South lost their lives. In a speech delivered on the battlefield in November 1863, President Lincoln eulogized the fallen Union soldiers in what became the famous *Gettysburg Address*.

In 1865, after five years of fighting, the loss of thousands of lives, and millions of dollars in property loss, the commander of the Confederate army, General Robert E. Lee, surrendered to General Ulysses S. Grant, commander of the Union forces. The Civil War took more American lives than any other war in U.S. history. The South lost nearly one-third of its soldiers, while the North lost about one-sixth. More than 50% of the deaths were attributed to the terrible conditions of field hospitals and to disease.

The loss of human life was not the only devastation, the economic losses were significant for both sides. The physical devastation, almost all of it in the South, was enormous: burned or plundered homes, pillaged countryside, untold losses in crops and farm animals, ruined buildings and bridges, devastated college campuses, and neglected roads all left the South in ruins.

### Reconstruction Era (1865–1877)

Post–Civil War physical reconstruction focused on the South. However, the emotional reconstruction and the reconstruction of American unity had to be done nationwide, and admission of rebel states back into the Union was not automatically granted. Because Lincoln was assassinated shortly after the end of the war, leadership of southern reconstruction fell to Lincoln's Vice-President, Andrew Johnson, a southerner who was disliked by both Northerners as well as Southerners. Eventually, Johnson was impeached and almost removed from power, surviving the removal vote in the U.S. Senate by one vote.

A major obstacle to reunification were the restrictive laws enacted immediately after the Civil War by every southern legislature. These Black Codes barred the newly freed slaves from free assembly, regulated black labor, and among other restrictions, denied Freedmen the right to vote, serve on juries, and testify against whites. After major electoral victories in the election of 1866, Republicans placed the South under military rule, and held new elections in which the Freedmen could vote.

By 1867, the U.S. Congress, still composed entirely of northerners, passed legislation to eliminate the black codes. On July 9, 1868, Congress passed the Fourteenth Amendment of the Constitution that provided universal male suffrage, made the Bill of Rights applicable to the states recognizing all substantive and procedural rights under the law, and provided equal protection under the law to all people in its jurisdiction. Furthermore, the U.S Congress required that each state ratify the Fourteenth Amendment as a prerequisite for reentry into the Union. Finally, in 1870, the last two states (Texas and Florida) having satisfied all requirements, were allowed back into the Union.

## Ku Klux Klan

The Ku Klux Klan first emerged as a secret society during Reconstruction, flourishing in the 1860s and dying out in the 1870s, only to reemerge in the 1920s and again in the 1950s and 60s. During reconstruction, Klan members enforced the Black Codes through violence and terror. Subsequent Klan activities, both overt and covert, upheld Jim Crow laws reinforcing segregation intimidation. Racial separation characterized life in the South and other parts of the nation throughout most of the twentieth century.

## Economic Development

After the reunification of the country, energy was redirected to the economic development and growth of the nation. New inventions, together with the development of the railroad, paved the way to economic recovery. The reconstruction that followed the war also played a vital role in the development of the United States as a solid economic and industrial nation.

## Temperance Movement—Prohibition

Early Americans drank in enormous quantities. Their yearly consumption at the time of the Revolution has been estimated at the equivalent of three-and-a-half gallons of pure, two hundred proof alcohol for each person. After 1790, American men began to drink even more. By the late 1820s imbibing had risen to an all-time high of almost four gallons per capita. This pattern was unchallenged until early in the nineteenth century, when local efforts to curb drinking by individual clergymen were amplified by the founding of the American Temperance Society in 1826, sponsored by a wide range of groups and individuals. Temperance reformers acted for a variety of reasons, but we can describe four powerful perspectives on temperance that motivated most advocates and shaped their arguments and campaigns. For many of them, of course, all four were linked together.

1.  *Social order.* Many reformers feared that drunkenness—particularly the increasing prevalence of binge drinking—was a threat to law-abiding society and economic prosperity. How could men act as responsible workers and vote as responsible citizens if they were insensible with drink?

2.  *Evangelical religion.* Religiously motivated temperance advocates came to see drinking as a sin—a way of giving in to the animal or depraved self that was incompatible with Christian morals, self-control, and spiritual awakening.

3.  *Damage to the family.* Looking at family destitution and violence, reformers reckoned the cost to American wives, mothers, and children of heavy drinking by their husbands and fathers. The Women's Christian Temperance League brought the concerns of religion and family together in the battle to outlaw alcohol.

4.  *Medical.* Health-minded reformers popularized a radically new way of looking at alcohol. Americans had traditionally considered strong drink to be healthy and fortifying; but after 1810, many physicians and writers on health were telling their patients and readers that alcohol was actually a poison.

By the end of the nineteenth and the beginning of the twentieth century, the alcohol abuse had reached such heights that the movement focused on an outright prohibition on the consumption of alcohol. In 1919, the U.S. Constitution was amended to prohibit alcohol consumption at the national level; this marked the adoption of the 18th Amendment (Cardinale, 2007). However, the prohibition was never fully enforced. Battles between law enforcements agents, like Eliot Ness, and organized crime characterized the prohibition era. Leaders of organized crime, like Al Capone, made millions bootlegging alcohol. After 14 years of prohibition and unsuccessful attempts to enforce the law, it was finally repealed in 1933 with the 21st Amendment.

## Civil Rights Movement

In the United States, the Constitution and the Bill of Rights guarantee civil rights to American citizens and residents. The first 10 amendments to the U.S. Constitution are known as the Bill of Rights. Following these initial amendments and as a result of the American Civil War, three additional amendments were ratified.

1.  The 13th Amendment freed all the slaves without compensation to slave owners;

2.  The 14th Amendment declared that all persons born in the U.S. were citizens (excluding Native Americans due to their legal sovereignty) and, that all citizens were entitled to equal rights, and that their rights were protected by due process;

3. The 15th Amendment granted universal male suffrage thereby granting black men the right to vote.

Even after the 13th, 14th, and 15th Amendments extended constitutional protections, blacks continued to be denied full civil rights through discriminatory laws and practices. These laws, known as Jim Crow laws, reenforced a strict racial separation in the South. African Americans were kept from voting by poll taxes and literacy tests. Segregation rules restricted blacks to separate facilities in public places such as theaters, restaurants, buses, restrooms, and schools. In 1896, *Plessy v. Ferguson* legalized segregation, allowing "separate but equal facilities" for black and white students.

In response to the horrific practice of lynching that undergirded the program of terror to enforce Jim Crow laws and specifically in reaction to the 1908 race riots in Springfield, Illinois, a group of white liberals issued a call for a meeting to discuss racial justice. Sixty people, seven of whom were African American (including W. E. B. Du Bois, Ida B. Wells-Barnett and Mary Church Terrell), signed the call, which was released on the centennial of Lincoln's birth. This heralded the birth, on February 12, 1909, of the National Association for the Advancement of Colored People (NAACP). Throughout the early twentieth century the NAACP saw enormous growth in membership, recording roughly 600,000 members by 1946. It continued to act as a legislative and legal advocate, pushing for a federal anti-lynching law and for an end to state-mandated segregation.

Several historic events marked the beginning of what is today known as the Civil Rights Movement. In 1947, Jackie Robinson became the first African American to play baseball on a major league team. In 1948, President Truman ordered the desegregation of the armed forces and introduced civil rights legislation in Congress. By the 1950s the NAACP Legal Defense and Educational Fund, headed by Thurgood Marshall, secured an important milestone through *Brown v. Board of Education of Topeka* (1954), which outlawed segregation in public schools.

The *Montgomery Bus Boycott* began in December 1955 when *Rosa Parks,* a well-known NAACP activist and respected citizen of Montgomery, Alabama, refused to give up her seat on a bus to a white man as Alabama's Jim Crow laws required. She was arrested and consequently sent to jail. Her actions prompted local community leaders of the NAACP to form a new organization called the Montgomery Improvement Association.

The association chose a young Baptist minister, *Dr. Martin Luther King, Jr.*, to lead the organization and to direct a boycott of the Montgomery bus company. The boycott began in December 1956 and ended about a year later when the U.S. Supreme Court ruled segregation on buses unconstitutional. This victory gained national attention and Dr. King became one of the most prominent figures of the civil rights movement. He founded the Southern Christian Leadership Conference (SCLC) with other African American leaders. The SCLC favored nonviolent forms of protest such as sit-ins, boycotts, and protest marches. On August 28, 1963, a march in Washington in support of the Civil Rights Act culminated in Dr. King's influencial and memorable "I Have a Dream" speech. The eloquent speech and orderly, large-scale demonstration gained more supporters for the cause.

President **John F. Kennedy** proposed new civil rights laws as well as programs to help the millions of Americans living in poverty. After his assassination in Dallas in 1963, President **Lyndon B. Johnson** urged Congress to pass the laws in honor of Kennedy, persuading the majority of Democrats and some Republicans. The **Civil Rights Act** passed in 1964 prohibited segregation in all public facilities and discrimination in education and employment. On April 4, 1968, Dr. Martin Luther King, Jr. was assassinated in Memphis, Tenn., taking his place alongside the other martyrs who lost their lives in the struggle for freedom during the modern Civil Rights Movement, which extended from 1954 to 1968.

### The Mexican American Civil Rights Movement

During the 1960s Mexican Americans were engaged in the struggle for human rights. As part of the process, the Mexican-American leaders initiated a movement called the **Chicano Movement**. This movement was cultural as well as political (Rosales Castañeda n.d.). It embraced four main goals: the restoration of land grants, the farm workers' rights, education, and political rights (Mendoza, 2001). The movement also sought to rescue the cultural and linguistic identity of Mexican Americans.

Activist **Reies López Tijerina** initiated the Chicano Movement in New Mexico with the land grant movement, which sought to recover the land taken from the Mexican Americans as a result of the Guadalupe Hidalgo Treaty of 1848 and the eventual annexation of the American Southwest. In Colorado, Rodolfo "Corky" Gonzales founded the Crusade for Justice as a platform for the political movement (Mendoza, 2001). He also defined the movement through his epic poem "Yo Soy Joaquín/I am Joaquin." In this poem he provided a historical development of Mexican-American identity and described their struggles in the United States.

As part of the effort to support the rights of farm workers, human rights leaders **Cesar Chávez** and **Dolores Huerta** founded the **United Farm Workers** (UFW) union. Through the UFW they fought for better working conditions and fair compensation for agricultural workers.

In Texas, the movement focused its attention on the educational and political rights of Mexican Americans. In Crystal City, students took a leadership role by organizing

Mexican-American voters and joining the political process. As part of this process, Mexican American Student Organization (MAYO), under the leadership of *José Ángel Gutiérrez* and *Mario Compean* founded the *Raza Unida Party* (RUP) in 1970. Through the RUP, they sought to bring greater economic, social, and political autonomy to Mexican Americans (Acosta, n.d.). As a result of this movement, the RUP nominated candidates for mayor, city councils, and school boards in three South Texas cities—Crystal City, Cotulla, and Carrizo. In these communities, the RUP won fifteen seats. This political awakening of the Mexican-American voters in Texas paved the way for better schools and programs for Mexican American and minority children in general.

## Women's Rights

While the 19th Amendment to the Constitution guaranteed women the right to vote in 1920, women remained the subject of discrimination. The civil rights movement provided a backdrop for the womens' movements of the 60s as women of varying classes and races, working in the civil rights movement and in the anti-war movement, began to recognize their own second class status. The middle class or liberal women's movement attained better employment and professional opportunities for women through legislation such as the Equal Pay Act of 1963, the Civil Rights Act of 1964, the Equal Credit Opportunity Act (1974) and the Pregnancy Discrimination Act of 1978. All prohibited discrimination based on gender. In 1966, *Betty Friedan*, author of *The Feminine Mystique*, and other women leaders founded the *National Organization for Women* (NOW) and the 1970s saw an exponential growth of organizations and associations formed to promote women's equality.

## Conflicts and Wars

### Spanish-American War of 1898

The war between Spain and the United States in 1898 made the United States a world power. As a result of this war, the United States established its power and influence in the Caribbean Sea and Pacific Ocean. Cuba became an independent nation, and the United States gained control of the Philippines, Guam, and Puerto Rico. Eventually, the Philippines became an independent nation, while Puerto Rico and Guam remained U.S. territories. Eventually, the people from Guam and Puerto Rico became American citizens.

### World War I

The first global war, World War I, began in Europe and involved two alliances: the Allies and the Central Powers. The Allies were England, France, Russia, and Italy. The

Central Powers were Germany, the Austria-Hungary Empire, Turkey, and Bulgaria. Initially, the Americans remained neutral and benefited extensively from trading with the Allies. America's neutrality was challenged, however, when the Germans developed a new weapon, the submarine, and used it successfully to destroy Allied ships. In 1915, the Germans sank a British liner, the Lusitania, killing more than 1,100 passengers, including 128 Americans. Additionally, American cargo ships were sunk, which forced President Wilson to ask Congress to declare war against Germany and the Central Powers. The influx of fresh American forces fostered the Allies' victory in 1918.

With the Treaty of Versailles, the war officially ended. In this treaty, the Central Powers were severely punished and forced to pay for the war. Additionally, the Austria-Hungary Empire was dismembered and new countries created. The punitive conditions of the Treaty of Versailles created the resentment among the Germans that eventually led to the second global confrontation, World War II.

### The Bolshevik Revolution in Russia

In 1917, the Communists, led by **Vladimir Lenin**, took over the government in Russia. As a result of this revolution, Russia underwent a period of governmental reconstruction to incorporate the communist philosophy in the nation. With a new government in power, Russia withdrew from World War I.

### The Great Depression

After World War I, the United States enjoyed a period of prosperity, the golden 1920s. However, it all came to an abrupt end on October 29, 1929, when the stock market crashed, initiating a ten-year period that we now call the Great Depression. During the Depression, millions of people lost their capital and jobs. Between 1933 and 1937, **President Franklin D. Roosevelt** implemented a series of government-sponsored programs, called the New Deal, designed to revitalize the economy and alleviate poverty and despair caused by the Depression.

### World War II

The emergence of totalitarian countries like Russia, Germany, and Italy created instability in Europe and eventually led to war. Communist Russia, under the leadership of Stalin, became a threat to European countries. Italy was a fascist, belligerent state where individual liberties were ignored. Germany, under the leadership of **Adolf Hitler**, was ready to avenge the humiliating treatment it suffered as a result of World War I. In the Pacific, Japan was building an empire that had already conquered parts of China. All these conditions promoted the creation of military alliances that eventually led to World War II. Germany, Italy, and Japan created the Axis powers, and Russia, France, and England became the Allies. The war started with the German invasion of Poland in 1939. Two days later, France and England declared war against Germany. Hitler conquered most of Europe in a relatively short time. France was occupied, and England was brought close to submission. The United States supported the Allies with supplies and weapons but did not send troops. Although it remained neutral for the first few years of the war, the United States joined the Allies when Japan attacked its naval base in Pearl Harbor, Hawaii, in 1941.

### D-Day

With Hitler in full control of Europe, the United States joined England and representatives of the French government to plan and execute the invasion of Europe in 1944. On June 6, **General Dwight D. Eisenhower**, together with a quarter of a million Allied soldiers, crossed the English Channel into France and launched one of the largest offensives ever seen against the German occupying forces. This massive attack was known as D-Day. As a result of the collective effort of the Allies, France was freed from German occupation. With the combined forces of England, Russia, Canada, and the United States, Hitler and the Axis forces were finally defeated.

### Yalta Conference

The Allies met in Yalta, Russia, to discuss the terms of the treaty to end the war in Europe. In this meeting, the leaders of the Allied forces—Winston Churchill, Joseph Stalin, and Franklin D. Roosevelt—met to discuss peace. Under the terms of peace agreed to at Yalta, Germany was to be divided into four sections, each controlled by an Allied country—Britain, France, Russia, and the United States. The Germans were to pay the Russians for war reparations in money and labor. Poland was divided, and the Russians received control of one section (later they took full control of the nation). Finally, plans were set to organize the United Nations to prevent future conflicts in the world.

### Hiroshima and Nagasaki

The United States was fighting the war on two fronts, and the Japanese appeared to be invincible. The best available option seemed to be the atomic bomb. By the order of **President Harry Truman**, the United States dropped two atomic bombs on the cities of Hiroshima and Nagasaki. The death and destruction caused by these two bombs forced the Japanese government to surrender in 1945, which officially ended World War II.

## Marshall Plan

The Marshall Plan was a U.S.-supported program to rebuild the economic infrastructure in Europe. The United States provided money and machinery for the reconstruction of the continent.

## The Holocaust and Creation of Israel

During World War II, Hitler devised a "master plan" to exterminate the Jewish population. Germany placed European Jews in concentration camps and systematically killed millions. This act of genocide is known today as the *Holocaust*. At the end of the war, under the leadership of Great Britain, the United States, and the United Nations, the state of Israel was created in Palestine. On that same day, the Arab Liberation Army (ALA) was created to fight the Jewish state. This liberation movement has resulted in several wars between Israel and the Arabs. Today, this conflict has expanded to include Europe and the United States, with many terrorist attacks committed during the new century.

## Truman Doctrine

In response to the threat of the Soviets, Harry Truman issued a proclamation warning communist countries that the United States will help any nation in danger of falling under communist control. This declaration was called the ***Truman Doctrine***. As a result of this doctrine, the United States became involved in two major military conflicts: the Korean War and the Vietnam War.

## Cold War

As a result of the Yalta agreement, Russia became the most powerful country in the region. After taking over Poland and East Berlin, and building the Berlin Wall, a new war emerged between the Soviet Union and the United States—***the Cold War***. Although war was never formally declared between the two nations, confrontations occurred from 1945 to 1991. In 1963, the two nations were on the verge of nuclear war after Premier Nikita Khrushchev ordered the deployment of nuclear missiles to Cuba. An intense negotiation between **Premier Khrushchev** and **President Kennedy** avoided war between the two countries. This most intense confrontation of the Cold War was called the ***Cuban Missile Crisis***.

The Cold War finally ended with the fall of the Soviet Union under the leadership of **Mikhail Gorbachev**. The fall of the Soviet empire resulted in the reunification of Germany and the creation of multiple smaller countries in Russia that gained independence.

## War on Terrorism

In 2001, terrorists from abroad attacked American soil. The attacks on the twin towers of the World Trade Center in New York and the Pentagon in Arlington, Virginia, on September 11 killed more than 3,000 people, including 40 in Pennsylvania, where one of three hijacked planes crashed after passengers' heroic attempt to wrest control from the hijackers. As a result of the attacks, the United States declared war on terrorism and attacked the Taliban regime in Afghanistan. American forces had some success in the country but failed to capture Saudi Arabian militant Osama bin Laden, the mastermind of the 9/11 attacks, until May 2011, when he was killed in a U.S. raid on his Pakistani compound. The search for weapons of mass destruction led the United States into war with Iraq, which toppled the dictatorship of and led to the eventual death of Saddam Hussein.

## Texas History

### Timeline

| | |
|---|---|
| 1519 | Álonso Alvarez de Pineda explores and maps the Texas coastline |
| 1528 | Spanish explorer Álvar Núñez Cabeza de Vaca explores the Texas interior on his way to Mexico |
| 1685 | French explorer, René-Robert Cavelier, Sieur de La Salle establishes Fort St. Louis at Matagorda Bay, establishing French claim to Texas territory |
| 1688 | French colony is massacred |
| 1689 | The French continue to claim Texas but no longer physically occupy any of the territory |
| 1690 | First mission in East Texas established by Alonso de Leon |
| 1700s | Spain establishes Catholic missions throughout Texas |
| 1718 | Mission San Antonio de Valero (the Alamo) founded |
| 1762 | As a result of the The Seven Years War (French and Indian War) the French give up their claims to Texas and cede Louisiana to Spain until 1800 |
| 1800 | North Texas territory is returned to French and later sold to the U.S. in the Louisiana purchase (1803) |
| 1821 | Texas becomes a Mexican state as Mexico becomes free from Spain |
| 1823 | Stephen Austin establishes the Old Three Hundred colony along the Brazos River |
| 1830 | Mexico bans emigration into Texas by settlers from the United States |
| 1832 | Battle of Velasco—first casualties of the Texas Revolution |

| 1835 | The Texas Revolution official begins at the Battle of Gonzales |
| 1835 | Texans lead by Jim Bowie win the Battle of Concepcion, near San Antonio |
| 1836 | The Convention of 1836 signs the Texas Declaration of Independence at Washington on the Brazos |
| 1836 | The Alamo—Texans under Colonel William B. Travis were defeated by the Mexican army after a two-week siege at the Battle of the Alamo in San Antonio |
| 1836 | The Battle of San Jacinto—Texans under Sam Houston defeat Santa Anna and win independence |
| 1837 | Sam Houston, the first President of the Texas Republic, moves the capital of Texas 5 times, ending in Houston |
| 1839 | Austin becomes the capital of the Republic of Texas |
| 1845 | Texas admitted as the 28th state in the Union. |
| 1846 | The Mexican-American War due to disputes over claims to Texas boundaries. The outcome fixed the southern boundary at the Rio Grande River. |
| 1850 | The compromise of 1850 adjusts the state boundary and assumes Texas' debts |
| 1861 | Texas secedes from the Union and becomes part of the Confederacy |
| 1865 | Texas slaves freed after Union soldiers land in Galveston and put the Emancipation Proclamation into effect |
| 1870 | Texas is readmitted into the union |
| 1900 | Hurricane destroys Galveston and kills 6,000+ people |
| 1901 | Oil discovered at Spindletop |

## Before European Colonization

Several Native American groups inhabited the territory known today as Texas. They adopted different customs, different farming, hunting, and gathering methods, and made slightly different weapons. At times they fought against one another and at other times they lived in cooperation. It is important to recognize that Native American tribes had established important cultural, social, and economic systems in the United States long before European colonizers arrived on the continent.

Archeologists have found evidence of Native American civilization in Texas dating back to at least 9,200 BCE. The three groups living in the coastal plains—the Coahuiltecans, Karankawas, and Caddos—were food gatherers, fishermen, and farmers. When the Spanish arrived in Texas, they made initial contact with these groups. The name

*Texas* came as a result of contact with the Caddos. Attempting to communicate to the Spaniards that they were not hostile, some Caddos identified themselves with the word *taysha*, which in their language meant "friend" or "ally." When the Spaniards heard the word *taysha*, they thought the Caddos were identifying the name of the region. From that exchange, the name Texas and the state motto, "Friendship," emerged.

A fourth group, the Jumanos, lived in the mountains and basins of West Texas. The information about this group is limited because they virtually disappeared before the Spaniards arrived in the area. The last two groups are the Comanches and the Apaches. These two groups coexisted with Europeans and resisted the colonization efforts. After they domesticated horses, previously introduced by the Spanish, the Comanches and Apaches became fearless warriors and successful buffalo hunters. The domestication of the horse allowed the development of the culture of the buffalo. When buffalo were later annihilated in the area, these two groups became practically extinct. Table 4.2 presents a summary of Native American groups in Texas.

### Table 4.2
### Native American Groups in Texas

| Regions | Native Group |
|---|---|
| Coastal plains, flatland | **Coahuiltecan** (Rio Grande Valley)<br>**Economic Activity:** Food gatherers and hunters—roots, beans of the mesquite tree, rabbit, birds, and deer<br>**Features:** Lived in family groups |
| | **Karankawa** (Southeastern Texas)<br>**Economic Activity:** Fishing and food gathering<br>**Features:** Lived as nomads and used canoes for fishing |
| | **Caddo** (East Texas, Piney Woods)<br>**Economic Activity:** Farming—squash, pumpkins, tobacco, and corn (good food supply)<br>**Features:** Built villages and lived in groups |
| Central plains, flatland, and hills | **Apache** (Central and western Texas)<br>**Economic Activity:** Farming and hunting<br>**Features:** Lived as nomads, built portable housing called tepees, domesticated horses, and hunted bison |
| Great Plains, flatland, and hills | **Comanche**<br>**Economic Activity:** Hunters<br>**Features:** Lived as nomads and built portable housing; also domesticated the horse and hunted the buffalo |
| Mountains and basins | **Jumano** (West Texas)<br>**Economic Activity:** Farming and hunting<br>**Features:** Mostly sedentary and built homes of adobe |

## European Colonization

### Cabeza de Vaca

The Spanish exploration of the territory today known as Texas began in 1528, when *Álvar Núñez Cabeza de Vaca* and three companions landed in the territory. The four Spaniards made contact with the Caddo in the southeastern part of the state, near modern-day Houston. In his account of the meeting, de Vaca described the Caddo as a very sophisticated Native American group. From there, de Vaca continued exploring the region of modern-day New Mexico and Arizona. No other significant events happened in the region until 1541, when *Francisco Vázquez de Coronado* explored Texas.

### Francisco Vázquez de Coronado

In response to reports of the mythical Seven Cities of Cibola, Coronado led an expedition of almost a thousand men in search of the golden cities. The expedition left Mexico City and explored the southwestern United States and northern Texas. In 1542, Coronado returned to Mexico empty handed. For the next 140 years, the Texas region remained isolated, and no other attempts were made to colonize it.

### Robert de la Salle and French Influence over Texas

In 1685, **Robert de la Salle**, a French explorer, established a French settlement at Matagorda Bay called Fort St. Louis. This settlement established France's claim on this region of Texas. A few years later, the French colony was massacred by Native Americans. Spain then established a series of missions in East Texas to control the French threat in the region. The French continued to claim Texas for decades following the massacre, even though they had no physical presence in the region. In 1762, France relinquished its claim on Texas, turning it over to Spain.

### Catholic Missions in Texas

In the 1682, the Spanish began establishing missions throughout Texas beginning with the Ysleta del Sur near the present-day city of El Paso. In 1690, *Alonso de Leon* established the San Francisco de los Tejas Mission in East Texas. Spain continued to establish missions throughout Texas through the 18th century. In 1718, the Spanish established a mission and a fort—San Antonio de Valero and Fort San Antonio de Bexar—near what is now the city of San Antonio. The Spanish missions were designed not only to promote religious conversion, but to provide territorial claim and protection over Texas. The Catholic missions established throughout Texas helped the Spanish maintain control over the region from 1682-1821.

## Mexican War of Independence

During the first part of the nineteenth century, the Spanish empire began crumbling. Mexico obtained its independence in 1821 and took control of the colony of Texas. Up until this point Texas had been a sparsely populated area that served as a buffer between the territories claimed by France and Spain. To encourage settlement in this area, Mexico invited European and American settlers to move to the region.

## Stephen F. Austin and Anglo Presence in Texas

In 1821, Moses Austin received permission from the Spanish government to bring Anglo-American families to settle in Texas. This agreement was voided when Mexico took control of the territory. Later, Austin's son, Stephen, negotiated with the Mexican government and obtained a similar agreement to allow Anglo-Americans to settle in Texas. Stephen F. Austin established a colony called the *Old Three Hundred* on the Brazos River, which opened the way for further settlement in this area. By 1835, the settlers were the majority in the region, which antagonized the Mexican government and eventually resulted in war.

## The Texas War for Independence

Conflicts between Texans and the Mexican government started as early as 1830. The colonists felt that the government was not providing adequate support and protection to Texas. Initially, they wanted to negotiate with the new president, **Santa Anna**, and sent Stephen Austin to Mexico City to represent the colony. The Mexican government was not willing to negotiate and jailed Austin for a year.

### Battle of Gonzales

The power struggle between the Mexican government and Texas settlers continued to escalate. The town of Gonzales had a cannon to protect the colonists from Native Americans. By order of the government, Mexican soldiers came to take the cannon from the colonists in October 1835. The Texans refused to relinquish their weapon and fired the cannon against the Mexican soldiers. With this incident in Gonzales, the war for Texas independence began.

## Battle of the Alamo and Goliad

The next major battle of the Texas war for independence took place near the present-day city of San Antonio in a small mission and fort known as the Alamo. When the battle began, fewer than 200 men, led by **Colonel William Travis**, protected the Alamo. Eventually, James Bowie and Davy Crockett joined Travis in defending the fort. In 1836, **General Antonio López de Santa Anna** and the Mexican army took the fort and killed all its defenders, including Texans of Mexican ancestry. Following this victory, Santa Anna continued marching against the rebels and took the city of Goliad, where more than 300 rebels were killed. These two battles provided the battle cry that resulted in the creation of a Texas army, led by Sam Houston.

## Texas Declaration of Independence

As fighting grew worse, another Convention of Texas delegates was called in 1836 at Washington-on-the-Brazos. This convention led to the creation of the Texas Declaration of Independence which established the Republic of Texas and the *Ad Interim* government with **David G. Burnet** as president and **Lorenzo de Zavala** as vice president. This document was signed on March 2, 1836, 2 days before the Battle of the Alamo ended.

## Battle of San Jacinto

While the colonists were fighting the Mexican army at the Alamo and in Goliad, General Sam Houston was strengthening the army of the new republic. The Texan army continued retreating ahead of the Mexican forces until they reached the San Jacinto River, near the city of Houston. In a battle that lasted less than twenty minutes, Houston's troops defeated the Mexican army and captured General Santa Anna. Texas President Burnet and Mexican President Santa Anna signed the Treaty of Velasco, with Santa Anna agreeing to withdraw his troops from Texas in exchange for safe conduct back to Mexico, where he would lobby for recognition of Texas independence. Santa Anna's commitment never materialized, and the Mexican government refused to recognize Texas as an independent republic. Nevertheless, Sam Houston became the president of the new republic, and from 1836 to 1845, Texas functioned as an independent nation. However, the Mexican government still considered it one of its rebellious provinces that it could one day reclaim (Barker & Pohl, 2009).

## The Republic Period (1836–1845)

Despite the economic hardship typical of new nations, Texas managed to remain independent for ten years and was recognized by several nations in the world, including the

United States. This period was marked by tensions between those who wished to remain independent and those who wished to become part of the United States. Sam Houston was one who advocated for Texas to join the union. Unable to secure its borders and reverse its financial situation, Sam Houston's vision would grain traction as the Republic of Texas sought the support of the United States.

### Texas Joins the United States

In 1845, Texas became the twenty-eighth state of the American union. Texas was admitted as a slave state. Immediately, the U.S. government sent troops to the Rio Grande (which Mexicans considered their territory) to secure the Texas border. The ensuing clashes between Mexican and U.S. forces resulted in Congress declaring war in May 1846.

### Mexican-American War

Between 1846 and 1848, Mexico and the United States waged a war that ended with a decisive victory and tremendous land acquisitions for the United States. As a result of the Treaty of Guadalupe Hidalgo, Mexico withdrew its claim over Texas and established the Rio Grande, or *Rio Bravo*, as it is known in Mexico, as the official border between the two countries. Mexico also ceded California and the territory known today as the American Southwest to the United States.

## Confederacy Period (1861–1865)

At the onset of the American Civil War, Texas left the union and joined the Confederacy as a proslavery state. Sam Houston, the governor of the State of Texas, refused to declare allegiance to the Confederacy and was thus replaced. After five years of war, the Confederate army, led by General Robert E. Lee, surrendered to General Ulysses S. Grant, the leader of the Union forces. With the Union victory came freedom for slaves. In June, 1865, news of the Emancipation Proclamation, which abolished slavery, reached Galveston. *Juneteenth* is a holiday that celebrates this event.

## Reconstruction Period (1865–1877)

After the war, the Union forces occupied the South for a period of 12 years (1865–1877). This era was called the Reconstruction Period. During Reconstruction, Texas was briefly under occupation by U.S. troops. Texas was allowed to rejoin the union in 1870. The Ku Klux Klan became very active at this time, terrorizing African Americans in Texas and the southern states.

## Economic Development after Reconstruction

### Cattle

After Reconstruction, the Texas economy flourished, largely based on the growth of the cattle industry. Barbed wire was introduced in 1880, and ranchers began using scientific cattle breeding to increase production and improve the quality of meat.

### Railroads

Railroads changed the way Texas farms. With increased access to railroads, farmers could ship their surplus goods to market and ranchers could ship cattle to other states. As such, the building of rail lines in Texas led to an increase in both commercial agriculture and cattle ranching.

### Oil

In 1901, oil was discovered in the Spindletop Oil Field near Beaumont. The development of the oil industry that ensued catapulted Texas to its position as the leading producer of oil in the United States. As a result of this boom, cities like Houston and Dallas became large urban and industrial centers.

### Military and Wartime Industry

As a result of World War I, Texas emerged as a leading military training center. Several military bases were established in the state, bringing economic growth. The rapid development of the aircraft industry and highly technological businesses led to rapid industrialization in the state. By World War II, Texas was a leading state in the defense industry. The modern economy of Texas still relies on agriculture, ranching, and oil production, but new high technology industries are rapidly becoming the top economic forces in the state.

### Six Flags over Texas

The phrase "Six flags over Texas" describes the different countries that have exerted control in Texas from 1519, when the first European exploration of the region by Cortés took place, to the present:

- Spain (1519–1821)
- France (1685–1690)

- Mexico (1821–1836)

- Republic of Texas (1836–1845)

- United States (1845–1861)

- Texas in the Confederacy (1861–1865)

- Back to the American union (1870–present)

## State Facts and Symbols

Texas has adopted the following symbols to represent the state:

- State flower      Bluebonnet

- State bird        Mockingbird

- State tree        Pecan

- State motto       Friendship

- Border states     Oklahoma, Louisiana, Arkansas, and New Mexico

- State song        "Texas, Our Texas," by William J. Marsh and Gladys Yoakum Wright

# Competency 030 Geography

*The teacher understands and applies knowledge of geographic relationships involving people, places and environments in Texas, the United States and the world, as defined by the Texas Essential Knowledge and Skills (TEKS).*

## Geographic Concepts

### Geography

Geography is the study of the Earth's surface, the organisms that populate it, and their interaction within the ecosystem. Geography consists of two main areas: physical geography and cultural geography. Physical geography refers to the physical characteristics of the surface of the Earth and how those features affect life. Cultural geography deals with the interaction of humans with their environment and how that interaction produces changes.

## Locating Places and Regions on a Map

There are two categories of maps: reference and thematic. Reference maps show the locations of places, boundaries of countries, states, counties, and towns. Atlases and road maps are examples of reference maps. Thematic maps show a particular topic such as population density or distribution of world religions, and physical, social, economic, political, agricultural, or economic features. A physical map shows the topography of the Earth including land features and elevations. A political map shows how a country is organized. An economic map shows the important resources of a country or region. A historical map is used to show historical events including places of the past. Population maps are used to show where people live in a particular region.

A globe is a scale model of the Earth shaped like a sphere. Because a globe resembles the actual shape of the Earth it shows sizes and shapes more accurately than a Mercator projection map (a flat representation of the Earth). However, the cylindrical shape and portability of Mercator projections makes them more useful than globes.

## The Grid System

A grid system is a network of horizontal and vertical lines used to locate points on a map or a chart by means of coordinates. This grid shows the location of places. Latitude and longitude lines form divisions in this grid system that consist of geometrical coordinates used in designating the location of places on the surface of the Earth on a globe or map. The lines measure distances in degrees.

Latitude lines are horizontal lines that run parallel around the Earth measuring the distance north and south of the equator. The equator is identified as the 0 degree line of latitude, and it divides the Earth into the Northern and the Southern hemispheres. The United States is located in the Northern Hemisphere, while Brazil is located in the Southern Hemisphere. Longitude lines are vertical lines that run north and south going east and west. The 0 degree line of longitude is known as the prime meridian. It goes through Greenwich, England, and it divides the Earth into the Eastern and Western hemispheres. The United States is in the Western Hemisphere and Japan in the Eastern Hemisphere.

## Geographic Symbols

A compass rose is a design printed on a chart or map for reference. It shows the orientation of a map on Earth and shows the four cardinal directions (north, south, east, and west). A compass rose may also show in-between directions such as northeast or northwest. Symbols are used for a map to contain a large amount of information that can be easily understood. Common symbols used on a map include dots, stars, and small pictures to represent cities or places. Some maps use different colors to represent features such as elevations and divisions. These symbols and colors are defined in the map's key, or legend. A map scale shows the distance between two places in the world. The scale to which a map is drawn represents the ratio of the distance between two points on the Earth and the distance between the two corresponding points on the map.

## Locations and Human and Physical Characteristics of Places and Regions

### Texas

As measured by area, Texas is the second-largest state in the United States, as only Alaska is larger. Covering 268,601 square miles, the state contains five geographic regions within its boundaries. Table 4.3 lists the regions and the key cities and main economic activities of each.

**Table 4.3**
**Regions and Economic Activity in Texas**

| Region | Key Cities | Main Economic Activities | Key Statistics |
|---|---|---|---|
| Coastal plains, flatland | Dallas Houston San Antonio Austin Corpus Christi Laredo | **Lumber:** East Texas (Piney Woods) **Oil:** Refineries in Houston **Farming:** Rice, oranges, cotton, wheat, milo Ranching: Cattle in Kingsville **Shipping:** Houston | **Population:** High; 1 of 3 Texans live here **Rainfall:** High **Distinguishing Mark:** Hurricanes |
| Central plains, flatland and hills | Fort Worth Arlington San Angelo Abilene | **Ranching:** Cattle, wool (mohair), sheep **Farming:** Grains | **Population:** High **Rainfall:** Medium **Distinguishing Marks:** Tornadoes, northerlies (cold winds), hailstorms; large ranches |
| Great Plains Flatland and hill country | Midland Odessa Lubbock Amarillo Texas Panhandle | **Ranching:** Cattle, sheep **Minerals:** Graphite **Oil:** Odessa and Midland **Farming:** Wheat | **Population:** Average **Rainfall:** Medium **Distinguishing Marks:** Snowstorms, dust storms, windmills, use of aquifers |

*(continued)*

Table 4.3
Regions and Economic Activity in Texas (continued)

| Region | Key Cities | Main Economic Activities | Key Statistics |
|---|---|---|---|
| Mountains and basins, Rocky Mountains, and Chisos | El Paso Fort Davis Guadalupe | **Ranching:** Limited large ranches | **Population:** Low; however, El Paso has high population density. **Rainfall:** Low; hard rain wears out the rocks and land **Distinguishing Mark:** Big Bend National Park |
| Chihuahuan Desert | | Mexico-U.S. border economy based on trading of goods produced by the industries established in Mexico: Maquiladoras. | |

## The United States

The concept of regions facilitates the examination of geography by providing a convenient and manageable unit for studying the Earth's human and natural environment.

## Regions in the United States

The continental United States typically divide into eight broad geographic regions:

- **Laurentian Highlands** are part of the Canadian Shield that extends into the northern United States and the Great Lakes area. This area has a hard winter, and agriculture is very limited.

- **Atlantic–Gulf Coastal Plains** are the coastal regions of the eastern and southern states. It includes New York in the North, the Mid-Atlantic states to Florida in the South, and all the way west to Texas on the Gulf Coast.

- **Appalachian Highlands** covers the Appalachian Mountains, the Adirondack Mountains, and New England—the states of Connecticut, Maine, Massachusetts, New Hampshire, Rhode Island, and Vermont.

- **Interior Plains and the Great Plains** cover the interior part of the United States. Included in this area are the states west of the Appalachians, south of the Great Lakes, and as far west as Montana, Wyoming, Colorado, New Mexico, and northwestern Texas. Most of the nation's wheat, corn, and feed crops are grown in this area.

- **Interior Highlands** are also part of the interior continental United States. This area includes the Ozark Mountains and the states of Missouri, Arkansas, Kentucky, and part of Oklahoma and Kansas.

- **Rocky Mountain System** is in the western United States and Canada, extending from British Colombia to Montana, Utah, Colorado, and New Mexico. The mountain range is called the *Continental Divide*, because it separates the eastward-flowing rivers from the westward-flowing rivers. The waters that flow eastward empty into the Atlantic Ocean, and those that flow westward empty into the Pacific Ocean.

- **Intermontane Plateaus** is a large region that includes the Pacific Northwest, the Colorado Plateau, and the basins of the southwestern United States. This area covers the states of Washington, Oregon, Idaho, part of Utah, New Mexico, and Arizona. Included are the areas of the Grand Canyon and Death Valley.

- **Pacific Mountain System** covers the west coast of the United States. This area extends from the Cascade Mountains in the north down the entire west coast through the states of Washington, Oregon, and California.

### Rivers in the United States

These are the largest and most important rivers in the United States:

- The *Mississippi* is the longest river in the United States and the fourteenth longest in the world. It begins in Minnesota and ends in the Gulf of Mexico.

- The Ohio River begins near Pittsburgh and runs southwest, ending in the Mississippi River on the Illinois and Missouri borders.

- The Rio Grande begins in the San Juan Mountains of southern Colorado and ends in the Gulf of Mexico. The river is the official border between the United States and Mexico, where it is known as the *Rio Bravo*.

- The Colorado River begins in the Rocky Mountains and ends in California.

- The Missouri River begins in the Rocky Mountains, flowing north first and then generally southeast across the central United States, ending at the Mississippi River, just to the north of St. Louis, Missouri.

For information about significant rivers in the continental United States, visit: *WorldAtlas.com*.

## Regions of the World

A world region is an area of the world that shares similar, unifying cultural or physical characteristics that are different from those of surrounding areas. The physical features refer to topographic characteristics like elevation, rivers, and mountains. The cultural features include all the features that distinguish different groups of people, for example: language, religion, government, economics, food, architecture, shared values, and family life.

Geographers divide the world into ten regions: North America, Central and South America, Europe, Central Eurasia, the Middle East, North Africa, Sub-Saharan Africa, South Asia, East Asia, and Australasia. These divisions are based on physical and cultural similarities. North America consists of Canada, the United States, and Mexico. It is the third-largest continent, and it is located between the Arctic Circle and the Tropic of Cancer. The Europeans colonized the North American region. Table 4.4 presents an overview of the world regions by physical and cultural features.

### Table 4.4
### World Regions

| World Region | Physical Features | Cultural Features |
|---|---|---|
| North America | • Consists of Canada, the United States, and Mexico.<br>• The United States is the fourth-largest country in the world.<br>• Oil is an important resource in the U.S.<br>• Most of the U.S. has a humid-continental or humid-subtropical climate<br>• Most of Canada has a subarctic or Tundra climate.<br>• Over 75% of Canadians live along the Southern border.<br>• The areas of greatest concentration of population in the U.S. are along the East Coast and California.<br>• The climate of Mexico ranges from humid tropical and subtropical to desert and highland.<br>• Mexico has rich mineral resources including oil. | • Europeans colonized this region.<br>• Languages spoken are predominantly English, Spanish, and French.<br>• A majority of people identify as Christian. |

*(continued)*

**Table 4.4**
**World Regions** (continued)

| World Region | Physical Features | Cultural Features |
|---|---|---|
| Central and South America | • Includes the countries of Central America, the Caribbean islands, and South America.<br>• The majority of this continuous mass of land is south of the Equator.<br>• South America extends from Point Gallinas in Colombia to Cape Horn.<br>• Part of South America lies closer to the South Pole than any other land mass of this size.<br>• Venezuela is one of the world's leading exporters of oil.<br>• Most of Eastern Central America and equatorial South America have a humid tropical climate. | • Most people speak Spanish, but many other languages are spoken: Portuguese, French, Dutch, English, and several Native American languages and dialects.<br>• Christian beliefs, the Roman Catholic religion historically more predominant; however, the region is becoming more religiously diverse.<br>• Architecture, law, religion, traditions, and language are strongly influenced by Europe's colonial rule of this region.<br>• The many ethnic groups in this region are separated by geographical barriers such as the Andes and the Amazon. |
| Europe | • Western section of the Eurasian continent<br>• Shares a mountain chain, the Alps.<br>• Most of Europe has a temperate climate.<br>• Europe's irregular coastline has many harbors that are important manufacturing and trade centers.<br>• The rivers of Europe are important resources for trade, water, and hydroelectricity.<br>• European population growth rates are the lowest in the world. | • Shares a common history in the Roman Empire and later the Catholic Church and Latin language.<br>• English is the most widely used language in Europe, German and French are also widespread.<br>• Cultural diffusion or shared cultural traits spread throughout Europe.<br>• Ninety percent of all adults ages 15–24 speak a second language and some countries are considered multilingual.<br>• Europeans practice many different religions.<br>• Roman Catholicism is the predominant religion of many European countries.<br>• Most of Northern and Central Europe is Protestant.<br>• Jews live in many parts of Western Europe. |

*(continued)*

### Table 4.4
### World Regions (continued)

| World Region | Physical Features | Cultural Features |
| --- | --- | --- |
| Central Eurasia | • Central Asia and Eastern Europe<br>• United around one continuous mass of land located in the center of the continent.<br>• Little access to the sea<br>• The borders of Eastern European countries have changed many times.<br>• From WWII to the late 1980s, the Soviet Union controlled Eastern Europe and introduced communism to the region. | • Conquered at different times by the Persians, Mongolians, Tartars, the French, the Germans, and the Russians.<br>• Slavic languages are predominant.<br>• Most people in the Eastern part of the region follow the Eastern Orthodox church, people in the Northern area are mostly Roman Catholic. |
| Middle East | • Consists of the area of southwest Asia and North Africa.<br>• Access to sea water<br>• The majority of the land is desert.<br>• Rich in oil | • While the majority of people follow the religion of Islam there are also groups that follow Christianity and Judaism.<br>• The religion defines the law in many places.<br>• The most ancient of human civilizations. Egyptians, Assyrians, Babylonians, Persians, Greeks, and Romans have left their mark in this region.<br>• This region has been the battleground for many religious wars. |
| North-Africa | • Part of the African continent<br>• Includes Egypt, Libya, Tunisia, Algeria, and Morocco<br>• Extensive coastline<br>• The Sahara desert and the Nile river are two important physical features of this area<br>• Rich in oil<br>• Egypt is undergoing rapid growth and urbanization, and industrialization | • The majority of people follow the religion of Islam.<br>• People speak Arabic predominantly.<br>• Religious issues influence the politics of this area. |

*(continued)*

**Table 4.4
World Regions** (*continued*)

| World Region | Physical Features | Cultural Features |
|---|---|---|
| Sub-Saharan | • Consists of Africa south of the Sahara<br>• Most of the area is a savanna<br>• Has abundant rain<br>• Extensive coastline<br>• Fertile land<br>• Most people live in the forest zone and the dry savannas<br>• Agriculture is the predominant activity in West Africa<br>• Livestock is the predominant economic activity in the northern area | • Cultural diversity reflects indigenous, Arab, and European influences.<br>• Majority follows tribal beliefs, Christianity, or a combination of both.<br>• Most people speak native African or European languages.<br>• Over 500 ethnic groups live in this region. |
| South Asia | • Consists of a large Indian peninsula that extends into the Indian Ocean.<br>• Abundant rainfall<br>• Strong seasonal winds called monsoons<br>• Rice is an important crop.<br>• One of the most populated regions in the world<br>• The world's highest mountains are located in the northern area of this region.<br>• Many major manufacturing and trade centers are located along the coast. | • People in South Asia speak many languages.<br>• Predominant beliefs are of Eastern origins such as Buddhism and Hinduism.<br>• Many South Asians are farmers who live in small villages.<br>• Many cultural influences<br>• Through the efforts of Mohandas Gandhi the region gained its independence from Britain in 1947. |
| East Asia | • Consists of China, Korea, Taiwan, and Japan.<br>• It is the most densely populated region in the world.<br>• Large expanse of coastline. | • Buddhism and Taoism are predominant religions.<br>• Confucian philosophy<br>• People speak Chinese, Japanese, Korean, Mongolian, and many other languages.<br>• Chinese Script or characters influence |
| Australasia | • It is composed of the Australian continent and surrounding islands.<br>• South of the equator | • English is the predominant language of most of the nations in this region.<br>• Population is largely Christian. |

## World Mountains

With the notable exception of the peak known as K2, which is part of the Karakoram Range, the tallest mountains in the world are located in the Himalayas, ranging across the countries of China, Pakistan, Nepal, and Tibet. Table 4.5 lists the top ten tallest mountains. Compared with the world's tallest peaks, the United States' mountains are small, with the highest mountain being Mt. McKinley in Alaska. In fact, the state of Alaska has the 16 highest peaks in the United States. A list of the world's mountains with elevations of 16,000 feet or above is presented in Table 4.5. For additional information about the world's mountains, go to *www.infoplease.com*.

### Table 4.5
### Tallest Mountains in the World

| Mountain | Location | Height (in feet) |
|---|---|---|
| Everest | Nepal/Tibet | 29,035 |
| K2 | Pakistan/China | 28,250 |
| Kanchenjunga | India/Nepal | 28,169 |
| Lhotse I | Nepal/Tibet | 27,940 |
| Makalu I | Nepal/Tibet | 27,766 |
| Cho Oyu | Nepal/Tibet | 26,906 |
| Dhaulagiri | Nepal | 26,795 |
| Manaslu I | Nepal | 26,781 |
| Nanga Parbat | Pakistan | 26,660 |
| Annapurna | Nepal | 26,545 |

## Deposition

Deposition is the process of carrying soil from one place to another, usually by means of water or wind. This process is responsible for the creation of beaches, sand dunes found in desert areas, and landforms created by glaciers.

## Human Adaptation, Modification, and Use of the Physical Environment

Humans can alter the physical environment of the Earth, but the physical environment can also shape humans and their culture. For example, the Incas built the capital of their empire, Cuzco, in the Andes Mountains in what is now Peru. This city has an altitude of 11,152 feet above sea level, where oxygen is scarce and agriculture is a challenge. However, the Incas managed to live and flourish under these conditions. They carved the land for agriculture and built roads and cities. In turn, the environment changed the Incas, who had to evolve to tolerate the low levels of oxygen. Studies conducted on the Indians from Peru suggest that people of the Andes developed genetic adaptations for high-altitude living (Discovery Channel, 2004 March 10). By adapting to the conditions of their environment, inhabitants of the area not only survived but also flourished in less-than-ideal conditions.

## How Regional Physical Characteristics and Human Modifications to the Environment Affect People's Activities and Settlement Patterns

The intended and unintended consequences of how humans modify the physical environment result in constant change to the human and physical world.

Advances in technology can bring a continuum of positive to negative consequences for people and for the environment. For example, humans often meet energy needs from the Earth. The U.S. has long relied on coal as an energy source. Much of U.S. coal comes from Pennsylvania and West Virginia. Humans cannot have the energy benefits of coal without altering the physical landscape from which the coal is taken. This physical reshaping of mining the Earth changes how rainfall runs, where people can build homes, and how they maintain safe drinking water.

Japan's recent weather affected how people assess the safety of nuclear energy. People relied on the nuclear energy to meet their needs, but it came at great human and ecological cost when tsunamis and earthquakes interfered with the stability of this country's main energy source. In addition to Fukushima, Japan, other nuclear incidents around the world serve as examples such as Chernobyl, Ukraine, and Three Mile Island, Pennsylvania. The greater the population density of an area, the greater the energy needs. Likewise, in order to plant and harvest food, humans redefine environmental systems as human activities reshape the Earth. Some farming methods feature greater measures for sustainability like intercropping, while other methods maintain a human-entered focus to maximize yield.

## How Location (Absolute and Relative) Affects People, Places and Environments

Both relative and absolute location tell us about where we are in the world. We use latitude and longitude to determine a global location. We use a street address to determine local location. Both of these are examples of absolute location. Often we describe a location by what is around a location. This is relative location. Referencing a landmark or the distance a location is from another well-known location would be examples of giving a relative location.

Most of us interact daily within intersects of location, people, and environments of a daily basis. If you buy dolphin safe tuna, bottled water, or sunscreen, then you have real-life examples. Geography, in part, helps us to understand the pattern of how humans organize space. To do this, we utilize location, place, territory, geo-politics, migration, gender, race, language, economic change, and power. We can examine a small, localized geography or worldwide effects and influences.

## Characteristics, Distribution and Migration of Populations

The global population is close to six billion people, with much of the growth occurring in the last two centuries. Population density of hyper-urban areas is also growing. For example, Tokyo, Japan, has over 36 million people. New York, and Sao Paulo, Brazil, both have over 20 million people. Mumbai and Delhi, both urban areas in India, have over 21 million people each! Increases in population places strains on cities, regions, countries, and on our Earth to keep up with their daily needs and wants from access to clean water and medical care to maintaining and growing schools and industry to support basic to extended quality of life. Population growth predicts migration. Population density shifts can also predict supply and demand. Likewise, word events from war to vaccines predict population. Migration is a dynamic function of human societies. Some migration is voluntary, as when humans search for a better quality of life. Other migration is involuntary, as when humans must move to maintain their culture or life such as cases of famine, war, or ecological devastation.

## Cultural Diffusion

The term *cultural diffusion* describes the exchange or transmission of cultural information and lifestyles from people around the world. For example, most people in the world use cotton, a fabric developed in India, and silk, developed in China. Chicken and pigs were originally domesticated in Asia, but by the process of cultural diffusion, these animals are common today in most countries in the world. Many countries are predominantly Christian today, but Christianity was born in the Middle East, a place where most people are Muslim. The Romans facilitated the cultural diffusion of Christianity around the ancient world. Travelers visiting Morocco, a Muslim country in North Africa, may be surprised to hear Puerto Rican salsa and Jamaican reggae music being played in local nightclubs. The popularity of Latin and Caribbean rhythms in a predominantly Muslim country is an example of the powerful effect of cultural diffusion.

# Competency 031 Economics

*The teacher understands and applies knowledge of economic systems and how people organize economic systems to produce, distribute, and consume goods and services, as defined by the Texas Essential Knowledge and Skills (TEKS).*

## Basic Principles of Economy

Economics is a social science that analyzes the principles that regulate the production, distribution, and consumption of resources in society. It emphasizes how these principles operate within the economic choices of individuals, households, businesses, and governments. Economics can be divided into two main areas: macroeconomics and microeconomics. Macroeconomics is the study of the economy at the world, regional, state, and local levels. Some of the topics include reasons and ways to control inflation, causes of unemployment, and economic growth in general. Microeconomics deals with specific issues related to the decision-making process at the household, firm, or industry levels.

The study of economics can be summarized into several key principles.

1. People choose.

2. People's choices have costs.

3. People respond to incentives in predictable ways.

4. People create economic systems that influence individual choices and incentives.

5. People gain when they trade voluntarily.

6. People's choices have consequences that lie in the future.

## Scarcity

Economics centers on the notion of scarcity. Scarcity refers to the reality that there are limited resources despite consumer's unlimited wants. The result is that people must choose among competing alternatives. The choices people make about which alternative to choose are generally purposeful and based on their desire to obtain the most utility or satisfaction from their choices. Time, money, and natural resources are all examples of scarce resources.

## Opportunity Costs

All choices have benefits and costs. Every time an investor, saver, consumer, or producer makes a decision, there is an alternative course of action that could be taken. Economists refer to the best-forgone alternative as the opportunity cost of a decision. Opportunity costs are both monetary and non-monetary in nature and are an important consideration in the choices people make. Let's consider your decision to read this book and study for the TExES exam. There are probably several other things you could be doing rather than reading this book and studying for the TExES exam, such as watching television, spending time with family or friends, or exercising. If you were to rank your alternatives in order, the alternative right behind your decision to read this book is the opportunity cost of your choice.

For instance, if you were to rank your choices in the following order, the opportunity cost of your decision to read this book would have been exercising.

1. Read this book (choice)

2. Exercise (opportunity cost: best forgone alternative)

3. Watch television

4. Spend time with family and friends

## Theory of Supply and Demand

This theory states that prices vary based on balance between the availability of a product or service at a certain price (supply) and the desire of potential purchasers to pay that price (demand). This balance of supply and demand can occur naturally or be created artificially. An example of an artificially created balance is the intentional destruction of a surplus of a given product on the world market to maintain the price level. Another way is to control the production and availability of the product to create a scarcity of a product. For instance, the Organization of Petroleum Exporting Countries (OPEC) often reduces its production of oil to cause an increase in price.

## Goods and Services

The use of machines increases the availability of goods and services to the population. This kind of production can decrease the cost of producing the goods and consequently its price. For example, as a result of the division of labor and the use of assembly lines developed by Eli Whitney in 1799, production costs of manufactured goods decreased and productivity increased. Mass production that came as a result of the Industrial Revolution made contemporary families and children more likely to become consumers rather than producers. However, before the Industrial Revolution, especially in colonial America, children were used to produce goods and contribute to the group.

## Factors of Production

The resources required for the production of goods and services are generally classified into four categories: natural resources, labor, capital, and entrepreneurship.

*Natural resources* include timber, land, fisheries, farms, oil, and other similar natural resources. Natural resources are generally a limited resource for many economies. Although some natural resources, such as timber, food and animals, are renewable, the physical land is usually a fixed resource. Nations must carefully use their natural resources by creating a mix of natural and industrial uses.

*Labor* represents the human capital available to transform raw or national resources into consumer goods. Human capital includes all able-bodied individuals capable of working in the economic system and providing various services to other individuals or businesses. This factor of production is a flexible resource as workers can be allocated to different areas of the economy for producing consumer goods or services. Human capital can also be improved through training or educating workers to complete technical functions or business tasks when working with other economic resources.

*Capital* has two economic definitions as a factor of production. Capital can represent the monetary resources companies use to purchase natural resources, land and other capital goods. Monetary resources flow through an economic system as individuals buy and sell resources to individuals and businesses. Capital also represents the major physical assets individuals and companies use when producing goods or services. These assets include buildings, production facilities, equipment, vehicles and other similar items.

*Entrepreneurship* is considered a factor of production because economic resources can exist in an economy and not be transformed into consumer goods. Entrepreneurs usually have an idea for creating a valuable good or service and assume the risk involved with transforming economic resources into consumer products. Entrepreneurship is also considered a factor of production since someone must complete the managerial functions of gathering, allocating and distributing economic resources or consumer products to individuals and other businesses in the economy.

## Gross Domestic Product (GDP)

The Gross Domestic Product is the total value of all goods and services produced in the country. In computing the GDP, only the value of the final goods and services are included. This means that only the value of the final product is included, and not all the individual factors of production that went into making that product. A house, for example, would only have its own value included in the GDP, and not the lumber, brick, wire, glass, cement, and shingles that went into building it. GDP is part of macroeconomics and is a primary indicator of an economy's overall health.

GDP consists of four broad sectors: consumers, businesses, government, and the foreign sector. To tabulate GDP, an economy's output can be measured in two ways, both of which yield the same result: the expenditure approach and the incomes approach. In the expenditures approach, GDP is determined by the spending in each sector. GDP equals the consumer consumption (C) plus investment expenditures (I) plus government spending (G) plus the difference between exports and imports in foreign sector spending (X-M). This formula includes only final goods and services, and not the value of intermediate goods.

$$GDP = C + I + G + (X - M)$$

The less used income approach to GDP, is calculated by adding up total compensation to employees, gross profits for incorporated and non-incorporated firms, and taxes, less any subsidies. Regardless of how GDP is calculated, this macroeconomic measure is an important indicator of the standard of living in various economies. For instance, GDP per capita (using purchase power parity) in the U.S. is $47,200 and in Mexico is $13,900.

## Economic Systems

Because resources are scare and wants are unlimited, societies often devise economic systems to help regulate this divide between demand and supply. Economic systems are generally created based on three important questions:

1. What goods and services to produce?

2. How to produce these goods and services?

3. How are these goods and services allocated?

The way a society answers these questions determines the type of economic system they will create. Examples of economic systems include market or free enterprise economies, centrally planned economies, and mixed economies.

### Market or Free Enterprise

Free enterprise is an economic and political doctrine of the capitalist system. The concept is based on the premise that the economy can regulate itself in a freely competitive market through the relationship of supply and demand, and with minimum governmental intervention. The three questions of economic systems are answered in the marketplace by the interaction of buyers and sellers. One of the main benefits of the system of free enterprise is the competition among businesses that results in a greater choice and better prices for consumers. The system of free enterprise has led to *globalization*. Globalization can be defined as a continuous increase of cross-border financial, economic, and social activities. It implies some level of economic interdependence among individuals, financial entities, and nations. As a result of globalization, trade barriers have been eliminated and tariffs imposed on imported products have been largely discontinued. In a global market, it is difficult to determine the origins of products. For example, Toyota from Japan and Ford from the United States joined forces to build cars using parts and labor from Mexico. The concept of economic interdependence describes a positive, close connection between producers and consumers of goods and services within a nation or across nations. This economic interdependence has guided nations to establish large markets of free trade zones like the European Union (EU) trade agreement and the North American Free Trade Agreement (NAFTA) for Canada, Mexico, and the United States. The European Union went a step further; in 2002 they adopted a common currency for the Union—the *euro*.

### Centrally Planned or Command Economy

The opposite of a market or free enterprise economy is called a centrally planned economy, once referred to as *communism*. In a planned economy, the means of production where supply and price are regulated by the government rather than market forces. government planners answer the three questions of economic systems and decide which goods and services are produced and how they are distributed. Most planned economies direct resources into the production of capital and military goods leaving little resources for consumer goods. A command economy discourages individualistic profit motives and consumeristic needs. Under such a planned system, rewards, wages, and perks are distributed based on the social value of the service performed. Certain sectors get preferential allocation at the expense of others, which may lead to shortages in some essential goods. Absence of profit motives precludes any need for competitiveness. This acts as a disincentive in individual contribution to collective efforts. The former Soviet Union was an example of a command economy. China also had a command economy . Today, countries using a command economy are rare. Remaining examples of countries with a command economy include Cuba and North Korea.

### Mixed Economies

In between market and planned economies are mixed economies. A mixed economy is an economic system that answers the three questions both in the marketplace and in the government. Planning is usually used to direct resources at the upper levels of the economy, with markets being used to determine prices of consumer goods and wages. The former Yugoslavia was a mixed or socialist economy. Although the United States government plays a role in our economy, a mixed economy usually involves producers working closer with the government than they do in the United States so the U.S. economic system is still a market economy.

### Money and Banking

Under the presidency of Woodrow Wilson, the Federal Reserve System was established. The main purpose of this institution is to keep the banking industry strong to ensure a supply of currency. The Federal Reserve is run by the Federal Reserve Board of Governors, a seven-member body appointed to a four-year term, with the option of being reappointed to a maximum of fourteen-year terms. **Alan Greenspan** served as chairman of the Federal Reserve Board from 1987 to 2006. He finished an unexpired term and then served for a full fourteen-year term for a total of eighteen and a half years. The current chair is **Ben S. Bernanke**. His term will expire in January 2014. The main function of the Federal Reserve Bank is to promote monetary stability and economic growth in the nation and to regulate inflation and deflation. The Board of Governors controls the flow of money and sets the interest rate that banks use to lend money. They increase the interest rate to control inflation and lower the interest rate when business slows down.

### Savings, Interest Rates, and Investment

All markets, including financial markets, function to create an efficient allocation of resources. In the financial market, the supply and demand of money is often tied to the loanable funds available to those who are willing to transact at the market price. The market price of loanable funds is the interest rate. The interest rate is determined by the Federal Reserve Bank. The supply of loanable funds comes from savings. Savings represents the dollar amount of the postponed spending of business and individuals. In order to save, people must have some incentive to postpone their spending and save money. The incentive to save money comes in the form of an interest rate. The higher the interest rate, the more money people are willing to save and the more money that is available to be loaned. The lower the interest rate, the less incentive people have to save and the less loanable funds that are available. The interest rate represents an **opportunity cost**. At higher interest rates, the opportunity cost of not saving is higher than at lower interest rates. As such, the supply of loanable funds is an upward sloping curve.

The funds created from savings are needed for individuals and businesses to invest in the production of goods and services. Often times individuals and businesses do not have the liquid funds available to invest, thus they must borrow funds. In order to borrow funds, investors must pay a price for the funds they borrow. This price is the interest rate. Thus, the lower the interest rate, the more money people are willing to borrow. This means that the demand for loanable funds is a downward sloping curve.

Investment is an important component of GDP. In order for economies to grow, individuals and businesses have to be willing to invest funds. Economies with higher rates of savings have higher rates of investment and therefore higher growth rates. When individuals save money, they free up resources for things such as investment, which leads to economic growth. Economies with lower investment rates have lower growth rates because there are fewer funds for investment and growth purposes.

## Inflation and Deflation

Inflation reduces the purchasing power of money, which technically affects the value of the currency. Countries generally devalue their currency to keep up with inflation. Deflation is the opposite of inflation: the purchasing power of money increases, thereby lowering the prices of goods and services. In a period of deflation, consumers benefit but industry suffers. The **Federal Reserve** controls the flow of money and keeps a healthy balance between inflation and deflation.

## Economic Indicators

Economic indicators reveal what is happening in the economy, including how well or poorly it is performing. Most measures of economic output are expressed in terms of dollars. However, the purchasing power of the dollar often changes due to inflation and economic growth. Thus, when comparing figures like GDP over time, there are fluctuations from year to year. To determine if these fluctuations in actual differences in output or if they are due to inflation or price changes, we must adjust for these possibilities in our calculation. To do so, we use what is called the **price index**. The price index equals the price in any year divided by the price in a base year multiplied by 100. This means we must select one year to be the base year and use that in our calculations to construct the price index. The Consumer Price Index (CPI) is a specific price index that measures the average change over time in the prices paid by consumers for a market basket of predetermined goods and services.

*Price Index* = *(Price in any year/price in base year)* × *100*

Once we have established a price index, we can then adjust for inflation and growth in our GDP comparisons. Real GDP is GDP adjusted for inflation. Nominal or unadjusted GDP is reported in current dollar figures and has not been adjusted for inflation. By adjusting for inflation and growth, we can make meaningful comparisons of GDP across time.

*Real GDP* = *(Nominal GDP/Price Index)*

Another important economic rate is the inflation rate. The inflation rate shows the decrease in purchasing power of the dollar in relation to the rise in the general level of prices. Essentially, the inflation rate simply means we cannot buy as much as we did before.

*Inflation Rate* = *(current year price index – previous year's price index)/previous year's price index*

The unemployment rate is another important economic indicator. The unemployment rate refers to the percentage of the labor force that is not working. It is calculating via the following method:

*Unemployment Rate* = *(Number of people unemployed/number of people in labor force)* × *100*

The labor force only includes those people who are capable of working, are willing to work, and are working or actively seeking work. The labor force is roughly one half of the U.S. population.

Real GDP, inflation, and unemployment figures provide important information about the state of the economy. An economy in recession needs to be stimulated with expansionary monetary and fiscal (government policy over taxation and spending) policy and an economy that is expanding too rapidly with inflation needs to be slowed down with contractionary monetary and fiscal policy. Government official and economists use these figures to determine what is the best course of action to maintain the health of an economy.

## American Federal Income Tax System

In 1913, the Sixteenth Amendment of the U.S. Constitution allowed the imposition of direct taxation of citizens. This direct taxation is known as the federal income tax. Federal income tax dollars are then used to fund various government agencies and projects.

## Economic History in the U.S.

It is important to understand the major events and trends that have shaped economic history. These events and trends helped shaped the economic system of Texas, the U.S., and the world.

### Agricultural Revolution

The invention of the plow led to a significant transformation in the way people lived and led to the agricultural revolution. The plow made large-scale agricultural production possible and facilitated the development of agrarian societies. In addition to the plow, the invention of the wheel and formalized writing structures helped shift hunter/gatherer societies towards more agricultural societies that were self-sustaining.

The continued advances in agricultural technology led to the ability of societies to produce surplus goods. The surplus of goods created a trade market in which people trading their surpluses for other desired goods. As such, traders and trade routes developed between different communities and villages. Protecting these surplus goods became a primary concern of societies and led to the construction of fortified communities.

### Industrial Revolution

The industrial revolution of the 18th and 19th centuries led to even greater changes in human societies and increased opportunities for trade, production, and the exchange of goods and ideas. The first phase of the industrial revolution (1750-1830) included improvements in mining, the invention of the steam engine, improvements in transportation including canals and railroads, and the mechanization of the textile industry. The second phase of the industrial revolution (1830-1910) resulted in improvement in the mechanization of a variety of industries. Important innovations of this time period included the Bessemer steel process, the steam ship, electricity, photography, hydroelectric power, and petroleum engineering. It was during phase of the industrial revolution that these ideas and inventions spread to the United States.

The industrial revolution led to some major economic shifts including: increase in productivity, specialization and division of labor, increase in global trade, mass production, growth in large corporations and monopolies. During this period of time, ideas and knowledge spread rapidly with the increase in mobility. Additionally, immigration to industrialized countries also increased. As immigration increased so did the clashing and blending of cultures. In the U.S., as the economy grew and developed, people began spreading north, south, and westward. Each of these regions developed unique economic systems. The southern states had economies based primarily around agriculture, planta-tions, and slave labor. The North developed into a primarily industrial economy.

## The Roaring Twenties to the Great Depression

Prior to World War I, the United States remained fairly isolationist with few trade partners. Following the war, international trade became an increasingly common reality for the U.S. After the war, the U.S. economy of the "roaring twenties" saw huge increases in mass production. Manufacturing output doubled during this period from 1918-1929. The building and loan sector also saw a huge boom. The stock market was booming with buying and selling with borrowed money, or, on margin. Unfortunately, when stock prices fell in 1929, many speculators could not meet their margin demands and this shortage eventually led to the Great Depression.

The Great Depression (1929 to early 1940s) had devastating effects in virtually every country. Personal income, tax revenue, profits and prices dropped, while international trade plunged by more than 50%. Unemployment in the U.S. rose to 25%, and in some countries rose as high as 33%. Cities around the world were hit hard, especially those dependent on industry. Construction was virtually halted in many countries. Farming and rural areas suffered as crop prices fell by approximately 60%.

## World War II (1939–1945)

Typically, war is seen as a way to jump-start a failing economy, because wartime efforts demand the production of various wartime goods and services. This demand for increased production also leads to increased employment opportunities. World War II led to a dramatic increase in GDP, the export of vast quantities of supplies to the Allies and to American forces overseas, the end of unemployment, and a rise in civilian consumption even as 40% of the GDP went to the war effort. This was achieved by workers moving from low-productivity occupations to high efficiency jobs, improvements in productiv-ity through better technology and management, by students, retired people, housewives, and the unemployed moving into the active labor force, and an increase in hours worked. Roosevelt's New Deal policies of public spending also helped lead the U.S. economy out of the Great Depression. Most durable goods became unavailable, and meat, clothing, and gasoline were tightly rationed. Prices and wages were controlled, and individual savings increased, which led to renewed growth after the war instead of a return to depression.

## The Texas Economy

Texas continues to play a unique role in the U.S. economy and in the world. Texas interacts with other states and the national government through trade and commerce. Cattle, livestock, and agriculture were important factors in the development of the Texas economy. As railroads and cities developed, the Texas economy continued to expand. Dallas became a trading post for grain and cotton. Houston's port location was at the heart of the sugar trade and later the oil industry. In 1901, the discovery of oil at Spindle Top also lead to increase economic production in Texas as it became the leading producer of oil in the U.S. In the 1940s, the Texas economy continued to grow as major corporations relocated to Texas providing more jobs.

Today, the Texas economy is still highly agricultural in nature and serves as the leading exporter of cattle and cotton in the U.S. High tech industries, defense contracting, telecommunications, biotechnology, oil, and tourism are also important economic activities in Texas. A large percentage of these products are exported to members of the North American Free Trade Agreement (NAFTA)—Mexico and Canada—and to the world markets. The Texas economy relies heavily on exports of goods and services. From 2002 through 2005, Texas was ranked as the number one state in terms of export revenues (BIDC 2006). Without its exports, the Texas economy could not sustain its growth. Because of the interdependence of state and global economies, political turmoil and economic problems in the world can have a direct impact on the Texas economy. For example, because part of the economy of Texas is based on petroleum, the decisions of OPEC have a direct impact on the state's economy. The Texas economy has weathered the most recent recession better than most states, but the unemployment rate have continued to climb in the state. In 2011, the jobless rate stood at almost 8.5%.

# Competency 032: Government and Citizenship

*The teacher understands and applies knowledge of concepts of government, democracy, and citizenship, including ways in which individuals and groups achieve their goals through political systems, as defined by the Texas Essential Knowledge and Skills (TEKS).*

## Forms of Government

Forms of government or political systems can be defined by the way nations govern themselves. The U.S. Department of State identifies 26 forms of governments in the world (CIA, n.d.). Some of the best-known forms of government listed are communism, socialism, democracy, monarchy, and oligarchy. A description of these types of government follows:

1. ***Communism*** is a system in which the state controls the economic activity in the nation. The state rejects free enterprise and capitalism; consequently, private ownership is discouraged and often prohibited. Usually the nation is ruled through a one-party system. In theory, communists believe that the country should not have social classes, as a way to avoid the oppressor–oppressed dichotomy that exists in the world.

2. ***Socialism*** is a system of government in which the central government controls the production and distribution of goods, services, and labor in the nation. The goal is to promote an equitable distribution of resources among the people. In theory, members of the working class should take over and administer collectively the resources for their benefit and the benefit of the nation as a whole.

3. ***Democracy*** is a form of government in which the majority rules. In practice, it becomes a representative democracy, in which the people elect candidates to represent them in the government.

4. ***Monarchy*** is a system in which a king or queen leads the nation. The monarch can have supreme powers and become dictator, or he/she can have limited or ceremonial powers limited by a parliament or a constitution.

5. ***Oligarchy*** is a type of government in which a small group of people controls the government. Generally, power rests with an elite class distinguished by royalty, wealth, family ties, commercial, and/or military legitimacy.

There are three main broad classifications for these forms of government based on the number of people in power—government by one person, a group, or by many people:

## Rule by One

In this form of government, one person becomes the supreme leader of the nation. Some of the terminology and concepts linked to this type of government are:

- **Autocracy:** Ruler has unlimited power, uses power in an arbitrary manner.

- **Monarchy:** Ruled by a king or queen who holds complete control over the subjects. Ruler sometimes claims birth and divine rights.

- **Dictatorship:** The ruler holds absolute power to make laws and to command the army.

### Ruled by a Few

In this system, a group of influential people takes control of the government. Traditionally, they appoint one of their own to function as the supreme leader of the government. Some examples of this type of government are:

- **Theocracy:** Ruled by a group of religious leaders, e.g., the Islamic Republic in Iran, or, the Taliban in Afghanistan.

- **Aristocracy:** A group of nobles controls the economy and the government.

- **Oligarchy:** A small group of powerful and wealthy people rule the nation with the support of the military.

- **Military:** A committee of military officers or a junta becomes the rulers of the nation.

### Rule by Many

In this type of government, the citizens of the nation, technically, become the government. In practice, the citizens elect members to represent them and become the government. Some examples of this type of government are:

- **Democracy**: The citizens of the nation directly or through elected members make important decisions, and become part of the government.

- **Constitutional Democracy**: It is a democratic form of government regulated by a constitution.

- **Parliamentarian Monarchy**: The monarch shares the power with the parliament. Often, the powers of the monarch are ceremonial in nature, like in Great Britain.

- **Federal Republic:** A constitutional government in which the powers of the central government are restricted to create semi-autonomous bodies (states or provinces) with certain degrees of self-governing powers, e.g., the United States.

## The American Government

The governmental system of the United States has been identified as a federal republic and constitutional representative democracy. It is a federal republic because the U.S. government is limited by law; in this case, the government is limited by the Constitution.

It is a constitutional representative democracy because the citizens elect senators and representatives to represent them in Congress. This combination is referred to as a Constitutional Republic in the revised social studies TEKS.

The American democratic system is based on popular sovereignty. *Popular sovereignty* grants citizens the ability to participate directly in their own government by voting and running for public office. This ideal is based on the notion that all citizens have equal rights to engage in their own governance. Certainly, over time, this notion of equal rights has expanded to include a respect for minority rights, including women and non-white citizens.

The American government is also based on majority rule. In public elections, the candidate who receives the most votes wins; in Congress, legislation is decided based on how the majority of the body votes. Majority rule ensures that authority cannot be concentrated in a small group of people. This majority rule system also shapes the two party system of the U.S. government. There are two major political parties in the U.S.: the Republican and Democratic parties.

## The U.S. Constitution

The Constitution is the supreme law of the nation. It contains a description of the government and the rights and responsibilities of its citizens. The document can be amended with the approval of two-thirds of the House and the Senate and the ratification of three-fourths of the individual state legislatures. Amendments to the U.S. Constitution have made it more democratic than the original document. The first ten amendments to the Constitution are known as the Bill of Rights.

The U.S. Constitution was based on four fundamental principles, which are listed below

1. *Federalism:* This is a system of in which government powers are divided between the national and state governments. This established four types of governmental powers: 1) delegated or expressed—those directly listed, 2) implied powers—those not stated directly, but suggested, 3) reserved powers—those not given to the national government but reserved for the people or for the states; and 4) concurrent powers—given to both national and state governments at the same time.

2. *Separation of Powers:* This constitutional principle is based on a system of checks and balances. The Constitutional writers wanted to protect their new nation from tyranny or the possibility of one branch of government becoming more powerful and influential than another. Thus, they created a three branch system and system of checks and balances.

3. ***Protection of individual rights and liberties:*** These provisions of the Constitution include: the prohibition of "ex post facto laws" or laws passed after the crime was commitment providing the penalty for an act that was not illegal at the time it was committed and "bills of attainder" or laws that give punishment to someone without a court trial first. Individual rights are protected through the "writ of habeas corpus" that required persons be released from jail if they had not been formally charged or convicted of a crime. The Bill of Rights also guarantees protection of individuals against federal action that would threaten their life, liberty, or property without proper legal proceedings.

4. ***Adaption to changing times and circumstances:*** This allows governing bodies to meet the needs of changing times through the process of amendments. The necessary and proper or elastic clause also provides Congress the power to make additional laws needed to implement other powers.

## Federalism: Power Sharing Between State and Federal Governments

One of the most significant principles of the U.S. Constitution is the concept of power sharing between the federal and state governments. Some of the powers reserved to the federal and state governments follow.

### Powers Reserved for the Federal Government

- Regulate interstate and foreign commerce
- Print money and regulate its value
- Establish the laws for regulation of immigration and naturalization
- Regulate admission of new states
- Declare war and ratify peace treaties
- Establish a system of weights and measures
- Raise and maintain armed forces
- Conduct relations with foreign nations

### Powers Reserved for State Governments

- Conduct and monitor local, state, and federal elections
- Provide for local government
- Ratify proposed amendments to the Constitution

- Regulate intrastate commerce

- Provide education for its citizens

- Establish direct taxes like sales and state taxes

- Regulate and maintain police power over public health and safety

- Maintain control of state borders

## Concurrent Powers of Federal and State Governments

- Both may tax

- Both may borrow money

- Both may charter banks and corporations

- Both may establish courts

- Both may make and enforce laws

- Both may take property for public purposes

- Both may spend money to provide for public welfare

In addition to the powers reserved to the states, the Tenth Amendment of the U.S. Constitution provides additional powers to the state. In this amendment, the powers not specifically delegated to the federal government are reserved for the states.

## Separation of Powers: Branches of Government

The U.S. Constitution set up a federal system of government, dividing up power between the state and national governments. The national government is further balanced through the three branches of government that provide checks and balances on each other's power. The three branches of government are the executive, legislative, and judicial branches. Each of the branches is described in more detail below.

### Executive Branch

The executive branch of the U.S. government is composed of a president and a vice president elected every four years by electoral votes. The President can be elected for a maximum of two terms. The president is the commander-in-chief of the armed forces. He or she appoints cabinet members, nominates judges to the federal court system, grants pardons, recommends legislation, and has the power to veto legislation. The President also appoints American representatives to carry out diplomatic relations in foreign lands and to serve in international organizations. The President also performs a variety of ceremonial duties.

### Legislative Branch

The legislative branch is composed of the Congress, which is bicameral, or divided in two parts— the Senate and the House of Representatives. The Senate is composed of two senators from each state for a total of a 100 members. Senators are elected for 6 year terms. The composition of the House is based on the population of people in each state for a total of 435 members who each serve two year terms. The Congress makes the laws of the nation, collects taxes, coins money and regulates its value, can declare war, controls appropriations, can impeach public officials, regulates the jurisdictions of federal courts, and can override presidential vetoes. The Vice President presides over the senate as its leader, while the Speaker of the House serves as the leader of the House of Representatives.

### Judicial Branch

The judicial branch is composed of a federal court system that includes the Supreme Court and a system of lower courts—district courts, appeals courts, bankruptcy courts, and special federal courts. Federal judges are nominated by the president of the United States and confirmed by the Senate. All federal judges are appointed for life. The Supreme Court is composed of nine judges, and their ruling is considered final. Under a process called "judicial review" (set forth in *Marbury v. Madison*, 1803), the Supreme Court has the power to declare unconstitutional any executive orders or legislative acts of both the federal and state governments. Some of the major responsibilities of this body are to interpret the Constitution, resolve conflicts among states, and interpret laws and treaties.

## System of Checks and Balances

The U.S. Constitution provides for a system of checks and balances among the three branches of the government. In this type of system, individual branches check the others to be sure that no one assumes full control of the central government. The legislative branch can check the executive branch by passing laws over presidential veto (by a two-thirds majority in both houses). This branch exerts control over the judicial branch by having to confirm the president's judicial appointments. The executive can check the legislative branch by the use of the veto and the judicial branch by appointing federal judges. The judicial branch can check the other two branches through the process of judicial review, which can declare legislation unconstitutional or illegal.

## Protection of Individual Rights and Liberties: The Bill of Rights

After the U.S. Constitution was enacted in 1783, the founders felt that additional measures were necessary to preserve basic human rights. The first ten amendments to the U.S. Constitution came to be the Bill of Rights. A summary of the first ten amendments follows:

- *First Amendment*—separation of church and state; freedom of religion, speech and press; and the right to peaceful assembly

- *Second Amendment*—right to keep and bear arms

- *Third Amendment*—makes it illegal to force people to offer quarters to soldiers in time of peace

- *Fourth Amendment*—rights to privacy and unreasonable searches or seizures

- *Fifth Amendment*—rights of due process, protection against self-incrimination, and protection from being indicted for the same crime twice (double jeopardy)

- *Sixth Amendment*—rights to speedy public trial by an impartial jury and to counsel for one's defense

- *Seventh Amendment*—right to sue people

- *Eighth Amendment*—protection against cruel and unusual punishment

- *Ninth Amendment*—enumeration of specific rights in the Constitution cannot be taken as a way to deny other rights retained by the people

- *Tenth Amendment*—rights not delegated to the federal government by the Constitution are reserved to the states or to the people

## Adapting to Change: The Amendment Process

When the Constitution was written, the writers knew their creation was not perfect. They knew that new ideas and changes would need to be considered. They wanted to make it possible to change the Constitution in a thoughtful and democratic process. Thus, the Constitution provides for an amendment process. An amendment to the Constitution is a change that can add to the Constitution or change an older part of it. An amendment can even overturn a previous amendment, as the Twenty-first did the Eighteenth. There are a few methods to amend the Constitution, but the most common is to pass an amendment through the Congress, on a two-thirds vote. After that, the amendment goes to the states, and if three-quarters of the state legislatures pass the amendment, it is considered a part of the Constitution and has been ratified. To date there are 27 amendments to the Constitution, the first 10 comprise the Bill of Rights.

## Landmark Supreme Court Cases

### Judicial Review Process—Marbury v. Madison (1803)

A dispute that occurred as the Thomas Jefferson administration came into power fundamentally altered the system of checks and balances of the American government. In this case, the judicial branch confirmed its power to review and assess the constitutionality of the legislation passed by Congress and signed by the president. This process is now called the judicial review.

### National Supremacy—McCulloch v. Maryland (1819)

A dispute occurred between the Bank of the United States and the State of Maryland. In 1819, the U.S. still had a federal bank, the Bank of the United States. The State of Maryland voted to tax all bank business not done with state banks. This was meant to be a tax on people who lived in Maryland but who did business with banks in other states and with the federal bank. Andrew McCulloch, who works in the Baltimore branch of the Bank of the United States, refused to pay the tax. The State of Maryland sued, and the Supreme Court accepted the case. Chief Justice Marshall wrote in his briefing, that the federal government did indeed have the right and power to set up the federal bank. He wrote that the state did not have the power to tax the federal government. Although the Bank of the United States would die out, the process of judicial review continued.

### Federal Regulation of Commerce—Gibbons v. Ogden (1824)

The New York Legislature in 1808 granted Robert Livingston and Robert Fulton a twenty-year monopoly to operate steamboats in New York waters. In 1811, Fulton in turn granted Aaron Ogden a license to operate steamboats between New York and New Jersey. In 1818, the U. S. Congress, using the power given it by the commerce clause of Article I, Section 8 of the Constitution, granted Thomas Gibbons a license to engage in the coastal trade and operate steamboats between New York and New Jersey. Claiming that his monopoly rights were being violated, Ogden obtained an injunction from a New York court forbidding Gibbons from continuing to operate his steamboats in these waters. After obtaining the services of Daniel Webster as his lawyer, Gibbons appealed to the U. S. Supreme Court. The majority opinion, written by Marshall, said that the U.S. Constitution had a commerce clause that allowed the federal government to regulate commerce, in this case trade, wherever it might be, including within the borders of a state. Previously, it was thought that the federal government had power over only *interstate commerce*. However, Marshall's opinion said that the commerce clause applied here, too. Thus, the Supreme Court extended the definition of interstate commerce and cemented the power of the federal government over the states when laws conflicted.

### Federal vs. States Rights in Indian Affairs—Worcester v. Georgia (1832)

In December 1829, President Andrew Jackson announced his Indian removal proposal in an address to the U.S. Congress. In 1830, the Congress passed the Indian Removal Act, which authorized the President to grant the Indians unsettled lands west of the Mississippi River in exchange for Indian lands within existing state borders. The Georgia Legislature meanwhile had passed a law requiring anyone other than Cherokees who lived on Indian territory to obtain a license from the state. Samuel Worcester and several other non-Cherokee Congregational missionaries settled and established a mission on Cherokee land at the request of the Cherokees and with permission of the United States government. The state of Georgia charged them with residing within the limits of the Cherokee nation without a license. They were tried, convicted, and sentenced to four years of hard labor. Worcester and the other missionaries appealed their convictions to the U.S. Supreme Court. The Supreme Court ruled in favor of Worcester and the Cherokees arguing that the Cherokee nation was a "distinct community" with self-government "in which the laws of Georgia can have no force." It established the doctrine that the national government of the United States, and not individual states, had authority in American Indian affairs.

### Slavery/Due Process—Dred Scott v. Sandford (1857)

Dred Scott, a slave in Virginia, was moved by his owner to Illinois, a non-slave (free) state. In 1836, they moved to Minnesota, which was part of the non-slave Wisconsin territory, before being moved to Missouri. Then, Dred Scott sued his owners, claiming that he was no longer a slave because he had become free when he lived in a free state. The jury decided that Scott and his family should be free. His owners did not like the decision and appealed to the Missouri Supreme Court in 1852. That court said that Missouri does not have to follow the laws of another state. As a slave state, Missouri's laws meant that Scott and his family were not free. Scott finally took his case to the U.S. Supreme Court who ruled that Scott and all other slaves were not state or U.S. citizens and thus had no rights. A slave was considered property, not a person or a citizen. Thus, Scott or other slave had no right to sue in state or federal court. Further, the court ruled that the federal government had no legal right to interfere with the institution of slavery.

### Separate But Equal—Plessy v. Ferguson (1896)

In 1890, Louisiana passed a law called the Separate Car Act. This law said that railroad companies must provide separate but equal train cars for whites and blacks. Two parties wanted to challenge the constitutionality of the Separate Car Act. A group of black citizens who raised money to overturn the law worked together with the East Louisiana Railroad Company, which sought to terminate the Act largely for monetary reasons. They chose a 30-year-old shoemaker named Homer Plessy, a citizen of the United States who was one-eighth black and a resident of the state of Louisiana. On June 7, 1892, Plessy purchased a first-class passage from New Orleans to Covington, Louisiana, and sat in the railroad car for "White" passengers. The railroad officials knew Plessy was coming and arrested him for violating the Separate Car Act. Plessy argued in court that the Separate Car Act violated the Thirteenth and Fourteenth Amendments to the Constitution. The Thirteenth Amendment banned slavery and the Fourteenth Amendment requires that the government treat people equally. After both a lower level court and the Supreme Court of Louisiana found Plessy guilty, he took his case to the Supreme Court of the United States. The U.S. Supreme court upheld the decisions of the two lower courts, arguing that separate but equal practices were constitutional. This decision legitimized the move towards segregation practices begun earlier in the South and provided an impetus for further segregation laws.

### Desegregation—Brown v. Board of Education of Topeka (1954)

In the early 1950s, many students went to different schools because of their race. Many other public facilities were also segregated. Segregation was legal because of the Plessy v. Ferguson case. Under segregation, all-white and all-black schools sometimes had similar buildings, buses, and teachers. Sometimes, the buildings, busses, and teachers for the all-black schools were lower in quality. Often, black children had to travel far to get to their school. In Topeka, Kansas, a black student named Linda Brown had to walk through a dangerous railroad switching station to get to her all-black school. Her family believed that segregated schools should be illegal. The Brown family sued the school system (Board of Education of Topeka). After losing their cases in two lower courts, the Browns took their case to the U.S. Supreme Court, who unanimously ruled that "separate educational facilities are inherently unequal." This case paved the way for integration and the civil rights movement.

## Local and State Governments

Most states in the United States follow the type of government established in the U.S. Constitution. State governments generally have three branches—executive, legislative, and judicial. The main difference is that the executive branch is led by a governor and the judicial branch is composed of a state court system subordinate to the federal court system. The city government is generally headed by a mayor or city manager with the support of a city council.

## Citizenship in the U.S.

Citizenship is membership in a political state such as a country or state. Citizenship allows the right to participate politically in a society. Anyone born in the United States is a U.S citizen, regardless of the nationality or citizenship of his or her parents. Additionally, children who are born on foreign soil, but whose parents are U.S. citizens are also considered citizens of the United States.

Citizenship in the U.S provides individuals with certain rights, including the right to life, liberty, and the pursuit of property. Along with rights, however, come specific responsibilities. In the U.S., citizens have the right to vote at the age of 18. With this right comes the responsibility to be an informed voter who makes wise decisions. Citizens of the U.S. are also eligible to run for public office. With this right comes the responsibility of representing one's constituents as well as possible. The right to free speech is also given to citizens of the U.S. This means that citizens also have the responsibility to allow others to speak freely. Additionally, the U.S. Constitution guarantees freedom of religion. This means that citizens have both the right to choose their religious affiliation and the responsibility to allow others to practice their religion. Being a good citizen means exercising one's own rights, meeting one's responsibilities, and allowing others to do the same.

Citizenship rights and responsibilities in Texas and the U.S include obeying state, local and national laws, to pay taxes, and vote in elections. Good citizens should also develop a respect that recognizes and values the feelings, interests, beliefs, and values of others. While citizenship involves being respectful of one another and obeying the laws of the land, it does not mean that we need to teach students to simply comply and conform. Dissent is an important part in any governmental system and provides necessary checks and balances on governmental authority. Dissent may be expressed in a number of ways including voting, protesting, writing to one's legislator, etc. Certainly there are some forms of dissent that are more socially and politically acceptable.

The development of civic ideas and practices is a lifelong process that begins in school by observing patriotic holidays, learning about the contribution of historical characters, and pledging allegiance to the American and Texas flags each day. Civic education and the principles of democracy are infused through active participation in community activities. To promote civic responsibility, students can get involved in discussions about issues that affect the community. Teachers guide students to suggest possible solutions to community problems, while students are guided to listen and analyze contributions.

Through this exchange, students are guided to practice principles of democracy and to value individual contributions to solve community problems.

Children in these grade levels should be developing civic responsibility. Teachers can promote this sense of responsibility by involving students in real-life situations in which they take civic responsibility. For example, teachers can make children aware of how producing trash can affect the environment. As part of this process, students can be guided to examine the amount of trash that they produce daily and explore ways to reduce it. Promoting a sense of responsibility to the well-being of everyone constitutes the main principle for developing responsible citizenship.

## American Symbols

### American Patriotic Symbols

Patriotic symbols are visible signs of national pride. The U.S. National Flag, the Pledge of Allegiance, the Statue of Liberty, the Liberty Bell, and the White House are important examples of patriotic symbols for Americans.

***The United States of America National Flag*** has 50 stars representing the 50 states of the Union. The color red represents hardiness and valor, the white symbolizes purity and innocence, and the blue symbolizes vigilance, perseverance, and justice. The Congress approved a new flag with 13 red and white alternating horizontal stripes and 13 stars representing the original colonies in 1777. A star and stripe were added to the flag each time a state entered the union. The Congress set the number of stripes at thirteen in 1818 and approved to continue to add a star for each new state.

***The Pledge of Allegiance*** is a declaration of patriotism. It was first published in 1892 in *The Youth's Companion* and was believed to be written by the magazine's editor, Francis Bellamy. The original purpose was for the pledge was to be used by school children in activities to celebrate the 400th anniversary of the discovery of America. The Pledge was widely used in morning school routines for many years and received official recognition by Congress on 1942. The phrase "under God" was added in 1954 with a law indicating the proper behavior to adopt when reciting the pledge, which includes standing straight, removing hats or any other headgear, and placing the right hand over the heart.

***The Star-Spangled Banner*** is the national anthem of the United States. It was originally a poem written by Francis Scott Key during the Battle of Baltimore in the War of 1812 against the British. In 1931, it was made the official national anthem of the United States.

*The Statue of Liberty* was a gift of friendship from the people of France to the people of the United States commemorating the United States' 100th anniversary. It is a universal symbol of freedom, democracy, and international friendship.

*The Liberty Bell* is a symbol of freedom and liberty. The Pennsylvania Assembly ordered the Liberty Bell to commemorate the 50th anniversary of Pennsylvania's original constitution, the William Penn's Charter of Privileges. It is traditionally believed that it was rung to summon the people of Philadelphia to hear the Declaration of Independence. It became an icon when the abolitionists adopted it as a symbol of freedom. The abolitionists changed its name from The State House Bell to the Liberty Bell.

*The White House* was originally planned by President George Washington in 1791 and was completed in 1800 when its first resident, President John Adams, moved in with his wife, Abigail. It was originally called the President's House. President Theodore Roosevelt christened it with the name The White House in 1901. For over 200 years, it has been the home of U.S. presidents and their families. It is recognized as a symbol of the Presidency of the United States throughout the world.

*Great Seal of the United States* consists of a bald eagle holding an olive branch and a bundle of arrows. The olive branch represents peace and the arrows represent military strength. The eagle holds a scroll in its beak with the nation's motto: "E Pluribus Unum" which means "Out of many, one."

For additional information about symbols of the United States, go to *http://www.ushistory.org*, a website created and hosted by the Independence Hall Association in Philadelphia.

## Competency 033 Culture; Science, Technology and Society

*The teacher understands and applies knowledge of cultural development, adaptation and diversity and understands and applies knowledge of interactions among science, technology and society, as defined by the Texas Essential Knowledge and Skills (TEKS).*

### The Role of Families in Meeting Basic Human Needs

While all young people need food, clothing, and shelter, families may have different ways of meeting these needs. Cultural, religious, and familiar traditions may influences families' preferences and choices in meeting basic needs.

## How Families and Cultures Develop and Use Customs, Traditions and Beliefs to Define Themselves

Educators should give students and families opportunities to share and express their culture throughout the social studies curriculum. Parents are children's first and constant teachers. Educators must realize that a student's cultural or religious beliefs could at time be incompatible with school activities and thus, students may opt not to participate in certain school events. Teachers should help students feel positively about their cultural differences. Family values and culture fuel children's self-esteem, identity, and pride surrounding who they are and who they aspire to become as educated adults. Schools should make space for students' cultural heritages to be respected, valued, and incorporated into their education.

## Knowledge of Institutions that Exist in All Societies and How Characteristics of These Institutions May Vary among Societies

Gay (2000) defines culturally responsive teaching as using the cultural knowledge, prior experiences, and performance styles of diverse students to make learning more appropriate and effective for them; it teaches to and through the strengths of these students. All societies have norms, rules, and laws; however, these may differ from one society to the next.

## People's Use of Oral Tradition, Stories, Real and Mythical Heroes, Music, Paintings and Sculpture to Create and Represent Culture in Communities

Stories, art, and music help people express and share culture. While some mythic archetypes exist across cultures, such as the hero's journey, the trickster, the quest, and creation stories, cultural aspects of stories vary from one culture to the next.

### In Texas

Texas has unique cultural traditions and celebrations such as Juneteenth. Juneteenth is uniquely Texan, representing the oldest celebration commemorating the end of U.S. slavery. On June 19, 1865, two and a half years after Lincoln's *Emancipation Proclamation*, Major General Gordon Granger landed in Galveston, Texas, and announced, "The people of Texas are informed that in accordance with a Proclamation from the Executive of the United States, all slaves are free."

### In the United States

Thanksgiving, Memorial Day, and Independence Day on the Fourth of July are holidays unique to the U.S. We have localized myths and folktales from various American

Indian tales to frontier folklore such as Paul Bunyan and Babe the Blue Ox. In addition to mythical heroes, all cultures, including the U.S., have real heroes of cultural expression. The Harlem Renaissance represents a uniquely U.S. convergence of cultural expression with many real-life cultural leaders and heroes.

### In The World

Cultural stories exist in any culture. Humans tell stories as part of cultural expression. *Beowulf, The Odyssey, The Aeneid, El Cid, Paradise Lost, Mahābhārata, Metamorphoses,* and *Epic of Gilgamesh* represent cultural stories from differing languages and origins that are still valued today.

## Relationships among World Cultures and Relationships between and among People from Various Groups, Including Racial, Ethnic and Religious Groups

According to the National Council for the Social Studies' *Curriculum Guidelines for Multicultural Education*, "A democratic society protects and provides opportunities for ethnic and cultural diversity at the same time having overarching values—such as equality, justice, and human dignity—that all groups accept and respect." (Banks, J. A., 2011)

## Relationships among Religion, Philosophy, and Culture & the Impact of Religion on Ways of Life in the United States and World Areas

While the Harlem Renaissance is perhaps best known for its artistic and religious movements, Harlem also had significant political movements at this same time period. Marcus Garvey, who ascribed to a Black Nationalist philosophy, founded the Universal Negro Improvement Association and was a proponent of a black migration back to Africa. He also founded African Orthodox Church. While Garvey advocated for separation, W.E.B. Du Bois favored integration. Du Bois was the leading African American politician and philosopher during the Harlem Renaissance. James Weldon Johnson was the first appointed African American officer in the NAACP. Louis Armstrong and Duke Ellington were noted musicians during this period.

## Concept of Diversity within Unity

"E Pluribus Unum" means "one from many." In 1776, John Adams, Benjamin Franklin, and Thomas Jefferson proposed this Latin saying as the motto to be printed on the first Great Seal of the United States. While the original intent involved a single unified nation from many states, the motto stands the test of time and still affirms U.S. identity. James Banks (2001) and several co-authors, published a document entitled, *Diversity within Unity Essential Principles for Teaching and Learning in a Multicultural Society* centered around 12 principles aligned to five key areas: (1) teacher learning; (2) student learning; (3) intergroup relations; (4) school governance, organization, and equity; and (5) assessment.

The concept of diversity within unity values that our cultural differences makes society stronger. We achieve unity through civic ideals and practices and an acknowledged commitment to the greater good. As citizens of the U.S., we share in common challenges and collective joys of our nation, bound by both geographic union and shared American identity, not by any such law that would impose a forced unity. Americans uphold and affirm citizens' rights to decent lives and publicly speak against policy via peaceful protest. In part, it is our affirmation and respect of differences that hold us in our unity.

## Effects of Scientific Discoveries and Technological Innovations

### In Texas

Some Texas leaders in science and technology include:

- *Walter Cunningham*—NASA's second civilian astronaut, fighter pilot, retired military physicist

- *Michael DeBakey*—Surgeon who helped develop innovative treatments in heart and vascular surgery

- *Denton Cooley*—Native Houstonian known for heart surgery and transplants, as well as adept surgical work with children

- *Benjy Brooks*—Native Texan and the first female pediatric surgeon in Texas. She conducted research on congenital defects, burn treatment, spleen reparation, and the prevention of hepatitis. A foundation set up in her name has advanced the surgical care of young children in Texas.

- *Michael Dell*—Founder of Dell Computer Corporation. He is a native Houstonian known for technology, business, and philanthropy.

- *Howard Hughes Sr.*—Designer of a drill bit that could drill through hard rock. Previously, oil drillers could not reach large pockets of oil lying beneath hard rock. He co-founded the Sharp-Hughes Tool Company, which held the patent for the new drill bit, manufactured the bit, and leased the bit to oil companies.

## Major Scientific, Mathematical, and Technological Discoveries throughout History

- *Archimedes*—One of the greatest mathematicians and scientists; worked in hydrostatics, static mechanics, the measurement of the volume or density; calculus

- *Copernicus*—Mathematician and astronomer; discovered that the earth revolved around the sun, which was stationary in the center of the universe; created a conceptualization of our universe as a place where the distances of the planets from the sun had direct relationship to the size of their orbits; often considered to be the initiator of the Scientific Revolution.

- *Eratosthenes*—A mathematician who worked on prime numbers and measuring the diameter of the earth

- *Galileo*—Scientist who formulated basic laws of falling bodies; constructed a telescope to study lunar craters; discovered four of Jupiter's moons

- *Pythagoras*—Philosopher and mathematician; contributed to math systems; however, none of his writings are known, so his contributions are not distinctly defined

- *Robert Boyle*—Chemist and philosopher; worked toward establishing chemistry as based on a mechanistic theory of matter

- *Marie Curie*—Scientist who discovered the radioactive elements polonium and radium; first person awarded two Nobel prizes. Her work influenced the development of medical research and treatment

- *Thomas Edison*—Scientist and inventor, most famous for developing the incandescent light bulb

- *Albert Einstein*—Physicist who heavily contributed to the modern vision of physics including his general theories of relativity.

- *Robert Fulton*—Artist, engineer, and inventor who made the steam boat designs viable and put this mode of transportation into actual practice

- *Sir Isaac Newton*—Philosopher, scientific theorist, and inventor of the infinitesimal calculus and a new theory of light and color. He transformed physical science through conceiving the three laws of motion and the law of universal gravitation

- *Louis Pasteur*—Biologist, chemist, and humanitarian, known for germ and immunization theories; he uncovered origins of rabies, anthrax, chicken cholera, and silkworm diseases; contributed to the development of the first vaccines; he described the scientific basis for fermentation

- *James Watt*—Engineer and inventor known for improvements made to Newcomen's atmospheric engine, which turned steam into the major power source of the Industrial Revolution

## Competency 034 Social Studies Foundations and Skills

*The teacher understands the foundations of social studies education and applies knowledge of skills used in the social sciences.*

### Social Studies Inquiry

Research in social studies involves the use of systematic inquiry. Engaging students in inquiry involves the ability to acquire information from various resources. Inquiry involves the ability to design and conduct investigations, which requires students to develop an understanding of key information in social studies content. To gather content information, students should become familiar with the various resources used in social sciences research. Those resources include primary and secondary sources, encyclopedias, almanacs, atlases, government documents, artifacts, and oral histories. Students need to apply critical-thinking skills to organize and use information acquired from a variety of sources including electronic technology.

Information about social studies is available from the Internet; however, students need to evaluate the scholarship of the many sources available and use only those known to be reliable. Teachers should equip middle grade social studies students to think, research, and communicate like historians, sociologists, geographers, and other social studies processionals do. Inquiry is the mechanism to achieve professional-level social studies skills.

### The Problem-Solving Process

Just like scientists, social scientists utilize the basics of the scientific method. Educators should guide students to:

1. identify a social science problem.

2. formulate research questions and hypotheses.

3. gather and analyze information.

4. raise discipline-appropriate question, identify possible positive and negative consequences.

5. test and report findings.

## Professionally Modeled Thinking

When studying history, an educator should guide students to think like historians. Likewise, when studying geography or culture, the teacher will prompt students to work like geographers and anthropologists. This approach builds core social studies skills while simultaneously preparing students with college and career readiness skills. Professionals who work in the field of social studies do not rely on memory skills alone, nor should students in the middle grades. Professionally modeled thinking involves leading students through the interrogation of primary and supporting secondary sources to test hypothesis. Often, students may come away with more questions than they started with in their initial hypotheses, which is natural for this type of educational experience. Professionally modeled thinking prompts students to be critical consumers of information and it empowers them to think critically about the social worlds around them. Students acquire life-long learning skills through classroom activities that foreground professionally modeled thinking.

## How Social Science Disciplines Relate to Each Other

Social studies is an umbrella term used to encompass the disciplines of history, geography, civics and government, economics, and psychology. All five components are intertwined with the standards or strands developed by the National Council for the Teaching of Social Studies in 1997 (NCTSS, 2006). The Texas Education Agency (TEA) used these strands and curriculum standards as a foundation to develop the state social studies curriculum for kindergarten through grade 12. In many ways, social studies is a hub at the center of all other disciplines. Social studies brings together reading, writing, and other linguistic processing skills with mathematical reading and thinking skills as students read and interpret maps, charts, and other social science data immersed in both linguistic and numerical data. Social studies subjects also relate to students' everyday life interactions with all subject areas. For example, when students encounter chemistry and health in the real world, it often takes laboratory science to the everyday social setting of the breakfast table where nutritional charts inform them about their own eating choices and where digestion becomes an internal body chemistry validation of what they read. When teachers overtly connect all the other disciplines linked to students' everyday worlds through their study of the social studies, then students begin to understand the applicability of the entire curriculum through the study of their own and others' social lives. Social studies can become the real-world connection hub for all other disciplines.

## Relates Philosophical Assumptions and Ideas to Issues and Trends in the Social Sciences

Core philosophical assumptions align with various historical and social traditions. For example, the Enlightenment pulls ideas from Jefferson, Locke, and Rousseau. The scientific revolution relies on ideas from Copernicus (Ptolemaic Astronomy; Earth's revolution around the sun), Galileo (refracting telescope, objects of various weights descend at the same rate), and Newton (universal gravitation, calculus, laws of motion). Political science origins relay on Aristotle, Plato, and Aquinas. Machiavelli and Hobbes contribute to ideas of power. Historical and philosophical trends go hand-and-hand. Students begin to understand the works of philosophers like Heidegger and Arendt more fully when they can process the information within the historical backdrop of that period in time.

In part, people think about philosophy as they do because of what is going on in the world around them. In powerful and transformative social studies classrooms, educators help students to explore and make sense of how social theory, philosophical development, and history intermingle and influence one another. Students can then apply the continuity of historical and philosophical ideas to the worlds of today and tomorrow.

## Sources of Information

Teachers should use various primary and secondary sources (e.g., databases, maps, photographs, media services, the Internet, biographies, interviews, questionnaires, artifacts, works of historical fiction, interviews, etc.) and information from a variety of sources to acquire social science information and answer social science questions. Students and teachers must evaluate the validity of social science information from primary and secondary sources regarding bias issues, propaganda, point-of-view, and frame of reference.

Educators should help students to formulate social studies research questions and use appropriate procedures to reach supportable judgments and conclusions in the social sciences, as well as analyze social science information (e.g., by categorizing, comparing and contrasting, making generalizations and predictions, drawing inferences and conclusions). Students should be able to pull together, synthesize, apply, and evaluate modern-day Internet resources, alongside historical sources. Teachers should always consider students' everyday worlds as sources or comparative sources to help make the study of social studies meaningful to students' lives. Likewise, educators should include familial and local oral histories and other historical and cultural documents and artifacts that make students' immediate geographies and histories relevant to the majority of the social studies curriculum.

See the National Archives (*www.archives.gov*) for more information on locating primary sources and lesson ideas related to social studies.

# Competency 035 Social Studies Instruction and Assessment

*The teacher plans and implements effective instruction and assessment in social studies.*

The teacher should plan and implement effective instruction and assessment in social studies, aligned to state content and performance standards for social studies that comprise the Texas Essential Knowledge and Skills (TEKS). Additionally, educators must understands the vertical alignment of the social sciences in the TEKS from grade level to grade level, including prerequisite knowledge and skills. Educators should account for the implications of stages of child growth and development for designing and implementing effective learning experiences in the social sciences and understand the appropriate use of technology as a tool for learning and communicating social studies concepts.

Educators should select and use effective instructional practices, activities, technologies and materials to promote students' knowledge and skills in the social sciences in order to promote students' use of social science skills, vocabulary and research tools, including technological tools. Prepared educators know how to communicate the value of social studies education to students, parents/caregivers, colleagues, and the community and how to provide instruction that relates skills, concepts, and ideas in different social science disciplines.

Optimally, educators should provide instruction that makes connections between knowledge and methods in the social sciences and in other content areas. Teachers will demonstrate knowledge of forms of assessment appropriate for evaluating students' progress and needs in the social science and use multiple forms of assessment and knowledge of the TEKS to determine students' progress and needs and to help plan instruction that addresses the strengths, needs, and interests of all students, including English-language learners.

## Texas Essential Knowledge and Skills (TEKS) in Social Studies

The Texas Essential Knowledge and Skills is the state curriculum for kindergarten to grade 12. The TEKS organizes the social studies content inductively, from the known to the unknown. In this vertical alignment, children begin learning about the self in kindergarten and expand their knowledge with each successive grade, eventually encompassing the community, the state, the nation, and the world.

### Grades 4 & 7 Focus—History of Texas

- History of Texas from its beginning to the present

- Events and individuals of the nineteenth and twentieth centuries

- Human activity and physical features of regions in Texas and the Western Hemisphere

- Native Americans in Texas and the Western Hemisphere

- European exploration and colonization

- Types of Native American governments

- Characteristics of Spanish and Mexican colonial governments

### Grade 5 & 8 Focus—United States History

- History of the United States from its early beginnings to the present

- Major events and significant individuals of the late 19th and 20th centuries including contributions of famous inventors and scientists

- Regions of the United States that result from physical features and human activity

- Characteristics and benefits of the free enterprise system

- Roots of representative government

- Important ideas in the Declaration of Independence

- Meaning of the Pledge of Allegiance

- Fundamental rights guaranteed in the Bill of Rights

- Customs and celebrations of various racial, ethnic, and religious groups in the nation

### Grade 6—People and Places of the Contemporary World

- People and places of the contemporary world

- Societies from the following regions in the world: Europe, Russia and the Eurasian republics, North America, Middle America, South America, Southwest Asia-North Africa, Sub-Saharan Africa, South Asia, East Asia, Southeast Asia, Australia, and the Pacific Realm

- Influence of individuals and groups from various cultures on selected historical and contemporary events

## Different Ways of Organizing Economic and Governmental Systems

### Using Maps and Globes

Symbolic representation can pose challenges for students through grade 4, and even students in grades 5 and 6. Maps and globes are tools for representing space symbolically. In the early grades, the main purpose for using globes is to familiarize children with the basic roundness of the Earth and to begin developing a global perspective. It can also be used to study the proportion of land and water. In grades 4 through 6, students can use a 16-inch globe containing additional details. Generally, seven colors are used to represent land elevation and three colors to represent water depth.

### Activities for Students in Grades 4–8

Teaching map concepts in grade 4 should include the following activities:

- Stress that the globe is a very small representation of the Earth.

- Show children how land areas and water bodies are represented on the globe.

- Identify major land and water bodies.

- Show the location of the North Pole and the concept of the Northern Hemisphere, where most of the world's land is located.

- Show the location of the South Pole and the concept of the Southern Hemisphere, where most of the world's water is located.

- Show the relationship and location of the Earth in the solar system.

- Use the globe to find the continent, the country, the state, and the city where the children live.

- Encourage children to explore the globe to find places by themselves.

- Compare the size of the continents represented on a globe with their representation on a Mercator projection—the flat representation.

Teaching map concepts in grades 5 and 6 should include the following activities:

- Create and interpret maps.

- Use maps and globes to pose and answer questions.

- Locate major historical and contemporary societies on maps and globes.

- Use maps to solve real-life problems, i.e., using road maps to plan a route to a specific destination.

### Latitude and Longitude—Developmental Considerations

The concepts of latitude and longitude are generally covered in grade 4 and up. However, these students may have difficulty understanding the mathematics involved in the grid system. Children might get confused with these concepts:

- The sizes of the meridians of longitude and the parallels of latitude on a globe and Mercator projection look different.

- The meridians of longitude have a consistent size, but the parallels of latitude vary in size, becoming smaller as they move away from the equator.

### Using Technology Information in Social Studies

Research in social studies involves the use of systematic inquiry. Engaging children in inquiry involves the ability to acquire information from various resources. Inquiry involves the ability to design and conduct investigations, which requires students to develop an understanding of key information in social studies content.

Information about social studies is available from the Internet; however, students need to evaluate the scholarship of the many sources available and use only those known to be reliable. In addition to sources available electronically, students can use commercially developed programs. These kinds of interactive programs can expose students to problem-solving skills and social studies content in a fun and supportive environment.

### Integration of Social Studies

As mentioned earlier, the teaching of social studies by definition implies integration of content from five disciplines: history, geography, civics and government, economics, and psychology. However, teachers can go beyond this integration and add components from other content areas. The use of a literature-based approach is an ideal way to integrate social studies with language arts. Using authentic multicultural literature, teachers can expose children to quality reading and the cultures of the many ethnic and linguistic groups living in the United States.

The use of thematic units can also help teachers to integrate the content areas. In this approach, a teacher or teachers select a theme and organize content area instruction around it. Thematic instruction can be done in a self-contained classroom or in a departmental format in which several teachers teach the content.

Thematic instruction is ideal for English language learners (ELLs) because the use of a common theme in multiple content areas makes content more cognitively accessible for them. For example, in a unit on the *solar system*, the names of the planets and the terminology used to describe the system can be introduced and repeated in several subjects through the duration of the unit. The presentation and repetition of content in different subjects and conditions allow students the opportunity to develop English vocabulary while learning content.

## Graphic Representations of Historical Information

Information in social studies can be presented in a visual form with graphs and charts to make content accessible to all children, including ELLs.

### Graphs

The most commonly used graphs are the pictorial graph, the bar graph, the pie or circle graph, and the line graph. The pictorial graph is the most concrete type of graph because it uses a picture of the object being represented. Bar graphs are more concrete than pie graphs. Although the pie graph appears to be simple, students need to understand the concept of percentages to interpret correctly the meaning of this type of graph, and the concept of percentages is not acquired until late in the elementary grades.

Teachers can use more sophisticated graphs like the pie to represent research information. For example, children can take 5 to 10 minutes a day to observe the types of transportation used by people in the neighborhood. Teachers can use this information to guide children to make inferences about the information contained in the graph. Why are so many people using pickup trucks as a mode of transportation? Why are only a small number of people walking?

### Charts

Charts can be used to record information and present ideas in a concise way. Charts are ideal for promoting concept formation in a concrete fashion. **Data retrieval charts** are used to gather and keep track of data gathered from research, observation, or experimentation. The chart is constructed to allow the easy comparison of two or more sets of data. **Narrative charts** are used to show events in a sequence. For example, students can develop charts showing the steps in making their favorite dishes. A narrative chart can also be used to present a time line of historical events. An example of a simple time line is one that shows a child's personal history. A **flowchart** shows a process involving changes at certain points.

## Addressing the Needs of English Language Learners

English language learners can find social studies instruction quite challenging; thus, teachers need to modify instruction to make the content comprehensible for this group. Some textbooks have been written with ELLs in mind. These books use numerous visual and graphic representations to make the content cognitively accessible to children learning English. For example, *Adventure Tales of America*, written by Jody Potts (1994), is an American history book that uses cartoons and illustrations to explain complex concepts like the processes of electing the president and making a bill into law. It also uses concrete time lines to represent the historical development of the nation. The illustrations give ELLs the fundamental meanings of important concepts from which teachers can develop lessons. Other books integrate language instruction with content to deliver both components in a contextualized format. One example is the ESL series titled *Avenues*, published by Hampton Brown (Schifini et al., 2004). This set of books presents ESL lessons in conjunction with content from other disciplines. The integration of content and language is one of the most effective strategies to promote content area mastery and language development.

## Cognates and Suffixes

English and most Western languages have been heavily influenced by the Greek and Roman civilizations. The association has resulted in the creation of multiple cognates—words that are similar in two languages. Most of the sophisticated English words in the content areas and especially in social studies are cognates of Spanish and other Western languages. Teachers can use these similarities to expand the vocabulary of students and enhance content area comprehension. Table 4.6 presents examples of the connection between English and Spanish words (Rosado and Salazar, 2002–2003).

Table 4.6
Common Greek and Latin Roots and Affixes

| Roots/Affixes | Meaning | English/Spanish Cognates |
|---|---|---|
| Phobia Xeno | Fear of Foreigners or strangers | Xenophobia/Xenofobia |
| Phono Logy(ia) | Sound Study of | Phonology/Fonología |
| Photo Graphy | Light Graph, form | Photography/Fotografía |
| Homo Sapiens | Same, Man Able to think | Homo sapiens/homo sapiens |
| Demo Cracy | People Government | Democracy/Democracia |

## Instructional Techniques to Support English Language Learners

Teachers need to implement a variety of activities to teach the state curriculum to English Language Learners (ELLs) at the grade level and complexity required of native English speakers. Scaffolding was originally used to describe the way in which adults support children in their efforts to communicate in the native language (L1). The same concept can be used to facilitate language and content development for ELLs. The term *scaffolding* alludes to the provisional structure used to provide support during the construction of a building. This support is eliminated when the structure is complete. Following this analogy, ELLs receive language support to make content cognitively accessible to them until they achieve mastery in the second language (L2); once that mastery is accomplished, the language support is eliminated.

**Graphic organizers** are visuals used to show relationships. These are the most common graphic organizers:

- A **semantic web** or **tree diagram** shows the relationship between main ideas and subordinated components.

- A **time line** presents a visual summary of chronological events and is ideal for showing historical events or events in a sequence.

- A **flowchart** shows cause-and-effect relationships and can be used to show steps in a process, like the process for admission to a school or program.

- A **Venn diagram** uses circles to compare common and unique elements of two or three distinct components, such as properties of numbers, elements of stories, or events, or civilizations.

The **SQ4R** is a study strategy in which the learner is engaged in the entire reading process. The acronym stands for **survey**, **question**, **read**, **reflect**, **recite**, and **review**. During the **survey** part, readers examine the headings and major components of the text to develop predictions and generate questions. Through these **questions**, students establish the purpose for reading. As they **read**, students look for answers to the questions they generated. They monitor their comprehension as they **reflect**, write a summary, and **recite** the content they learned. Finally, they **review** to evaluate how much they learned about the content.

## Academic Vocabulary in Social Studies

Academic vocabulary is the vocabulary needed to understand the concepts of school. In other words, it is the vocabulary of teaching and learning. Marzano and Pickering (2005) emphasize the importance of teaching academic vocabulary to English language learners and recommend a six-step systematic approach that includes direct instruction as well as practice and reinforcement. The steps to teach academic vocabulary are presented next.

- The teacher provides a description, explanation, or example of the new term.

- Students restate the description, example, or explanation in their own words.

- Students create a representation of the word by drawing a picture, symbol, or graphic of the word.

- Students periodically participate in activities that help to add to their knowledge of terms.

- Students discuss terms with one another.

- Students participate in games and activities that reinforce the new term.

Cooperative learning is a teaching strategy designed to create a low-anxiety learning environment in which students work together in small groups to achieve instructional goals. As a result of this instructional arrangement, students with different levels of ability or language development work collaboratively to support each other to ensure that each member masters the objectives of the lesson. This approach can easily be used to deliver content and language instruction. Traditionally, the strategy is delivered in specific steps (Arends, 1998):

1. **Present Goals**—The teacher goes over the objectives of the lesson and provides the motivation.

2. **Present Information**—The teacher presents information to students either verbally or with text.

3. **Organize Students into Learning Teams**—The teacher explains to students how to form learning teams and helps groups make an efficient transition.

4. **Assist Teamwork and Study**—The teacher assists learning teams as they do their work.

5. **Test Students on the Content**—The teacher tests students' knowledge of learning materials as each group presents the results of its work.

6. **Provide Recognition**—The teacher finds ways to recognize both individual and group efforts and achievements.

To emphasize the cooperative nature of the strategy, specific methods were developed to enrich the lessons. These specialized methods are described in the sections that follow.

## Student Teams Achievement Division (STAD)

1. The teacher presents new academic information to students.

2. Students are divided into four- or five-member learning teams.

3. Team members master the content and then help each other learn the material through tutoring, quizzing one another, or carrying on team discussions.

4. Each student receives an improvement score that helps show the growth he or she has made.

5. Daily or weekly quizzes are given to assess mastery.

6. Each week, through newsletters or a short ceremony, groups and individual students are recognized for showing the most improvement (Slavin, 1986).

## Think-Pair-Share

This activity was developed as a result of the wait-time research. Wait-time research suggests that pausing for a few seconds to allow children to reflect on the question can improve the quality of the response and the overall performance of children (Rowe, 1986).

1. **Think**—The teacher poses a question and asks students to spend a minute thinking alone about the answer. No talking or walking is allowed.

2. **Pair**—Students pair off and discuss what they have been thinking about, sharing possible answers or information.

3. **Share**—Students share their answers with the whole class. The teacher goes around the classroom from pair to pair until a fourth to a half of the class has a chance to report (Lyman, 1981).

## Numbered Heads Together

This activity was designed to involve more students in the review of materials covered in class.

1. **Number**—The teacher divides the students into teams with three to five members each and assigns a number to each member.

2. **Question**—The teacher asks a question.

3. **Heads Together**—Students put their heads together to figure out the answer and to be sure everyone knows the answer.

4. **Answer**—The teacher calls a number, and students from each group with that number raise their hands and provide the answer (Kagan, 1985).

## References

Acosta, T. P. 2009. Raza Unida Party. *The Handbook of Texas Online. Texas State Historical Association.*

Arends, R. 1998. *Learning to Teach.* 4th ed. Boston: McGraw-Hill.

Barker, E. C. and J. W. Pohl. 2009. Texas Revolution. *The Handbook of Texas Online. Texas State Historical Association. www.tshaonline.org* (accessed April 2, 2012).

CIA World Fact Book. Central Asia: Russia.

Echevarria, J., M. Vogt, and D. Short. 2000. *Making content comprehensible for English language learners: The SIOP model.* Needham Heights, MA: Allyn and Bacon.

Fry, P. L. "Origin of Name." *The Handbook of Texas Online. Texas State Historical Association.*

Ganeri, A., H. M. Martell, and B. Williams. 1999. *The World History Encyclopedia.* Bath, UK: Parragon.

Gay, G. 2000. *Culturally Responsive Teaching: Theory, Research & Practice.* New York: Teachers College Press.

Kagan, S. 1985. *Cooperative learning resources for teachers.* Riverside, CA: Spencer Kagan.

Kerr, A. 2006. Temperance and prohibition. History Department, Ohio State University.

Lyman, F. T. 1981. The responsive classroom discussion: The inclusion of all students. In *Mainstreaming Digest,* ed. A. S. Anderson, 109–113. College Park: University of Maryland Press.

Marzano, R., and D. Pickering. 2005. *Building academic vocabulary: Teacher's manual.* Alexandria, VA: ASCD.

National Council for the Social Studies (NCSS) 2006. Expectations of Excellence: Curriculum Standards for Social Studies—Executive Summary.

Nieto, S. 1996. *Affirming diversity: The sociopolitical context of multicultural education* (2nd ed.). White Plains, NY: Longman.

Parker, W. C. 2001. *Social Studies in Elementary Education.* 11th ed. Columbus, OH: Merrill Prentice-Hall.

Potts, J. 1994. *Adventure Tales of America*. Dallas, TX: Signal Media.

Rosado, L., and D. Salazar. 2002–2003. La Conexión: The English/Spanish connection. *National Forum of Applied Educational Research Journal* 15(4): 51–66.

Rosales Castañeda, O. 2006. *The Chicano Movement in Washington State* HistoryLink. org  (Accessed April 2, 2012). *1967-2006.*

Rowe, M. B. 1986. *Wait Times: Slowing Down May Be a Way of Speeding Up. Journal of Teacher Education*, 37, 43–50.

Schifini, A. 1985. *Sheltered English: Content area instruction for limited English proficiency students*. Los Angeles County Office of Education.

Schifini, A., H. García, D. J. Short, E. E. García, J. Villamil Tinajero, E. Hamayan, and L. Kratky. 2004. *Avenues: Success in language, literacy and content*. Carmel, CA: Hampton-Brown.

Seattle Civil Rights and Labor History Project. 2006.

Sheppard, D. E. *Cabeza de Vaca in North America*. Floridahistory.com.

Slavin, R. 1986. *Student Learning: An Overview and Practical Guide*. Washington, DC: Professional Library, National Education Association.

# CHAPTER 5

# Science

The National Science Teachers Association (NSTA) Standards for Science Teacher Preparation (2003) emphasize that all generalist teachers should teach science emphasizing "observation and description of events, manipulation of objects and systems, and identification of patterns in nature across subjects" (p. 6). For students to learn science, they must be consistently engaged in hands-on, manipulative activities. Teaching practices focusing on experience and direct investigation will best promote students' science learning.

NSTA strongly supports the idea that scientific inquiry should be a basic component of the curriculum in every grade in American schools (NSTA 2002). A position paper of the organization published in 2002 emphasizes the importance of offering students early experience in problem solving and scientific thinking. The report indicates that children learn science best under the following conditions:

- Students are actively involved in firsthand exploration of scientific concepts.

- Instruction is related and built on the abilities and experiences of the learners.

- Instruction is organized thematically.

- Mathematics and communication skills are integrated.

The report also contends that curriculum should emphasize the contributions of people from a variety of cultures. Finally, the NSTA (2002) states that science education can be successful if teachers receive adequate professional development and school administrators show a genuine interest in science education.

Further, the National Academies report titled *A Framework for K-12 Science Education: Practices, Crosscutting Concepts, and Core Ideas* (National Research Council [NRC], 2011) emphasizes that "one of the principal goals of science education has been to cultivate students' scientific habits of mind, develop their capability to engage in scientific inquiry and teach them how to reason in a scientific context" (p. 3-1). It is important that teachers provide direct experiences so students may develop the knowledge they need through these experiences. Accordingly, "a narrow focus on content along has the unfortunate consequence of leaving the students with naïve conceptions of the nature of scientific inquiry and the impression that science is simply a body of isolated facts" (NRC 2011, p. 3-4).

To be most effective in helping students learn science, teachers need to understand both the content and process of science. Importantly, teachers must understand and develop skill in implementing experiential, inquiry-based science as the primary teaching practice in all K-12 classrooms.

## Competency 036: The Teacher Understands how to Manage Learning Activities to Ensure the Safety of All Students

Teachers need to develop and communicate safety guidelines to students, model and implement safe practices in the classroom, and ensure all students follow the safety guidelines at all times. Teachers should prepare a safety contract for students listing all guidelines and behavioral expectations to be read aloud in class, and signed by both the student and parents. Safety rules should be clearly posted in the classroom and periodically reviewed, particularly before engaging in laboratory activities. Safe practices to consistently implement and enforce in the classroom include the following.

- Require students to use appropriate personal protective gear, like goggles, laboratory coats, and gloves.

- Use appropriate procedures for cleaning and disposing of materials.

- Adhere to appropriate disciplinary procedures to avoid accidents; for example, do not allow children to play with water or other lab materials.

- Substitute less hazardous equivalent materials when possible; for example, use cleaning products instead of chemicals in their pure form; use mild acids such as vinegar instead of more dangerous acids if appropriate.

- Use polyethylene or metal containers in place of glass.

- Advise children to avoid tasting or ingesting substances or materials.

- Label containers appropriately to avoid confusion.

- Control the distribution of materials to students and provide appropriate containers to safely transport materials.

- Control the use of sharp objects that can puncture the skin, providing strict rules and monitoring behavior at all times.

- Supervise the use of living organisms and ensure humane treatment of organisms is practiced.

- Monitor the cleaning of instruments used to ensure proper sanitation and avoid breakage.

- Avoid experimenting with human cells and bodily fluids.

- Share the responsibility for the safety of the students with the whole group; that is, students should motivate each other to follow safety procedures.

- Make provisions for the movement and handling of equipment and materials for students with special needs.

- Prepare, review, and send home an age-appropriate safety contract requiring parent/guardian signature.

- Organize all materials to be used in class by placing them in separate bins for a member of each student group to pick up for use for the lab activity and for returning materials after the lab activity.

- Clearly label and demonstrate the use of safety equipment with students, such as the eyewash station and fire blanket.

- Prepare and practice an emergency plan with students should an accident occur.

- Document all accidents, regardless of how minor, and have another teacher sign as witness if possible.

- Clearly write and read to students the safety precautions for the laboratory before beginning the activity. Ensure all students understand by responding to their questions before beginning.

- Place posters around the room emphasizing the safety rules of the classroom and laboratory.

- Keep all chemicals, glassware and other laboratory materials in locked cabinets with no unsupervised student access.

- Maintain regular inventory of all laboratory materials and chemicals.

- Store acids and other caustic chemicals in cabinets close to the floor in case they fall when retrieving for use.

- If using an open flame, such as lit candles, students must tie long hair back and tape or roll up loose sleeves to avoid contact with the fire.

- Caution students on the use of hot plates and placing materials on the hot plates reminding students that it remains warm long after it has been turned off.

The use of dangerous chemical substances in the middle level classroom may be generally limited in scope. Many laboratory chemicals can be substituted with household products. However, care needs to be taken even when handling household chemicals. It is important to demonstrate safe laboratory procedures for the classroom because household products are still chemicals and pose some level of risk to students. Safety management of chemicals in the classroom requires teachers to have knowledge of those chemicals and their properties. For example, teachers need to be aware that a simple tool like a mercury thermometer can break and pose a danger to students.

The National Science Teachers Association has an official position and guidelines on animals in the classroom. This information can be found at: *www.nsta.org/about/positions/animals.aspx*. NSTA contends that using animals in the classroom sparks interest and curiosity among students, and therefore important to their science education experience. However, animals must be cared for and treated in a humane and ethical manner. This includes all animals that are sometimes not recognized as falling within these guidelines, from ants in ant farms, to mealworms, to guinea pigs and rabbits. Below are a few important guidelines in the treatment of animals in the classroom.

- Send permission slips home to be signed by parents if you anticipate the children will be handling the animals. This permission can go along with the safety contract previously described.

- Research and learn as much as possible about the animals, their typical behaviors, diet, sleep patterns, and habitats in advance of housing the animals in the classroom.

- Instruct students on how to handle animals and monitor their handling of animals at all times.

- Ensure the animals' habitats, including cages or other living quarters, are clean and regularly maintained. With instruction, cleaning animal housing can be done on a rotating basis by the students, teaching them important lessons on responsibility and fulfilling necessary chores.

- Feed and water the animals on a regular schedule according to the dietary needs of the animal.

- Demonstrate safe and humane treatment, and strictly enforce this treatment among all who have access to the animals.

When animals are used in dissection, it is critical that students learn to respect that this animal was a once living organism, and that the dissection is for their learning. Monitor the dissection to ensure students treat the specimen with respect (e.g., do not "play" with internal organs). Have a back-up plan for students who may object to participating in animal dissection, or have low tolerance for the activity.

In addition to NSTA, the American Psychological Association provides guidelines for the ethical treatment of animals. These guidelines can be found at: *www.apa.org/science/leadership/care/guidelines.aspx*. Most of the information presented deals with using animals in scientific research; however, the guidelines also present useful information on caring for animals.

## Competency 037: The Teacher Understands the Correct Use of Tools, Materials, Equipment and Technologies

Scientific experimentation requires careful observation and precise measures beyond what we can determine through our senses alone. To extend what can be observed with our senses scientific instruments are used such as balances, microscopes, beakers, electronic probes, and graduated cylinders to allow precise observations and measurements are made. Science requires the use of standard measuring devices to be sure that the information is clear, accurate, and able to be replicated in experimental settings.

In selecting the appropriate tools to use for a given observation and measurement consider the task that is needed and match that with the instrument as follows.

- To take an object's *mass* (amount of matter in an object) use triple beam or electronic balance and obtain the measurement in grams or kilograms. If taking the mass of a liquid or object that will not stay on the balance or scale, use a container such as a beaker or plastic cup in which to place the liquid or object. First measure and record the mass of the container minus the liquid or object. Then place the liquid or object in the container and measure the mass of both objects together. Subtract the mass of the container from the mass of both the container and liquid or object together to obtain the measure of only liquid or object.

- To measure the *volume* (amount of space something occupies) of a liquid, use a graduated cylinder for a precise measure in milliliters. Liquids that are polar molecules such as water cling to the walls of the container forming a downward arc shape or meniscus. The lowest point in the arc or meniscus is the accurate reading of liquid volume. It is best to have students view the meniscus at eye level to obtain an accurate reading.

- To measure the *volume* of an irregular object such as a rock, place water in a graduated cylinder to allow room for the object when dropped into the liquid, typically up to about half-way to three-quarters of the way to the top. Measure the water level as described above, reading and recording the water level at the meniscus. Then place the object into the graduated cylinder, being careful not to allow water to splash. The water will rise to a new level according to the volume of water that was displaced by the object. Measure the new volume of water with the object in the graduated cylinder then subtract the beginning volume of water to obtain the volume of the irregular object. One milliliter (ml) is a liquid volume measure that is equal to one cubic centimeter (cc) that is a solid volume measure.

- Measuring the volume of a cube is accomplished by taking the length × width × height of the object using a metric tape measure or meter stick. The volume is typically recorded in cubic centimeters (cc).

- Beakers are usually used to hold liquids, with a less precise measure of volume. Beakers are useful in making solutions.

- Compound light microscopes are used in observing very small specimens, and provide fairly high magnification. Specimens must be very thin when placed on a slide on the stage of the microscope in order that light may pass through.

- Dissecting microscopes have lower magnification than compound microscopes and are used for observing larger specimens such as whole insects, leaves, and rock minerals.

The United States uses a combination of the English system of measurement (standard) and the metric system. The United States is the only technologically developed country in the world that uses the English system for business transactions and for day-to-day activities. However, for international business, engineering, and natural sciences, all countries use the more standardized, precise system of weights and measurement, the metric system. The English system uses pounds, gallons, and inches for measurement, while the metric system uses grams or kilograms, liters, and meters. The metric system uses a system of fractions and multiples of units that are related to each other by powers of 10, allowing conversion and comparison of measures simply by shifting a decimal point, and avoiding the lengthy arithmetical operations required by the English system.

The TEKS requires the teaching of both the metric and the English systems; however, all scientific data are to be reported using the metric system.

It is best that students become comfortable with using metric measurements. To help them learn metric, it is important to show them exactly what a gram or kilogram for example, looks and "feels" like, along with meters, centimeters, liters and milliliters. Have students measure and make items according to these standards as a reference for all to use in the classroom.

## Competency 038: The Teacher Understands the Process of Scientific Inquiry and the History and Nature of Science

One common misunderstanding about scientific inquiry is that scientific investigations are limited to one method, the scientific method. Many science classrooms support this idea with a poster that describes this single method, the experimental method. These posters often describe a number of "steps" including a hypothesis, control, and variable to be manipulated. However, science has more than one way to carry out investigations, with experimental science as just one of several recognized forms of scientific inquiry accepted by the scientific community. Some of these forms of scientific inquiry include: descriptive studies, controlled experiments, and comparative data analysis. The experimental method attempts to find causal relationships among variables within a particular phenomenon. However, this method is typically not the goal of astronomers or ecologists, for example. An astronomer and ecologist cannot work from a hypothesis, establish controls or manipulate variables, although they are still engaging in scientific inquiry and, in this case, descriptive studies. In contrast, scientists using the experimental method, such as a chemist experimenting on the effects of a certain chemical on bacterial growth, may start with a hypothesis and experimental controls in a more structured manner. However, it should be noted that experiments do not always precisely follow the linear set of steps of the scientific method from hypothesis to the reporting of results. Instead, the process is often a cyclical and non-linear endeavor to establish causal relationships. Comparative investigations are more open but there is no control group; data is being compared among different existing situations, such as collecting data on two different populations. It is important to note that there is at least one aspect of science inquiry that all types of scientific investigations share and that aspect is a *question*. The type of scientific inquiry to engage in is always dependent upon the nature of the question(s) and the best way to respond to the question(s) (e.g., using experimental methods, descriptive studies, comparative data analysis).

In the classroom there are multiple ways to implement inquiry science, often referred to as *structured*, *guided*, or *open*. These instructional methods vary primarily in the amount of control of the teacher in the inquiry process, along with the nature of the scientific research question.

Scientific research and information must be disseminated to other scientists and the general public using strong communication skills. Therefore it is critical that students learn to effectively communicate their work to others, defending the results and explanations derived from their investigations. Students must use logical scientific reasoning and present sound arguments for their findings based on evidence. These communication skills can best be developed and promoted by engaging students in collaborative, inquiry-based science in the classroom, and providing students with regular opportunities to present their findings in written and oral forms using a variety of delivery mechanisms (posters, technical papers, technology). The National Research Council promotes the need for strong communication among students as stated in the publication, *Inquiry and the National Science Education Standards* (NRC, 2000). In this document, the NRC (2000) specifically states that students' scientific explanations "must adhere to criteria such as: a proposed explanation must be logically consistent; it must abide by the rules of evidence; it must be open to questions and possible modification; and it must be based on historical and current scientific knowledge" (p. 20). The book addresses several of the ideas and responsibilities encountered by students while conducting scientific inquiry.

Ethical standards are an important aspect of science to preserve the scholarship and rigor of the discipline. As such, scientists' research and reporting of research is guided by a strict code of ethics; a practice that should also be followed in the classroom. The following list is a summary of principles of scientific ethics recognized and practiced by the scientific community (Resnik, 2008):

1. **Scientific Honesty:** Do not commit scientific fraud, i.e., do not fabricate, fudge, trim, cook, destroy, or misrepresent data.

2. **Carefulness:** Strive to avoid careless errors or sloppiness in all aspects of scientific work.

3. **Intellectual Freedom:** Scientists should be allowed to pursue new ideas and criticize old ones. They should be free to conduct research they find interesting.

4. **Openness:** i.e., share data, results, methods, theories, equipment, and so on.

5. Allow people to see your work, be open to criticism.

6. **The principle of assigning credit:** Do not plagiarize the work of other scientists; give credit where credit is due (but not where it is not due).

Teachers should understand the potential sources of error or uncertainty in inquiry-based investigations. Two common sources of error that students might encounter are systematic and random error. Systematic errors, for example, are due to faulty instruments. Random errors are not predictable and could be due to a variety of errors including human error in interpreting data, recording data incorrectly, or inaccurate readings of measurements.

Teachers should understand the historical development of science and the contribution that diverse cultures and individuals of both genders have made to scientific knowledge. Although the 'modern science' we practice today finds its origins in the European Renaissance it was the 'reawakening' to the work of many non-western cultures (e.g., Arab philosophers and scholars) that led to the knowledge and technological advances of today in medicine and nearly all other fields of science. These contributions and contributions from the diverse populations and regions of the world need to be regularly introduced and discussed in the classroom.

In addition to diverse cultures, women have made tremendous contributions to the body of scientific knowledge. For example, it was astronomer Celia Payne who challenged the assumptions of the prevailing opinion that the sun was composed primarily of iron. It was her spectroscopic work that suggested the sun was actually composed primarily of hydrogen and helium. As it was then, her work is often ignored in the classroom today. And, yet she is credited with providing a basis for the discovery of how the sun produces its energy (i.e., through fusion).

It is necessary for teachers to know about and use the history of science in teaching however, it is not sufficient. The integration of the diversity of scientists and scientific contributions within the history of, and in present-day science is one way to also address the goal of equity. At the crux of this competency is the idea that teachers should provide equitable science learning opportunities. That is, science and science education is for *all students* regardless of gender, culture, or ethnicity. Teachers need to ensure the examples they provide, students called upon to respond, the opportunity to experience inquiry, and treatment of all students is equitable and fair at all times. It is important for the students to see *themselves* as scientists and as capable of solving problems and engaging in the inquiry process.

## Competency 039: The Teacher Understands How Science Impacts the Daily Lives of Students and Interacts with and Influences Personal and Societal Decisions

Teachers need to remain knowledgeable of the influences of science and technology on the lives of students and the extent to which it permeates their lives. The functioning of their bodies, the potential threat of diseases, issues of sustainability and the natural environment around them, and their everyday use of electrical appliances, computers, and cell phones are examples of biological and physical science in their lives. Many of these topics and technologies can be used productively in classroom science instruction, as they are intertwined in the lives of students. However, teachers need to be aware that students tend to keep the science they learn in school separate from the science they experience in everyday life. Instead of teaching science and technology in isolation and maintaining this pervasive separation, teachers need to help students connect the science they are learning in school to the world around them. Integrating everyday life experiences and personal and societal topics into the classroom through science teaching will broaden students' conceptual understandings and promote the usefulness, value, and applicability of science. In inquiry science, the optimal time to make connections with everyday life phenomena is either after, or while students experience a hands-on lab activity and construct an understanding of the concept. To make sense of science, the student must have the background needed to relate the newly learned concept to their everyday lives and see how the concept works in differing contexts. Connecting newly learned concepts to the students' life experiences makes the learning more meaningful for students and helps them retain understanding of the concept for later use. Relating science to what students already know and experience in life helps bridge the disconnections between "school science" and science they observe and experience in everyday life.

Another approach is to place the entire societal and everyday life connections in the context of science through Project Based Learning or PBL (Krajcik, et al., 1994). In PBL, a societal topic is selected as the overarching theme, and the teacher leads the students in, or the students initiate their own, inquiry based science experiences connected to the overarching theme, or project. Project-Based Learning engages students in authentic learning activities that is motivating, and designed to answer a question or solve a problem. PBL provides students with experiences that are consistent with learning and workplace activities that are present in the everyday world. More specifically PBL is defined as: "a systematic teaching method that engages students in learning essential knowledge and life-enhancing skills through an extended, student-influenced inquiry process structured around complex, authentic questions and carefully designed products and tasks" (The Buck Institute for Education and Boise State University, 2012).

Science has brought society many advantages that have served to increase the health and longevity of human lives, and to improve the quality of life for all. However, there may be consequences, often unforeseen, to scientific discovery and invention that impacts society and the natural environment, as well as the habitats and survival of the living organisms that share this planet. To better understand these issues, students need to gain scientific knowledge and evidence of what is known. Armed with appropriate background knowledge, students will be in the position to weigh the pros and cons of various scientific discoveries and debate issues that prevail in our global community. Students should be apprised of issues such as global warming, for example, but before taking a position on the topic, they must be prepared with accurate scientific information on the topic. When students are given opportunities to use scientific concepts as support for sound logic and reasoning to debate or evaluate a scientific issue, they are operating at high cognitive levels important to their intellectual development. Equally important is student awareness of the ethical, personal, societal, and economic implications of science, from both positive and negative perspectives. Students need to realize the trade-offs often present in scientific discovery and experimentation, for example, laboratory testing on animals. Many new and important discoveries have improved the quality of life at the cost of animals' lives. In order to best understand the complexity of how science interfaces with personal and societal issues, students need to be engaged in electronic and library research on impactful science topics and take part in discussion with peers and experts in the science fields. Topics such as cloning, global warming, alternative and fossil fuels, and space exploration are just a few additional topics tied to ethical, personal, societal, and economic concerns. It is important that students fully understand the scientific knowledge that underlies all such complex issues, and can formulate decisions based on this knowledge.

The scientific processes are skills that last a lifetime, applicable to a vast array of everyday life decisions and experiences. Teachers need to help students apply the scientific processes to real world situations. Making careful observations, experimenting, collecting data and information, and drawing conclusions, as examples, are important in everyday life decisions. Determining which presidential candidate to vote for, which doctor to see and after, knowing if the diagnoses are correct, what product to buy, or what to determine is true as presented in the media all require proficiency in using scientific processes and the associated reasoning skills. Teachers must provide students with opportunities to apply scientific processes in everyday life decisions so they may see the importance and benefits of learning these skills.

Natural resources and the consumption of natural resources has been a dominant issue in society over the past 100 years. Currently, energy as a source of fuel and electricity is a major issue threatening the economic, environmental, and personal status of living in the U.S. and global society. It is important to know about fossil fuels, their origin, how they are obtained, and how they are used for energy consumption. In addition, fossil fuels are nonrenewable and will one day be expended. Therefore, science must continue to develop and improve upon alternative sources of energy such as wind, hydroelectric, and geothermal. Teachers must be knowledgeable about these other sources of energy and be able to guide students toward understanding how these alternative, renewable energy sources are used and how they impact our society's energy needs.

A significant impact of science on daily life relates to fitness and health. Childhood obesity is a serious crisis in the U.S., and teachers can play an important role in educating children on the negative health issues associated with poor nutrition and a lack of exercise. Teachers need to help students learn about factors that impact physical and psychological health and about how to make good choices on regarding nutrition, hygiene, physical exercise, smoking, drugs and alcohol. Understanding human biology will help students realize how obesity and other factors such as substance use/abuse affect their physical and mental health. The topics of heart disease, diabetes, and cancer should be included in the curriculum as ways to help students understand the detrimental effects of unhealthy life choices.

## Competency 40: The Teacher Knows and Understands the Unifying Concepts and Processes that Are Common to All Sciences

Science is a way of knowing, a process—it is a systematic way of looking at the world and how it works. This competency focuses on how science uses a regular, consistent method of collecting and reporting data about scientific phenomena. Science is a way of organizing observations and then seeking patterns and regularity in order to make sense of the world. In science we organize evidence, create models, and explain observations in a logical form. We may make predictions and hypotheses and test our predictions and hypotheses through controlled experimentation, meaning all variables of the experiment remain constant except for the variable being tested. We repeat experiments multiple times and seek constancy in our findings in form and/or function. We seek patterns and consistency in our observations and data in order to construct explanations and make new predictions. We employ different forms of scientific inquiry to best respond to our research questions, including experimental, descriptive, and comparative methods, recognizing that experiments do not always progress as planned.

Science embraces a broad spectrum of subject matter, such as life science, physical science, and earth science, all of which is interrelated. For example, in studying the ecosystem, teachers must understand the biological aspects (e.g., the living organism) and how they interact, as in predator-prey relationships and symbiotic relationships (e.g., parasitism, commensalism), as well as the chemical aspects of the ecosystem (e.g., nitrogen cycle), the geologic or earth science aspects (e.g., the landscape, the water, and the climate) and the physics aspects (e.g., energy transfer, motion). Ecosystems, for example, regardless of location on earth, share unifying components and characteristics, and teachers must understand this unity. In life science, there is unity of what makes organisms "living"—they all must carry on life functions and are composed of one or more cells. These are the criteria that unify life forms and classify something like a virus, for example, as non-living (it does not carry on the life functions and is not composed of cells).

All scientific observations can be described by their characteristics or "properties." These properties organize the observations according to commonalities, or classification. Observed properties and patterns are centered on space, time, energy, and matter. Unifying concepts in teaching science in Texas at each grade level are articulated in the *Texas Essential Knowledge and Skills for Science* document, found at: *www.tea.state.tx.us*.

## Competency 41: The Teacher Understands Forces and Motion and Their Relationships

*Universal forces include gravity, electricity, and magnetism, which are important to understanding this competency.*

Force is defined as the action of moving an object by pulling or pushing it. Force can cause an object to move at a constant speed or to accelerate. When force is applied over a distance, work is done. Work is the product of the force acting in the direction of movement and causing displacement. Energy is defined as the ability to do work; when a tow truck uses force to pull a car and move it to a different location, energy is used and work is accomplished. Newton's laws of motion are important to understand in fulfilling this competency. Newton's first law is that an object at rest will remain at rest unless acted upon by an (unbalanced) force, and an object in motion will continue to stay in motion with the same speed and in the same direction unless acted upon by an (unbalanced) outside force. This first law is also called inertia. Newton's second law is that acceleration is produced when a force acts on mass and the greater the mass of the object being accelerated, the greater the amount of force needed to accelerate that object. Newton's third law of motion is that for every action there is an equal and opposite reaction.

Force and motion, as well as changes in motion, may be measured through hands-on activities in which variables such as time, speed, distance, and direction can be recorded and graphed, and teachers need to know how to do so. For example, teachers can have students experience and record what happens when an object with higher mass (such as a large marble or ball bearing), collides with an object with less mass (e.g., a small marble or ball bearing). Teachers should also know what happens when the rate of speed is high when the objects collide compared to when the rate of speed is low. The game of pool or billiards is a good example. When forces are unbalanced, it may cause the object to change its motion or position.

Magnetism is the force of attraction or repulsion between objects that results from the positive and negative ionic charges of the objects. Usually, the objects are metals, such as iron, nickel, and cobalt. Magnets have two poles that have opposing charges or forces: north (+) and south (−). When the north pole of a magnet is placed close to the north pole of a second magnet, repulsion occurs. When poles of different kinds (north and south) are placed close, they attract one another. The strength of the forces depends on the size and the proximity of the magnets. The charged area around a magnet is called a magnetic field. The Earth is like a large magnet, with opposing forces—the North Pole and South Pole, and the magnetic field of attraction of Earth that we know as gravity is like that of a magnet. Without gravity, all objects on Earth, including the atmosphere, would not be held onto its surface. Planets and other celestial objects that are more massive than Earth, such as Jupiter, have stronger gravitational forces, and those that are less massive and/or dense, such as our moon, have weaker gravitational forces.

A machine is something that makes work easier. Machines can be as simple as a wedge or a screw or as sophisticated as a computer or gas engine. A simple machine has few or no moving parts and can change the size and direction of a force. A screw, hammer, wedge, and incline plane are examples of simple machines. Simple machines are part of our daily activities. For example, children playing on a seesaw are using a simple machine called a lever. Thus, teachers and their students should know the practical use of these simple machines in everyday life. A complex machine is two or more simple machines working together to facilitate work. Some of the complex machines used in daily activities are a wheelbarrow, a can opener, and a bicycle.

Force and motion is what keeps the sun, Earth, moon, and planets in their orbits and explains the structure and changes of the universe. On Earth, force and motion are found in all geologic processes, explaining phenomena such as tides and tsunamis.

# Competency 42: The Teacher Understands Physical Properties of and Changes in Matter

Matter has physical, thermal, electrical, and chemical properties. These properties are dependent upon the molecular composition of the matter.

The physical properties of matter are the way matter looks and feels. It includes qualities like color, density, hardness, and conductivity. Color represents how matter is reflected or perceived by the human eye. Density is the mass that is contained in a unit of volume of a given substance. Hardness represents the resistance to penetration offered by a given substance. Conductivity is the ability of substances to transmit thermal or electric current.

Matter is sensitive to temperature changes. Heat and cold produce changes in the physical properties of matter; however, the chemical properties remain unchanged. For example, when water is exposed to cold temperature (release of heat), it changes from liquid to solid; and when water is exposed to heat, it changes from solid to liquid. With continued heat, the water changes from liquid to gas (water vapor). Water vapor can be cooled again and turned back into liquid. However, through all these states, water retains its chemical properties—two molecules of hydrogen and one molecule of oxygen or $H_2O$.

Matter can be classified as a conductor or nonconductor of electricity. Conductive matter allows the transfer of electric current or heat from one point to another. Metals are usually good conductors, while wood and rocks are examples of nonconductive matter.

Matter can exist in four distinct states: solid, liquid, gas, and plasma. Most people are familiar with the basic states of matter, but they might not be familiar with the fourth one, plasma. Plasmas are formed at extremely high temperatures when electrons are stripped from neutral atoms (University of California, 2006). Stars are predominantly composed of plasmas. Solids have mass, occupy a define amount of space or *volume* or have a definite shape, and are denser than liquids. Liquids have mass, occupy a definite volume, do not have a definite shape, but instead take the shape of their container. Gases have mass, do not have a definite volume, have no definite shape but take the shape of their container, and are the least dense of the three states of matter. Plasma has no definite shape or volume, and is a substance that cannot be classified as a solid, liquid, or gas. When substances change from one state of matter to another, such as ice melting, it is a physical change, and not a chemical change.

A physical change is a change in a substance that does not change what that substance is made of. Examples of physical changes are melting ice (boiling water), tearing paper, chopping wood, writing with chalk and mixing sugar and water together. In the mixing of sugar with water, or salt with water, even though the sugar or salt may not be visible to the naked eye in the water, it is still there and still has the same composition—that is, the molecules that make up the sugar or salt and water are still the same as when you mixed them. You can evaporate the water and you will recover your sugar or salt crystals.

A chemical change is when the substances that were combined are no longer the same molecules—they have changed to new substances. For example, burning wood, mixing baking soda and vinegar, or a rusting nail, which is when the iron of the nail (Fe) combines with oxygen (in the presence of water) to form a new substance—that is, a new molecule is formed, iron oxide $Fe_2O_3$.

Physical changes can be reversed, whereas chemical changes generally cannot be reversed. Evidence of a chemical change include that the combination of the substances gives off a gas (bubbles are observed), it changes color (not always a chemical change, but may be if the other evidences are also present), gives off heat and becomes warmer, or absorbs heat and becomes colder (temperature change), and forms a precipitate (a solid substance). When heat is given off in a chemical change, it is an exothermic reaction; and when heat is absorbed in a chemical change (the combination becomes colder), it is an endothermic reaction. Everyday examples of exothermic reactions are firewood burning or the use of a hand warmer used by many mountain climbers and snow skiers. Examples of endothermic reactions are a cold pack used for sports injuries or the combination of baking soda and vinegar (try it with a thermometer in the vinegar during the reaction and see!).

## Competency 43: The Teacher Understands Chemical Properties of and Changes in Matter

Matter is anything that takes up space and has mass. The mass of a body is the amount of matter in an object or thing, and volume describes the amount of space that matter takes up. Mass is also the property of a body that causes it to have weight. Weight is the amount of gravitational force exerted over an object. It is important not to confuse mass and weight. What students are measuring on their balances in the laboratory is an object's *mass*. Weight changes as an object goes from one level of gravitational force to another, for example, from Earth to the moon, because the amount of "pull" on that object is different; but the mass of the object—how much matter or material is in the object—does not change unless we do something to actually take away or add matter to that object.

There are 118 basic kinds of matter, called elements, which are organized into the periodic table. An element is composed of sub-microscopic components called atoms. Atoms are made up of particles called electrons, neutrons, and protons. The mass of the atom is located mostly in the nucleus, which is made up of protons, which have a positive charge, and neutrons, which are neutral or have no charge. The atomic mass of atom is its protons plus neutrons, where each has a mass of 1 atomic mass unit (AMU). The electron contains little mass (which has a negligible contribution to the overall atomic mass), carries a negative charge, and follows an orbit with a specific distance and shape around the nucleus (electron energy level or shell). The atomic number is the number of protons in the nucleus of the atom. The number of protons is the distinction between one type of atom and another, e.g. Hydrogen, which has 1 proton, and Helium, an entirely different atom with different properties, which has 2 protons. The number of electrons is equal to the number of protons in a stable atom, so the negative and positive charges are balanced. An ion is an atom or molecule that has lost or gained one or more electrons and thus has negative or positive charge (because there are either more or less protons, or positive charges, compared to electrons, or negative charges).

Molecules are two or more atoms bonded together in a chemical bond. There are two types of chemical bonds, ionic bonds and covalent bonds. In ionic bonds electrons are transferred from one atom to the other that it is bonding with, for example Na (sodium) gives its outer shell electron to Cl (chlorine) to make NaCl (sodium chloride) or table salt. In covalent bonding electrons are shared, equally or unequally, between the different atoms in the molecule. For example, Carbon and two oxygen atoms share outer shell electrons to form covalent bonds to the molecule $CO_2$ (carbon dioxide). In bonding, the atoms are chemically seeking to fill their outer shell of electrons, usually with the full complement of 8 electrons (2 electrons in the case of hydrogen).

The atoms of a molecule can be more than one of the *same kind* of atom, as in the naturally occurring oxygen molecule, $O_2$, or a molecule can be two or more *different kinds* of atoms as in carbon dioxide, $CO_2$, ammonia, $NH_3$, and glucose, $C_6H_{12}O_6$. Compounds are when you have two or more *different* kinds of atoms in the molecule and you have a given amount of that substance. In other words, compounds consist of matter composed of atoms that are chemically combined with one another in molecules in definite weight proportions. An example of a compound is water; water is oxygen and hydrogen combined in the ratio of two hydrogen molecules to one molecule of oxygen $H_2O$. So, you can also call it *one* $H_2O$ a molecule.

The chemical properties of one type of matter (element) can react with the chemical properties of other types of matter. In general, elements from the same groups will not react with each other, while elements from different groups may. The more separated the groups, the more likely they will cause a chemical reaction when brought together. A type of matter can be chemically altered to become a different type of matter; for example, a metal trashcan will rust if it is left out in the rain.

Mixtures are combinations of two or more substances, where each substance is distinct from the other that is, made up of two or more types of molecules and not chemically combined. The two substances in the mixture may or may not be evenly distributed, so there are no definite amounts or weight proportions. Mixtures may be *heterogeneous*, which means an uneven distribution of the substances in the mixture throughout. A mixture may be *homogeneous,* which means the components are evenly distributed throughout. Examples of mixtures include milk, which is a heterogeneous mixture of water and butterfat particles. The components of a mixture can be separated physically. For example, milk producers and manufacturers remove the butterfat from whole milk to make skim milk.

Solutions are *mixtures* that are *homogeneous*, which means that the components are distributed evenly and there is an even concentration throughout. The solute is the substance in the smaller amount that dissolves and that you add into the substance that is in the larger amount—the solvent. Water is a common solvent. Solids, liquids, and gases can be solutes. Examples of solutions are seawater and ammonia. Seawater is made up of water and salt, and ammonia is made up of ammonia gas and water. In these examples, the salt and the ammonia ($NH_3$) are the solutes; water is the solvent.

Chemical reactions occur in everyday life and are an essential part of our physical and biological world. The burning of gasoline in automobiles is a chemical change—and burning of any kind for that matter. Burning is the combination of oxygen from the atmosphere with substances containing the carbon atom. The proper temperature has to be reached in order to begin this exothermic reaction, but once started, the chemical reaction can continue until the oxygen is used up or is prevented from entering into the reaction. So since gasoline is a fossil fuel (a once living organism), it contains carbon. When we provide the energy it needs to begin the reaction, called activation energy, as long as oxygen is present, the carbon substance will burn. Burning is a chemical reaction because the carbon and oxygen combine to form new substances such as carbon monoxide (CO) and carbon dioxide ($CO_2$). The same reaction occurs in burning wood, candles, and even in cell respiration—the oxygen we breathe and carry through our bloodstream is combined in our cells with carbon-containing glucose molecules in a type of "controlled" burning. Our bodies give off heat from this reaction, which is why we are able to maintain a fairly high temperature of about 98.6 degrees Fahrenheit. Other examples of chemical reactions in everyday life include chemical batteries, the digestion of food, and cooking/baking. Moreover, the process of photosynthesis, where plants use sunlight to convert carbon dioxide gas and water into food for the plant known as glucose (a simple sugar), is also an important chemical reaction responsible for providing food for and sustaining all life on Earth.

# Competency 44: The Teacher Understands Energy and Interactions Between Matter and Energy

Energy is available in many forms, including heat, light, solar radiation, chemical, electrical, magnetic, sound, and mechanical energy. It exists in three states: potential, kinetic, and activation energies. An object possessing energy because of its ability to move has kinetic energy. The energy that an object has as the result of its position or condition is called potential energy. The energy necessary to transfer or convert potential energy into kinetic energy is called activation energy. All three states of energy can be transformed from one to the other. A vehicle parked in a garage has potential energy. When the driver starts the engine using the chemical energy stored in the battery and the fuel, potential energy becomes activation energy. Once the vehicle is moving, the energy changes to kinetic energy.

Heat is a form of energy. Temperature is the measure of heat. The most common device used to measure temperature is the thermometer. Thermometers are made of heat-sensitive substances—mercury and alcohol—that expand when heated.

The most common form of energy comes from the sun. Solar energy provides heat and light for animals and plants. Through photosynthesis, plants capture radiant energy from the sun and transform it into chemical energy in the form of glucose. This chemical energy is stored in the leaves, stems, and fruits of plants. Humans and animals consume the plants or fruits and get the energy they need for survival. This energy source is transformed again to create kinetic energy and body heat. Kinetic energy is used for movement and to do work, while heat is a required element for all warm-blooded animals, like humans. Cold-blooded animals also require heat, but rather than making it themselves through the transformation of plant sugar, they use solar energy to heat their body. Energy transformation constitutes the foundation and the driving force of an ecosystem. In addition to heat and solar radiation, energy is available in the forms of electricity and magnetism.

When you arrange an energy source, such as a battery, a wire, and a light bulb (or motor, or bell, or any electrical device) such that all metal parts are touching (metal is a good "conductor" of energy) in a circle—the bulb will light (the motor will run, the bell will ring, and so on). What has been created by arranging the items in this circle is known as an "electric circuit." The energy from the battery or other energy source is able to "flow" or be transferred through the metal wires and parts of the circuit. A closed circuit is when all metal parts are touching and the electrical charge is able to continue to be transferred through the circuit. A light switch or other "on button" closes the circuit and allows the electricity to flow. An open circuit is when there is a break someplace in the flow of electricity through the circuit. A switch or "off button" opens the circuit and stops the electricity flow. When you ring a door bell, you are closing the circuit or allowing all metal parts to touch and send electricity through it to make the bell ring; when you let go of the doorbell button, the circuit is open, and so the flow of electricity stops and so does the bell's ringing.

Lightning is a form of static electricity, which means it is not "flowing" or being transferred in the way it is through a metal wire, but is instead caused by friction, much the same as walking across a carpet in socks and getting a shock when a metal doorknob is touched. In both kinds of electricity, the electrons in the atoms of the substance, which are negatively charged, are pulled away from their atom's nucleus, giving the object, or cloud, a negative charge. The negative charge is quickly attracted to a positive charge—in the case of lightning, that positive charge could be something (or someone!) on the ground. The positive charge quickly jumps toward the negative charge and the negative charge quickly jumps toward the positive charge, and a flash of lighting and clap of thunder is heard; or in the case of the doorknob, a spark and a snap sound. Electric circuits are just a way to channel the electricity and the opposing charges through a conductor such as metal wires to allow us to use the energy to do work and to transform the energy into different forms such as sound (a radio), light (light bulbs), mechanical (machinery), and/or heat energy.

Light energy, and all energy for that matter, travels in waves and in a straight-line path. The electromagnetic spectrum shows the different wavelengths and frequencies of energy, including the small portion that is visible light. The electromagnetic spectrum includes, for example, micro-waves, x-rays, radio waves, infrared radiation, visible light waves, and ultraviolet radiation, all of which have different wavelengths and frequencies that distinguish one type of wave from another.

Visible light is the wavelength of light we can see, which our eyes see as white light. However, this white light is composed of a host of other wavelengths of light that our eyes cannot always distinguish, which we know as the visible light spectrum, or a rainbow. The colors of white light include red, orange, yellow, green, blue, indigo, and violet (although some sources now eliminate indigo as separate from violet), or ROYGBIV. When light, again, traveling in a straight line, hits an object or substance and is bent, it is called refraction. The bending of light waves may result in the colors of light in the spectrum becoming visible, as when we see a rainbow in the sky (the water molecules in the air bend the light) or when light travels through cut glass such as with a prism. Reflection is when light waves bounce back, as when looking in a mirror. The principles of reflection and refraction are used in periscopes and telescopes in order to be able to see objects we may otherwise not be able to see. They are often popular in magic shows when objects are said to "disappear." In actuality, the light of the object has been refracted or reflected to a place away from our eyes so that we can no longer see it.

Refraction is also used to our advantage through concave and convex lenses. Concave or convex lenses work such that when light passes through it changes the focal point. The eye contains a lens, but when light passing through the eye cannot properly focus on the "screen" known as the retina, the object being viewed may be blurred. Concave or convex lenses are used in eyeglasses to adjust and correct the focal point. These lenses are also used in cameras, microscopes, and telescopes. A spoon is an example of both a concave and a convex lens—if you look into the concave side, you will see yourself upside down. If you look into the convex side of the spoon, you will see yourself right side up. This is due to refraction (and reflection) of light.

Sound also travels in waves. Sounds are caused by vibrations, such as a guitar string (or a rubber band), or banging on a drum or cymbal. Sound has a certain wavelength, frequency, pitch, and amplitude (loudness). Sound waves must travel through a medium, which may be solid, liquid, or gas. Sound travels best through solids because there are more molecules (particles) to vibrate, and least well through gases.

The types of sound waves are longitudinal and transverse. Longitudinal waves move parallel to the direction the wave moves, and transverse waves move perpendicular to the direction of the wave.

## Competency 45: The Teacher Understands Energy Transformations and the Conservation Of Matter and Energy

The sun is the source of energy that sustains life on earth. It is one of billions of stars in our galaxy, the Milky Way, and of the countless trillions of stars in the universe. The sun is actually quite an ordinary star, falling somewhere in the middle range in size. The sun is largely composed of the gases hydrogen and helium and generates energy by nuclear fusion, or the combining of atoms in high speed collisions releasing tremendous amounts of energy.

Electricity is the flow of electrons or electric power or charge. The basic unit of charge is based on the positive charge of the proton and the negative charge of the electron. Energy occurs naturally in the atmosphere through light. However, it is not feasible to capture that type of energy. The electricity that we use comes from secondary sources because it is produced from the conversion of primary (natural) sources of energy like fossil fuels that are nonrenewable (natural gas, coal, and oil) and nuclear, and renewable resources such as wind and solar energy. All sources of energy are used to produce a common result—to turn a turbine that generates electricity. Electricity that is generated can then be sent through wires for human use, and can be transformed into other forms of energy, including sound, light, heat, and force.

The main principle of energy conservation states that energy can change form but cannot totally disappear. For example, the chemical energy stored in a car battery is used to start the engine, which in turn is used to recharge the battery. Another example of energy conservation is placing merchandise on shelves. Energy was used to do the work (placing merchandise on a shelf) and it was stored as potential energy. Potential energy in turn can be converted to kinetic energy when the merchandise is pushed back to the floor. In this case, work was recovered completely, but often the recovered energy is less than the energy used to do the work. This loss of energy can be caused by friction or any kind of resistance encountered in the process of doing the work. For example, as a vehicle's tires roll across the pavement, doing the work of moving forward, they encounter friction. This friction causes heat energy to be released, as well as kinetic energy.

In essence, energy cannot be created or destroyed, only changed in form (law of conservation of energy). Likewise, matter cannot be created or destroyed, only changed in form (law of conservation of matter). Thus, energy from the sun is changed, for example, to chemical energy when plants use the energy to make glucose in photosynthesis. The energy from the sun is stored in the chemical bonds of the glucose molecule and will be released for use by the organism—the plant itself, or any organism that eats the plant and its glucose—when the molecule's chemical bonds are "broken" by oxygen in cell respiration and/or stored in another chemical form known as ATP. Likewise, electrical energy comes from burning, or breaking the bond of carbon-based molecules as in fossil fuels. This electricity generated is then transformed to another form by first capturing and sending that electrical energy through metal wires originating at the power generating plant, and sending it in a complete, closed circuit to homes, businesses, and industries. There the electrical energy may be transformed to sound, heat, light, and/or mechanical energy. In all cases the energy is not lost it is changed in form.

It is important to conserve matter and energy generated from fossil fuels as these are non-renewable sources and will one day be expended. It is also important to continue exploring alternative, renewable forms of energy and electricity generation to meet our society's energy demands and maintain our Earth's clean air and water supplies.

# Competency 046: The Teacher Understands the Structure and Function of Living Things

## Major Taxonomic Groups

Living things are divided into five groups, or kingdoms: Monera (bacteria), Protista (protozoans), Fungi, Plantae (plants), and Animalia (animals).

*Monera* consists of unicellular organisms. It is the only group of living organisms made of prokaryotic cells—the cells with a primitive organization system. Some examples of this organism are bacteria, blue-green algae, and spirochetes.

*Protista* contains a type of eukaryotic cell with a more complex organization system. This kingdom includes diverse, mostly unicellular organisms that live in aquatic habitats, in both freshwater and saltwater. They are not animals or plants but unique organisms. Some examples of Protista are protozoans and algae of various types. The Amoeba, Paramecium, and Euglena are in the Protista Kingdom.

*Fungi* are multicellular organisms with a sophisticated organization system—that is, containing eukaryotic cells. Fungi exist in a variety of forms and shapes. Because they do not have chlorophyll, they cannot produce food through photosynthesis. Fungi obtain energy, carbon, and water from digesting dead materials. Some examples of these types of organisms are mushrooms, mold, mildews, and yeast.

*Plants* are multicellular organisms with a sophisticated organization system. In addition to more familiar plants, moss and ferns also fall under this category. Plant cells have chloroplasts, a component that allows them to trap sunlight as energy for the process of photosynthesis. In photosynthesis plants use carbon dioxide from the atmospheric environment and as the by-product of this process, supply the oxygen needed for the survival of animals.

*Animals* are also multicellular with multiple forms and shapes, and with specialized senses and organs. The Animalia kingdom is composed of organisms like sponges, worms, insects, fish, amphibians, reptiles, birds, and mammals. Animals are the most sophisticated type of living organisms and represent the highest levels of evolution. Animals live in all kinds of habitats, and they are as simple as flies or as sophisticated as humans.

## Life Functions and Cells

All living things carry on life functions, such as, respiration, nutrition, response, circulation, growth, excretion, regulation, and reproduction, all of which characterize them as *living* as opposed to nonliving. In addition, all living things are composed of the basic unit of life known as *cells*. Organisms, as well as individual cells of an organism and single-celled organisms, carry on these life functions using specialized structures. For example, earthworms carry on respiration through their moist skin; plants excrete gases from tiny pores on the underside of leaves called stomata; a single-celled Amoeba ingests food by use of a "false foot" or pseudopodia; and insects respond to chemical attractants called pheromones of the opposite-sex insect for mating.

Cells are the basic unit of all living organisms. Within cells there are specialized organelles that carry on all of the life functions at a microscopic/chemical level. For example, the mitochondria carries on cell respiration, and ribosomes assemble proteins for use both inside the cell and out. Teachers should know the parts of the cell, called organelles, and their functions, particularly, the nucleus, mitochondria, chloroplasts (plants only), ribosomes, Golgi, endoplasmic reticulum, vacuoles, and cell membranes.

Animal and plant cells are similar in appearance, but they do have certain distinctions. Animal cells contain mitochondria, small round or rod-shaped bodies found in the cytoplasm of most cells. The main function of mitochondria is to produce the enzymes for the metabolic conversion of food to energy. This process consumes oxygen and is termed aerobic respiration.

Plants cells also contain mitochondria, which allow plants to carry on respiration where they use oxygen and excrete carbon dioxide and water just like animals. However, plants also have specialized organelles called chloroplasts that are used for taking in sunlight and using this energy to convert the gas, carbon dioxide, and water taken in from the roots to make glucose—a simple sugar that is the food for the plant. Chloroplasts contain chlorophyll, which is used in this process of converting light into chemical energy. This process is called photosynthesis. Photosynthesis is the process by which chlorophyll-containing organisms convert light energy to chemical energy. Through the process of photosynthesis, a plant containing chlorophyll captures energy from the sun and converts it into chemical energy. Part of the chemical energy is used for the plant's own survival, and the rest is stored in the stem and leaves.

The cell is the basic unit of living organisms and the simplest living unit of life. Living organisms are composed of cells that have the following common characteristics:

- Have a membrane that regulates the flow of nutrients and water that enter and exit the cell

- Contain the genetic material (DNA) that allows for reproduction

- Require a supply of energy

- Contain basic chemicals to make metabolic decisions for survival

- Reproduce and are the result of reproduction

There are two kinds of cells—prokaryotic and eukaryotic. Prokaryotic cells are the simplest and most primitive type of cells. They do not contain the structures typical of eukaryotic cells. Prokaryotic cells lack a nucleus and instead have one strand of deoxyribonucleic acid (DNA). Some prokaryotic cells have external whip like flagella for locomotion or a hair-like system for adhesion. Prokaryotic cells come in three shapes: cocci (round), bacilli (rods), and spirilla or spirochetes (helical cells). Bacteria (of the Kingdom Monera) are prokaryotic cells.

Eukaryotic cells evolved from prokaryotic cells and in the process became structurally and biochemically more complex. The key distinction between the two cell types is that only eukaryotic cells contain many structures, or organelles, separated from other cytoplasm components by a membrane. The organelles within eukaryotic cells are the nucleus, mitochondria, chloroplasts, and Golgi apparatus. The nucleus contains the deoxyribonucleic acid (DNA) information. The mitochondria have their own membrane and contain some DNA information and proteins. They generate the energy for the cell. The chloroplast is a component that exists in *plants only*, allowing them to trap sunlight as energy for the process of photosynthesis. The Golgi apparatus secretes substances needed for the cell's survival.

An organism may consist of only one cell, or it may comprise many billions of cells of various dimensions. For example, cells are complete organisms, such as the unicellular bacteria; others, such as muscle cells, are parts of multicellular organisms. All cells have an internal substance called cytoplasm—a clear gelatinous fluid—enclosed within a membrane. Each cell contains the genetic material containing the information for the formation of organisms. Cells are composed primarily of water and the elements oxygen, hydrogen, carbon, and nitrogen.

## Structures and Functions

Moving outward from the *cell*, it is important to know that cells communicate with one another on a chemical level and work together to perform specific functions. The shape of these groups of cells and activity levels differ according to their particular function in the body; for example, muscle cells are long and narrow so they may better respond to stimuli and contract. Groups of cells with similar functions are called *tissues*. Tissues are organized together to perform a specific life function. A complex system of tissues working together to carry on one of the body's life functions is an *organ*. A group of different organs working together to support and help carry out a life function and keep the organism alive is called an *organ system*. Examples of systems include the digestive system, the respiratory system, the immune system, the muscular system, the skeletal system, the nervous system, and the circulatory system. Organ systems are organized into an *organism*. The order of organization is as follows:

Cells → Tissues → Organs → Systems → Organ Systems → Organism

## Musculoskeletal System

The human skeleton consists of more than 200 bones held together by connective tissues called ligaments. Movements are effected by contractions of the *skeletal muscles*, and skeletal muscles are arranged in pairs, such as the biceps and triceps of the upper arm. When one of the pair contracts, it causes a certain movement of the bones; in the meantime the opposing muscle relaxes. When the opposing pair of muscle contracts, a different movement of the bones occurs, and the original muscle of the pair relaxes. For example, when the biceps (the muscle on top of the upper arm) contracts, the arm bends upwards; when the opposing muscle of the pair, the triceps, contract, the arm extends. Skeletal muscles are attached to bones with specialized connective tissue called tendons.

The specialized connective tissue that attaches bones to other bones is called ligaments. The soft spongy tissue on the ends of bones is called cartilage. Muscular contractions are controlled by the nervous system.

In addition to skeletal muscle, the body also has muscles that are not part of the musculoskeletal system, thus not attached to bones. One such muscle type is called *smooth muscle*. Smooth muscle forms the inner linings of our digestive system and is controlled involuntarily by our autonomic (automatic) nervous system. A third type of muscle is *cardiac muscle*, which is the muscle of the heart, and is also controlled by our autonomic nervous system.

## Nervous System

The nervous system has two main divisions: the somatic and automatic. The somatic allows the voluntary control of skeletal muscles, and the automatic, or involuntary, controls cardiac and glandular functions. Voluntary movement is caused by nerve impulses sent from the brain through the spinal cord to nerves to connecting skeletal muscles. Involuntary movement occurs in direct response to outside stimulus. Involuntary responses are called reflexes. For example, when an object presents danger to the eye, the body responds automatically by blinking or retracting away from the object.

## Circulatory System

The circulatory system follows a cyclical process in which the heart pumps blood through the right chambers of the heart and through the lungs, where it acquires oxygen. From there it is pumped back into the left chambers of the heart, where it is pumped into the main artery (aorta), which then sends the oxygenated blood to the rest of the body using a system of veins and capillaries. Through the capillaries, the blood distributes the oxygen and nutrients to tissues, absorbing from them carbon dioxide, a metabolic waste product. Finally, the blood completes the circuit by passing through small veins, which join to form increasingly larger vessels. Eventually, the blood reaches the largest veins, which return it to the right side of the heart to complete and restart the process.

## Immune System

The main function of the body's immune system is to defend itself against foreign proteins and infectious organisms. The system recognizes organisms that are not normally in the body and develops the antibodies needed to control and destroy the invaders. When the body is attacked by infectious organisms, it develops what we know as a fever. Fever is the body's way of fighting invading molecules. The raised temperature of a fever will kill some bacteria. The major components of the immune system are the thymus, lymph system, bone marrow, white blood cells, antibodies, and hormones.

## Respiratory System

Respiration is carried out by the expansion and contraction of the lungs. In the lungs, oxygen enters tiny capillaries, where it combines with hemoglobin in the red blood cells and is carried to the tissues through the circulatory system. At the same time, carbon dioxide passes through capillaries into the air contained within the lungs.

Animals inhale oxygen from the environment and exhale carbon dioxide. Carbon dioxide is used by plants in the process of photosynthesis, which produces the oxygen that animals use again for survival.

## Digestive and Excretory Systems

The energy required for sustenance of the human body is supplied through the chemical energy stored in food. To obtain the energy from food, it has to be fragmented and digested. Digestion begins at the moment that food is placed in the mouth and makes contact with saliva. Fragmented and partially digested food passes down the esophagus to the stomach, where the process is continued by the gastric and intestinal juices. Thereafter, the mixture of food and secretions makes its way down the small intestine, where the nutrients are extracted and absorbed into the bloodstream. The unused portion of the food goes to the large intestine and eventually is excreted from the body through defecation.

### Reproductive System

Students in the middle grades should know some basic biological facts about human reproduction. They should know that the body matures and develops in order for child-bearing to occur. The menstrual cycle should be understood by students, including what occurs in ovulation to prepare the egg cell, namely, the process of meiosis. In males, the process of meiosis occurs to produce the sperm cell. Students should know that these specialized cells, called gametes (egg and sperm), unite to form a fertilized egg, which grows and develops in distinct stages to produce new offspring.

### Energy and Matter

Plants make glucose during the process of photosynthesis. Plant cells' chloroplasts capture energy from the sun, take in carbon dioxide ($CO_2$) from the atmosphere, and absorb water ($H_2O$) up through its roots and restructuring these molecules into glucose ($C_6H_{12}O_6$). The glucose is used to make its own body structures and stored in chains, which when assembled together make carbohydrates or starch. The starch is stored in roots, stems and leaves, and may also be transformed into other substances made by the plant such as oils, waxes, and fruits. Photosynthesis is the way plants make food, but it is not the way they metabolize food for energy. The sugars plants make are metabolized by oxygen in respiration to produce the energy needed for plants to carry on their own life functions (excretion, growth). Thus, it is important to know that similar to animals, *plants carry on respiration* (along with photosynthesis) taking oxygen into their cells and into the mitochondria—the respiratory centers of their cells—where they break the bonds of the glucose molecule ($C_6H_{12}O_6$) to release stored energy in the form of ATP. Note that it is a common misconception of students who may think that plants only carry on photosynthesis – plants also carry on cellular respirations just like animals. Note however that the processes of photosynthesis and respiration are the reverse of one another, only with sunlight as the source of energy in photosynthesis, and energy in the form of ATP being produced in respiration.

Animals need the sugars and stored starches made by plants in order for its own cells to carry on life functions and produce the energy needed to sustain the animal's life. Animals therefore must ingest food from plants, or from animals that had ingested plants. Once the food is digested into its smallest components in the small intestine, the glucose enters the bloodstream and is carried to the cells. In the cells, and inside the mitochondria of the cells, oxygen that entered the bloodstream and ultimately the cells through respiration combines with the glucose to break the chemical bonds of the molecule and produce energy in the form of ATP. This energy is needed for the animal to sustain its own life functions.

**Photosynthesis**

(Chloroplasts of plant cells)

Sunlight energy + $6CO_2$ + $6H_2O$ → $C_6H_{12}O_6$ + $6O_2$

**Plant *and* Animal Respiration**

(Mitochondria of both plant and animal cells)

$C_6H_{12}O_6$ + $6O_2$ → $6CO_2$ + $6H_2O$ + ATP energy

In addition to aerobic cellular respiration, which requires the use of oxygen in the process, organisms or certain cells of organisms may carry on anaerobic respiration, a form of respiration that does not use oxygen. Anaerobic respiration occurs in organisms such as yeast, called fermentation, and in the muscle cells of animals when the demands for energy are high, as during strenuous exercise. Anaerobic respiration yields less energy than aerobic respiration, therefore it occurs in small organisms (yeast, certain bacteria). In animals, it provides a little extra energy to the muscles in the form of ATP during exercise when extra energy is needed. The by-products in anaerobic respiration for yeast and certain bacteria (e.g., those used in making wine) are different than in muscle cells. In yeast and wine-making bacteria anaerobic respiration is called fermentation and the by-products are alcohol and carbon dioxide gas. The carbon dioxide gas is what makes bread dough containing yeast to rise (the alcohol burns off during baking). In the muscle cells the anaerobic respiration that takes place during strenuous exercise results in the production of lactic acid.

**Anaerobic Respiration in Yeast and Certain Bacteria (as Fermentation)**

$C_6H_{12}O_6$ (Glucose) is Broken down to → Energy (ATP) + Ethanol + Carbon dioxide ($CO_2$)

**Anaerobic Respiration in Muscle Cells**

$C_6H_{12}O_6$ (Glucose) is Broken down to → Energy (ATP) + Lactic acid

## Chemical Compounds of Life

All living things contain and/or need four main carbon-based compounds for life, also known as organic molecules. These four compounds or organic molecules are carbohydrates, proteins, lipids, and nucleic acids.

Carbohydrates are stored as starches, with the simplest form or basic building block a simple sugar or monosaccharide, such as glucose. Carbohydrates are ultimately digested into simple sugars and used in cellular respiration to produce energy for all life functions. The type of carbohydrate or starch is a factor of the number of monosaccharides in the chain, along with the types of monosaccharides. Plant substances contain starch in their roots, stems, leaves, and fruit in particular, with an abundance of starch often stored in the roots. Potatoes, carrots, turnips, corn, peas, celery, spinach and apples are examples of foods that store sugars and starches, or carbohydrates. Carbohydrates are composed of carbon, hydrogen, and oxygen atoms.

Proteins are complex molecules that are made of a repeating, and an often turned and twisted chain of its smallest component, amino acids. Proteins can be immense in size and perform a variety of essential functions and purposes in the body. Proteins are in cell membranes, and make up connective tissue, bones and muscles, and are the enzymes and hormones that control the body's metabolism and internal actions that maintain life. There are 20 different amino acids that exist on earth that make proteins. Proteins are found in meats, eggs, and cheese, as examples. In addition to carbon, oxygen, and hydrogen atoms, proteins contain nitrogen.

Lipids are fats, and the basic building block or smallest component is one to three fatty acid molecules and one glycerol molecule bonded together. Lipids are stored as energy reserves in the fat of animals, or stored in the form of oils in plants. The stored in the body, provides insulation for animals in cold climates, and is also believed to be important for brain development. Lipids can be found marbled within meats, and in substances like butter and oils. Lipids contain carbon, hydrogen, and oxygen molecules.

Nucleic acids include deoxyribonucleic acids (DNA) and ribonucleic acids (RNA) found inside of cells. These nucleic acids provide hereditary information and instructions or "blueprints" that direct the cell's life functions. The smallest component of DNA and RNA are nucleotides, which consist of a sugar, a phosphate group, and a nitrogen base. In DNA the sugar is deoxyribose and the nitrogen base in a nucleotide can be adenine (A), thymine (T), cytosine (C), or guanine (G). DNA is shaped as a "double helix" or twisted ladder, with the rungs of the molecular ladder being paired nitrogen bases, and the sides being the sugars and phosphate groups. The nitrogen bases from one side of the ladder are weakly bonded or attracted to the nitrogen bases on the other side of the ladder by hydrogen bonds. The pairing of nitrogen bases is important: DNA nucleotides with the nitrogen base *thymine* only bonds in the center of the ladder with nucleotides carrying the nitrogen base *adenine*, whereas nucleotides with *cytosine* only bond with nucleotides that have the nitrogen base *guanine* (A-T or G-C). The differing sizes of the nitrogen bases, A, T, G, and C cause the ladder to twist, thus forming the twisted double-helix shape. The particular sequence of DNA nucleotides with their nitrogen bases code for traits and characteristics of the organism. The sequence in a section of DNA that codes for a trait is called a *gene*.

Ribonucleic acid (RNA) is similar to DNA, only it is single stranded rather than double, the sugar in the nucleotide is ribose instead of deoxyribose, and the nitrogen bases are adenine, uracil, cytosine, and guanine (no thymine). In RNA adenine pairs with uracil, and cytosine pairs with guanine. RNA is important in making proteins (e.g., enzymes, hormones) in the cell to be used for a particular life function such as making the enzyme lipase in pancreatic cells to digest the sugar in milk known as lactose.

Nucleic acids are composed of carbon, hydrogen, and oxygen, and also phosphorus, nitrogen and sometime sulfur.

## Competency 047: The Teacher Understands Reproduction and the Mechanisms of Heredity

### Asexual and Sexual Reproduction

There are two forms of reproduction, asexual and sexual reproduction. Asexual reproduction has one parent cell that divides by a process called mitosis or binary fission into two daughter cells with identical DNA as the parent and as each other. This type of reproduction occurs in simple, one-celled organisms and in body cells when they undergo growth and repair, and takes place through a series of steps in the cell's life cycle. Growth in most organisms is caused by mitosis. The importance of mitosis is that the daughter cells are an exact copy of the original. Through mitosis, new cells are made, for example, to form a scar after an injury, new bone cells, muscle cells, blood cells, and any cell that is needed by the body throughout life and growth. In single-celled organisms, mitosis is the cell's form of reproduction—making exact copies of the DNA in each of the two "daughter" cells, and is often called binary fission. Only one organism (the single cell) is involved and there is no exchange of genetic material or DNA. Thus, the two offspring cells, or daughter cells, are identical to the original or parent cell.

In mitosis, the entire DNA within each chromosome in the cell makes a copy of itself (replicates). The replicated chromosomes containing DNA line up along the equatorial plane of the cell, and through a series of events, prepare to be separated from each other. When the cell divides, one copy of each strand or chromosome of DNA goes into one of the daughter cells, and one goes into the other daughter cell. This process preserves the DNA of the parent, but does not allow for much variation in the offspring (daughter cells).

Sexual reproduction requires two parent cells, and the combination DNA from parent with the DNA from the other parent in the new cell or offspring. Sexual reproduction occurs in more complex organisms. The process of producing the cells that will ultimately join together to form the new offspring is meiosis. Meiosis occurs only in specialized cells of the parents – namely within the sex organs or gonads, known as the ovary in females and testicles in males. Meiosis is somewhat similar to mitosis but there are important distinctions. Meiosis is how sperm and egg cells are formed in preparation for being combined in the process of fertilization.

Each species of organism has a certain number of chromosomes (containing DNA and thus the genetic code) in each of its cells, for example, humans have 46 chromosomes, arranged in 23 pairs. Any new offspring of that species must have the same number of chromosomes as the parent cells. Thus, in the case of humans, the specialized beginning cells (oocytes and spermatocytes) in the gonads have 46 chromosomes, but they must make cells that have half the number of chromosomes (23 in total), which are called *gametes*. Again this reduction to half the number of chromosomes occurs because when the gamete from one parent (female egg or ovum) combines with the gamete from the other parent (male sperm cell) the full number of 46 chromosomes (arranged in 23 pairs) is restored in the fertilized egg. In sum, meiosis is the process that reduces the number of chromosomes in half to prepare the new daughter cell(s), namely the egg cell in females and sperm cell in males, to join together in the process known as fertilization to produce a new offspring.

In meiosis the chromosomes duplicate as they do in mitosis however, the cell divides twice, preserving one of each pair of chromosomes in the resulting four daughter cells (in humans, 23 chromosomes). The result of meiosis, therefore, is four cells with half the number of chromosomes as the original parent cell. In the female, only one of the four daughter cells becomes a viable egg cell, whereas in males all four daughter cells are viable sperm cells. After the egg cell has been fertilized by the sperm, it is called a zygote. The zygote immediately begins to divide by *mitosis* to grow and develop into a new offspring; first forming a structure called the morula, then a blastocyst (ball of cells) and then differentiating its cells into what will become the various structures and organs of the new offspring, called the gastrula. Soon the gastrula, with its rapidly dividing and differentiating cells, becomes an embryo, and later a fetus that is growing and developing (by mitosis) into the new offspring.

Sexual reproduction allows for more variation in offspring because they have a combination of genetic material (DNA) from each parent.

Many animals carry out sexual reproduction and therefore come from eggs. For some animals, the egg is inside the female animal and is fertilized by the male sperm cells within the body. For other animals such as most fish species, the eggs are fertilized by the male after they have been expelled from the female's body. When fertilized internally, the fertilized egg may be laid externally from the female as in many insects, reptiles, and birds, or it may remain in the body of the female until birth. The egg has an outer lining to protect the animal growing inside. Bird eggs have hard shells, while the eggs of amphibians, like the turtle, have hard but flexible coverings. With the appropriate care and heat, an egg will hatch. After hatching, in some species, the parents protect and feed the newborn until it can survive on its own; in other species, the eggs are left on their own to survive. On reaching adulthood, females begin laying eggs, and the cycle of life continues. Mammals are also conceived through egg fertilization, but the resulting embryo is kept inside the mother until it is mature enough for life outside the womb.

The reproduction of plants can also be divided into asexual and sexual mechanisms. Asexual reproduction of plants takes place by cutting portions of the plant and replanting them. Tubers or the eyes of potatoes and the bulbs of tulips grow into roots and are also a form of asexual reproduction.

Sexual reproduction in plants involves seeds produced by flowers of female and male plants, which are cross-pollinated with help from insects or other animals. The flower is the reproductive organ of the plant and consists of several parts that are the male and female reproductive organs. Some flowers may have only the male part, and likewise, some flowers contain only the female part of the same species of plant/tree. So there actually can be a "male" tree and a "female" tree for example. In the flower, the male reproductive organ is the *stamen*, which is divided into filament and anther. The filament simply holds up the anther, and the anther contains the pollen and in the pollen are the sperm nuclei. Flowers may also contain the female reproductive organ, the *pistil*, which consists of the ovary, style, and stigma. The ovary contains the egg cells, which in the flower are called ovules. The style is the tube above the ovary, and the stigma is the top of the style which has a sticky substance. The pollen needs to either be manually placed on the stigma, or blown there by the wind, or what usually happens, it needs to stick to the body of a bee or butterfly (who are actually in search of sugary nectar in the flower and not the pollen). When the pollen sticks to the body of the insect, it may then be transferred from the anther (male part) to the stigma (female part). In essence, the sperm nuclei then travel down the style to reach the ovules, where fertilization occurs. The fertilized egg then becomes the seed. The ovary of the flower may swell and become the fruit (as in a peach or apple). This process helps protect the seeds and also helps with seed dispersal (animals eat the fruit, the seed has a seed coat that protects it and is indigestible, the animals excretes the seed, unharmed, in its fecal matter). Seed germination—where the seed sprouts into a plant—requires the appropriate quantity of air, water, and heat.

## Heredity

Hereditary information is contained in the specific sequence of DNA in areas called genes, on chromosomes within the cells of organisms. Traits are inherited from the parent cells to the offspring, according to the genes the offspring receive from the parents for particular traits. More than one trait can be determined by a single gene, and one or many genes can determine a particular trait. For example, the gene for human eye color is located on several genes. However, there may be several different physical expressions of genes, such as eye color, with brown, blue, green and hazel eye colors appearing in offspring, as examples. There are also three genes called alleles, for blood type, A, B, and O that exist in the human population. According to the National Human Genome Institute, an allele is one of two or more versions of a gene however offspring inherit two alleles for each gene. One allele was inherited from each parent, one from the original sperm cell, and one from the original egg cell.

Recall that sperm and egg cells each contain one of each pair of chromosomes from the original parent cell. When the egg is fertilized the pairs are restored, but a random combination from the mother (egg) and father (sperm). The genes inherited by the parent cells may be *dominant* or *recessive* for certain traits in the offspring. In the pair of chromosomes, dominant gene is the trait that is expressed in the offspring when paired with another dominant gene or with a recessive gene. The recessive gene is only expressed when paired with another recessive gene for a trait. Gene pairs are often shown in science as letters, for example, Brown fur color = B (dominant is shown as a capital letter), and white fur color = b (recessive is shown as a lower case letter of the dominant gene). Genetic problems are solved using Punnett square diagrams. These Punnett diagrams help predict the gene combinations and expressed traits in the offspring. The genotype is the actual gene combination, and the phenotype is the trait that is expressed or that "shows up" in the offspring. Recall that the egg or sperm cell will have only one of each allele, whereas the fertilized egg (offspring) will have two, and that number will be maintained in every cell in the offspring throughout its lifetime (except for its own sperm and egg cells when an adult). Two dominant traits may be shown as two capital letters (BB), a dominant and recessive pair may be shown as a capital letter with a lower case (Bb), and two recessive genes are shown as two lower case letters (bb). Two of the same, e.g., two dominant genes or two recessive genes, is called homozygous for that trait and one dominant and one recessive together is termed heterozygous (hybrid).

A Punnett square problem is solved by placing the egg cell genes along one top (or side) of the diagram, and sperm cell genes along the side (or top). Then the genes are combined within the boxes of the diagram, representing fertilization, to predict the probabilities of certain gene combinations occurring in the offspring.

B = dominant for brown fur

b = recessive for white fur

A mother guinea pig is homozygous dominant for brown fur. She is mated with a heterozygous male with brown fur color. What are the expected genotypes and phenotypes of the offspring? The solution is shown in the Punnett square diagram below.

|  | mother | |
|---|---|---|
| father | B | B |
| B | BB | BB |
| b | Bb | Bb |

In this problem, the mother's genotype is BB and she has brown fur. The father's genotype is Bb and he also has brown fur, however carries the gene for white fur. Fifty percent of the offspring will be homozygous dominant (BB), and fifty percent will be heterozygous (Bb). One hundred percent of the offspring will have the phenotype of brown fur color.

In addition to the genotype and phenotype directly inherited in offspring, environmental factors may contribute to how, or sometimes even whether, the gene is expressed. Some genes may not be expressed until an environmental condition or stressor triggers the gene into action. It is believed that autoimmune diseases, a situation where antibodies are formed to attack otherwise normal body cells, as in certain forms of hypothyroidism, are triggered by environmental stressors. In addition, factors in the environment such as viruses or carcinogens may activate susceptible inherited genes in an individual in the development certain cancers, food intolerances, or allergies.

Genetics has somewhat recently been transformed into an industry, where crops and cattle are genetically engineered for example, to produce greater quality specimens at higher yields. The health industry has been able to use genetics to produce vaccines and medications that have vastly improved the quality of human life, however sometimes impinging on socially controversial areas such as stem cell research and cloning. By changing the DNA sequence in genes, scientists may, for example, be able to grow limbs and organs to replace those lost, develop humans with pre-specified desired characteristics, or increase the human lifespan. Thus, genetics has been beneficial to the quality of life, however if unchecked, could also create controversy and possible dangerous results.

## Competency 048: The Teacher Understands Adaptations of Organisms and the Theory of Evolution

### Survival in the Environment

Genetics plays an important role in the ability of organisms to be able to survive and thrive in their environment and, ultimately, produce new offspring such that they pass on similar genetic material, *like* that which allowed them to survive and thrive, and maybe survive and thrive even better. Some inherited traits, called adaptations, could allow the organisms to better survive in their environment or could lead to their demise (and thus prevent the prospect of future offspring). It is important to note that adaptations do not suddenly arise or develop in the lifetime of organisms. They occur gradually in the species over time. For example, if a certain deer-like animal thousands of years ago were particularly fast—that is, it was born with stronger muscle tissue than most, and a better bone and muscle physical structure—perhaps it was better able to run away from predators and survive. Therefore, this deer-like animal was able to survive long enough for it to have offspring with similar genetic material. At the same time, those deer-like animals that were not born with the same muscular and structural soundness as this one were killed as prey before they could reproduce. The animal that was best adapted to its environment (needing to run from predators) was the first deer-like animal. In time, those animals that are best suited in this, as well as in other ways, are the organisms who survive, as do their offspring. Those not well adapted perish. It is also the case that the organism that survives will breed with another that also has better adapted characteristics, and was also able to survive in the natural environment. A change or mutation in the genetic material, that is, the genes that direct the development of a trait, may give rise to a new characteristic that either is or is not better suited for the environment. In the case that it is better suited, the organism will survive and produce offspring with this same mutation. Over the years, mutations that are better suited to the environment may make the organism appear quite different than it did hundreds, thousands, and millions of years earlier. If the environment itself changes, however, organisms that were able to survive under the previous conditions (climate, water supply, vegetation, landscape) may be unable to survive in the new environmental conditions. Thus, a catastrophic event, such as perhaps a large asteroid striking the Earth, could change the environmental conditions and either lead to the extinction of organisms, or the survival of organisms that would not have survived under the conditions before the strike. Likewise, selective breeding, which is human selection of which organisms breed with another, and which controls the genetic material that is passed onto offspring, also effects the change over time of organisms. The combination of genetics, adaptations, changes over time, mutations, selective breeding, and environmental conditions/changes contribute to the concept known as evolution.

It is important to understand that adaptations come about in a random manner. Though it was not known how adaptations occurred in Darwin's writings or Gregor Mendel's studies (the father of heredity) it was later discovered that adaptations occurred due to random mutations of gene sequences that code for certain traits. For a multitude of reasons, chance, environmental conditions, exposure to toxic material, genetic codes may change. The change in genetic code may give rise to a variation in a trait that turns out to be more favorable that the original trait. If the change prolongs the life of the species with the mutation, then the mutated species more likely to survive long enough to produce new offspring with the same favorable mutation.

There are several lines of evidence for evolution. Paleontology contributes to our understanding of past organisms, specifically fossils.

- Fossils found in more recent layers of rock are similar or identical to existing organisms.

- In older rock layers, fossils significantly differ from present day organisms.

- Discoveries are regularly being made that fill gaps in the fossil record.

- Scientists are finding fossils that have the features they predicted based on known, older and younger fossils

- Fossils of any species have only been found in rock layers younger than their ancestor species, and not found in rock layers older than their ancestors.

Because the Earth is constantly changing, plates shifting and colliding, continents being uplifted, and seas being buried, fossils of once-living organisms have been found in all places over the Earth, called biogeography. Scientists have been able to reveal from fossils that species originate in one place and spread out to other places from that source. Fossils have been found to do exactly that—where a fossil is found it can be traced back to its source point.

Another source of evidence of evolution, known as developmental biology, studies how vertebrate embryos develop. During their development from embryos, all vertebrates tend to share common features. Some of these features, such as a tail, appear only in the embryo stage of some species and then disappear or are incorporated into the body, whereas the same feature may remain in another species.

Animals can be grouped according to commons physical structures or morphology. Organisms are grouped, for example, as vertebrates and invertebrates due to the presence or absence of a backbone.

Homologous and analogous structures exist in organisms. Homologous structures are of the same origin but have different functions. For example, the bone structure of the wing of a bat is very similar to the bone structure of the human arm. Analogous structures developed from unrelated evolutionary lines, but the structure was a positive adaptation to the environment, so both survived and were carried on to offspring in their respective species. An example of analogous structures is the wing of a bird and the wing of a house fly. Both serve as a beneficial adaptation, even though the species are not related.

With more precise and detailed information now available on genomes and particular gene sequences that make an organism's genetic code, we are better able to show how closely species may be related due to similarities and differences in the sequence. For example, humans have been found to be more closely related to chimpanzees according to similarities in the genetic code, than to gorillas—a finding that was at first surprising.

## Competency 049: The Teacher Understands Regulatory Mechanisms and Behavior

### Response to Stimuli

All living organisms respond to stimuli from within and outside in the environment. Stimuli within the organism are internal stimuli, including feeling hungry or needing food; stimuli outside of the organism are external stimuli such as warmth or cold, light or dark. Even the tiniest organisms such as Bacteria have sensory mechanisms called chemoreceptors in its cell membrane that allow it to sense and move toward food in its environment. Plants have chemical hormone substances called auxins, which cause a variety of growth and movement patterns called tropisms. Auxins in plants root tips sense and cause the roots to grow toward water, called hydrotropism, and downward toward gravity (geotropism). Auxins in the stem tips sense light and cause the stems and leaves to grow toward light (phototropism). Other auxins cause plants twining plants to seek anchors, some flowers to open during the day and close at night, and growth patterns called circadian rhythms.

Animals respond to external stimuli using their senses, with many responses to stimuli being automatic, such as the pupils of the eyes dilating in the dark and constricting in light (external stimuli). The nervous system in animals controls responses, sending signals to the spinal cord (if present in the organism) and/or to the brain, which then instructs the appropriate muscles or organs to respond. For example, if one accidentally touches a hot stove with the hand, the nervous system immediately sends a signal to the spinal cord, which sends a signal to the correct muscle (biceps) to pull the hand away. It is only after the hand is pulled away from danger that the signal is sent on to the brain and that the hand was burned is realized. Once the individual verbalizes pain (ouch!), the hand has already been pulled away. The action of the nerves in the hand to the spinal cord to the muscle is called a 'reflex' arc. The purpose of the reflex arc is for protection.

## Maintaining Stable Internal Conditions

Organisms respond to stimuli to maintain a stable internal condition called homeostasis. Homeostasis mechanisms maintain the organism's proper temperature, pH, respiratory rates, and other important factors that protect the balance of life functions in the organism. Maintaining homeostasis is important for an organisms' survival.

In addition to the nervous system, hormones within the body also act to regulate life functions and maintain homeostasis. Hormones are produces in glands in the body within the endocrine system. For example, adrenalin is secreted from the adrenal glands (located on top of the kidneys) in high stress or fear situations, such as being chased by a viscous dog, that triggers a series of other responses in the body to that allow the organism to experience "flight or fight" reactions. For example, respiration and heart rate is increased and the brain is more alert. Some have reported sudden bursts of strength in such situations allowing them to survive or escape the stressful or fearful situation. Other hormones, for example, those secreted by the thyroid and pituitary gland, control growth and metabolism, and in females, hormones including estrogen and progesterone control menstrual cycles and pregnancy.

## Feedback Mechanisms

Regulatory feedback mechanisms can be positive or negative. Positive feedback mechanisms causes reactions to increase, such as eating when hungry, whereas negative feedback causes reactions to slow down such as to stop eating when full. The examples already described in this section, such as secretion of adrenalin in the body, describe feedback mechanisms, in this case, a positive feedback mechanism where the stimulus causes a reaction, rather than slows or stops a reaction.

## Evolution and Behavior

Organisms have long developed and displayed behaviors that contribute to its survival as a species. In ant colonies, for example, individual organisms have specific roles that ensure the survival of the entire colony, e.g., workers, soldiers. Other behaviors, such as mating dances of some animals, echolocation in bats, differing bird calls, are behaviors that have evolved over time that serve an important role in survival.

## Competency 050: The Teacher Understands Relationships Between Organisms and the Environment

Ecology studies the relationship of organisms with their physical environment. The physical environment includes light, heat, solar radiation, moisture, wind, oxygen, carbon dioxide, nutrients, water, and the atmosphere. These factors of the physical environment are the *abiotic* (nonliving) components of the ecosystem. The *biotic* components are the living and nonliving organisms in the ecosystem. There are three main biotic components of an ecosystem:

- *Producers* are green plants that produce oxygen and store chemical energy for consumers.

- *Consumers* are animals, both herbivores and carnivores. The herbivores take the chemical energy from plants, and carnivores take the energy from other animals or directly from plants.

- *Decomposers*, like fungi and bacteria, are in charge of cleaning up the environment by decomposing and freeing dead matter for recycling back into the ecosystem.

A successful ecosystem requires a healthy balance among producers, consumers, and decomposers. This balance relies on natural ways to control populations of living organisms and is maintained mostly through competition and predation. Predation is the consumption of one living organism, plant or animal, by another. It is a direct way to control population and promote natural selection by eliminating weak organisms from the population. As a consequence of predation, predators and prey evolve to survive. If an organism cannot evolve to meet challenges from the environment, it perishes.

Living organisms like plants and animals need to have ideal conditions for their survival. They need nutrients, the appropriate temperature, and a balanced ecosystem to survive and reproduce. A healthy ecosystem must contain an appropriate system for energy exchange or a food chain. The right combination of herbivorous and carnivorous animals is necessary for a healthy ecosystem. The food chain generally begins with the primary source of energy, the sun. The sun provides the energy for plants; plants in turn are consumed by animals; and animals are consumed by other animals. These animals die and serve as food sources for decomposing bacteria, fungi and plants. In the food chain, or more accurately, food web, energy from the sun is captured by plants in photosynthesis to make sugars stored as starches. Some of this energy is transferred to the consumers when eaten, however energy was lost to the plant itself when used in its own life processes. Each level along the food chain receives less and less energy because of the use of some of the energy by the organism itself to sustain its life functions. It is estimated that each level of consumer only receives about 10% of the energy from the producer or consumer it ingests, whereas 90% was used in that organism's own life functions. A food chain is shown as follows. Decomposers digest dead organisms and return them to soil so that, with proper sunlight and water conditions, new producers may begin the food chain/web again.

**Food chain/web:**

Sun → producers → 1st order consumers → 2nd order consumers →
3rd order consumers → decomposers

**Example:**

Sun → wild corn → mouse → snake → hawk → decomposing bacteria

When the balance of the ecosystem's food chain/web is disrupted either by the removal of organisms or the introduction of nonnative species, the ecosystem is affected, forcing animals and plants to adapt or else die. Thus, the common basic needs of all living organisms for survival are: *air, water, food,* and *shelter.* When a shared resource is scarce, organisms must compete to survive. The competition, which occurs between animals as well as between plants, ensures the survival of the fittest and the preservation of the system.

Changes in the environment have led to certain adaptations to arise in organisms that are favorable to the new environment, and did allow the organisms without that adaptation to survive. The behaviors or physical features of organisms that developed due to mutations that were more favorable to the changes in the environment allowed greater chances of survival and so were carried on to future generations. For example, over thousands of years, the anteater species and its offspring were able to survive better if they had a long snout to be able to reach for ants, and frogs developed a long, sticky tongue to catch flies. Adaptation for animals, plants, and even humans is a matter of life and death. As another example, in analyzing the skulls of predators versus prey a pattern in the placement of the eye sockets and shapes of teeth becomes clear. Predators such as wolves, foxes, and lions have eye sockets in the front of their skull, which helps them focus on their prey when hunting. Prey such as rabbits and squirrels have eyes on the sides of their skull, which helps them see on both sides of their body at once in order to escape predation. Predators have sharp, pointed teeth for tearing the flesh of their prey, whereas prey (those that are primary or first order consumers) have flat teeth for chewing and grinding plants they consume. It is important to note that plants and other non-animal organisms also adapt their environment. For example, coniferous trees have thin but strong needles rather than leaves to protect it against the cold, whereas plants in the tropics have broad leaves allowing it to absorb the abundant sunshine for photosynthesis and release excess water through transpiration. In bacteria, a mutation in its genetic code may result in the bacteria being resistant to antibiotics; bacteria without the mutation are killed by the antibiotic, whereas the mutated variety survives. When the bacterium divides in binary fission, its offspring or replicated bacteria contains the mutated DNA, so is also resistant to the antibiotic. This new, mutated variety of bacteria becomes predominant, whereas the former variety dies off. This is why scientists work to make new and different antibiotics in order to eliminate the new mutated species of bacteria.

Changes in the food chain of animals often lead to modifications in behaviors and the predominance of certain inherited traits that are favorable adaptations to new conditions. For example, because their habitats are destroyed when land is developed by humans, raccoons and opossums have learned to coexist with humans and to get new sources of food. Bears have managed to successfully adapt to colder climates by hibernating during the winter and living on the fat they accumulate during the rest of the year. Other animals, like the chameleon and the fox, have developed camouflage to hide from predators. Humans are not exempt from the need to adapt to new situations. For example, humans have had to adapt and use tools to produce, preserve, and trade the food supplies they needed to sustain them. All these examples represent ways in which organisms adapt to deal with challenges in their ecosystem.

## Competency 051: The Teacher Understands the Structure and Function of Earth Systems

The formation of deserts, mountains, rivers, oceans, and other landforms can be described in terms of geological processes. Mountains are formed by colliding plates. For example, the Appalachian Mountains in the United States were formed 250 million years ago when the tectonic plate carrying the continent of Africa collided with the plate carrying the North American continent (Badder et. al., 2000). Rivers and natural lakes form at low elevations where rainfall collects and eventually runs down to the sea. The sediment gathered by the rivers in turn accumulates at river mouths to create deltas. These are both constructive and destructive processes that form the Earth. *Constructive processes* include those that build mountains, such as the gradual (over millions of years) collision and crushing together of the earth's tectonic plates. *Destructive processes* include weathering and erosion—the wearing down of mountains and rock by forces such as water, wind, and ice.

## Layers of the Earth

The average circumference of the Earth at the equator is 25,902 miles, and its radius is about 3,959 miles. The Earth is divided into three main parts:

- The crust is the outer portion of the Earth where we live. The thickness of the crust varies from about 3 miles to 40 miles, depending on the location. It contains various types of soil, metals, and rocks. The crust is broken down into several floating tectonic plates. Movements of these plates cause earthquakes and changes in landforms.

- The mantle is the thickest layer of the Earth located right below the crust. It is composed mostly of rocks and metals. The heat in the mantle is so intense that rocks and metals melt, creating magma and the resulting lava that reaches the surface.

- The core is the inner part of the Earth. It is composed of a solid inner core and an outer core that is mostly liquid. The inner core is made of solid iron and nickel. Despite temperatures in the inner core that resemble the heat on the surface of the sun, this portion of the Earth remains solid because of the intense pressure there.

## Continental Drift

In 1915, the German scientist Alfred Weneger proposed that all the continents were previously one large continent but then broke apart and drifted through the ocean floor to their present locations. This theory was called the Continental Drift, and it was the origin of today's concept of plate tectonics.

## Tectonic Plates

Based on the theory of plate tectonics, the surface of the Earth is fragmented into large plates. The upper crust, or lithosphere rides on top of the layer beneath, called the asthenosphere. The lithospheric plates are in continuous motion, floating on more liquid-like asthenosphere and always changing in size and position. The edges of these plates, where they move against each other, are sites of intense geologic activity, which results in earthquakes, volcanoes, and the creation of mountains. The generator for the movement of the continents/Earth's plates is the mid-Atlantic ridge—a huge volcanic mountain range on the floor of the Atlantic Ocean that is continuously erupting and pushing the plates apart in opposite directions from each other.

## Forces That Change the Surface of the Earth

Three main forces and processes change the surface of the Earth: weathering, geological movements, and the creation of glaciers.

### Weathering

Weathering is the process of breaking down rock, soils, and minerals through natural, chemical, and biological processes. Two of the most common examples of physical weathering are exfoliation and freeze thaw.

- Exfoliation occurs in places like the desert when the soil is exposed first to high temperatures, which cause it to expand, and then to cold temperatures, which make the soil contract. The stress of these changes causes the outer layers of rock to peel off.

- Freeze-thaw breaks down rock when water gets into rock joints or cracks and then freezes and expands, breaking the rock. A similar process occurs when water containing salt crystals gets into the rock. Once the water evaporates, the crystals expand and break the rock. This process is called salt-crystal growth.

Weathering can be caused by chemical reactions. Two of the most common examples of chemical weathering are acid formation and hydration. Acid is formed under various conditions. For example, sulfur and rain are combined to create acid rain, which can weather and change the chemical composition of rock. Hydration occurs when the mineralso in rock absorb water and expand sometimes changing the chemical composition of the rock. For example, through the process of hydration, a mineral like anhydrite can be changed into a different mineral, namely gypsum.

### Erosion

After weathering, a second process called erosion can take place. Erosion is the movement of sediment from one location to the other through the use of water, wind, ice, or gravity. The Grand Canyon was created by the processes of weathering and erosion. The water movement (erosion) is responsible for the canyon being so deep, and the weathering process is responsible for its width (Badder et al., 2000).

### Earthquakes and Geologic Faults

The movement of the Earth's plates has forced rock layers to fold, creating mountains, hills, and valleys. This movement causes faults in the Earth's crust, breaking rocks and reshaping the environment. When forces within the Earth cause rocks to break and move around geologic faults, earthquakes occur. A fault is a deep crack that marks the boundary between two plates. The San Andreas Fault in central California is a well-known origin of earthquakes in the area. The epicenter of an earthquake is the point on the surface where the quake is the strongest. The Richter scale is used to measure the amount of energy released by the earthquake. The severity of an earthquake runs from 0 to 9 on the Richter scale. Small tremors occur constantly, but generally every few months, a major earthquake occurs somewhere in the world. Scientists are researching ways to predict earthquakes, but their predictions are not always accurate. There are various types of earthquake faults lines. These fault lines include normal fault, thrust fault, and strike-slip fault and are named according to how the two sides of the fault interface to cause the earthquake.

### Volcanoes

Volcanoes are formed by the constant motion of tectonic plates. This movement creates pressure that forces magma from the mantel to escape to the surface, creating an explosion of lava, fire, and ash. The pressure of the magma and gases creates a monticule, or a small cone, that eventually grows to form a mountain-like volcano. Volcanic activity can create earthquakes, and the fiery lava can cause destruction. There are several types of volcanoes with different characteristics, including cinder cones, composite volcanoes, shield volcanoes, and lava domes.

### Gravity

Gravity is the force of attraction that exists between objects. Gravity keeps the Earth in its orbit by establishing a balance between the attraction of the sun and the speed at which the Earth travels around it. However, gravity is also responsible for many of the Earth's forces that change the land. For example, when ice melts on the tops of mountains, it is because of gravity that the water will form streams and rivers that flow down the mountain, eventually making its way to the lowest point. Some of the main functions of gravity are listed here:

- Keeping the Earth's atmosphere, oceans, and inhabitants from drifting into space
- Pulling the rain to the rivers and eventually to the sea
- Guiding the development and growth of plants

- Affecting the way that our bones and muscles function

For information about the Earth and space, go to the official website of the National Aeronautics and Space Administration (NASA) at *www.nasa.gov*. The site includes special sections for students from kindergarten through grade 12 and teachers.

## Surface Water and Groundwater

Surface water is the water in streams, lakes and rivers, and all water that is on the surface of the land. Ground water is water that seeps beneath the surface of the land and forms an underground "river" of water. The groundwater seeps into the soil until it reaches an impermeable layer of rock. The water stays on top of this layer and is a source of drinking water. This water may be tapped into via aquifers and wells.

## The Earth's Atmosphere

The Earth is surrounded by a large mass of gas called the atmosphere. Roughly 348 miles thick, this gas mass supports life on the Earth and separates it from space. Among the many functions of the atmosphere are these:

- Absorbing energy from the sun to sustain life

- Recycling water and other chemicals needed for life

- Maintaining the climate, working with electric and magnetic forces

- Serving as a vacuum that protects life

The atmosphere is composed of 78 percent nitrogen, 21 percent oxygen, and 1 percent argon. In addition to these gases, the atmosphere contains water, greenhouse gases like ozone, and carbon dioxide. The Earth's atmosphere has five layers. The layer closest to the Earth is called the troposphere, and the weather we experience occurs in this layer.

## Natural and Human Influences on Earth Systems

It is important to understand that many natural processes on Earth can change its systems. For example, earthquakes and volcanoes can be destructive and change the structure and composition of the landscape. Tsunamis, an enormous wall of water that crashes into shorelines caused by earthquakes under bodies of water such as oceans, can create a dramatic change in that shoreline. However, human influences may also change Earth systems. The destruction of the rainforests, called deforestation can change the structure and composition of the land, and on a larger scale, affect the balance of atmospheric gases including carbon dioxide and oxygen levels. Carbon dioxide emissions from factories, automobiles, and airplanes, as examples, may play a role in changing the atmospheric composition as well. Carbon dioxide, called a *greenhouse gas*, tends to trap heat energy and result in an overall warming of the atmosphere, which has an impact on climate and plant growth that in turn affects all living organisms on Earth. There are many natural and human influences that contribute to the increase of greenhouse gases in the atmosphere producing what is known as *global warming*. Other greenhouse gases include methane ($CH_4$) and ozone, which is the molecule $O_3$ that when at the surface of the Earth are components of smog.

It is important to distinguish global warming and the ozone that is in smog from the destruction of the ozone layer (hole in the ozone layer) which is a different phenomenon. Ozone forms a layer at the top of the atmosphere that blocks harmful ultraviolet rays from the sun from reaching the Earth's surface ("good ozone"). The "hole" in the ozone layer means there is a destruction of this ozone layer, and now harmful ultraviolet radiation is reaching Earth's surface where this hole is present. Chlorofluorocarbons, which are found in aerosols, contribute to the destruction of the ozone layer.

## Energy Transfer

The transfer of heat is accomplished in three ways: conduction, radiation, and convection.

Conduction is the process of transferring heat or electricity through a substance. It occurs when two objects of differing temperatures are placed in contact with each other and heat flows from the hotter object to the cooler object. For example, in the cooling system of a car, heat from the engine is transferred to the liquid coolant. When the coolant passes through the radiator, the heat transfers from the coolant to the radiator, and eventually, out of the car. This heat transfer system preserves the engine and allows it to continue working.

Radiation describes the energy that travels at high speed in space in the form of light or through the decay of radioactive elements. Radiation is part of our modern life. It exists in simple states as the energy emitted by microwaves, cellular phones, and sunshine or as potentially dangerous energy as X-ray machines and nuclear weapons. The radiation used in medicine, nuclear power, and nuclear weapons has enough energy to cause permanent damage and death.

Convection describes the flow of heat through the movement of fluid matter, meaning gases and liquids, from a hot region to a cool region. In its most basic form, the concept of convection is that warmer gases or liquids rise and colder gases or liquids sink. The colder gases or liquids contract and so are denser and sink; the warmer gases or liquids expand, meaning particles become more spread out, and so are less dense and rise. Thus, convection occurs when the heating and circulation of a substance changes the density of the substance. A good example is the heating of air over land near coastal areas coupled with the influx of cooler sea breezes offshore. The heated air inland expands and thus decreases in density, causing the cooler, more dense air to rush in to achieve equilibrium. A more common example of convection is the process of heating water on a stove. In this case, heat is transferred from the stove element to the bottom of the pot by conduction, which heats the water. Heat is transferred from the hot water at the bottom of the pot to the cooler water at the top by convection. At the same time, the cooler, denser water at the top sinks to the bottom, where it is subsequently heated. This circulation creates the movement typical of boiling water. Convection currents created by the combining or colliding of cold and warm air masses is one factor responsible for storms and circular rotation of the air in tornados and hurricanes. Ocean currents are also caused by the collision of cold water and warm water masses in the oceans (Cavallo, 2001). Convection currents occur in the molten or partially molten rock of the mantle causing plates to move and the crust to have seismic and volcanic activity.

## Competency 052: The Teacher Understands Cycles in Earth Systems

### Rock Types

The hard, solid part of the Earth's surface is called rock. Rocks are made of one or more minerals. Rocks like granite, marble, and limestone are extensively used in the construction industry. They can be used in floors, buildings, dams, highways, or the making of cement. Rocks are classified by the way they are formed.

On earth there are three types of rock:

- *Igneous* rocks are crystalline solids that form directly from the cooling of magma or lava. The composition of the magma determines the composition of the rock. Granite is one of the most common types of igneous rocks and is created from magma (inside the Earth). Once magma reaches the Earth's surface, it is called lava. Lava that has cooled forms a rock with a glassy look, called obsidian.

- *Sedimentary* rocks are called secondary rocks because they are often the result of the accumulation of small pieces broken off from preexisting rocks and then pressed into a new form. There are three types of sedimentary rocks:

▶ Clastic sedimentary rocks are made when pieces of rock, mineral, and organic material fuse together. These are classified as conglomerates, sandstone, and shale.

▶ Chemical sedimentary rocks are formed when water rich in minerals evaporates, leaving the minerals behind. Some common examples are gypsum, rock salt, and some limestone.

▶ Organic sedimentary rocks are made from the remains of plants and animals. For example, coal is formed when dead plants are squeezed together. Another example is a form of limestone rock composed of the remains of organisms that lived in the ocean.

• *Metamorphic* rocks are also secondary rocks formed from igneous, sedimentary, or other types of metamorphic rock. When hot magma or lava comes in contact with rocks or when buried rocks are exposed to pressure and high temperatures, the result is metamorphic rocks. For example, exposing limestone to high temperatures creates marble. The most common metamorphic rocks are slate, gneiss, and marble.

## Rock Cycle

The formation of rock follows a cyclical process. For instance, rocks can be formed when magma or lava cools down, creating igneous rocks. Igneous rocks exposed to weathering can break into sediment, which can be compacted and cemented to form sedimentary rocks. Sedimentary rocks are exposed to heat and pressure to create metamorphic rocks. Finally, metamorphic rocks can melt and become magma and lava again (Badder et al., 2000).

## Minerals

Minerals are the most common form of solid material found in the Earth's crust. Even soil contains bits of minerals that have broken away from rock. To be considered a mineral, a substance must be found in nature and must never have been a part of any living organism. Minerals can be as soft as talc or as hard as emeralds and diamonds. Dug from the Earth, minerals are used to make various products:

• Jewelry—Gemstones such as amethysts, opals, diamonds, emeralds, topazes, and garnets are examples of minerals commonly used to create jewelry. Gold and silver are another type of mineral that can be used to create jewelry.

• Construction—Gypsum boards (drywall) are made of a mineral of the same name—gypsum. The windows in homes are made from the mineral, quartz.

- Personal Use—Talc is the softest mineral and it is commonly applied to the body in powder form.

## Water Cycle

The hydrologic cycle describes a series of movements of water above, on, and below the surface of the Earth. This cycle consists of four distinct stages: storage, evaporation, precipitation, and runoff. It is the means by which the sun's energy is used to transport, through the atmosphere, stored water from the rivers and oceans to land masses. The heat of the sun evaporates the water and takes it to the atmosphere from which, through condensation, it falls as precipitation. As precipitation falls, water is filtrated back to underground water deposits called aquifers, or it runs off into storage in lakes, ponds, and oceans.

## Tides

The word *tides* is used to describe the alternating rise and fall in sea level with respect to the land, produced by the gravitational attraction of the moon and the sun. Additional factors such as the configuration of the coastline, depth of the water, the topography of the ocean floor, and other hydrographic and meteorological influences may play an important role in altering the range, interval, and times of the arrival of the tides.

## Nutrient Cycles

Nutrient cycles include the carbon and nitrogen cycle. The carbon cycle is the capture of carbon from carbon dioxide in the atmosphere by plants to make glucose. When this glucose is used as food for the plant or other organisms, it is digested, then by respiration, broken apart again into carbon dioxide and returned back to the atmosphere. The process continues in a life sustaining process.

For the nitrogen cycle it is important to recognize that most of the air we breathe is nitrogen, but it is not useful to us in that form, so it is exhaled. Lightning causes nitrogen in the air to combine with oxygen. Certain bacteria that live on the roots of certain plants, called nitrogen-fixing bacteria, are able to take nitrogen in this combined form with oxygen and make it available for use by plants. The plants can incorporate the nitrogen into their plant structure, and when eaten by animals and other organisms, this nitrogen becomes available for use. The nitrogen returns to the soil when the plant or other living organism dies and decays, releasing nitrogen gas back into the atmosphere. Nitrogen is important to all living things because it is a major component of DNA, RNA, and amino acids, which are the building blocks of proteins.

# Competency 053: The Teacher Understands the Role of Energy in Weather and Climate

## Weather

The elements of weather include interactions between wind, water (precipitation), wind speed and direction, air pressure, humidity, and temperature. Wind is caused by air masses that have different amounts of heat (temperatures), where there may be a warm air mass that is moving toward a cold air mass for example. Air pressure is related to both the amount of water in the air mass and its temperature (heat content), in that warm air has higher pressure than cold air—warm, high pressure air masses move toward cold, low pressure air masses. One simple rule is that energy always moves from *warmer to colder*. So, if you open a window on a hot summer day when your air conditioning is on, the cold does *not go out*—the *warm air comes in*. The same is true on a larger scale with warm and cold air masses.

Humidity is a measure of the percentage of water that is in the air. Dew point is the temperature at which the air needs to be for the water to condense out of the air in liquid form as precipitation; or it may be observed as "dew." In other words, air has a certain amount of water vapor (water in the gas state) in it (the percent is measured as humidity). That water vapor will turn to liquid water as temperatures drop overnight, in which we observe dew, or when a cold front moves in that lowers the temperature, which can result in a rain or snow storm.

Wind is measured by an instrument called an *anemometer*. Air pressure is measured by a *barometer*; *rain gauges* and other instruments measure precipitation. Temperature is measured by a *thermometer*. Relative humidity is measured by a *psychrometer*.

## Climate

Weather is the conditions of the atmosphere at a given, relatively short period of time. Climate, however, is the long-term weather conditions in an area on a continuous, seasonal basis. The climate is more complex and can be measured by the average variety of weather conditions, such as temperature and precipitation, that occur seasonally in that geographic region of the world over a period of time.

## Predicting Weather

Weather can be predicted by tracking weather patterns using maps and charts. These maps have special symbols that indicate, for example, warm and cold air masses, air pressure, and relative humidity in a region. By knowing how air behaves, such as the fact that cold air goes down and warm air rises, warmer air always moves toward colder air, and high pressure always moves outward toward lower pressure, we can track the weather and make predictions. Clouds are also an indication of the type of weather occurring in an area.

Interpreting weather maps is an important skill for weather prediction. It is important that teachers know the various symbols, including warm fronts, cold fronts, stationary fronts, wind speed and direction symbols, high and low pressure systems, and others.

## The Earth's Surface and Position as a Factor in Weather and Climate

The Earth's surface is primarily water, and bodies of water affect the weather and climate of an area. Water has a high specific heat, which means that it takes longer to take in heat and longer to release the heat it has absorbed than any other material on Earth. Therefore, coastal areas tend to be warmer than areas inland or away from water, because the water moderates the temperature, even if the locations are at the same latitude. In the U.S., for example, areas in the middle of the country will have greater extreme differences in the cold temperatures in the winter and warm temperatures in the summer compared to a location at the same latitude near the ocean.

Large lakes, such as the Great Lakes also create a situation called "lake effect" in the winter—the air over the lake is relatively warm, and so can carry water vapor (evaporation). As soon as that air carrying water moves over land, however, it rapidly cools and releases its water (precipitation) in the form of snow over the land. Mountains and other landforms also have an effect on the weather. When air holding water hits a mountain side, it is forced upward which makes the air cool and therefore rain (or snow) on that side of the mountain. This is typically the western side of the mountain in the U.S. as in the mountain ranges of the Rocky Mountains. Once the precipitation is gone from that air mass and the air mass crosses the mountain to the other side, it drops back down and warms, but now it is dry air and so may result in an arid region or desert. The Gobi Desert of the U.S. is a result of this phenomenon.

On a much larger scale, the tilt of the Earth itself—as a planet—is responsible for weather and climate. The Earth is on a 23.4° tilt on its axis in space. This tilt means the Earth's North Pole is pointed *away* from the sun when it is in one location in its orbit (path around the sun), and *toward* the sun when it is in the opposite orbital location. This tilt of the Earth results in the seasons, with extreme changes being in locations closer to the North and South poles. For example, when the North Pole is pointing toward the sun in its orbit, it is summer in the Northern Hemisphere, and when the North Pole is pointing away from the sun in its orbit it is winter in the Northern Hemisphere.

# Competency 54: The Teacher Understands the Characteristics of the Solar System and Universe

The sun is the center of our solar system, which is composed of eight planets, many satellites that orbit the planets, several dwarf planets, and a large number of smaller bodies like comets and asteroids. Short definitions of these terms follow.

- Planets are large bodies orbiting the sun.

- Dwarf planets are small bodies orbiting the sun.

- Satellites are moons orbiting the planets. Our planet has one moon whereas other planets may have no moons (Mercury, Venus), or many moons (Jupiter, Saturn).

- Asteroids are small dense objects or rocks orbiting our star, the sun. The Asteroid Belt of our own solar system is located between Mars and Jupiter. Some theorize that the asteroids could be the remains of an exploded planet.

- Meteoroids are fragments of rock in space, most originating from the debris left behind by comets that burn up/vaporize upon entering Earth's atmosphere due to friction from the air molecules.

- Comets are small icy objects traveling through space in an elongated, elliptical orbit around the sun.

The objects in our solar system revolve around our star, which we call the sun. The *inner* solar system contains the planets Mercury, Venus, Earth, and Mars, in this order. The *outer* solar system comprises the planets Jupiter, Saturn, Uranus, and Neptune, and a number of dwarf planets, including Pluto, Ceres, Eris and others, with likely more yet to be found (see Table 5.1).

### Table 5.1
### Planets and Dwarf Planets of our Solar System

| | |
|---|---|
| **Inner Planets** | Mercury, Venus, Earth, Mars |
| **Outer Planets** | Jupiter, Saturn, Uranus, Neptune |
| **Dwarf Planets** | Pluto, Ceres, Eris, Haumea, Makemake |

Galaxies are large collections of stars, hydrogen, dust particles, and other gases. The universe is made up of countless galaxies. The solar system that includes Earth is part of a galaxy called the Milky Way.

Stars like the sun are composed of large masses of hydrogen pulled together by gravity. The hydrogen, with strong gravitational pressure, creates fusion inside the star, turning the hydrogen into helium. The liberation of energy created by this process causes solar radiation, which makes the sun glow with visible light, as well as forms of radiation not visible to the human eye.

Earth performs two kinds of movement: rotation and revolution. Rotation describes the spinning of Earth on its axis. Earth takes approximately 24 hours to make a complete (360°) rotation, which creates day and night.

While Earth is rotating on its axis, it is also following an orbit around the sun. This movement is called revolution. It takes a year, or 365¼ days, for Earth to complete one revolution. The tilt of Earth as it moves around the sun and its curvature create climate zones and seasons. The zones immediately north and south of the equator are called the tropics—Cancer (north) and Capricorn (south). The Arctic Circle (North Pole) and Antarctic Circle (South Pole) are the area surrounding Earth's axis points. Latitude lines are imaginary horizontal lines around the Earth, and longitude lines are likewise vertical lines around the Earth from the North to the South Poles. These lines form a grid that helps us locate positions on Earth according to the locations specific latitude and longitude.

During each lunar orbit around Earth (about 28 days), the moon appears to go through several stages based on the portion of the moon visible from Earth. The moon does not have its own source of light but reflects the light from the sun. The shape of the moon varies from a full moon, when Earth is between the sun and the moon, to a new moon, when the moon is located between the sun and Earth.

The most prominent scientific theory for the origin of the universe is called the big bang. This theory is based on the observations of scientists such as Edwin Hubble. He provided evidence that galaxies and other celestial objects appear to be moving away from a central point in our universe. Scientists theorized that a great explosion occurred as a result of the compression of all the matter and energy in the universe.

## Competency 55: The Teacher Understands the History of the Earth System

Until the 18th century, it was commonly believed that the Earth was a few thousand years old. However, radiometric dating has now placed the Earth at approximately 4.5 billion years old. This amount of time is difficult to imagine, especially since humans have only been on Earth for about 200,000 years. Geologic time is divided into Precambrian and

Cambrian expanses of time, and further divided into Eons, Eras, Periods and Epochs. The division of geologic time is based on geologic features of the Earth and events, and may also be characterized by the living organisms that dominated the Earth during that time.

The Earth originated from a cloud of dust that as with all celestial objects, originated from the big bang and over time, rotated and condensed into its current form. The condensation of dust and rock particles in space that formed the Earth was caused by molecular attractions between the particles, just as dust balls seem to clump together on the floor of a home. More and more particles collided with Earth, also generating much heat. In its early history, the Earth consisted primarily of hot liquid, which cooled over time, as particle collisions subsided. It is believed that the first, primitive living organisms, likely single celled bacteria, originated on earth 3 billion years ago.

As discussed in Competency 051, in the early 1900's it was proposed that all the continents were previously one large continent but then broke apart and drifted through the ocean floor to their present locations. This theory was called the Continental Drift, and it was the origin of today's concept of plate tectonics, that is, that the surface of the Earth is fragmented into large plates. The collision of plates is the cause of many geologic features on Earth, and the cause of catastrophic events such as volcanoes and earthquakes. The edges or boundaries of the plates are the sites of much seismic activity and the location of most of the "fault lines" on earth. The "Ring of Fire" is known as the boundaries of the Pacific plate, in particular, because the seismic activity forms a circle around the edges of the continents surrounding the Pacific ocean, and this is where most volcanic and earthquake activity occurs.

As the plates collide they produce a variety of geologic results. One example that occurs when plates collide is that one plate is forced beneath the other creating a subduction zone. The plate that rides over the top pushes upwards and forms mountains, whereas the plate that plunges underneath forms a deep sea trench. This type of boundary exists off the west coast of South America and is responsible for forming the Andes Mountains. In subduction zones plates are destroyed. Another plate boundary is a convergent zone, where island chains may arise.

As mentioned in Competency 051, the movement of the continents/Earth's plates is caused by a huge "generator" known as the mid-Atlantic ridge. This ridge is a significantly large volcanic mountain range on the floor of the Atlantic Ocean running north and south, extending through the center of Iceland. The mountains in the ridge are continuously erupting and pushing the plates apart in opposite directions from each other, at a rate of about 1 cm per year. Evidence exists that the mid-Atlantic ridge is responsible for pushing the continents apart when they were (at several times in geologic history), joined together as one large supercontinent.

The theory of continental drift was supported by the existence of common preserved remains of organisms along the continents, known as fossils. For example, according to the theory, the continents have been joined together at various times throughout history. Fossils of the same time period have been found on the western coast of Africa that are identical to fossils of the same time period found on the east coast of South America, where the two continents would have been joined. The continents joined together formed a supercontinent, often referred to as Pangaea.

## Competency 056: The Teacher Has Theoretical and Practical Knowledge About Teaching Science and About How Students Learn Science

### Developmentally Appropriate Practices

Children's processing of scientific inquiry can begin as early as age three or four. However, teachers must be aware of the stages of cognitive, social, and emotional development of children to appropriately introduce children to science concepts. For example, observing and experimenting with water and colors can easily be done by three- or four-year-olds, but using microscopes to observe and analyze animal or vegetable cells might be more appropriate for children in third and fourth grades. Students in EC-6 need direct experiences in order to understand concepts. According to Piaget (1964), children are transitioning through stages of development that require direct involvement to make sense of their experience. The model of teaching known as the learning cycle and 5-E model are based upon promoting the intellectual development of children. Thus, these models of teaching were designed to be consistent with the nature of science—and importantly, to match how children naturally learn (Marek and Cavallo, 1997; Renner and Marek, 1990). It is important that teachers understand the theory and research that underlie such models, as well as know how to use these models in teaching.

Misconceptions or alternative conceptions are a pervasive problem in science teaching and learning. Children tend to view the world from their own perspectives and draw conclusions based on their limited experiences. Once misconceptions are established in learners' minds, they are difficult to change. Therefore, teaching needs to allow children the opportunity for direct experience and collecting evidence. The learning cycle has been established as a teaching model that promotes conceptual change, helps students resolve misconceptions, and leads to more scientifically accurate understandings (Sandoval, 1995).

Teachers need to begin lessons with direct, concrete activities giving students experience with objects. After concept understandings are established in learners, then teachers can move them from the concrete to more abstract reasoning. For example, in learning the concept of density, it is important that students have objects to touch, feel, weigh (take the mass of) and measure first, as in the exploration phase of the learning cycle. From direct experience with the objects, students should construct the concept that "a certain amount of matter (mass) is packed into a given amount of space (volume)." The term that labels this concept is "density." As application, teachers help students develop their abstract-thinking abilities by having them solve problems using the formula for density, $D=M/V$. Teachers need to select instruction appropriately such that concrete experiences are used first, leading the students to later use abstract reasoning. Teachers need to select learning experiences that will promote the students scientific knowledge, skills, and use of inquiry. Further, the students are able to use the prior knowledge they have formed about density to learn more extended, related concepts such as buoyancy. This example demonstrates the instructional knowledge and skills teachers need to have to prepare the best possible science learning experiences for students. The learning cycle or 5-E model are consistent with the goals of this competency.

The use of good questions by the teacher is critical to promoting logical thinking and scientific reasoning among students. Good questioning causes students to reflect upon the logic of their data and observations with confidence and also identifies possible misinformation or misunderstanding of important concepts. Students learn to effectively use scientific argumentation and respond to challenges to their findings in order to support their conclusions. Teachers use questioning to reveal student learning and assess their progress in forming sound scientific frameworks of understanding. Questioning is the hallmark of science inquiry and should be used throughout inquiry instruction. In the learning cycle/5-E model, questioning must be designed to lead students toward being able to state the concept, so it is especially critical in the concept invention or "explain" phase.

Teachers can guide students at various levels of development to observe events; and through questioning teachers can help students develop high-order thinking skills. For example, a teacher can lead children to make predictions while conducting experiments with objects that float or sink in water. By asking students to predict and explain why an object might sink or float, the teacher is leading students to analyze the properties of the object and the water to make an evaluative decision; that is, the children are using analysis and evaluation to complete that simple task. The following guide will help teachers best promote and elevate logical thinking abilities among students.

**1. USE KEY QUESTIONING TERMS AIMED AT THE FULL RANGE OF THE COGNITIVE DOMAIN** (Bloom & Krathwohl, 1956; Anderson & Krathwohl, 2001).

## LEVEL 1: Remember

Recall of factual information

**Examples**    *List* the five Kingdoms.

*Label* the parts of the cell in the diagram provided.

*Write* the formula for density.

## LEVEL 2: Understand

Communicate an idea in a different form

**Examples**    *Explain* heat transfer through conduction.

*Restate* what an ecosystem is in your own words.

*Submit* a definition of photosynthesis in your own words.

## LEVEL 3: Apply

Use what is known to find new solutions or apply in new situations

**Examples**    *Relate* the concept of convection to plate tectonics.

*Utilize* your understanding of density to explain why pennies sink in water but battleships float.

*Making use of* the clothes you are wearing, how can you stay afloat for several hours?

## LEVEL 4: Analyze

Break things and ideas down into component parts and find their unique characteristics

**Examples**    *Examine* blueprints of the electrical circuitry of your school building and explain how it works to bring electricity to your laboratory station.

*Study* the diagram of human digestion and *reason* what the organ marked #7 might be and explain its function.

Using the given laboratory materials, *deduce* the identities of the substances labeled "A," "B," and "C."

### LEVEL 5: Evaluate

Use what is known to make judgments and ratings; accept or reject ideas; determine the worthiness of an idea or thing

**Examples**     *Decide* whether or not you agree with the production of more nuclear power plants and provide justification for your decision.

*Make a ruling* you would give to car manufacturers on global warming and provide support for your ruling.

*Rank* the top five greatest discoveries in scientific history and *explain* why you have chosen those discoveries and ranked them in that particular order.

### LEVEL 6: Create

Use what is known to think creatively and divergently; make something new or original; pattern ideas or things in a new way

**Examples**     *Create* a burglar alarm system for the classroom.

*Build* an interactive display for a hands-on science museum that demonstrates at least one important concept you have learned in science class this year.

*Develop* a plan for cleaning the pollutants in the Trinity River.

### 2. AVOID YES/NO QUESTIONS (UNLESS PART OF A GAME) AND QUESTIONS WITH OBVIOUS ANSWERS.

**Examples**     a.    Showing students a picture of a cell:
*Not effective*

Is this a cell?
*Better*

What is this structure and how do you know?

b.    Students watching a chemical reaction in which the solution turns blue:
*Not effective*

Did it turn blue?
*Better*

What happened? What did you observe? Why did this happen?

**3. USE QUESTIONS BEGINNING WITH THE WORDS *WHY, HOW, WHAT, WHERE,* AND *WHEN* THAT PROBE STUDENTS' THINKING.**

**Examples**   How do you know?

Why do you think that? Where did you see a change?

What is your explanation for this observation? When did you notice the change occur?

What do you think?

## Competency 057: The Teacher Understands the Process of Scientific Inquiry and the History and Nature of Science

### Planning and Implementing Scientific Inquiry

Scientific inquiry is promoted through students engaging in hands-on activities and experimentation. From their experiences conducting scientific experiments, students acquire information firsthand and develop problem-solving skills. Children in grades EC-6 are inquisitive and want to understand the environment around them. Teachers can use this interest to provide students with opportunities to use electronic and printed sources to find answers to their questions and to expand their knowledge about the topic. It is important for children to develop inquiry skills. This can only be accomplished by allowing them to experience science for themselves in hands-on investigations. By doing so, students develop important science inquiry and thinking skills (Table 5-2).

### Table 5-2
### Science Thinking Skills (FOSS, 2000)

| |
|---|
| **Observing:** Using the senses to get information |
| **Communicating:** Talking, drawing, and acting |
| **Comparing:** Pairing and one-to-one correspondence |
| **Organizing:** Grouping, seriating, and sequencing |
| **Relating:** Cause-and-effect and classification |
| **Inferring:** Super-ordinate/subordinate classification, if/then reasoning, and developing scientific laws |
| **Applying:** Developing strategic plans and inventing |

The model of inquiry that best supports science learning is a model known as the *learning cycle*, consisting of three phases: *exploration*, *concept invention*, and *application* (Lawson, Abraham, and Renner, 1989; Marek and Cavallo, 1997). Over time the learning cycle was extended with the addition of two new phases becoming what is known as the 5-E model (Bybee 1989). What follows is some history on the development of inquiry-based teaching via the learning cycle and 5-E model.

The original three-phase learning cycle model developed by Robert Karplus in the early 1960s was based upon the following theoretical foundation:

1. Science must be taught in a way that is *consistent with the nature of science.* Science is discovery and investigation, and that means science must be taught as an active process—as something we *do*. The children need to have the opportunity to experience the true nature of science by doing science exploration for themselves through direct experiences and hands-on investigations.

2. Science teaching must be focused on promoting the main purpose of education, namely, to promote the development in our students the *ability to think*—to be critical and independent thinkers. Science must be taught in a way that promotes the students use of independent, critical, and higher-level thinking abilities (e.g., logic). Promoting this purpose of education is best accomplished by *not* giving or telling students the "answers" or information (e.g., as in giving a lecture); but instead by first giving students hands-on, direct experiences in which they use logic and reasoning to find "answers" or explanations for themselves; further discussion and teacher guidance can follow the students' direct experiences.

3. Science must be taught in a way that *matches how students learn,* described as the mental functioning model by Piaget (1964). How individuals learn is through mentally experiencing the following three-phase mental process. We first *assimilate* or "take in" information with our senses from our environment and what we are experiencing in our environment. During assimilation, we may have a sense of "disequilibrium," which is confusion or "cognitive conflict" as we try to make sense of our experiences. When in disequilibrium, we need to go back and *assimilate* more information—make more observations and gather more data, for example. When we have assimilated enough information and made sense of the information we have gathered, our minds experience *accommodation*. That is the "aha!" moment, the point when we ultimately feel "cognitive relief"—we figured it out, or what we have observed/experienced now makes sense! Third, our minds take that newly accommodated information and we *organize* it into our mental structures. That is, we connect the new idea or what we have just figured out/made sense of to what we already know, what we experience in everyday life, and/or to new related concepts.

The three phases of learning described by Piaget, assimilation-accommodation-organization, *match* the original learning cycle's three phases: Exploration-Concept Invention-Application. The logic in developing the learning cycle in these three phases was that, given what we know about how children (people) *learn*, we should be *teaching* in a sequence or way that matches this learning pattern. To do so, teachers should first provide children with an *Exploration* phase in which students can assimilate information using their senses. The students may or may not experience disequilibrium, but, as teachers, we should guide them (not tell them!) through the sense-making process. We should then carry out a discussion in the *Concept Invention* phase in which students share their observations and findings. With careful questioning, teachers guide students to review their data/observations toward helping them reach the "aha!" moment or accommodation. The summarizing statement the students are to write, post on the board, and/or state aloud to others in this phase represents their accommodation or understanding of the concept. The teacher then helps students organize the new concept by guiding them through *Application* of the concept in new contexts, in which students can connect the concept with what they observe in everyday life, or what they already know, for example.

Furthermore, by teaching via the learning cycle, we are teaching in a way that is consistent with the nature of science—as an active, hands-on process characterized by investigation and discovery—and we are teaching in a way that supports the purpose of education, that is, we are promoting children's development of higher level thinking abilities. The learning cycle and its origins and theory base is more fully described in a book by Marek and Cavallo (1997) titled *The Learning Cycle: Elementary School Science and Beyond.*

Over time, science educators added some additional phases to the learning cycle, namely, the *Engage* phase, with the idea that teachers need to do something that will gain the students' attention before beginning the exploration phase. Engage can be a demonstration (without explanation) or simply posing a question, challenge, or problem. So the original learning cycle model's first phase, *Exploration*, became two phases, *Engage* and *Explore*. Though identical, the *Concept Invention* phase's name was changed to *Explain* and *Application* phase had the name changed to *Elaborate*, to sustain the alliteration. Assessment or the measurement of learning in the original three-phase model was to take place throughout the learning cycle. However, science educators at the time preferred to have assessment articulated as an additional phase, which again to keep the "E" pattern, was termed *Evaluate*. So the three-phase learning cycle model was expanded into a 5-E Model: *Engage, Explore, Explain, Elaborate, Evaluate.*

The two models are basically the same and grew out of the same underlying philosophy and theoretical foundation. However, the three phases more closely follow the model of learning—assimilation, accommodation and organization—as first described by Piaget; whereas the 5-E incorporates two additional essentials of classroom teaching, namely gaining students focus and attention, and measuring student learning.

Most importantly, in both models, the learning cycle and 5-E, students are *not told* the science concept or information before beginning the inquiry, but must discover the concept themselves through hands-on investigation, observation, and collection of data. In using the *Engage* phase (from 5-E) the students' learning experience begins with the teacher posing one or more questions, giving an interesting demonstration, or providing a laboratory guide; but in all of these, this phase captures their curiosity and motivates them to learn. Whether or not an *Engage* phase is used, students next (or first) experience an *Exploration* phase—and it must be a student-centered hands-on activity, investigation, or experiment. In the *Exploration* phase, students make observations and gather data on a science idea or topic area. In this phase, students can determine the experimental design or it can be pre-determined by the teacher. The main aspect, however, is that students are doing the lab activity themselves, and have not been told the expected outcome beforehand. For example, students may grow plants in the light and in the dark, and make observations, draw and/or take photos, and measure the plants grown under the two differing conditions over a period of time. All other variables are controlled (soil, water, air); only the light received by the plants is different, which is the variable.

After the observations have been made and data has been gathered by students, the teacher begins the next instructional phase called *Concept Invention*, or in the 5-E model, the *Explain* phase. In this phase the students present and share data with their classmates in a teacher-guided discussion of findings. The teacher uses questions to guide students' thinking and encourages the use of logic and reasoning as they interpret their data. For example, students may post the photos or drawings of plants grown in the dark and in the light, make line graphs of plant height over time, or share qualitative information about how the plant appeared after grown under the two conditions (e.g., plants in the light were green, whereas plants in the dark were yellow and pale). At the end of this phase, the students construct an overall statement that summarizes their data and observations, which is the central science *concept*. The science vocabulary is then linked to the concept students "invented."

Next the teacher helps students through the *Application* (from the learning cycle) or *Elaborate* (from the 5-E model) in which students use the new concept they learned as it is applied in new contexts. For example, students can create new questions to investigate or hypotheses to test based on what they just learned (the concept) and develop a way to answer their questions or test their hypotheses (e.g., what color of light is best for plants to grow?).They can also go to the Internet to learn more about the concept they just invented. In this phase the teacher can engage students in additional hands-on laboratories, readings, discussions, field trips, and/or writing activities that extend and expand upon the concept. These models of inquiry science teaching and learning are endorsed by NSTA (NSTA, 1998, 2003).

The diagram in Figure 5-1 shows the inquiry-based learning cycle model as it corresponds to the 5-E model of science teaching. The template shown in Table 5-4 explains each phase of the learning cycle as it relates to the 5-E Model for structuring inquiry-based science teaching for all students.

**Figure 5-1**
**The Learning Cycle and 5-E Model**

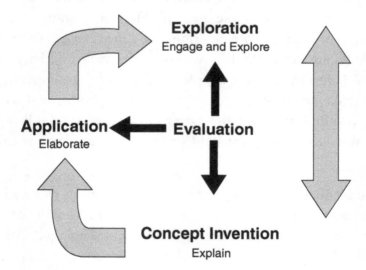

# Table 5-4
## Description of the Phases of the Learning Cycle and 5-E Model

| Phase | The Student | Activities | The Teacher |
|---|---|---|---|
| **ENGAGE** the student in the learning task. The student mentally focuses on an object, problem, situation, or event. The activities of this phase should make connections to past and future activities. The connections depend on the learning task and may be conceptual, procedural, or behavioral. | Asks questions such as:<br>• Why did this happen?<br>• What do I already know about this?<br>• What can I find out about this?<br>• How can this problem be solved?<br>Also:<br>• Shows interest in topic.<br>• Responds to questions demonstrating their own entry point of understanding | Initiate the learning task. The activity should make connections between past and present learning experiences, and anticipate activities and organize students' thinking toward the learning outcomes of current activities.<br>• Generate interest<br>• Access prior knowledge<br>• Connect to past knowledge<br>• Set parameters of the focus<br>• Frame the idea | • Raises questions and problems.<br>• Elicits responses that uncover students' current knowledge about the concept/topic.<br>• Generates interest.<br>• Generates curiosity. |
| **EXPLORE:** Once the activities have engaged students, they need time to explore their ideas. | • Thinks creatively within the limits of the activity.<br>• Tries alternatives to solve a problem and discusses them with others.<br>• Suspends judgment.<br>• Conducts activities, predicts, and forms hypotheses or makes generalizations<br>• Becomes a good listener<br>• Shares ideas and suspends judgment<br>• Records observations and/or generalizations<br>• Discusses tentative alternatives | Provide students with a common base of experiences from which current concepts, processes, and skills are identified and developed.<br>• Experience key concepts<br>• Discover new skills<br>• Probe, inquire, and question experiences<br>• Examine students' thinking<br>• Establish relationships and understanding | • Elicits responses that uncover students' current knowledge about the concept/topic.<br>• Raises questions and problems.<br>• Acts as a facilitator<br>• Observes and listens to students as they interact<br>• Asks good inquiry-oriented questions<br>• Generates interest.<br>• Generates curiosity. |
| **EXPLANATION** means the act or process in which concepts, processes, or skills become plain, comprehensible, and clear. The process of explanation provides the students and teacher with a common use of terms relative to the learning experience. | • Explains possible solutions or answers to other students.<br>• Listens critically to other students' explanations.<br>• Questions other students' explanations.<br>• Listens to and tries to comprehend explanations offered by the teacher.<br>• Refers to previous activities.<br>• Uses recorded observations in explanations.<br>• Uses previous observations and findings.<br>• Provides reasonable responses to questions. | Focus students' attention on a particular aspect of their engagement and exploration experiences, and provide opportunities to demonstrate their conceptual understanding, process skills, or behaviors. This phase also provides opportunities for teachers to introduce a concept, process, or skill.<br>• Connect prior knowledge and background to new discoveries<br>• Communicate new understandings<br>• Connect informal language to formal language | • Formally provides definitions, explanations, and new vocabulary.<br>• Uses students' previous experiences as the basis for explaining concepts.<br>• Encourages students to explain their observations and findings in their own words<br>• Provides definitions, new words, and explanations<br>• Listens and builds upon discussion from students<br>• Asks for clarification and justification<br>• Accepts all reasonable responses |
| **ELABORATE:** Once the students have an explanation of their learning tasks, it is important to involve them in further experiences that apply, extend, or elaborate the concepts, processes, or skills. | Applies new labels, definitions, explanations, and skills in new, but similar, situations.<br>• Uses previous information to ask questions, propose solutions, make decisions, design experiments.<br>• Draws reasonable conclusions from evidence.<br>• Provides reasonable conclusions and solutions.<br>• Records observations, explanations, and solutions. | Challenge and extend students' conceptual understanding and skills. Through new experiences, the students develop deeper and broader understanding, more information, and adequate skills.<br>• Apply new learning to a new or similar situation<br>• Extend and explain concept being explored<br>• Communicate new understanding with formal language | • Expects students to use vocabulary, definitions, and explanations provided previously in new context.<br>• Encourages students to apply the concepts and skills to new situations.<br>• Reminds and refers students of alternative explanations.<br>• Uses previously learned information as a vehicle to enhance additional learning<br>• Encourages students to apply or extend the new concepts and skills<br>• Encourages students to use terms and definitions previously acquired |
| **EVALUATE:** At some point, it is important that students receive feedback on the adequacy of their explanations. Informal evaluation can occur from the beginning of the teaching sequence. The teacher can complete a formal evaluation after the elaboration phase. | • Demonstrates an understanding or knowledge of concepts and skills.<br>• Answers open-ended questions by using observations, evidence, and previously accepted explanations.<br>• Evaluates his or her own progress and knowledge.<br>• Asks related questions that would encourage future investigations.<br>• Provides reasonable responses and explanations to events or phenomena. | • Encourage students to assess their understanding and abilities and provide opportunities for teachers to evaluate student progress.<br>• Demonstrate understanding of new concept by observation or open-ended response<br>• Apply within problem situation<br>• Show evidence of accomplishment | • Assesses students' knowledge and skills<br>• Observes students as they apply new concepts and skills.<br>• Looks for evidence that students have changed their thinking.<br>• Allows students to assess their learning and group process skills.<br>• Asks open-ended questions such as, Why do you think...? What evidence do you have? What do you know about the problem? How would you answer the question?<br>• Encourages students to assess their own learning |

## Interpreting Findings in Science Inquiry

In planning and conducting experiments, teachers should guide children to develop an appropriate procedure for testing hypotheses, including the use of instruments that can yield measurable data. Even at the early stages of scientific experimentation, the procedure must be clear and tangible enough to allow replication by other students or scientists. Help students understand the concept of controlling variables and testing only one variable at a time. Students need to learn to be precise in the collection of data and measurements. Ensure the use of the metric system in obtaining all measurement data.

Allowing students to gather their own data and observations for interpretation promotes their critical and logical thinking abilities. It also gives them experience with using appropriate tools, resources, and technology of science that will lead to accurate organization and analysis of data. The students will be able to experience and practice science skills by verifying their findings, basing findings on evidence, and analyzing sources of error. Having students collect and report their own data also brings the teacher opportunities to discuss scientific ethics with students.

In explaining data collection procedures and display of findings to English language learners, the teacher needs to demonstrate and provide a model of what the end results should look like. In using inquiry, students work in groups, which is particularly helpful for second language learners as they interpret and exchange ideas about data and scientific reasoning.

When students complete their experiments, teachers need to engage them in the process of analyzing their own, and other groups' data for similarities, differences, and variations including error. This occurs in the concept invention or "explain" phase of the learning cycle and 5-E model, and again in any application or "elaborate" activities in which data has been collected. After data has been collected from students' explorations, they display their data in charts and graphs, for example, and communicate their observations and, ultimately, concept statements to the class by posting them on the board and/or through an oral presentation. The data helps them develop conclusions and form new research questions or hypotheses as they evaluate their findings, setting the foundation for new explorations. Students should be able to present pertinent data using graphic representations, and communicate their findings in written and oral forms to others.

In using scientific inquiry as in the learning cycle and 5-E model, scientific vocabulary is introduced *after* students have had hands-on experiences in the (engage and) exploration phase *and* have used their observations and data to construct meaning from their experiences in the *concept invention* or "explain" phase. Once students have had the hands-on direct experience with the concept, and have stated the meaning of their observations, the scientific vocabulary or terms that label the concept can be introduced by the teacher. In the application or elaborate phase, the teacher and students use the new vocabulary in extended experimentation, discussion, readings, writing, and other learning activities. Introducing terms after students have directly experienced the science inquiry and constructed meaning from their experiences by making a concept statement is especially important for second language learners in facilitating the development of understanding of science concepts. For all students, but especially for second language learners, this helps them understand concepts when terms are later *re-introduced*. By giving students the experience—something they *do*—and then allowing them to form meaning from their experience in ways that make sense to them, then when the term that labels what they learned is introduced, they are able to link it to prior knowledge and learning experiences in their minds. The terms are now able to build their background knowledge, which is critical for second language learners to understand the language of science. Making a connection between the hands-on activities and scientific vocabulary is beneficial to all students but especially to English language learners (ELLs), who can link the actions with the appropriate concept and vocabulary words without engaging in translations.

## Promoting Logical Thinking and Scientific Reasoning

Interpreting results is one of the most challenging phases of scientific inquiry for the middle grades. Students can easily discuss the observable results but might have difficulty interpreting their meaning. Teachers have to use developmentally appropriate practices to guide students to make extrapolations and infer information from the data, which involves the teachers' use of questioning, as addressed previously, in Competency 056.

## Scientific Tools and Equipment for Gathering and Storing Data

Various tools or instruments are used in scientific experimentation in the middle-level grades. The classroom should be equipped with measuring devices like graduated cylinders, beakers, scales, dishes, thermometers, meter sticks, and micrometers. They might also have anatomical models showing the body systems. Teachers need to learn to use these tools and equipment properly in order to help their students know how to use them and to collect accurate data in their inquiry investigations.

The TEKS requires students to gather information using specific equipment and tools. Examples of the tools required in grades 4 through 8 are presented in Table 5-5.

### Table 5-5
### Sample Tools and Equipment for the Middle-Level Science Classroom

| Tools and Equipment | 4th | 5th | 6th | 7th | 8th |
|---|---|---|---|---|---|
| Nonstandard measurements | | | | | |
| Hand lenses | √ | √ | √ | √ | √ |
| Computers | √ | √ | √ | √ | √ |
| Balances | √ | √ | √ | √ | √ |
| Cups and bowls | √ | √ | √ | √ | √ |
| Thermometers | √ | √ | √ | √ | √ |
| Clocks | √ | √ | √ | √ | √ |
| Meter sticks | √ | √ | √ | √ | √ |
| Light Microscopes | √ | √ | √ | √ | √ |
| Dissecting Microscopes | √ | √ | √ | √ | √ |
| Safety goggles | √ | √ | √ | √ | √ |
| Magnets | √ | √ | √ | √ | √ |
| Compasses | √ | √ | √ | √ | √ |
| Timing devices | √ | √ | √ | √ | √ |
| Calculators | √ | √ | √ | √ | √ |
| Sound recorders | √ | √ | √ | √ | √ |
| Hot plates | | √ | √ | √ | √ |
| Burners | | √ | √ | √ | √ |
| Beakers | | √ | √ | √ | √ |
| Graduated cylinders | | √ | √ | √ | √ |
| Flasks (Erlenmeyer and Florence) | | √ | √ | √ | √ |
| Test tubes and holders | | √ | √ | √ | √ |

## Competency 058: The Teacher Knows the Varied and Appropriate Assessments and Assessment Practices to Monitor Science Learning in Laboratory, Field and Classroom Settings

### Measuring Student Learning

Teaching cannot occur without student *learning*, and in order to determine that learning is occurring, student progress needs to be assessed on a regular basis. Assessment of learning should occur on some scale, large or small, *every class day*, to monitor students' progress in the learning of concepts, as in the learning cycle and 5-E models. Measuring learning as it is occurring is "authentic assessment" and allows teachers to adjust the instruction according to student learning and immediately and routine address potential difficulties and/or misconceptions in learning. Alternative, *informal* assessment methods, in addition to the more traditional, *formal* testing formats (e.g., multiple-choice) should be used to obtain a full picture of what students know and do not know, or can and cannot do. Alternative assessments include techniques such as verbal reports, laboratory practical exams, story writing, developing advertisements or brochures, constructing concept maps, writing essays, creating drawings or models, and developing plays or skits. In each assessment, the concepts to be learned are represented in alternative ways—yet clearly communicate what students have learned and understand.

It is essential that teachers monitor and assess students' understanding of concepts and skills on a regular, consistent basis and use this information to adjust instruction. The results of frequent informal and formal/traditional and alternative assessments should be used as a tool for planning subsequent instruction. Teachers must communicate progress to students so they can learn to self-monitor their own learning and understand what is needed to achieve learning goals.

Formative assessments are assessments that take place during the learning process that allow teachers to regularly monitor learning, and provide measures of student learning at various times and in various manners throughout the process. Summative assessments are tests given at the end of instruction to measure learning, typically by an exam or standardized test. Formative assessments provide teachers with more information and insight into the students' thinking and learning compared to summative assessments, which provide a culminating measure of achievement. It is important that teachers use both forms of assessment, and prepare students on taking a variety of assessments, so the most accurate measure of their learning and accomplishments can be obtained.

## Assessing the Science Curriculum

As part of the accountability system, Texas has a very comprehensive assessment system to measure the state uniform curriculum. This system, new in spring 2012, centers on the STAAR exam. Beginning in spring 2012, the State of Texas Assessments of Academic Readiness (STAAR) replaced the Texas Assessment of Knowledge and Skills (TAKS). The STAAR program at grades 3–8 assesses the same subjects and grades that were assessed on TAKS. See: *www.tea.state.tx.us* under *Student Assessment/STAAR*. On the STAAR, students are assessed on both content understanding and process skills (TEA, 2012).

In this system, students take the STAAR test in grades 3 through 12. However, the science component of STAAR is assessed only in grades 5, 8, and 10. The fifth-grade and eighth grade science tests are available in Spanish; thus, Spanish-speaking ELLs can take the test in Spanish. In addition to the required science STAAR examinations, students are assessed through teacher- and district-developed tests in kindergarten through grade 12.

## References

Anderson, L. W., D. R. Krathwohl, et al. Eds. 2001. *A Taxonomy for Learning, Teaching, and Assessing: A Revision of Bloom's Taxonomy of Educational Objectives*. Boston, MA: Allyn & Bacon (Pearson Education Group)

Badder, W., D. Peck, L. J. Bethel, C. Sumner, V. Fu, and C. Valentino. 2000. *Discovery works*. (Texas ed.). Boston: Houghton Mifflin.

Bloom, B. S. and D. R. Krathwohl. 1956. *Taxonomy of Educational Objectives: The Classification of Educational Goals, by a committee of college and university examiners. Handbook I: Cognitive Domain*. NY, NY: Longmans, Green

Bybee, R., Buchwald, C.E., Crissman, S. Heil, D., Kuerbis, P., Matsumoto, C. & McInerney 1989. *Science and Technology Education for Elementary Years: Frameworks for Curriculum and Instruction*. Washington, DC: The National Center for Improving Science Education.

Cavallo, A.M.L. 2001. Convection connections: Integrated learning cycle investigations that explore convection—the science behind wind and waves. *Science and Children, 38*, 20–25.

Full Option Science System (FOSS). 2000. Lawrence Hall of Science, University of California, Berkeley, CA.

Krajcik, J., Blumfield, P., Marx, R. & Soloway, E. 1994. A Collaborative Model for Helping Middle Grade Science Teachers Learn Project-Based Instruction. *Elementary School Journal, 94*, 483-97.

Lawson, A.E., M.R. Abraham, and J. W. Renner. 1989. *A theory of instruction: Using the learning cycle to teach science concepts and thinking skills*. NARST Monograph No. 1.

Marek, E. A., & Cavallo, A. M. L. 1997. *The Learning Cycle: Elementary School Science and Beyond* (Rev. ed.). Portsmouth, NH: Heinemann.

National Science Teachers Association. 2003. *Standards for Science Teacher Preparation: Skills of Teaching* (Revised Version). Washington, DC: National Science Teachers Association.

National Science Teachers Association. 1998. *Standards for Science Teacher Preparation: Skills of Teaching*. Washington, DC: National Science Teachers Association.

National Research Council. 2011 *A Framework for K-12 Science Education: Practices, Crosscutting Concepts, and Core Ideas*. Washington, D.C.: National Academy Press.

National Research Council. 2000. *Inquiry and the National Science Education Standards*. Washington, D.C.: National Academy Press.

National Research Council. 1996 *National Science Education Standards*. Washington, D.C.: National Academy Press.

Piaget, J. 1964. Cognitive development in children: Piaget, development and learning. *Journal of Research in Science Teaching,* 2, 176–80.

Renner, J. W., and Marek, E. A. 1990. An educational theory base for science teaching. *Journal of Research in Science Teaching*. 27(3): 241–46.

Resnik, D. (1993). "Philosophical Foundations of Scientific Ethics," in *Ethical Issues in Physics: Workshop Proceedings*, Marshall Thomsen (ed.), Workshop: July 17–18, 1993, Eastern Michigan University, Ypsilanti Michigan. Ann Arbor, MI, 1994.

Sandoval, J. S. 1995. Teaching in subject matter areas: Science. *Annual Review of Psychology*, 46, 355–74.

Texas Education Agency 2010. *Title 19, Part II, Chapter 112*: *Texas Essential Knowledge and Skills for Science*. Texas Administrative Code (TAC) Retrieved from: *www.tea. state.tx.us* (Assessed April 3, 2010).

Texas Education Agency. 2012. *STAAR Science Resources*. Retrieved from: *www.tea. state.tx.us* (Assessed April 3, 2012).

# PRACTICE TEST 1

# TExES Generalist 4-8 (111)

**Also available at the REA Study Center** (*www.rea.com/studycenter*)

This practice test is also offered online at the REA Study Center. Although the TExES Generalist 4-8 (111) exam is offered in both paper- and computer-based formats, we recommend that you take the online version of the test to receive these added benefits:

- **Timed testing conditions** – helps you gauge how much time you can spend on each question
- **Automatic scoring** – find out how you did on the test, instantly
- **On-screen detailed explanations of answers** – gives you the correct answer and explains why the other answer choices are wrong
- **Diagnostic score reports** – pinpoint where you're strongest and where you need to focus your study

# Answer Sheet

1. (A) (B) (C) (D)
2. (A) (B) (C) (D)
3. (A) (B) (C) (D)
4. (A) (B) (C) (D)
5. (A) (B) (C) (D)
6. (A) (B) (C) (D)
7. (A) (B) (C) (D)
8. (A) (B) (C) (D)
9. (A) (B) (C) (D)
10. (A) (B) (C) (D)
11. (A) (B) (C) (D)
12. (A) (B) (C) (D)
13. (A) (B) (C) (D)
14. (A) (B) (C) (D)
15. (A) (B) (C) (D)
16. (A) (B) (C) (D)
17. (A) (B) (C) (D)
18. (A) (B) (C) (D)
19. (A) (B) (C) (D)
20. (A) (B) (C) (D)
21. (A) (B) (C) (D)
22. (A) (B) (C) (D)
23. (A) (B) (C) (D)
24. (A) (B) (C) (D)
25. (A) (B) (C) (D)
26. (A) (B) (C) (D)
27. (A) (B) (C) (D)
28. (A) (B) (C) (D)
29. (A) (B) (C) (D)
30. (A) (B) (C) (D)
31. (A) (B) (C) (D)
32. (A) (B) (C) (D)
33. (A) (B) (C) (D)

34. (A) (B) (C) (D)
35. (A) (B) (C) (D)
36. (A) (B) (C) (D)
37. (A) (B) (C) (D)
38. (A) (B) (C) (D)
39. (A) (B) (C) (D)
40. (A) (B) (C) (D)
41. (A) (B) (C) (D)
42. (A) (B) (C) (D)
43. (A) (B) (C) (D)
44. (A) (B) (C) (D)
45. (A) (B) (C) (D)
46. (A) (B) (C) (D)
47. (A) (B) (C) (D)
48. (A) (B) (C) (D)
49. (A) (B) (C) (D)
50. (A) (B) (C) (D)
51. (A) (B) (C) (D)
52. (A) (B) (C) (D)
53. (A) (B) (C) (D)
54. (A) (B) (C) (D)
55. (A) (B) (C) (D)
56. (A) (B) (C) (D)
57. (A) (B) (C) (D)
58. (A) (B) (C) (D)
59. (A) (B) (C) (D)
60. (A) (B) (C) (D)
61. (A) (B) (C) (D)
62. (A) (B) (C) (D)
63. (A) (B) (C) (D)
64. (A) (B) (C) (D)
65. (A) (B) (C) (D)
66. (A) (B) (C) (D)

67. (A) (B) (C) (D)
68. (A) (B) (C) (D)
69. (A) (B) (C) (D)
70. (A) (B) (C) (D)
71. (A) (B) (C) (D)
72. (A) (B) (C) (D)
73. (A) (B) (C) (D)
74. (A) (B) (C) (D)
75. (A) (B) (C) (D)
76. (A) (B) (C) (D)
77. (A) (B) (C) (D)
78. (A) (B) (C) (D)
79. (A) (B) (C) (D)
80. (A) (B) (C) (D)
81. (A) (B) (C) (D)
82. (A) (B) (C) (D)
83. (A) (B) (C) (D)
84. (A) (B) (C) (D)
85. (A) (B) (C) (D)
86. (A) (B) (C) (D)
87. (A) (B) (C) (D)
88. (A) (B) (C) (D)
89. (A) (B) (C) (D)
90. (A) (B) (C) (D)
91. (A) (B) (C) (D)
92. (A) (B) (C) (D)
93. (A) (B) (C) (D)
94. (A) (B) (C) (D)
95. (A) (B) (C) (D)
96. (A) (B) (C) (D)
97. (A) (B) (C) (D)
98. (A) (B) (C) (D)
99. (A) (B) (C) (D)

100. (A) (B) (C) (D)
101. (A) (B) (C) (D)
102. (A) (B) (C) (D)
103. (A) (B) (C) (D)
104. (A) (B) (C) (D)
105. (A) (B) (C) (D)
106. (A) (B) (C) (D)
107. (A) (B) (C) (D)
108. (A) (B) (C) (D)
109. (A) (B) (C) (D)
110. (A) (B) (C) (D)
111. (A) (B) (C) (D)
112. (A) (B) (C) (D)
113. (A) (B) (C) (D)
114. (A) (B) (C) (D)
115. (A) (B) (C) (D)
116. (A) (B) (C) (D)
117. (A) (B) (C) (D)
118. (A) (B) (C) (D)
119. (A) (B) (C) (D)
120. (A) (B) (C) (D)
121. (A) (B) (C) (D)
122. (A) (B) (C) (D)
123. (A) (B) (C) (D)
124. (A) (B) (C) (D)
125. (A) (B) (C) (D)
126. (A) (B) (C) (D)
127. (A) (B) (C) (D)
128. (A) (B) (C) (D)
129. (A) (B) (C) (D)
130. (A) (B) (C) (D)

## Mathematics Definitions and Formulas

| CALCULUS |
|---|

First Derivative: $f'(x) = \dfrac{dy}{dx}$

Second Derivative: $f''(x) = \dfrac{d^2 y}{dx^2}$

| PROBABILITY |
|---|

$P(A \text{ or } B) = P(A) + P(B) - P(A \text{ and } B)$

$P(A \text{ and } B) = P(A)P(B|A) = P(B)P(A|B)$

| GEOMETRY |
|---|

### Congruent Angles
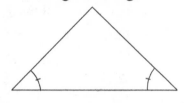

### Congruent Sides

### Parallel Sides
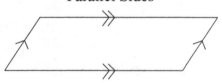

Circumference of a Circle
$C = 2\pi r$

| ALGEBRA |
|---|

$i$ $\qquad\qquad i^2 = -1$

$A^{-1}$ $\qquad$ inverse of matrix $A$

Compound interest: Where $A$ is the final value
$P$ is the principal
$A = P\left(1 + \dfrac{r}{n}\right)^{nt}$ $\quad$ $r$ is the interest rate
$t$ is the term
$n$ is the number of divisions within the term

$[x] = n$ $\quad$ Greatest integer function, where $n$ is the integer such that $n \le x < n + 1$

| VOLUME |
|---|

Cylinder: (area of base) × height

Cone: $\dfrac{1}{3}$(area of base) × height

Sphere: $\dfrac{4}{3}\pi r^3$

Prism: (area of base) × height

| AREA |
|---|

Triangle: $\dfrac{1}{2}$(base × height)

Rhombus: $\dfrac{1}{2}$(diagonal$_1$ × diagonal$_2$)

Trapezoid: $\dfrac{1}{2}$height(base$_1$ + base$_2$)

Sphere: $4\pi r^2$

Circle: $\pi r^2$

Lateral surface area of a cylinder: $2\pi rh$

| TRIGONOMETRY |
|---|

Law of Sines: $\dfrac{\sin A}{a} = \dfrac{\sin B}{b} = \dfrac{\sin C}{c}$

Law of Cosines: $c^2 = a^2 + b^2 - 2ab\cos C$
$b^2 = a^2 + c^2 - 2ac\cos B$
$a^2 = b^2 + c^2 - 2bc\cos A$

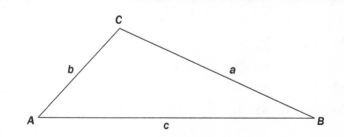

# Practice Test 1

**Time:** 5-hour time limit
130 questions: 30 Social Studies (23%)
      30 Science (23%)
      30 Math (23%)
      40 English Language Arts (31%)

**Directions**: Read each item and select the best response.

1. The model below represents what number?

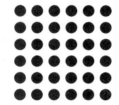

   A. 6
   B. $6 \times 2$
   C. $6^2$
   D. $6^3$

2. Economics is BEST described as the study of

   A. how different political systems establish systems for production and consumption.

   B. how individuals and groups with limited resources make decisions to best satisfy their needs and wants.

   C. how currency is used in different societies.

   D. how trade has developed through a historic and systematic process.

3. During literature circle discussion, Mr. Smith's fourth graders bring a response journal with their ideas about the novel they read to share with their peers. In small groups, the students share their ideas about the text in an open-ended discussion. The purpose of having students bring the written response journal to the group would be to develop the students' ability to

   A. express their thoughts in an imaginative way with others.

   B. plan and organize their thinking in writing before sharing their thoughts with the group.

   C. use grammar, spelling, and punctuation in conventional ways.

   D. share ideas, especially for the less talkative students.

4. Students in fifth grade are practicing reading their reader's theater scripts for a performance presentation on Friday. Their teacher encourages them to read with prosody, or expression. This instructional activity primarily fosters development in the key area of reading that is called

   A. Comprehension.
   B. Vocabulary.
   C. Fluency.
   D. Structural Analysis.

5. What is the motto of the United States?

   A. One nation under God
   B. *Carpe diem*
   C. In God we trust
   D. Freedom and justice for all

6. _____ is the economic and political system in which a country's trade and industry are controlled by private owners for profit rather than by the state.

   A. Socialism
   B. Republicanism
   C. Communism
   D. Capitalism

7. While giving a reading assessment to his sixth graders to test their oral reading, Mr. Tompkins notes that one student, Gerald, consistently reads at a rate much slower than the grade-level norms. He also lacks confidence in reading. Which of the following activities would help him to develop his fluency in reading?

   A. Repeated reading of independent-level text

   B. Guided reading and pausing to discuss the meaning

   C. Repeated reading of frustrational-level text

   D. Guided reading and completion of a graphic organizer

8. The rectangular array model shown below represents what multiplication problem?

   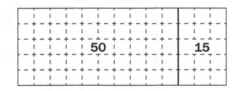

   A. $5 \times (10 + 3)$

   B. $50 \times 15$

   C. $50 + 15$

   D. $5 \times 15$

9. The comprehension strategy of reciprocal teaching develops students' ability to discuss and analyze a shared text through use of

   A. summarizing, connecting, revising, and sharing.

   B. summarizing, inferring, visualizing, and recalling.

   C. summarizing, questioning, clarifying, and predicting.

   D. questioning, knowing, wanting to know, and learning.

10. The purpose of having a teacher-led discussion prior to having students engage in small-group discussions might be to primarily do which of the following?

   A. To provide additional scaffolding for students who may need the explicit modeling prior to engaging in their own discussions

   B. To be sure that behavior management is under control before the teacher puts students into small groups

   C. To be sure that students are capable of engaging in small group discussion

   D. To be in control of the lesson rather than letting students take control of their conversations

11. A teacher wants to meet with students individually during writing workshop time in her fifth-grade classroom. A *primary* purpose of conferring with students would be to

   A. motivate them to want to write more.

   B. edit and proofread their work for spelling and mechanics.

   C. give them a final grade for their finished product.

   D. check in with them to monitor their progress and assist their writing process.

12. One activity used for pre-reading and post-reading is the KWL chart by which students discuss and list what they know, what they want to know, and what they learned about the topic. A rationale for conducting this activity would be to

   A. help students compare and contrast main ideas in the text.

   B. provide a structured assessment tool to grade understanding of the text.

   C. help students better understand the story grammar of the text.

   D. activate background knowledge and generate interest in the text.

13. To help her students acquire research skills, a fifth-grade teacher wants her students to understand how to evaluate credible sources of information from a variety of sources by using the Internet. Which of the following lessons would help them most as they seek out multiple sources of information?

    A. Teach students how to critically evaluate sources of information for accuracy and credibility as potential sources

    B. Teach students how to use multiple web browsers to search for different sources

    C. Teach students how to summarize the article in a paragraph

    D. Teach students how to read charts, tables, and graphs in different sources

14. The density of silver is 10.5 grams per cubic centimeter. What is the mass of a cube of silver that measures 1.8 cm on each side?

    A. 0.17 grams

    B. 5.83 grams

    C. 18.90 grams

    D. 61.24 grams

15. A major conflict between colonial Americans and the British occurred over a series of British Acts of Parliament dealing with

    A. taxes.

    B. slavery.

    C. farming.

    D. Native Americans.

16. Which of the following instructional activities would best assist students with the aspect of phrasing for fluency?

    A. Require students to explain why reading with expression is important

    B. Have students read silently during guided reading groups

    C. Provide a rubric for oral expression and reading and penalize students who deviate from the rubric

    D. Model reading by doing expressive read-alouds

17. To use structural analysis to decode, the reader would use which of the following?

    A. Syntactic clues

    B. Initial consonant sounds

    C. Initial, medial, and final sounds

    D. Roots, prefixes, and suffixes

18. Christina is drawing figures using circles. The table below shows how many circles are used to create each new figure. Which of the following expressions can be used to determine how many circles are in the $n$th figure?

| Fig. 1 | Fig. 2 | Fig. 3 | Fig. 4 | ... | Fig. $n$ |
|--------|--------|--------|--------|-----|----------|
| 1      | 5      | 14     | 30     | ... | ?        |

    A. $\dfrac{n(n+1)}{2}$

    B. $\dfrac{n(n+1)(2n+1)}{6}$

    C. $n^2$

    D. $n!$

19. Which of the following would help students to self-assess their correct use of writing conventions during the writing process?

    A. An editing checklist

    B. A retelling checklist

    C. A mentor text

    D. A revision checklist

20. Which item below is true of arteries?

    A. They carry blood away from the heart.

B. They carry blood toward the heart.

C. They contain valves to prevent backflow of blood.

D. They always transport oxygenated blood.

21. The first thing a teacher should do when a student's eye has been exposed to hazardous chemical is to

   A. remove any eyewear, including contact lenses, and wait for emergency personnel.

   B. flush the affected area with water to dilute the hazardous chemical.

   C. place safety goggles on the student to contain the hazardous chemical.

   D. call 911 and wait for emergency personnel.

22. Which movement was most influential to the crafting of the U.S. Declaration of Independence and the U.S. Constitution?

   A. Scientific revolution

   B. Industrialism

   C. Enlightenment

   D. Renaissance

23. The parts of any scientific investigation (observations, question, procedure, etc.) are collectively referred to as

   A. an experiment.

   B. the scientific method.

   C. scientific inquiry.

   D. a six-step approach.

24. What was NOT a major tension between settlers in Texas and the Mexican government that led to the Texas War of Independence?

   A. Texas settlers and Mexicans both believed themselves to be racially superior to one another.

   B. Texas settlers wished to retain slavery, which had been outlawed in Mexico.

C. Texas settlers were upset by Santa Anna's Siete Leyes (seven laws), which abolished the Mexican Constitution.

D. Santa Anna wanted to tax the Texas settlers

25. A teacher wants to read traditional stories to his class to help them learn more about this genre. What is another name for the larger genre that includes the subgenre of traditional stories?

   A. Folklore

   B. Historical fiction

   C. Science fiction

   D. Poetry

26. A dog can run 5.25 times as fast as a child. Which equation can be used to find $r$, the speed of a dog, given $s$, the speed of the child?

   A. $r = 5.25s$

   B. $r = s + 5.25$

   C. $r = \dfrac{5.25}{s}$

   D. $r = \dfrac{s}{5.25}$

27. If a parent function is $f(x) = x^2$, what transformation occurred to the graph of the new function $f(x) = (x + 3)^2$?

   A. The function was translated up vertically by 3 units.

   B. The function was translated down vertically by 3 units.

   C. The function was shifted horizontally to the right by 3 units.

   D. The function was shifted horizontally to the left by 3 units.

28. Why do scientists use models?

   A. To aid in understanding and testing concepts and phenomena that are very simple

   B. To aid in understanding and testing concepts and phenomena that involve animate objects only

C. To aid in understanding and testing concepts and phenomena that involve inanimate objects only

D. To aid in understanding and testing concepts and phenomena that involve high complexity, a very long or very short time duration, or a very large or small scale

29. When seventh-grade students are presenting a formal speech about research in class, they should be required to do which of the following, according to the Texas Essential Knowledge and Skills?

A. Include evidence that justifies the conclusions

B. Retell a personal narrative that relates to the findings

C. Share their report in a five-paragraph essay format

D. Provide information from only one source

30. The presence of many metamorphic rocks in an area is an indication that the area has been subjected to

A. intense heat and pressure.

B. lack of volcanic activity.

C. significant weathering.

D. extended periods under water.

31. The most meaningful way to teach students about potential sources of error is to

A. ask the students to conduct an investigation that follows one procedure and leads to only one conclusion.

B. provide a lecture of sources of error in famous investigations from the history of science.

C. perform a demonstration and identify sources of error for students.

D. ask the students to conduct an investigation that is likely to result in instrument error, random results, and/or unsupported personal opinion.

32. Ms. White wants to use a "mentor text" to exemplify the writing trait of voice. She selects several texts in which the authors use dialogue and character development to teach this writing trait. What part of the language arts block would be most useful to model and share these examples of the selected writing trait?

A. Guided reading

B. Independent reading

C. Read-aloud

D. Partner reading

33. Consider the function $f(n) = \dfrac{5n^3 - 6n + 1}{7n^4}$. If you evaluate the function for $n$, what is the value of the function when $n$ becomes exceptionally large?

A. 0

B. $\infty$

C. $-\infty$

D. $\dfrac{5}{7}$

34. Astronomers have discovered vast differences in stars through their observations. One theory that is used to explain these differences is that

A. the distances between stars in the universe are extremely large.

B. stars in space are at different points in their life cycles.

C. Earth's atmosphere alters our view of the stars.

D. the high light pollution on Earth changes how stars appear to the human eye.

35. A train traveling from New York to Seattle passes a kilometer marker and then reaches the next kilometer marker in one minute. What is the velocity of the train?

A. 60 kilometers per hour

B. 1 kilometer per hour

C. 1 kilometer per hour in a westerly direction

D. 60 kilometers per hour in a westerly direction

36. Which of the following was NOT a result of the Industrial Revolution?

    A. Growth of urban areas

    B. Increased economic production

    C. Rise in small craft labor

    D. Specialization and division of labor

37. A scientist crosses a male and female guinea pig, both having a brown coat. Brown coat color is dominant over white coat color. Among the offspring, 75% have brown coats and 25% have white coats. The scientist can conclude that the genotypes of the parent guinea pigs were most likely:

    A. BB × BB

    B. BB × Bb

    C. Bb × Bb

    D. bb × bb

38. Water, or $H_2O$, is one of the few known chemicals that

    A. expands when frozen.

    B. contracts when frozen.

    C. contracts when heated.

    D. evaporates more rapidly when cooled.

39. Mr. Falvey provides students with a graduated cylinder and asks each student to measure the volume of water in the graduated cylinder. Students report a variety of different measurements. This is an opportunity for the teacher to discuss the importance of all of the following EXCEPT

    A. science generally has only one correct answer.

    B. measurement error.

    C. the importance of systematic observations and measurements.

    D. the importance of clear communication among investigators.

40. In Ms. Hernandez's class, the students are studying what plants need to survive. The students generate ideas to share. One need they identify for survival is food. When Ms. Hernandez asks the students where they think plants get their food, she notices that several students respond, "Plants get food from [eating] the soil." What is the *best* way to help students change this misconception that plants "eat the soil" to the scientifically accepted conception that plants make their own food from carbon dioxide and water through photosynthesis?

    A. Have students conduct an experiment in which they plant seeds in two different containers, place one in the dark and one in the light, and make observations over time

    B. Conduct a lecture/discussion session with students, explaining the process of photosynthesis by using pictures and diagrams

    C. Have students conduct an experiment in which they measure the mass of two pots of dry soil before planting seeds in the two pots; then after plants have grown, then measure the mass of the pots of dry soil again to see whether there has been a change.

    D. Ask students to read the textbook and search the Internet for information on how plants get food.

41. Which of the following was the purpose of the poster below?

Source: National Museum of American History, Smithsonian Institution

A. To encourage young women to go back to school

B. To encourage women to stand up for themselves

C. To encourage women to take factory jobs during World War II

D. To encourage men to recognize the rights of women

42. Why is sight word practice important to reading instruction?

A. It gives students a chance to decode CVC words and build word recognition.

B. It builds vocabulary and helps students with their conceptual understanding of the text.

C. It builds automaticity, as sight words are not spelled in phonetically regular ways and must be memorized.

D. It develops skills at problem solving and higher-level comprehension.

43. A seventh-grade language arts teacher has her students write and respond to one another about a novel on a class blog (web log). This way of having students represent information would primarily include which of the following types of media?

A. Media literacy

B. Print media

C. Visual media

D. Electronic media

44. The constitutional provision that allows one branch of government to amend or veto the decisions of another branch of government is referred to as what?

A. Judicial review

B. Checks and balances

C. Constitutional amendments

D. Due process

45. Which of the following aspects of writing is used to assess whether the writer engaged the reader sufficiently with her or his writing style to keep the reader's attention?

A. Organization

B. Conventions

C. Ideas

D. Voice

46. During independent reading, Mr. Murphy encourages his students to self-select expository text in addition to narrative text. Which of the following is an example of expository text?

A. A short story

B. A poem from a poetry anthology

C. A feature story in the daily newspaper

D. A young adult novel

47. Susan was measuring two angles with a protractor and found their sum to be 88 degrees. What is her percentage of error if the two angles were complementary?

A. 0.04%

B. 2.00%

C. 2.22%

D. 2.27%

48. Use the figure below to determine which triangle congruence property can be used to justify that $\triangle DEF \cong \triangle GHF$?

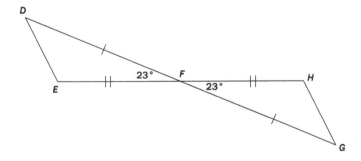

A. Angle-Angle-Side: if two angles and a side of one triangle are congruent to two angles and a side of another triangle, then the triangles are congruent.

B. Angle-Side-Angle: if two angles and the included side of one triangle are congruent to two angles and the included side of another triangle, then the triangles are congruent.

C. Side-Angle-Side: if two sides and the included angle of one triangle are congruent to two sides and the included angle of another triangle, then the triangles are congruent.

D. Side-Side-Side: if three sides of one triangle are congruent to three sides of another triangle, then the triangles are congruent.

49. On Earth, more solar energy reaches the equatorial regions than the polar regions because the equatorial regions

A. have more vegetation to absorb sunlight.

B. have days with more hours of light.

C. receive sun rays closest to vertical.

D. receive sun rays closest to horizontal.

50. A teacher gives a one-minute timed fluency check each week for students who are reading below grade level to measure their reading rate and to check for progress. What type of assessment technique is the teacher using?

A. Criterion-based assessment

B. Formal assessment

C. Curriculum-based assessment

D. Standardized assessment

51. Which of the following most accurately explains why scientific advances in farming equipment resulted in increased urbanization?

A. Farms lacked qualified people to operate the new equipment.

B. Farms required less human labor to produce crops.

C. Farmers could live in cities and commute to farms.

D. Manufacturing plants required more people to make new equipment.

52. Ms. Conway wants to help her seventh graders to effectively give oral instructions to perform a task. Which of the following lessons would best help prepare students to be successful with this task?

A. Model for students how to hold the audience's interest

B. Provide a blank graphic organizer for students to plan their speeches

C. Pair students to practice their speeches with classmates.

D. Teach students sequence words, such as *first*, *next*, *then*, to organize their writing.

53. Students are given a mirror and the figure below. On which edge should students place the mirror to create a rectangle from the original shape and the reflected shape?

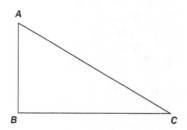

A. *AB*

B. *BC*

C. *CA*

D. *CB*

54. The writing process includes which of the following components?

A. brainstorming, mapping, rehearsal, drafting, editing

B. brainstorming, organizing, editing, spelling, grammar

C. brainstorming, drafting, revising, editing, publishing

D. brainstorming, sharing, listing, mapping, sub-mitting

55. Scientific investigations must involve all of the following EXCEPT

   A. verifiable evidence.

   B. peer review.

   C. logical reasoning.

   D. predictions.

56. Using a compass, a student creates the markings below next to ∠CAB. What is the student trying to construct?

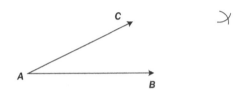

   A. A congruent angle to ∠CAB

   B. A supplementary angle to ∠CAB

   C. An angle bisector of ∠CAB

   D. A perpendicular bisector of ∠CAB

57. Mr. Smith is working with a group of fifth-grade students who are below grade level in reading. He wants to monitor their progress every six weeks to get a comprehensive measure of both their de-coding and comprehension skills. Which of the following assessment tools would best be used to monitor reading skills in these domains?

   A. An informal reading inventory

   B. A timed one-minute oral reading test

   C. A running record

   D. A phonics screening tool

58. Which of the following court cases overturned the conditions of segregation represented by the picture below?

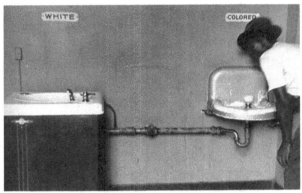

Source: National Archives and Records Administration

   A. *Plessy v. Ferguson*

   B. *Marbury v. Madison*

   C. *Brown v. Board of Education of Topeka*

   D. *Dred Scott v. Sandford*

59. A poster with a length of 21 inches and a width of 35 inches is reduced to the size of a notecard. The poster and notecard are similar. The length of the notecard is 3 inches, what is the width of the notecard?

   A. 1.8 inches

   B. 5 inches

   C. 7 inches

   D. 9 inches

60. According to the state standards for English Lan-guage Arts Reading, teaching sixth-grade students about writing conventions is best when done

   A. in the context of meaningful writing and ap-plication.

   B. using isolated drill and practice editing tech-niques.

   C. through weekly editing tests.

   D. by using lots of corrective feedback and edit-ing.

61. Geothermal energy, a possible energy resource, is based on which phenomenon?

    A. There are concentrations of heat in some places of Earth's crust.

    B. Earth's internal energy heats its surface more than the Sun does.

    C. Heat energy from the Sun penetrates deep into Earth.

    D. Fossils deep below Earth's surface have transformed over time to oil and coal.

62. While reading a novel with his seventh-grade language arts class, Mr. McBride asks his students to analyze character. He asks the class, based on the actions and dialogue of the main character, to identify several character traits of this character. He also asks them to refer back to direct evidence in the text for a specific example to support each character trait. Mr. McBride is helping his students to develop skills in

    A. connecting.

    B. inferencing.

    C. visualizing.

    D. synthesizing.

63. The economy of the southern colonies was primarily based on what?

    A. Cotton and tobacco

    B. Farming, shipping, and fishing

    C. Tobacco and shipping

    D. Trading

64. A dilation contracted the hexagon, shown on the left below, creating a similar figure, shown on the right below. What is the measure of *x*?

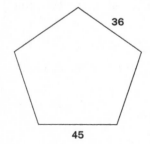

    A. 9

    B. 6

    C. 5

    D. 4

65. When teaching viewing and representing, the concept of design and selection of images to be used in a media presentation generally includes the study of each of the following aspects EXCEPT

    A. color.

    B. shapes.

    C. texture.

    D. hyperlinks.

66. According to the sixth-, seventh-, and eighth-grade Texas Essential Knowledge and Skills, the skills that should be taught as part of making oral presentations includes all of the following EXCEPT

    A. using eye contact.

    B. enunciation.

    C. a variety of natural gestures.

    D. including a personal story.

67. The term *manifest destiny* connotes a culture of

    A. ancestral harmony.

    B. territorial expansion.

    C. geographic isolationism.

    D. economic capitalism.

68. Oxygen gas ($O_2$) is an example of a(n)

    A. compound.

    B. heterogeneous mixture.

    C. homogenous mixture.

    D. element.

69. Marco surveyed his class last week and found 20% of his classmates have black hair, 25% have blond hair, 25% have dark brown hair, 20% have light brown hair, and the rest have red hair. Which circle graph best shows the results from Marco's survey?

A.

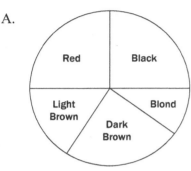

B.

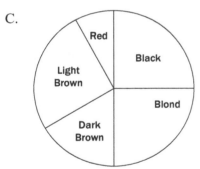

C.

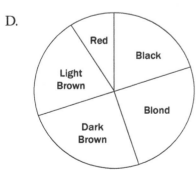

D.

70. To facilitate comprehension for the English language learners in his class, a language arts teacher wants to help students become more metacognitive at checking whether they understand what they read. Asking students to practice "chunking" the text at designated stopping points and having them explain what they read to a partner is a good way to support them in

A. self-monitoring.

B. increasing reading rate.

C. motivating them to read more.

D. developing their productive language skills.

71. The skill of phonemic awareness fosters literacy development in emergent and beginning readers primarily because

A. it helps students to produce rhyming words.

B. it is a predictor of learning to read.

C. it helps students to read with expression.

D. it helps students to read with comprehension.

72. Mr. Freeman conducted an inquiry lesson in which his class of 30 students worked in groups of three and first read and recorded the room temperature of two thermometers. The student groups then each taped one thermometer on the walls of the classroom near the floor, and the second thermometer on the walls of the classroom near the ceiling. After an hour, the students collected their thermometers and again read and recorded the temperature on each. What would be the best strategy to next use to help students reach the desired conclusion that the air at the ceiling is warmer than the air at the floor (demonstrating that warm air rises and cold air sinks, or the concept of convection)?

A. After students have collected their starting and ending temperatures on their thermometers, show a well-designed Powerpoint presentation with diagrams describing and showing convection. Follow the PowerPoint with discussion about other examples of convection, such as hot air balloons and a film about tornadoes.

B. After students have collected their starting and ending temperatures on their thermometers, ask each student group to review their starting and ending temperatures. Then ask each group to make a graph of their findings and develop a conclusion based on their group's measurements and results.

C. After students have collected their starting and ending temperatures on their thermometers, ask one student from each group to enter their starting and ending temperatures for their floor and ceiling thermometers on a class spreadsheet. Using all class data, ask students to make a line graph with one line showing starting and ending floor temperatures and another line showing the same for ceiling temperatures. Ask students to calculate the average starting and ending temperatures for ceiling and floor thermometers using class data.

D. After students have collected their starting and ending temperatures on their thermometers, have students conduct an experiment using a beaker filled with ice. Students measure the temperature of the ice and then place the beaker on a hot plate. After turning on the hot plate, the students measure and record the temperature of the ice every 30 seconds as it changes state from solid to liquid and then reaches the boiling point. The student groups record, share, and analyze findings in class discussion.

73. A coin is flipped and then a die is rolled. What is the probability that the outcome shows heads on the coin and an even number on the die?

A. $\dfrac{1}{12}$

B. $\dfrac{1}{6}$

C. $\dfrac{1}{4}$

D. $\dfrac{1}{3}$

74. Which branch of government is responsible for creating the nation's laws?

A. Executive

B. Legislative

C. Judicial

D. Fiscal

75. As part of the writing process, eighth-grade students are expected to be able to do all of the following EXCEPT

A. draft an essay with the audience in mind.

B. develop coherence in a piece of writing.

C. use compound and complex sentences.

D. write primarily in narrative prose.

76. Mr. Terry uses miscue analysis to assess each student's accuracy. He then looks for patterns in the types of miscues each student might make. All of the following are types of miscues that are measured in the decoding part of such an assessment technique EXCEPT

A. substitution.

B. omission.

C. mispronunciation.

D. prosody.

77. Which of the following helped to extend the border of the United States westward toward the Pacific Ocean?

A. The 1848 Annexation of Colorado

B. The 1845 Annexation of Mississippi

C. The 1803 Louisiana Purchase Treaty

D. The 1846 Washington Purchase

78. The scatter plot below shows the daily temperatures during the first 12 days in July. Which statement best represents the data?

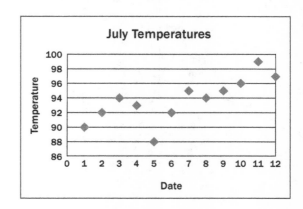

A. There is a positive relationship between temperature and date.

B. There is a negative relationship between temperature and date.

C. There is no relationship between temperature and date.

D. The warmest day was July 6.

79. During the writing process, students are encouraged to add, change, and/or delete ideas in their composition. This process is known as

A. brainstorming.

B. revision.

C. editing.

D. drafting.

80. Which constitutional amendment guaranteed women the right to vote?

A. Thirteenth

B. Eighteenth

C. Nineteenth

D. Twenty-second

81. Samantha was investigating properties of quadrilaterals and noticed the diagonals of rectangles and squares bisect each other. Samantha conjectures this statement is true for all quadrilaterals. Which step is the most reasonable for Samantha to take to evaluate the validity of her conjecture?

A. Generalize the conjecture to apply to other quadrilaterals

B. Find a counterexample to the conjecture

C. Find more examples supporting the conjecture

D. Prove the conjecture

82. The process by which energy is generated in the Sun is called

A. fission.     C. fusion.

B. combustion.     D. plasma.

83. What does the ability of a lizard to lose its tail when pulled represent?

A. An adaption for survival when attacked by predators

B. A mechanism of reproduction of a new lizard from the tail

C. A form of molting as the lizard grows in size

D. An indication of environmental stress such as drought

84. Select the best choice to the following question. What is the primary role of science notebooks in the science classroom?

A. An opportunity for students to reflect on the day's activities, similar to a diary

B. An opportunity for students to act like a scientist by recording and exploring ideas related to investigative inquiries

C. An opportunity for the teacher to assess grammar skills

D. An opportunity for students to act like scientists by writing to inform, explain, persuade, and explore

85. What is the arrangement of the Sun, Earth, and Moon during a solar eclipse?

A. The Earth is directly between the Sun and Moon, casting a shadow on the Moon.

B. The Moon is directly between the Sun and Earth, casting a shadow on Earth.

C. The Moon is present during the day at the phase known as first quarter.

D. The Sun emits solar flares that reach both the Moon and Earth, slightly increasing the overall temperature.

86. Mrs. Jones has three fourth graders who are at the early stages of their reading development. She wants to help her students move from the emergent stage of reading to understanding some basic sight words and the conventions of print. She uses a technique called "shared writing," in which students dictate their thoughts orally and she writes them down. This is followed by the group of students doing a repeated reading aloud of the shared text. The *primary purpose* in doing this activity with these students would be to

    A. demonstrate the conventions of writing such as punctuation, spelling, and grammar rules.

    B. engage students with a high-interest activity that will motivate them to want to write more.

    C. develop the students' ability to engage in listening, speaking, reading, and writing to further their reading development.

    D. foster a sight word vocabulary that will help them with spelling in future writing.

87. On October 1, a pair of cowboy boots was priced at $120. On November 1, the price was reduced by 15%. In December, the price was further reduced by 25% of the November 1 price and marked as *final*. What percentage of the original price was the final price?

    A. 76.5%

    B. 63.75%

    C. 40%

    D. 30%

88. A social studies teacher should expect students in grades 4–8 to do which of the following?

    A. Focus on traditional ways of finding, organizing, and displaying information

    B. Focus exclusively on history

    C. Focus primarily on memorization strategies

    D. Focus on making connections with the real world and between academic subjects

89. The difference between heat and temperature is that

    A. heat is the movement of thermal energy, whereas temperature is the measure of the average molecular movement of matter.

    B. heat is the measure of average molecular movement of matter, whereas temperature is the measure of how hot or cold something is.

    C. heat is the movement of energy through some medium, whereas temperature is the measure of the movement of energy from one source to another.

    D. heat is the movement of thermal energy, whereas temperature is the measure of state of matter.

90. Below is a model of a factored polynomial. Identify the polynomial and the factorization.

    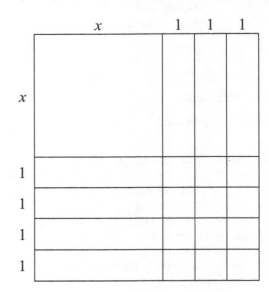

    A. $x^2 + x - 12$; $(x - 3)(x + 4)$

    B. $x^2 + 7x + 12$; $(x + 3)(x + 4)$

    C. $x^2 + 6x + 9$; $(x + 3)(x + 3)$

    D. $x^2 - 7x + 12$; $(x - 3)(x - 4)$

91. Which of the following represents a symbiotic relationship known as mutualism?

    A. Mistletoe growing on a tree and using the food and nutrients from the tree for its own growth

B. A clown fish living among a type of sea anemone, where the fish aggressively protects the anemone from predators and the anemone's poison protects the fish from predators

C. Poison ivy producing a toxin that irritates the skin of many animal species, therefore protecting the plant from predation

D. Spiders building their web on plants to capture insects for food and to have a protective shelter

92. _____ and _____ are two related key concepts that are seen across the science disciplines.

A. Empirical; supernatural

B. Constancy; change

C. Form; function

D. Both (B) and (C)

93. Consider the case in which an independent scientist received funding by a pharmaceutical company to conduct an investigation determining the effectiveness of a particular medication manufactured by the company. This is a situation to generate discussion with students about scientific ethics because

A. it provides an example of how scientists are often dishonest.

B. it provides an example of how scientists can work independently of society's ethics.

C. it suggests that the results of scientific investigations can be trusted.

D. it suggests a possible issue of conflict of interest.

94. Convection current is

A. transfer of heat energy in a fluid.

B. a form of electricity transfer in conductors.

C. direct transfer of heat energy from one substance to another.

D. radiation from the Sun that causes Earth to warm.

95. A teacher recently began teaching a unit on similar triangles. Which of the following topics is a teacher most likely to have students explore?

A. Area formulas for right and equilateral triangles

B. Pythagorean theorem

C. Proportional relationships

D. Angle measures

96. What are the distinguishing features of an experiment that differentiates it from other types of investigations?

A. Prediction, observations, and analysis of data

B. Prediction, observations, and conclusion

C. Testable hypothesis, variables identified and manipulated, and the aim of determining causal relationships

D. Testable hypothesis, variables identified and manipulated, and the aim of determining correlations among variables

97.

Source: National Archives and Records Administration

In reference to the photograph above, Eleanor Roosevelt said, "The destiny of human rights is in the hands of all our citizens in all our communities." From a social studies teacher's perspective, this quote applies

A. only to U.S. citizens in the 20th century.

B. only to U.S. citizens from early civilizations through today.

C. only to any human living after the 20th century.

D. to any human from early civilizations through today.

98. In a middle school math class, students have begun activities exploring area relationships among rectangles, triangles, parallelograms, and trapezoids. The classroom teacher wants to identify any aspects of the content that challenge the students in order to adjust future lessons on this topic. Which of the following assessment methods would be most appropriate for achieving this goal?

A. Regular observations and interviews among teacher and student

B. Periodical peer reviews of partner work

C. Pretest and posttest

D. Pop quizzes after future lessons

99. In a blinding snowstorm in Vermont, the air temperature and dew-point temperature are both 30°F. Meanwhile, under clear skies in Arizona, the air temperature is 85°F and the dew-point temperature is 38°F. From this information you could conclude that

A. there is more water vapor in the air in Arizona.

B. there is more water vapor in the Vermont snowstorm.

C. the same amount of water vapor is found in the air in Vermont and Arizona.

D. Vermont and Arizona are both located next to the ocean.

100. Simplify the expression $i^{10}$.

A. $i$

B. $-i$

C. 1

D. $-1$

101. Which of the following is an example of an activity that students could do to conduct *primary research* for a social studies project?

A. Create a poster report using Internet resources

B. Conduct a survey to gather information

C. Synthesize facts from multiple informational texts

D. Evaluate websites for accuracy of information

102. Mr. Morrissey noticed his seventh-grade students are consistently confusing the plural and the possessive in their written compositions. He wants to provide some guided practice in correcting this error. Which of the following would best help practice this convention?

A. Require students to complete practice worksheets with editing exercises

B. Provide direct instruction in the correct use of each with specific examples and have students practice writing sentences using each correctly

C. Model using the correct use of each and deduct points each time students use it incorrectly

D. Emphasize to students that using correct grammar will help them to be more effective writers

103. Article 55 of which document calls for "universal respect for, and observance of, human rights and fundamental freedoms"?

A. The U.S. Constitution

B. The Declaration of Independence

C. The United Nations Charter

D. The Texas Constitution

104. An eighth-grade social studies teacher wants to develop her students' understanding of cause and effect in major historical events. Which of the following graphic organizers would best help in facilitating this type of comprehension?

A. T-chart

B. Venn diagram

C. Semantic map

D. Inquiry chart

105. Simplify the expression below.

$$6i^7 \times 5i^{-5} + \frac{8i^{11}}{4i^9}$$

   A. −32

   B. 32$i$

   C. 30$i$ + 2$i^2$

   D. 28

106. Ms. Adams wants to assess reading comprehension by posing questions about the short story the students are reading. She begins her questioning by asking some basic recall questions to assess understanding. These types of questions are also known as

   A. literal questions.

   B. evaluative questions.

   C. inferential questions.

   D. applied questions.

107. What are the three American Indian groups remaining in Texas that are federally recognized tribes?

   A. The Alabama-Coushatta Tribe in east Texas; the Comanche Tribe in far west Texas; and the Kickapoo Traditional Tribe in southwest Texas along the Texas-Mexico border

   B. The Alabama-Coushatta Tribe in east Texas; the Kickapoo Traditional Tribe in southwest Texas along the Texas-Mexico border; and the Ysleta del Sur Pueblo, or Tigua, in far west Texas

   C. The Alabama-Coushatta Tribe in southwest Texas along the Texas-Mexico border; the Comanche Tribe in north and central Texas; and the Ysleta del Sur Pueblo, or Tigua, in far west Texas

   D. The Alabama-Coushatta Tribe in southwest Texas along the Texas-Mexico border; the Kickapoo Traditional Tribe in east Texas; and the Ysleta del Sur Pueblo, or Tigua, in far west Texas

108. Juneteenth is the celebration that recognizes which event in Texas history?

   A. Texas's independence from Mexico

   B. Freeing of slaves

   C. The cotton harvest

   D. Texas's secession from the Union

109. Fossils of clamlike shells have been found deep in the sedimentary rock in Texas. What do these fossils indicate?

   A. The state of Texas was once covered with small streams.

   B. Texas was once covered by a sea or ocean.

   C. The state of Texas was once seismically active.

   D. There once were mountain ranges across the state of Texas.

110. Mr. Marshall arranged chairs for a school function in rows of the same length, with more than one chair in each row and more than one row. Which of the following could NOT be the number of chairs he arranged?

   A. 99

   B. 81

   C. 73

   D. 27

**Use the information in this scenario to answer the next two questions.**

*Scenario:* Answer the following two questions about chlorofluorocarbons (CFCs). CFCs are nonflammable hydrocarbons containing both chlorine and fluorine used as solvents, refrigerants, cleaning fluids, and fire-extinguishing agents. We classify CFCs as halocarbons, a class of compounds that contain atoms of carbon and halogen atoms.

111. What statement is true about environmental changes brought about by scientific discoveries and technological innovations associated with increased use of CFCs?

    A. CFCs brought about scientific discoveries and technological innovations that improved the quality of food refrigeration, but the increased use of CFCs caused geological degradation.

    B. CFCs brought about scientific discoveries and technological innovations that improved the quality of life through air conditioning while having minimal negative effects on the environment.

    C. CFCs brought about scientific discoveries and technological innovations that improved the quality of food refrigeration, but they caused acid rain.

    D. CFCs brought about scientific discoveries and technological innovations that improved the quality of life through air conditioning, but they caused stratospheric ozone depletion.

112. CFCs were first synthesized in 1928 to

    A. make the refrigeration of food safer after a series of fatal accidents in the 1920s where methyl chloride leaked out of refrigerators.

    B. make the refrigeration of food safer after a series of food poisoning incidents in the 1920s where refrigerators failed to keep food at a safe storage temperatures.

    C. keep offices cooler after a large number of women joined the U.S. workforce in the 1920s and demanded more humane working conditions.

    D. keep houses cooler after the number of fatal heat stokes spiked in the 1920s due to increases in global warming.

113. Mr. Jones has his fifth-grade students examine some photographs of dust storms from the Great Depression. He asks the students to discuss details from the photos and to consider what life must have been like during that era and place. Students are asked to write a paragraph describing what life must have been like from the perspective of those who lived through it. What type of analysis are students doing while engaging in this instructional activity?

    A. Predicting

    B. Taking notes

    C. Comparing and contrasting

    D. Drawing inferences

114. Which of the following holidays most significantly contributes to the conceptualization of being American?

    A. Valentine's Day

    B. Memorial Day

    C. Christmas

    D. New Year's Day

115. Gerald wants to graph the equation: $3x + 6 - 4y - 4 = 18$. He chooses to first solve for $y$, to graph the line by using the slope-intercept form. Gerald's work is shown below.

$$3x + 6 - 4y - 4 = 18$$
$$3x - 4y + 2 = 18$$
$$?$$
$$3x - 4y = 16$$
$$3x - 3x - 4y = -3x + 16$$
$$\frac{-4y}{-4} = \frac{-3x + 16}{-4}$$
$$y = \frac{3}{4}x - 4$$

Which of the following equations best describes the missing step in Gerald's work?

    A. $3x - 4y - 4 = 18 - 4$

B. $3x - 4y + 2 - 2 = 18 - 2$

C. $3x - 4y - 6 = 18 - 6$

D. $3x - 4y + 4 - 2 = 18 - 2$

116. Which is the correct syllabication for the word *structure*?

A. str-uc-ture

B. struct-ure

C. struc-ture

D. stru-c-ture

117. The graph of the line $y = -2x + (-6)$ is shown below.

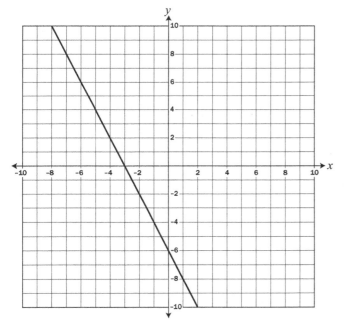

Which table of ordered pairs contains only the points on the line displayed on the previous page?

A.

| x | y |
|---|---|
| −2 | 2 |
| −1 | 4 |
| 0 | 6 |
| 1 | 8 |

B.

| x | y |
|---|---|
| −6 | −6 |
| −3 | 0 |
| 0 | 6 |
| 3 | 12 |

C.

| x | y |
|---|---|
| 6 | −6 |
| 0 | −3 |
| −6 | 0 |
| −12 | 3 |

D.

| x | y |
|---|---|
| −6 | 6 |
| −3 | 0 |
| 0 | −6 |
| 3 | −12 |

118. Which of the following are imaginary lines on the Earth's surface?

A. Only the equator

B. Only the International Date Line

C. Only lines of longitude and latitude

D. The equator, the International Date Line, longitude lines, and latitude lines

119. Bean seeds are planted in a cup inside a shoe box standing upright on its side with a 3-inch diameter circle cut out of the center of the shoe box close to the bottom of the box, as shown below.

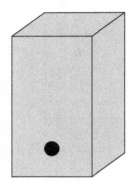

The box is placed in a sunlit room, and the plant is watered regularly without exposing it to sunlight for any length of time. Over time, what will the researcher most likely observe has happened to the bean seeds, and why?

A. The bean seeds will not have germinated and will die due to lack of sunlight.

B. The bean seeds will germinate and grow straight up to the top of the box but the plant will be brown, shriveled and soon die due to lack of sunlight.

C. The bean seeds will germinate and the plant will be observed to bend and grow out of the cutout circle due a phototropism reaction.

D. The bean seeds will germinate and the plant will be observed to bend and grow out of the cutout circle due to a geotropism reaction.

120. Which of the following activities fosters development in phonological awareness?

A. Repeated reading

B. Oral retelling

C. Tongue twisters

D. Think-pair-share

121. A way to use picture books to teach the Texas Essential Knowledge and Skills that focus on viewing might include which of the following?

A. Examine the ways that the art and design impact the mood of the story

B. Take turns discussing revision choices that students made during peer editing

C. Hold up the book during the read-aloud so students can properly view the pictures

D. Have students discuss their favorite pictures within the story

122. Authors who captured the cultural voice of societal change during the Harlem Renaissance included

A. Walter Dean Myers, Christopher Myers, Nikki Giovanni, Zoë Lewis, and Gail Carson Levine.

B. Aaron Douglas, Lois Jones, William H. Johnson, Jacob Lawrence, and Romare Bearden.

C. Langston Hughes, Countee Cullen, James Weldon Johnson, Jessie Redmon Fauset, and Zora Neale Hurston.

D. Marcus Garvey, W.E.B. DuBois, James Weldon Johnson, Louis Armstrong, and Duke Ellington.

123. Vince can read 20 pages in 30 minutes. If he continues reading at this rate, how many pages can he read in 1.5 hours?

A. 60 pages

B. 90 pages

C. 600 pages

D. 900 pages

124. A fifth-grade student can read a grade-level passage aloud with 94% accuracy in decoding. This grade level passage is at the student's _____ reading level.

A. frustrational

B. independent

C. comprehensive

D. instructional

125. Discovery of which natural resource led to the economic growth of Texas cities, including Houston and Dallas?

    A. Oil

    B. Natural gas

    C. Gold

    D. Limestone

126. What is a primary historical source?

    A. A document or piece of evidence produced during the period being studied

    B. A historian's analysis of the past

    C. The first document produced about a particular historical event

    D. A website that summarizes the key events of a major historical figure

127. The rectangular prism shown below was created by stacking 18 blocks together, all of which are the same size. What are the dimensions of each block?

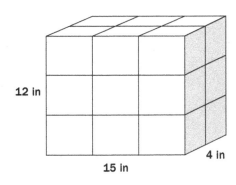

12 in
15 in
4 in

    A. $4 \times 4 \times 5$

    B. $2 \times 3 \times 5$

    C. $3 \times 4 \times 5$

    D. $2 \times 4 \times 5$

128. How can a teacher promote critical thinking in the social studies?

    A. Guide students toward a single perspective

    B. Prevent students from practicing evidence-based decision making

    C. Help students memorize key facts

    D. Encourage students to apply their knowledge to the real world

129. In the figure below, lines $l$ and $m$ are parallel. If $y° = 4x°$, what is the value of $x$ in degrees?

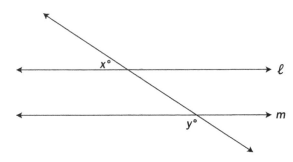

    A. 36

    B. 45

    C. 60

    D. 144

130. The circle graph below shows the distribution of recycled material, by weight, for the city of Smithville. If approximately 40 tons of recyclable materials are glass, approximately how many tons of the recyclable materials are paper?

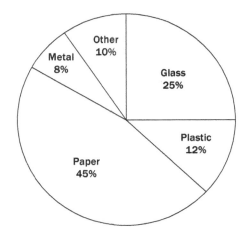

    A. 160 tons

    B. 72 tons

    C. 48 tons

    D. 40 tons

# Answer Key

| Question | Answer | Competency | | Question | Answer | Competency |
|----------|--------|------------|---|----------|--------|------------|
| 1 | C | 010 | | 32 | C | 007 |
| 2 | B | 031 | | 33 | A | 016 |
| 3 | B | 001 | | 34 | B | 054 |
| 4 | C | 003 | | 35 | D | 041 |
| 5 | C | 032 | | 36 | C | 029 |
| 6 | D | 031 | | 37 | C | 047 |
| 7 | A | 003 | | 38 | A | 042 |
| 8 | A | 011 | | 39 | A | 037 |
| 9 | C | 004 | | 40 | C | 056 |
| 10 | A | 001 | | 41 | C | 029 |
| 11 | D | 007 | | 42 | C | 003 |
| 12 | D | 005 | | 43 | D | 009 |
| 13 | A | 009 | | 44 | B | 032 |
| 14 | D | 012 | | 45 | D | 007 |
| 15 | A | 029 | | 46 | C | 005 |
| 16 | D | 003 | | 47 | C | 017 |
| 17 | D | 003 | | 48 | C | 018 |
| 18 | B | 013 | | 49 | C | 053 |
| 19 | A | 006 | | 50 | C | 002 |
| 20 | A | 046 | | 51 | B | 033 |
| 21 | B | 036 | | 52 | D | 001 |
| 22 | C | 029 | | 53 | C | 020 |
| 23 | C | 038 | | 54 | C | 007 |
| 24 | D | 029 | | 55 | D | 038 |
| 25 | A | 005 | | 56 | C | 018 |
| 26 | A | 014 | | 57 | A | 002 |
| 27 | D | 015 | | 58 | C | 029 |
| 28 | D | 040 | | 59 | B | 019 |
| 29 | A | 001 | | 60 | A | 006 |
| 30 | A | 052 | | 61 | A | 051 |
| 31 | D | 038 | | 62 | B | 004 |

*(continued)*

# Answer Key (continued)

| Question | Answer | Competency |
|----------|--------|------------|
| 63 | A | 031 |
| 64 | D | 020 |
| 65 | D | 008 |
| 66 | D | 001 |
| 67 | B | 030 |
| 68 | D | 043 |
| 69 | D | 021 |
| 70 | A | 004 |
| 71 | B | 002 |
| 72 | C | 057 |
| 73 | C | 022 |
| 74 | B | 032 |
| 75 | D | 007 |
| 76 | D | 003 |
| 77 | C | 030 |
| 78 | A | 023 |
| 79 | B | 007 |
| 80 | C | 032 |
| 81 | B | 024 |
| 82 | C | 045 |
| 83 | A | 048 |
| 84 | D | 058 |
| 85 | B | 054 |
| 86 | C | 002 |
| 87 | B | 025 |
| 88 | D | 035 |
| 89 | A | 044 |
| 90 | B | 026 |
| 91 | B | 050 |
| 92 | D | 040 |
| 93 | D | 039 |
| 94 | A | 051 |
| 95 | C | 027 |
| 96 | C | 038 |

| Question | Answer | Competency |
|----------|--------|------------|
| 97 | D | 033 |
| 98 | A | 028 |
| 99 | B | 053 |
| 100 | D | 010 |
| 101 | B | 009 |
| 102 | B | 006 |
| 103 | C | 030 |
| 104 | A | 005 |
| 105 | A | 011 |
| 106 | A | 004 |
| 107 | B | 030 |
| 108 | B | 029 |
| 109 | B | 055 |
| 110 | C | 012 |
| 111 | D | 030 |
| 112 | A | 033 |
| 113 | D | 034 |
| 114 | B | 033 |
| 115 | B | 013 |
| 116 | C | 003 |
| 117 | D | 014 |
| 118 | D | 030 |
| 119 | C | 049 |
| 120 | C | 002 |
| 121 | A | 008 |
| 122 | C | 033 |
| 123 | A | 015 |
| 124 | D | 004 |
| 125 | A | 031 |
| 126 | A | 034 |
| 127 | D | 017 |
| 128 | D | 034 |
| 129 | A | 018 |
| 130 | B | 021 |

# Practice Test 1 Answer Explanations

**1.    C**

The model shown is a square comprising 36 dots in the arrangement of 6 × 6. (C) is the correct answer since 6 × 6 is $6^2$ or 36 dots. Answer option (A) is incorrect because 6 is only one dimension of each side. (B) is incorrect because it gives only two rows of dots, or 12. Finally, (D) is incorrect because $6^3$ represents 6 × 6 × 6 = 216. **Competency 010**

**2.    B**

Economics is BEST described as the study of how individuals and groups with limited resources make decisions to best satisfy their needs and wants. Choice (A) is incorrect because examining how political systems establish systems for production and consumption is only one part of economic study. Choice (C), how currency is used in different societies, might be of interest to anthropologists or sociologists, but is not the primary responsibility of economists. Choice (D,) how trade has developed through a historic and systematic process, would be of interest to historians, but not the primary interest of economic study. Thus, (B) is the best general description of economic study. **Competency 031**

**3.    B**

The primary purpose of having a response notebook is to organize thinking about the key ideas and themes relating to the book. Organizing written notes also connects to students' ability to share these ideas orally. Choice (A) is incorrect because expression, although important, is not the primary purpose of the writing component and its connection with sharing ideas orally in the literature circles. Choice (C) is incorrect because grammar development and a focus on mechanics and conventions are not the primary objectives of the written component. What is key is the ability to express ideas. Choice (D) is incorrect because writing and planning don't necessarily assist shy students in their ability to express themselves. **Competency 001**

**4.    C**

Reader's theater involves the act of repeated reading. Evidence from research suggests that repeated reading builds automaticity and fluency in reading. Therefore, reader's theater fosters development in fluency. Even though comprehension (A) and vocabulary (B) might incidentally be developed, the act of repeated reading is primarily to develop fluency. Structural analysis (D) is a vocabulary tool used to decode and make sense of the meaning of individual words. **Competency 003**

**5.    C**

*E pluribus unum* is a Latin phrase that means "out of many, one." The United States used it as an unofficial motto from 1782–1955. This motto appears in the official Great Seal of United States on the banner in the bald eagle's beak. While both (A) "one nation under God," and (D) "freedom and justice for all," are phrases found in the U.S. Pledge of Allegiance, neither are official mottos of the United States. Choice (B), *Carpe diem,* which is Latin for "seize the day" is incorrect because it has never been recognized as the official motto of the United States. "In God we trust" was adopted as the official motto in 1956. **Competency 032**

**6.    D**

Capitalism is the economic and political system in which a country's trade and industry are controlled by private owners for profit, rather than by the state. Choice (A) is incorrect because socialism is an economic system in which the means of production are primarily owned by the state or cooperative groups, and members are given equal shares regardless of their contributions. Choice (B), republicanism, is incorrect because it is a political ideology that embraces a form of government in which leaders are elected for a specific period by the majority of the citizenry. Choice (C), communism, is incorrect because it is an economic and political system in which the economy is centrally planned to ensure that property is owned collectively and that control over the distribution of property is centralized in order to achieve both classlessness and statelessness. **Competency 031**

**7. A**

Repeated reading is the best approach to developing fluency in reading. By focusing on independent-level text, the reader is able to build upon success and is encouraged to continue reading the same text. Choice (D) focuses on an activity that would be intended to develop comprehension rather than fluency. **Competency 003**

**8. A**

The array model shown in the figure has dimensions 5 by 13 and the rectangular array is separated into two regions with areas of 50 and 15 square units. The first area region of 50 square units derived from $5 \times 10$, and the other area region represents $5 \times 3$, or 15, square units. Answer (A) is correct because the model represents the distributive property $5 \times (10 + 3) = (5 \times 10) + (5 \times 3) = 50 + 15 = 65$. Answers (B) and (D) are incorrect because their products are 750 and 75, respectively; neither equals 65. Although answer (C) results in 65, $50 + 15$ is an addition problem, and the directions ask to identify the multiplication problem modeled in the figure. **Competency 011**

**9. C**

Reciprocal teaching is a collaborative, small-group comprehension activity in which students work together to read and discuss a selected text. Each student has a role in processing and leading a discussion about the text, so the correct choice is (C). In these four roles, one student serves as the summarizer, another student poses questions to the group and encourages other students in the group to do so as well, a third student leads the group in predicting before and throughout the reading, and a fourth student helps the group to clarify tricky or confusing parts of the text. Together, the students work to comprehend the text at a deeper level. **Competency 004**

**10. A**

Choice (A) is correct because it fits with the concept that teachers need to first effectively model the types of discourse patterns and discussions they wish students to use in small group discussions. Choice (B) is incorrect because behavior management, although important, is not a primary consideration for choosing to use whole-class instruction. Choice (C) is incorrect because student discussion is an expectation of the state standards. Choice (D) is incorrect because

teachers need to allow students the responsibility and expectation of engaging in small group dialogue across different instructional activities to facilitate their development of oral language and expression. **Competency 001**

**11. D**

Conferring gives the teacher a chance to work with students for different purposes. A primary purpose is to give students individualized feedback on their written work. Choice (D) is correct because it focuses on this chance to monitor individual student progress. **Competency 007**

**12. D**

KWL stands for "Know," "Want to know," and "Learned," and relates to the types of discussion and questioning that would take place before, during, and after a story was read. In the "Know" part, the teacher guides students to consider what background knowledge they have that relates to the text. After these are shared, students pose questions about what they hope to know and learn from the text prior to reading it. After the text is read, or, while it is read, the teacher can discuss with students what they are learning or have learned as a result of reading the text. These activities help students anticipate what it is they will be reading prior to reading it, as well as activate their schema or background knowledge prior to reading. Answer (D) is the correct choice because it best fits this purpose of building and activating background knowledge while helping students to anticipate the key ideas in the text. The other choices don't directly relate to this purpose. **Competency 005**

**13. A**

Students need to critically evaluate and judge credibility and accuracy of information located online. This skill is primary in helping students to understand that not everything that is located online is highly accurate. Choice (B) is incorrect because using multiple web browsers won't guarantee that students can critically examine and evaluate the text they are reading. Choice (C) is incorrect because summarizing also doesn't necessarily lead to the skills needed to judge or evaluate the credibility of a source. Choice (D) is incorrect because, even though reading charts, tables, and graphs might develop overall comprehension of what is read, it doesn't directly lead to the primary objective of critically evaluating the sources. **Competency 009**

## 14.  D

To determine that answer (D) is correct, it is necessary to find the number of cubic centimeters in a cube with side lengths of 1.8 cm. The term "cubic centimeters" can also be referred to as the volume of the cube, which is found by the formula $V = s \times s \times s$ or $V = s^3$. Therefore, the volume of the silver cube is $(1.8)^3 = 5.832$ cubic centimeters. Since the density of silver is 10.5 grams per cubic centimeter, multiply 5.832 cm$^3$ by 10.5 to get 61.236 grams, which rounded to the nearest hundredth is 61.24 grams. Answer (A) is incorrect, but obtained by dividing 1.8 by 10.5. Answer (B) is incorrect since it is only the volume of the silver cube, and not the mass. Answer (C) was obtained by multiplying the two numbers in the problem together. **Competency 012**

## 15.  A

The British imposition of taxes on colonial Americans (A) provoked major conflicts between these two groups. The colonists were upset with the British for implementing taxes when they felt they did not have any direct representation in the British Parliament. For choice (B), even though slavery continued in the colonies after it was abolished in England (1833), it was not a huge source of contention between the colonists and the British because the American Revolution had already occurred and the United States was free from British control. For choice (C), colonial farming was an industry, which received little interference from the British. Choice (D) is incorrect because no British Acts of Parliament were passed that dealt with Native Americans. **Competency 029**

## 16.  D

Modeled reading provides a powerful example of fluent reading, including rate, accuracy, and expression. The idea of phrasing for fluency involves many aspects of reading with expression, including pausing, intonation, and adjusting reading rate. Students need to hear examples of phrasing to engage in it independently. By engaging in silent reading during read-aloud (B), students may not get the feedback they need to use the strategy effectively. A rubric alone (C) is not sufficient to give students the input and examples they need to engage in phrasing for fluency independently. The ability to explain something (A) does not mean that students will necessarily be able to engage in the task. **Competency 003**

## 17.  D

Structural analysis helps students to examine the meaning of words by analyzing the affixes that may make up the word. For instance, the word *biology* contains the prefix *bio-*, which means "life." Students can use this knowledge to ascertain the meaning of words. They can also use the structure to decode the words. Choice (A) is incorrect because it draws students' attention to grammar clues, which are part of the sentence level of reading. Choices (B) and (C) are incorrect because they are not focused on units of meaning, such as prefixes, suffixes, and root words. **Competency 003**

## 18.  B

Investigate the pattern in the table. The number of circles for the next consecutive figure increases. Evaluate each expression by using the figure numbers for $n$, to obtain the corresponding number of circles. For example, answer (A) is incorrect since substituting $n = 3$ in $\dfrac{n(n+1)}{2}$ gives $\dfrac{3(3+1)}{2} = \dfrac{3(4)}{2} = \dfrac{12}{2} = 6$. According to the table, Figure 3 has 14 circles, so evaluating this expression for $n = 3$ does not give the desired result. Using this process will show (B) as correct, whereas (C) and (D) are incorrect. **Competency 013**

## 19.  A

An editing checklist (A) is typically used to assist students in using correct mechanics and conventions of writing. This includes spelling, grammar, and punctuation. A retelling checklist (B) is primarily used to check reading comprehension rather than check an aspect of the writing process. A mentor text (C) is a text used by the teacher to model effective writing, but is not a tool used by students to check conventions. a revision checklist (D) is more for adding, deleting, and changing ideas and composition in the text rather than mechanics and conventions only. **Competency 006**

## 20. A

Arteries always carry blood away from the heart. Veins always carry blood to the heart. There is one artery—the pulmonary artery—that carries blood away from the right side of the heart directly to the lungs and thus does not carry oxygenated blood, making choice (D) incorrect. Choices (B) and (C) are incorrect because only veins contain valves to prevent backflow of blood as the blood is returning to the heart from all parts of the body. **Competency 046**

## 21. B

The most important thing a teacher can do is to take action right away. Choices (A) and (D) are incorrect because, although it is important to remove the external eyeware before flushing, removing contact lenses should follow an initial flushing, and waiting for someone else to do something is not acceptable. Choice (B) is correct because most of the time the chemical can be diluted. Choice (C) is incorrect because containing the hazardous chemical is secondary to treating the student, and keeping the chemical in the student's eye may cause irreparable harm. **Competency 036**

## 22. C

Of the four movements listed, the Enlightenment (C) was the most influential on the writing of the U.S. Declaration of Independence and the U.S. Constitution, particularly the notion of the social contract. The scientific revolution (A) was an important movement in the sixteenth and seventeenth centuries that had a fundamental impact on Europeans view of the natural world, but did not directly influence the crafting of these documents. Industrialism (B) is incorrect because this revolution occurred in the nineteenth century after the crafting of the Declaration of Independence and U.S. Constitution. The Renaissance (D) which began in Italy and lasted from the fourteenth to seventeenth centuries, was a period of rebirth for literature, language, art, and culture, but had little impact on the crafting of these documents. **Competency 029**

## 23. C

Choice (A) is not correct because not all scientific investigations use an experimental method. Choice (B) is not correct because there is no single scientific

method. Choice (D) is incorrect because there is no specific number of steps or sequence that makes an approach a scientific investigation. This leaves scientific inquiry, choice (C), as the correct answer because it is general enough to describe all scientific investigations. **Competency 038**

## 24. D

All of the reasons listed, except (D), were major tensions between Texans and the Mexican government. For choice (A), Texas settlers and Mexicans had difficulty valuing the unique cultural heritages of one another, each believing themselves to be better than the other. For choice (B), Texas settlers wished to maintain their rights to hold slaves despite Mexico's attempt to abolish this practice. Texans were enraged by the Siete Leyes (C) because they created an antifederalist and more centralized political structure, which threatened the freedom and power of Texas settlers. Thus, (D) is the correct answer because Santa Anna did not want to place any tax on Texas settlers. **Competency 029**

## 25. A

Traditional stories are part of the larger genre of folklore. Folklore draws on both oral and written literature and includes traditional stories as well as legends, mythology, and tall tales. **Competency 005**

## 26. A

Identifying key vocabulary terms can be essential for solving word problems. In this problem, the term "times" in the phrase, "5.25 times as fast as," implies the operation of multiplication. Answer (A), $r = 5.25s$ is the only option that shows multiplication in the equation and can be verified by substituting a value for $s$, the speed of the child. For example, if the speed of the child is 10, then the speed of the dog is $5.25(10) = 52.5$, and 52.5 is 5.25 times as fast as the child's speed of 10. Answer (B) is incorrect since the equation represents an addition problem. Similarly, (C) and (D) are incorrect since their equations include division. **Competency 014**

## 27. D

When a constant is added or subtracted within a function, the graph is shifted horizontally. When a value is added or subtracted outside of a function, the graph is translated vertically. In this problem, the constant is being added to the inside of the function, $f(x) = (x \pm c)^2$. When a constant is added within a function, the graph is shifted horizontally to the left, whereas when a constant is subtracted within the function, the graph is shifted horizontally to the right. Answer (D) is correct since 3 is being added within the parent function. Answers (A) and (B) are incorrect since the new function was not adding or subtracting 3 outside of the parent function. Answer (C) is incorrect since 3 is not being subtracted within the parent function. **Competency 015**

## 28. D

Choice (D) states the three primary reasons for using models in science. Choice (A) is incorrect because a model would be unnecessary if the phenomenon was simple. Choices (B) and (C) are incorrect because the phenomenon under study may be animate or inanimate. That is irrelevant to the primary reasons why scientists use models. **Competency 040**

## 29. A

The ability to support an argument with evidence and facts is a key component of oral presentations. The ability to share a personal narrative (B) may not support the conclusion or thesis of the research and is more of an appeal to emotion. Choice (C) is incorrect because the structure of the essay doesn't relate to the criteria that are necessary to present research. Choice (D) is incorrect because students should support their research with multiple sources and not limit their support to one source. **Competency 001**

## 30. A

Metamorphic rock is rock that has been deep beneath Earth's surface, has been heated and partially melted, and has been subjected to strong pressure due to actions of plate tectonic activities, such as mountain building where the rock has been folded. Answer (B) is incorrect because volcanic activity *is* typically associated with metamorphic rocks due to the heat and pressure present in these areas. Answer (C) is incorrect because weathering is a process of breaking down rock and not forming rock types. Answer (D) is incorrect because water is not associated with metamorphic rocks; rock under a body bodies of water would be sedimentary. **Competency 052**

## 31. D

The best way to teach students about potential sources of error is to have the students experience it themselves. This is what makes (B) and (C) incorrect. Answer (A) is incorrect because types of error will likely be limited to errors associated with the procedure or techniques. Allowing students to do more open inquiry will likely lead to more error personally experienced by nearly every student. **Competency 038**

## 32. C

The correct choice is (C) because read-aloud provides the best opportunity for the teacher to model the teaching focus of a writing mini-lesson using one or more mentor texts. During read-aloud, the teacher can point out different characteristics of quality writing and encourage students to apply these same characteristics in their own writing. **Competency 007**

## 33. A

When dividing a polynomial by a polynomial, look only at the highest powers of the numerator and denominator. In this function, that would be $\dfrac{5n^3}{7n^4}$, which is $\dfrac{5}{7n}$. As $n$ gets exceptionally large, $\dfrac{5}{7n}$ goes to 0, or answer (A). **Competency 016**

## 34. B

The stars have a life cycle from birth to death, and their appearance differs depending on their stage in the life cycle. Answer (A) is incorrect because distance does not impact appearance from Earth. Answers (C) and (D) are both incorrect because powerful telescopes, including those on satellites circling Earth, are not impacted by atmosphere or light pollution. **Competency 054**

## 35. D

The train travels 1 kilometer in 1 minute. In 60 minutes the train will travel 60 kilometers. Therefore, it is traveling at 60 kilometers per hour. That is the train's speed but not its velocity. Velocity always indicates direction. This makes choice (D) the only correct answer. **Competency 041**

**36. C**

A rise in small craft labor is the only answer choice that was NOT a result of the Industrial Revolution. During the Industrial Revolution, small craft labor, including family-owned and local businesses, actually decreased as large-scale factories were introduced in urban areas. Choices (A), growth of urban areas; (B), increased economic production; and (D) specialization and division of labor, were all direct outcomes related to the increase in industrial activity occurring during industrialization. **Competency 029**

**37. C**

In using the Punnett square diagram, the parental genotypes can be determined as follows:

|            |   | Parent 1 |    |
|------------|---|----------|----|
|            |   | B        | b  |
| Parent 2   | B | BB       | Bb |
|            | b | Bb       | bb |

As shown in the Punnett square, the result of the cross of Bb for one parent and Bb for the other parent is 75% with BB and Bb and 25% bb. The "B" allele for *brown* coat is dominant over the "b" allele for *white* coat, so the physical appearance or *phenotype* of 3 out 4 or 75% of the offspring will be a brown coat. The recessive gene will appear in 1 out of 4, or 25% of the offspring, which is represented in the Punnett square diagram as "bb." Any other cross will not produce these percentages of brown and white coats in the offspring. Answers (A) and (B) result in 100% of the offspring with the phenotype of brown coats. Answer (D) results in 100% of the offspring with the phenotype of white coats. **Competency 047**

**38. A**

Choice (A) is the only correct answer. The crystalline structure formed when water freezes increases the volume of the water. Other chemicals, such as alcohol, actually contract. This has implications for geology; for example, ine floats on liquid water, and when transitioning from a liquid to a solid can open cracks in rock. **Competency 042**

**39. A**

This scenario gives the teacher the opportunity to discuss the importance of each of answers (B), (C), and (D). However, a teacher should never communicate the idea that science generally has only one correct answer. Most of the time, competing theories, interpretations, techniques or procedures can cause different results. This is why answer (A) is incorrect and should therefore be selected for this item. **Competency 037**

**40. C**

This investigation provides a concrete experience for students to observe that there is no change in the mass of the soil from the beginning to the end of the experiment. They observe that the plant must not be "eating" the soil, but the source of food must be something else. This experiment should be followed by a series of investigations designed to help students discover the source of food as a combination of carbon dioxide and water in the presence of light, thereby constructing the concept of photosynthesis. Answer (A) is incorrect because, although student-centered, the concept discovered would be that "plants need light to grow." The seeds planted and placed in the dark will germinate but later die due to lack of sunlight, whereas those placed in the light will germinate, grow, and thrive. This experiment would help students discover the role of light in photosynthesis. Answer (B) is incorrect because students do not learn best through lecture/discussion, which is often abstract and meaningless to them. Further, students do not tend to alter their misconceptions when they are simply "told"—they need to discover for themselves. Answer (D) is incorrect because students will not know what to focus on in their readings and online searches and will likely be inundated with too much information, making a change from misconception to a more scientifically accepted conception unlikely. **Competency 056**

**41. C**

The purpose of the Rosie the Riveter poster produced in the early 1940s was (C), to encourage women to take factory jobs during World War II. As men were deployed to fight in the war abroad, and war efforts demanded the production of more military machinery, women were encouraged to fill the increased demand for factory workers. Using critical and historical thinking skills, we can examine the image by analyzing the clothing and appearance of the woman represented, the choice of words used, and the agency that produced the poster. In examining the image, we can conclude that the poster was not designed to encourage young women to go back to school (A), encourage women to stand up for themselves (B), or encourage men to recognize the rights of women (C). **Competency 029**

**42. C**

Sight words are words that are not spelled in phonetically regular ways. Learning them helps build automaticity in word recognition and overall fluency in reading. Examples might include "the," "of," and "many." They must simply be memorized. Choice (A) is incorrect because sight words are not CVC (consonant-vowel-consonant) words and are irregular. Choice (B) is incorrect because, even though learning sight words can also help build vocabulary or knowledge of word meanings, it is not the primary focus of sight word practice. Choice (D) is incorrect because sight word practice is primarily a word recognition strategy and is only incidentally related to comprehension. **Competency 003**

**43. D**

Using the Internet to compose, read, or write is an example of electronic media. The first choice, (A), is a broader category that includes a wider variety of media and focuses more on how the media are generally used. Print media, (B), focuses more on nonelectronic media. The third choice, (C), includes both print and electronic media, whereas the final choice, (D), is the most specific to the type of media used while reading and writing on the computer and Internet. **Competency 009**

**44. B**

Checks and balances involves the constitutional provision that allows one branch of government to amend or veto the decisions of another branch of government. Checks and balances provide assurances that one branch of government does not abuse its constitutional power. Judicial review (A) refers to the process whereby the Supreme Court can block laws that may be unconstitutional from being enacted. Constitutional amendments (C) refer to the process in which the constitution may be changed or amended based on the decisions of the legislative branch of government. Due process (D) is a term that refers to the notion that legal proceedings will follow a fair and just format. **Competency 032**

**45. D**

When students write a composition, they are often assessed by using a rubric that focuses on the key features of writing. The feature of writing that focuses on engaging the reader is the writer's voice. Writing with a strong voice allows the writer to have style. It is this style that engages the reader. Organization (A) focuses on the arrangement of ideas in the text. Conventions (B) focus on the writer's correct use of mechanics, such as spelling, punctuation, and grammar. Ideas (C) focus on development, but might not necessarily engage the reader with style or voice. **Competency 007**

**46. C**

Expository text means nonfiction or informational text. Examples used in the classroom typically include magazines with information-based text, newspapers with feature or news stories, and nonfiction books. The other answer choices are examples of narrative, or story-like, text, and would not be examples of expository text. **Competency 005**

**47. C**

Two complementary angles have a sum of 90 degrees. Therefore, if a student used a protractor and found the sum of two angles was only 88 degrees, the measure was inaccurate by 2 degrees. To find the percentage of error, divide the error amount by the total number of degrees possible, $\frac{2}{90} = 0.0\overline{222}$ or $0.0\overline{222}$. To represent a decimal as a percentage, multiply the decimal by 100. Therefore, (C) is the correct answer, 2.22%. **Competency 017**

**48. C**

To determine the congruence property, look carefully at the figure. Notice that in each triangle there are two sides with congruency marks and the angle between each is the same measure. This shows a Side-Angle-Side congruency between the two triangles, which is answer (C). **Competency 018**

**49. C**

The Sun's rays are more direct between the Tropic of Cancer and Tropic of Capricorn, with the equator in between due to the sun's position relative to Earth. Answer (A) is incorrect as it does not relate to the angle of the sun's rays on Earth. Answer (B) is incorrect because the hours of light are related to the Earth's tilt and its location in its orbit during the year (seasons). Answer (D) is incorrect because the Sun's rays at the equator are not horizontal. **Competency 053**

**50. C**

Choice (C) is correct because curriculum-based measurement uses a quick and efficient method of measuring an aspect of the learning process. Choices (A), (B), and (D) focus on other types of assessment techniques. **Competency 002**

**51. B**

Choice (B) is the correct answer, as scientific advances in farming equipment directly resulted in increased urbanization because farms required less human labor to produce crops. Choice (A) is incorrect because even though farms did occasionally lack qualified people to operate the new equipment, this did not substantially contribute to increased urbanization. More commonly, family farmers used the older equipment if they did not have the money or training for new equipment. Choice (C) is incorrect due to an illogical geographic construct. Farmers most often live on farms due to the round-the-clock demands of farming; thus, farmers did not move to urban areas and commute to farms. Although choice (D) is plausible, it is not the best answer option. Manufacturing plants required more people to make new equipment. However, this phenomenon does not account for or accurately explain why scientific advances in farming equipment resulted in increased urbanization. **Competency 033**

**52. D**

Choice (D) is correct because it ties directly with using explicit language to sequence steps, making it a more effective, coherent, and cohesive "how-to" essay. The other answer choices suggest the type of instruction that is more generic to supporting instruction in speaking in general, but are not specifically related to the type of rhetorical tools that best support the oral structure of a "how-to" speech. **Competency 001**

**53. C**

By placing a mirror along *CA*, the reflected shape shown in the mirror paired with the original shape will create a composite rectangle. Choices (B) and (D) are incorrect since they are the same side length, and if a mirror is placed along that side, an equilateral triangle would be formed between the reflected and original shapes. Choice (A) is incorrect as an equilateral triangle would be formed between the reflected and original shapes. **Competency 020**

**54. C**

Choice (C) is correct because the writing process begins with brainstorming and ends with publishing or some type of written final product. Students work through the different aspects of the writing process but don't always have to go through them in the exact sequence specified. **Competency 007**

**55. D**

Choice (D) is correct because not all investigations involve making predictions (e.g., observation and descriptive). Verifiable evidence (A) is necessary to support some conclusion that can be repeated by others. Peer review (B) is necessary because mutual skepticism is a part of scientific inquiry and an important part of negotiation that takes place among scientists concerning scientific claims. Logical reasoning (C) is a necessary component for making a rational argument. This is what a scientist does when reporting the results of an investigation. **Competency 038**

**56. C**

The small arcs were made by placing the point of a compass on point *C* to make a small arc, and doing it again on point *B*. By drawing a line from point *A* through the intersection of the small arcs, $\angle CAB$ will become bisected. **Competency 018**

**57. A**

A variety of measurement tools are used to assess reading growth and progress in decoding and comprehension. The correct choice is (A), an informal reading inventory, as it specifically measures accuracy in decoding and comprehension of text at both the literal and inferential levels. A timed test (B) is used to measure the fluency rate (accuracy and rate) of decoding but doesn't specifically measure comprehension. A running record (C) is used more for beginning readers and usually measures just the decoding aspect of reading, although it can also give insight into the processes a student uses to decode. Similarly, a phonics screening tool (D) might help the teacher to assess the decoding aspect, but would not let the teacher know how the student was developing in terms of comprehension. **Competency 002**

## 58. C

The conditions represented in the photograph were overturned by the 1954 ruling in *Brown v. Board of Education of Topeka* (C). In this case, the Supreme Court overturned the "separate but equal" conditions ruled constitutional in the 1896 (A) *Plessy v. Ferguson* case; thus, (A) is incorrect. The 1803 Supreme Court ruling in *Marbury v. Madison* (B) established the process of judicial review, but had nothing to do with conditions of racial oppression and segregation in the United States. In 1857, the Supreme Court ruled in *Dred Scott v. Sandford* (D) that people of African descent, slaves or not, were not protected by the U.S. Constitution and could never be U.S. citizens. **Competency 029**

## 59. B

Corresponding side lengths of similar figures have the same ratio. Setting up a proportion comparing lengths and widths of the poster and notecard would be appropriate. Such a proportion could look like: $\frac{21}{35} = \frac{3}{x}$. The numerators represent the lengths of the poster and notecard, and the denominators represent the measures of the widths. Through cross multiplication we can solve for $x$, or we can look for a multiplicative relationship between the numerators, the two known quantities. Since $21 \div 7 = 3$, then $35 \div 7 = x$, and answer (B), $x = 5$, is correct. **Competency 019**

## 60. A

The state standards (Texas Essential Knowledge and Skills) emphasize that teaching about conventions should be done in the context of meaningful instruction. This would exclude choice (B) because it focuses on isolated skills practice. Choice (C) is incorrect because weekly tests don't focus on instructional practice. Choice (D) is incorrect because corrective feedback

doesn't guarantee students can practice the use of mechanics in meaningful work, as specified in the state standards. The TEKS standards focus on student application of conventions. **Competency 006**

## 61. A

In certain areas of Earth's crust, the heat generated by the Earth's core that rises through convection currents beneath the surface is more readily accessible than in other areas. This heat can be used to generate electricity. Answers (B) and (C) are both incorrect because the Sun's energy is not relevant to geothermal energy. Answer (D) is incorrect because geothermal energy is not related to fossil fuels such as oil and coal. **Competency 051**

## 62. B

The ability to draw conclusions about character requires students to think beyond the literal meaning of the text. By being able to draw conclusions about apt descriptors that tell what a character is like, students are engaged in the comprehension strategy of making inferences. **Competency 004**

## 63. A

The economy of the southern colonies was primarily based on the production of (A) cotton and tobacco in large-scale plantations using slave labor. Farming, fishing and shipping (B) is incorrect because that was basis of the economy of the middle colonies. Tobacco and shipping (C) is incorrect because the South lacked the large-scale shipping ports necessary to cultivate this industry. Trading (D) is incorrect because trading was a part of the middle colonies economy due to their shipping abilities. **Competency 031**

## 64. D

The dilation contracted the large hexagon and formed the smaller hexagon, keeping the relationships among similar parts proportional. To find $x$, solve the proportion $\frac{36}{45} = \frac{x}{5}$. Many students will favor cross multiplication to solve proportions. However, logical reasoning can be an efficient method to solve this proportion. By simplifying $\frac{36}{45}$ we get $\frac{4}{5}$; therefore, $x = 4$, or choice (D) is correct. **Competency 020**

## 65.  D

The study of design includes the visual components of images. This would include what makes an image or picture visually appealing, so the consideration of color, shapes, and texture are important. However, hyperlinks are a functional tool that might or might not be used within a media representation. Therefore, choice (D) is not included and is the correct choice. **Competency 008**

## 66.  D

Students are expected to use the conventions of oral speaking such as eye contact, enunciating clearly, and using gestures in a natural and effective way. However, the state guidelines do not require that students include a personal narrative with their oral presentation. Although it is helpful and might hook the attention of the audience, it is not required, as the other components are. **Competency 001**

## 67.  B

*Manifest destiny* is defined as a nineteenth century doctrine that the United States had not only the right, but also the duty, to expand throughout North America. This brought about core American cultural attributes of geographic expansion, so (B) is the correct response. In many cases, *manifest destiny* worked against cultural practices of ancestral harmony, as its enactment broke families apart and moved many native peoples from their cultural connections to ancestral lands; thus, answer (A) is incorrect. Answer (C) is wrong because m*anifest destiny* resulted in geographic expansion and engagement, which are the antithesis of geographic isolationism. Economic capitalism (D) had a relationship to *manifest destiny* as an economic influence and often a result, but it does not connote any cultural aspects of *manifest destiny*. **Competency 030**

## 68.  D

The correct choice is (D) because diatomic molecules are, by definition, elements. **Competency 043**

## 69.  D

According to the information given, 25% of the students have blond hair, which is a quarter of the circle. Similarly, 25% have dark brown hair, or another quarter of the circle represent these students. Investigate the four circle graphs, looking for these portions of the graphs. (D) represents this information, and the remaining data are proportionally correct as well. Answer (A) can be ruled out since it does not show 25% students with blond hair. Answers (B) and (C) are incorrect since they do not show dark brown as 25% of their graphs. **Competency 021**

## 70.  A

When students can regulate their own understanding of whether they comprehend a text, they are engaging in self-monitoring (A). Answer (B) is incorrect because students are attending more to comprehension than the development of fluency. Answer (C) is incorrect because motivation to read may or may not be related to the skill of being metacognitive while reading. Answer (D) is incorrect because the focus of the lesson is more on comprehension than oral speech production. **Competency 004**

## 71.  B

Phonemic awareness is an important prerequisite skill in learning to read. It involves being able to hear, identify, and manipulate the smallest individual units of sound in words. As such, the ability to do this predicts (but is not the only predictor for) learning to read. Choice (A) is incorrect because rhyming words is part of the broader skill of phonological awareness. Choices (C) and (D) are incorrect because phonemic awareness is not directly related to reading fluency or comprehension development in reading text; it is an auditory skill primarily. **Competency 002**

## 72.  C

In this scenario, students use the data collected to make sense of their findings. They are using a larger set of data because they are sharing with all groups. Science requires many trials of the same experiment before conclusions can be drawn. Collecting data in several repeated experiments helps the researcher discover patterns and also errors and outliers. The data in this scenario are represented graphically and mathematically, which also promotes sound interpretations. Answer (A) is incorrect because students did not use their own collected data to draw conclusions and gain understanding of the concepts—their work was not *used*, so it became an irrelevant activity. Answer (B) is incorrect because sound scientific conclusions cannot be drawn based on one set of data but are accomplished by repeating the experiment several times or days in a row or using the whole class's set of data. Answer (D) is incorrect because interpretations of the first experiment were not made, and no conclusions were drawn. In addition, the second experiment is not related to the first experiment—the first leads to the concept of convection, whereas the second leads to concept of phase changes in water. **Competency 057**

## 73. C

When flipping a coin two options are possible, obtaining a head or a tail. Rolling a die results in obtaining 1, 2, 3, 4, 5, 6. A tree diagram can be helpful to visualize each possibility.

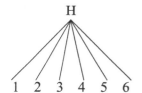 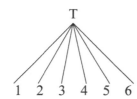

Overall, there are 12 possible combinations, but only three combinations satisfy tossing a head and rolling an even number. Those combinations are: H2, H4, and H6; hence, 3 combinations out of 12 total combinations is $\frac{1}{4}$, or answer (C). **Competency 022**

## 74. B

The legislative branch of government (B), comprising the two houses of congress, is responsible for creating the nation's laws. The executive branch of government (A) is primarily concerned with carrying out the laws of the country. The judicial branch of government (C) is responsible for interpreting and enforcing the nation's laws. The fiscal branch (D) is incorrect because this is not one of the three branches of government. **Competency 032**

## 75. D

Choice (D) is the exception because, as part of the writing process, students should be able to compose in

*both* narrative and expository types of prose. Choices (A), (B), and (C) focus on aspects of the writing process that are covered in the state standards. **Competency 007**

## 76. D

Miscue analysis was designed to help teachers attend to the types of cues a student might use during the reading process. When a student is reading and says something other than what is printed in the text, it is termed a *miscue*. The first three choices, (A), (B), and (C), focus on common types of miscues a student might make. Substitution (A) occurs when a student substitutes a real word for the printed word. Omission (B) occurs when a student leaves out a word. Mispronunciation (C) occurs when a student pronounces a word badly or incorrctly. Finally, prosody (D) is not a type of miscue, but is the aspect of fluency in which students read with expression, and is therefore, the exception. **Competency 003**

## 77. C

The Louisiana Purchase Treaty was a transaction with France allowing the United States to purchase 828,000 square miles of land west of the Mississippi River, which doubled the size of the country. It expanded the nation westward toward the Pacific Ocean, making (C) the correct answer. Answer (A) is incorrect because there was never a unified annexation of Colorado. The United States acquired Colorado through three distinct purchases, ranging in time from 1803 to 1850. Likewise, there was no annexation of Mississippi, so (B) is also incorrect. Answer (D) has some correct and some incorrect information. Washington did become part of the United States in 1846, but it was part of the Oregon Treaty of 1846, not the "Washington Purchase." There is no singular Washington Purchase. **Competency 030**

## 78. A

Examining the scatter plot, the data points tend to increase with each day in the month. This would represent a positive relationship between the temperature and date in July (A). Answer (B) is incorrect since the data points for temperature are not decreasing while the days in July increase. Answer (C) is incorrect since the scatter plot is not widely dispersed, showing no clustering of data points. Answer (D) is incorrect since the temperature on July 6 was about 92 degrees, and on July 11 the temperature peaked around 99 degrees. **Competency 023**

**79. B**

In the writing process, students are encouraged to proceed through the following phases: brainstorming, revision, editing, and drafting. Revision (B) involves the adding, deleting, or changing of ideas. Editing (C) is incorrect because it involves changing the mechanics or conventions rather than the writer's ideas. Brainstorming (A) and drafting (D) are initial stages of writing in which the writer is getting ideas organized and initially putting them on paper (or digitally on a computer or other device). **Competency 007**

**80. C**

The Nineteenth Amendment, passed in 1920, guarantees women the right to vote. The Thirteenth Amendment (A) abolished slavery. The Eighteenth Amendment (B) established the prohibition of alcohol. The Twenty-second Amendment (D) limits the presidency to two elected terms or a maximum of 10 years. **Competency 032**

**81. B**

Although Samantha found bisecting diagonals in rectangles and squares, she did not consider all other types of quadrilaterals, which include rhombi, parallelograms, trapezoids, and kites. Answer (B) is correct because finding a counterexample among one of the other quadrilaterals, such as a kite or trapezoid, would be the most reasonable next step. **Competency 024**

**82. C**

The correct choice is (C) because the process of combining two hydrogen atoms into one helium atom produces a great deal of energy and this process, fusion, is what occurs inside our Sun. Choice (A) is incorrect because it describes the reverse process—splitting atoms. **Competency 045**

**83. A**

Lizards tails easily drop off when touched or pulled as a form of adaption that allows the lizard to survive by escaping from predators. The tail will grow back in time. However, a new lizard will not grow from the detached tail (B). Lizards do not undergo molting (C); this is a characteristic of some insects and crustaceans. The lizard also does not lose its tail due to environmental stresses (D). **Competency 048**

**84. D**

The most correct answer is (D) because it describes the major outcomes desired of students in their writing and is also consistent with how scientists use their science notebooks. Choice (A) is not correct because scientists do not use science notebooks as a diary but as reflection focused on the ongoing investigation. Choice (B) is reasonable, but it leaves students only with the act of recording their observations and "exploring their ideas." Choice (D) includes the range of purposes seen in scientists' notebooks. **Competency 058**

**85. B**

A solar eclipse occurs when the Moon is between Earth and the Sun such that the Moon casts a shadow on Earth; in those regions that can see the eclipse, the Sun is blocked from view by the Moon. Answer (A) is incorrect because if Earth is blocking the Sun's rays and casting a shadow on the Moon, that is termed a lunar eclipse. Answer (C) is incorrect because the Moon is not blocking the Sun's rays nor casting a shadow on Earth. Answer (D) is incorrect because solar flares are not relevant to the occurrence of an eclipse. **Competency 054**

**86. C**

Shared writing is also known as the language experience approach. The purpose is to integrate reading, writing, listening, and speaking in a holistic way for students to make connections between speech and print. By engaging in this activity, students can learn about both the reading and writing processes in an authentic and holistic way. Choices (A), (B), and (D) are incorrect because they focus on more narrow and specific aspects of the purpose of the activity. The broader and primary reason to do shared writing is, therefore, Choice (C). **Competency 002**

**87. B**

Begin the problem solving process by calculating the cost of the cowboy boots after the first price reduction. If the original cost is reduced by 15%, a customer would pay 85% of the original cost (85% of

$120 is $102). If this price is reduced by 25%, then a customer would pay 75% of the list price (75% of $102 is $76.50). Therefore, the customer would purchase the cowboy boots for $76.50. The percentge of the original price is 76.50 ÷ 120 = 0.6375, or 63.75%, choice (B). **Competency 025**

## 88.  D

A social studies teacher should expect students in grades 4–8 to focus on making connections with the real world and between academic subjects (D). Answer choice (A) is incorrect because teachers should encourage students to focus not only on traditional ways of finding, organizing, and displaying information, but also on new technologies to do the same. Answer choice (B) is also incorrect because teachers should encourage their students to focus on other aspects of social studies education beyond history. Answer choice (C) is incorrect because teachers should not expect students to simply memorize, but to comprehend, analyze, and synthesize information. **Competency 035**

## 89.  A

The correct choice is (A) because, by definition, heat is the movement of thermal energy through some medium (at two different temperatures), whereas temperature is the measure of the average molecular movement of matter. **Competency 044**

## 90.  B

The figure representing the polynomial can be created by using common manipulatives called algebra tiles. In essence, to determine the area of a rectangle formed using various pieces, we begin by looking at the notation for each side length. The top horizontal side of the rectangle is denoted by $x + 1 + 1 + 1 = x + 3$, and the left vertical side of the rectangle is represented by $x + 1 + 1 + 1 + 1 = x + 4$. Therefore, the area of the rectangle representing the polynomial is the product of $(x + 3)(x + 4)$. The square within the picture represents one $x^2$ since $x \times x = x^2$, where each rectangle represents one $x$ since $x \times 1 = x$, and finally each small square represents one single unit since $1 \times 1 = 1$. Answer (B) is correct since altogether there is one $x^2$, 7 $x$'s, and 12 single units, or $x^2 + 7x + 12$. **Competency 026**

## 91.  B

Mutualism is a form of symbiosis in which both organisms benefit from the relationships (B). Answer (A) is an example of another form of symbiosis called parasitism, in which one organism benefits from the relationship at the expense of the other. Answer (C) is not a form of symbiosis. Answer (D) is a form of symbiosis called commensalism, in which one organism benefits and the other organism neither benefits nor is harmed. **Competency 050**

## 92.  D

Choices (B) and (C) are both correct because they are related and are key concepts in science. Therefore, the correct answer choice is (D). Choice (A) is incorrect due to the limit placed on science to study the physical world. **Competency 040**

## 93.  D

Answer (D) is correct because there is a conflict of interest in the study, and the rest of the choices are, ideally, not true of science and scientists. **Competency 039**

## 94.  A

Convection current refers to gases or liquids that, as heated, expand and rise, and as cooled, contract and sink, creating "current." Answer (B) is related to electrical energy transfer through a solid (conductor) and is not related to convection. Answer (C) describes conduction—heat transfer through solid objects—rather than convection. Answer (D) describes a form of energy transfer through empty space—radiation. **Competency 051**

## 95.  C

Two or more triangles are similar if their angle measures are the same and their corresponding sides are proportional. Answer (C) is correct because exploring proportional relationships is needed to learn about similar triangles. Answer (A) is incorrect since area formulas are not needed to learn about similar triangles. Answer (B) is incorrect since the Pythagorean theorem is used to explore side lengths of right triangles. Answer (D), exploring angle measures, is incorrect even though it is important in identifying corresponding congruent angles, but the study of angle measures in general is not the major focus of exploring similar triangles. **Competency 027**

## 96. C

An experiment has at least three distinguishing elements: testable hypotheses, variables identified and manipulated, and the aim of determining a causal relationship. Choice (C) has all these elements. Choices (A) and (B) are missing these elements and (D) has only two of the three elements. In addition, (D) states that correlations are determined; this is true of a correlational investigation but not an experiment. **Competency 038**

## 97. D

When Eleanor Roosevelt said, "The destiny of human rights is in the hands of all our citizens in all our communities," we understand that she was referencing any human from early civilizations through today (D). The photograph gives us clues to the answer in that we have a United Nations logo and a headline about human rights. Human rights extend beyond the borders of the United States, which eliminates responses (A) and (B). This is affirmed in 4–8 social studies teachers' familiarity with the preamble to the declaration of human rights, which begins, "Whereas recognition of the inherent dignity and of the equal and inalienable rights of all members of the human family is the foundation of freedom, justice and peace in the world." Although the United Nations General Assembly adopted the universal declaration of human rights on December 10, 1948, upon the end of World War II, it pulls from deep and ancient histories of human rights dating before that era, making response (C) incorrect. The Hindu Vedas, the Babylonian Code of Hammurabi, the Bible, the Quran (Koran), and the Analects of Confucius all address people's duties, rights, and responsibilities. Native Americans also addressed human rights via documents, including the Inca Aztec codes of conduct and justice and an Iroquois constitution. **Competency 033**

## 98. A

Frequent observations and interviewing students during observation (A) provide a quick informal opportunity to judge the progress of student learning, and then decide whether adjustments to the lessons are necessary. Choice (B) is incorrect because periodical peer reviews of partner work will not allow the teacher to make adjustments to lessons early in a unit. Choice (C) is incorrect because a pretest will provide a teacher with information to plan lessons, but a posttest shows what students know at the end of a unit, so this type of assessment does not allow for adjustments during the lessons. Choice (D) is incorrect since the quizzes would occur after future lessons, and the adjustments need to happen before future lessons. **Competency 028**

## 99. B

The air in Vermont is fully saturated because the dew-point temperature is equal to the air temperature. Dew point is the temperature at which there is 100% humidity in the air—the temperature where water will come out of the air in the form of precipitation. Answers (A) and (C) are incorrect because in Arizona the dew-point temperature is 38 degrees—divide this number by the air temperature (85 degrees) and multiply by 100 to obtain the percent humidity: $38 \div 85 \times 100 = 44.7\%$ humidity. In Vermont, the dew-point temperature must be 30 degrees (because it is precipitating out in the form of snow) and the air temperature is 30 degrees: $30 \div 30 \times 100 = 100\%$ humidity. Answer (D) is irrelevant to the question, and besides, both states are landlocked. **Competency 053**

## 100. D

To simplify $i^{10}$, first we need to review some properties of complex numbers.

$$i = \sqrt{-1}$$
$$i^2 = (\sqrt{-1})^2 = -1$$
$$i^3 = i \times i^2 = -i$$
$$i^4 = i^2 \times i^2 = (-1)(-1) = 1$$
$$i^5 = i \times i^4 = i \times 1 = i$$

So $i^{10} = i^5 \times i^5 = i \times i = -1$.

**Competency 010**

## 101. B

In doing primary research, the student should gather original information from either a primary source document or by gathering information directly from someone. In this case, a survey would be primary research and a way of gathering information that was not collected by someone else. The remaining choices, (A), (C), and (D), are examples of secondary research, or using documents of information that has already been collected. **Competency 009**

## 102. B

In developing editing skills, students would benefit most from clear and explicit instruction in the conventional use of both plural and possessive words. Having a direct application to a real sentence would provide the independent practice that is most closely related to using the correct form in their own writing. Choice (A) is incorrect because it doesn't ensure transfer to the student's own writing and composition. Choice (C) is incorrect because simply penalizing students doesn't promote the application and use of the correct written expression in the student's own writing. Choice (D) is incorrect because it is not direct enough to help students engage in guided practice or application of the rule to their own writing. **Competency 006**

## 103. C

Article 55 of The United Nations Charter, calls for "universal respect for, and observance of, human rights and fundamental freedoms" (C). Responses (A), the U.S. Constitution; (B), the Declaration of Independence; and (D), the Texas Constitution, although seemingly plausible, are incorrect answers to this fact-based question. **Competency 030**

## 104. A

Graphic organizers help students to represent the text structure and organization of the key ideas in the text. If a teacher wants students to understand some of the underlying ideas that relate to cause and effect, a T-chart would be the best way to organize the causes (on the left side of the T-chart) and the effects (on the right side of the T-chart). In contrast, Venn diagram (B) is typically used to show comparison and contrast, and a semantic map (C) is more broadly used to conceptualize key ideas in the text, but not necessarily those that are causally related. Finally, (D) is incorrect because an inquiry chart is used to show common aspects of a story or topic across multiple texts. **Competency 005**

## 105. A

To simplify the expression $6i^7 \times 5i^{-5} + \dfrac{8i^{11}}{4i^9}$, it is important to follow the order of operations. First, complete the multiplication portion by multiplying the whole numbers and applying rules of exponents to obtain $30i^2 + \dfrac{8i^{11}}{4i^9}$. Similarly, complete the division portion by dividing the whole numbers and applying rules of exponents to obtain $30i^2 + 2i^2$. Since $i^2 = -1$, we now have $-30 + (-2)$ or $-32$. **Competency 011**

## 106. A

Basic recall questions in a narrative text test whether a reader understands the basic aspects of the story, such as who was in it, what the main events were, and what happened so (A), literal questions, is the correct choice. Evaluative questions (B) test what a reader's judgment of a certain aspect of the story is and tests a higher level of understanding. Choices (C) and (D) also test higher-order comprehension beyond the literal or basic understanding of the story. **Competency 004**

## 107. B

The Alabama-Coushatta Tribe in east Texas; the Kickapoo Traditional Tribe in southwest Texas along the Texas-Mexico border; and the Ysleta del Sur Pueblo, or Tigua, in far west Texas are the three American Indian groups remaining in Texas are listed among the nation's many federally recognized tribes. Thus, response (B) is the correct reply. Response (A) is incorrect because most Comanche people live in Oklahoma today; thus, they are not an American Indian group remaining in Texas listed among the nation's many federally recognized tribes. Additionally, this response is missing the Ysleta del Sur Pueblo, or Tigua, in far west Texas. Response (C) is also incorrect for the same reasons as response (A), in wrongly inserting the Comanche Tribe. Additionally, it is missing the Kickapoo Traditional Tribe in southwest Texas along the Texas-Mexico border. Response (D) has the correct tribe names, but they are aligned to incorrect geographical references, making it an incorrect option. **Competency 030**

## 108. B

Juneteenth occurs on June 19 and is the celebration that recognizes the freeing of the slaves (B). News of the Thirteenth Amendment did not arrive in Texas until nearly two years after it was passed. Juneteenth celebrates the arrival of that news. Texas independence (A) is incorrect because it is recognized on March 2 to commemorate Texas's break from Mexico and the subsequent creation of the Republic of Texas. Although cotton (A) was an important commodity in Texas, it is not recognized as part of the Juneteenth celebrations. Texas's secession from the Union (D) occurred in February 1861 and is not part of the Juneteenth celebrations. **Competency 029**

## 109. B

Clamlike shells would live in oceans; thus, fossils of these once-living organisms in the earth indicates there must have been an ocean in that location in an earlier time in Earth's history, so answer (B) is correct. Fossils of oceanic organisms are found in sedimentary rock layers. The sedimentary rock layers are formed at the bottom of large bodies of water when particles in relatively still water settle out of solution and fall to the bottom. The organism, when it dies, falls to the bottom of the ocean and is covered by sediment. Answer (A) is incorrect because clams would not live in fast-moving, shallow streams. Answer (C) is incorrect because a seismically active area (e.g., one with volcanoes and earthquakes) is not relevant to the question of finding fossils, especially those that are clamlike. Answer (D) indicates that clams once lived in mountain ranges, which is incorrect. **Competency 055**

## 110. C

Chairs arranged in rows with an equal number of chairs in each row would imply that the total number of chairs has two whole number factors. The question asks to determine which of the numbers could NOT be the possible number of chairs Mr. Marshall arranged. Answer (C) is correct since 73 is a prime number, meaning the only factors of 73 are one and itself. Since the problem stated there was more than one row and more than one chair in each row, Mr. Marshall could have not used 73 chairs since they can only be arranged as 1 row of 73 chairs, or 73 rows of 1 chair in each row. Answers (A), (B), and (D) are not prime, so they are arrangement possibilities and thus not correct answers. **Competency 012**

## 111. D

This question asks what environmental changes were brought about by scientific discoveries and technological innovations associated with increased use of CFCs. Response (A) is only partially accurate. CFCs cause stratospheric ozone depletion in the air, not geological degradation on the ground. Thus, (A) is an incorrect option because not all of the information is accurate. Response (B) is also incorrect. CFCs destroy ozone in the stratosphere, which poses increased environmental health risks to humans. Response (C) is incorrect. Acid rain is precipitation containing a diluted solution of sulfuric acid and nitric acid. Pollution, mostly involving fossil fuels, is what causes acid rain, not CFCs. Response (D), CFCs brought about scientific discoveries and technological innovations that improved the quality of life through air conditioning, but they cause stratospheric ozone depletion, is the correct response. **Competency 030**

## 112. A

CFCs were first synthesized in 1928 to (A) make the refrigeration of food safer after a series of fatal accidents in the 1920s where methyl chloride leaked out of refrigerators. While incorrect food temperature can be a reason for food poisoning, the historical context does not fit the question; thus, answer (B) is incorrect. Answer (C) offers untrue and sexist information, which makes it incorrect. Global warming does not fit with the timeframe or the context of the question, thus (D) is also incorrect. **Competency 033**

## 113. D

Response (D) is correct because students have to make inferences about what life must have been like. Students must use visual information and prior knowledge to come up with new ideas (drawing inferences); this information is not stated directly in the photographs. Choice (A) is incorrect because students are not making predictions about what will happen next. Choice (B) is incorrect because students are not simply engaging in note-taking. Rather, their brainstorming takes place orally and they are using writing to synthesize their ideas and make inferences. Finally, choice (C) is incorrect because students are not explicitly asked to contrast what they are seeing with another time and place. **Competency 034**

## 114. B

Response (B), Memorial Day, is an American holiday designated to remember those who died defending our country. This holiday helps to build and strengthen our national unity and identity. Other nations have memorial days, but not on the same day or honoring the same fallen soldiers of the same conflict that the U.S. Memorial Day represents. Many Americans celebrate Christmas; however, some Americans do not follow the Christian religion to which this holiday aligns. Christmas is a special day to many, but it does not uniquely contribute to the identity conceptualization of all Americans, so response (C) is incorrect. Many nations celebrate New Year's Day on January 1. However, some Americans come from traditions that observe a cultural New Year's Day on a date other than January 1. This makes response (D) incorrect. Response (A), Valentine's Day, is also incorrect, as it does not directly connect with the conceptualization of being an American. **Competency 033**

## 115. B

To identify Gerald's missing step, first analyze the line above the missing step, which is $3x - 4y + 2 = 18$. The next visible step is $3x - 4y = 16$. The differences between these two steps are in regard to the constants. Gerald had subtracted 2 from both sides of the equations, isolating the variables on the left-hand side; so (B) is the correct answer, as it shows the subtraction of 2 on both sides of the equation. **Competency 013**

## 116. C

The word *structure* is syllabicated before the final stable syllable, -ture. Each syllable should also have one distinct vowel sound, so (C) is the correct response. **Competency 003**

## 117. D

Identifying the $x$- and $y$-intercepts is a great starting point for solving this problem. The $x$-intercept is located at $(-3, 0)$ and the $y$-intercept is located at $(0, -6)$. This eliminates (A) and (C) as possible answers. Choice (B) is incorrect because $(-6, -6)$ and $(3, 12)$ are not points on the graph of the line. Choice (D) is the correct solution, as each point in the table is located on the line. **Competency 014**

## 118. D

Answer choice (D) is correct because the equator, the International Date Line, and latitude and longitude lines are all imaginary lines on Earth's surface. Thus choices (A), only the equator at 0° longitude; (B) only the International Date Line at 180° longitude; and (C) only longitude and latitude are incorrect because *all* of these choices represent human-imposed, imaginary lines on Earth's surface. Latitude lines are imaginary lines running horizontally around Earth. Longitude lines are imaginary running vertically around Earth. The equator is an imaginary line spanning horizontally around Earth at 0° latitude, equidistance from the poles and perpendicular to Earth's axis of rotation. The International Date Line is an imaginary line mostly at 180° longitude. Locations to the east of the International Date Line are one calendar day earlier than locations to the west of it. **Competency 030**

## 119. C

The plant will grow and bend toward the light due to chemicals called auxins that create specific responses to stimuli in the plant from the environment. The environmental stimulus that produces a chemical response directing plant stems and leaves to grow toward light is called a phototropism, so (C) is correct. Answer (A) is incorrect because seeds do not need sunlight to germinate, only the proper temperature for that particular plant species, water, and air (oxygen). Answer (B) is incorrect because there will be some light entering the box through the circle cutout opening at the bottom, so although it may not be the healthiest of plants, it will not be entirely shriveled and will likely survive. Answer (D) is incorrect because a geotropism is a plant's response to gravity, typically presented by the roots growing downward toward gravity. **Competency 049**

## 120. C

Phonological awareness involves listening and the ability to hear and make distinctions in oral language. It includes the ability to hear distinct sounds, use alliteration, distinguish rhymes, and develop skills in phonemic awareness. Choice (C) is correct because tongue twisters involve alliteration, or the ability to hear and use words that begin with the same initial sound. Repeated reading (A) primarily develops fluency, whereas oral retelling (B) and think-pair-share (D) help to develop comprehension. **Competency 002**

**121. A**

Choice (A) focuses on the skills students will need to view images and have a better understanding of the ways that images can be effectively used in text. It focuses on the teacher's intent in using a picture book with older students to teach viewing. Choice (B) focuses on an aspect of composition that is not related to the viewing standard. Choice (C) focuses only on properly displaying the text but doesn't have a clear instructional focus aligned with the state standards. Choice (D) fosters a reader response among the students; however, it also doesn't have a clear instructional focus aligned with the viewing standard. **Competency 008**

**122. C**

The Harlem Renaissance produced many prolific and famous writers who capture the cultural voice of societal change, including, but not limited to, those mentioned in the correct response (C) containing Langston Hughes, Countee Cullen, James Weldon Johnson, Jessie Redmon Fauset, and Zora Neale Hurston. Choice (A) includes authors and illustrators of children's books about the Harlem Renaissance who wrote about it at a later point in time; thus, it is the incorrect choice. These are all secondary sources that teachers may use to teach about the Harlem Renaissance in an age-appropriate framing. Choice (B) includes famous artists from the Harlem Renaissance, not authors; thus, this response is incorrect. Choice (D) includes social activists and musicians associated with the time and place of the Harlem Renaissance, but not authors who influenced change in traditional cultural ways, such as through poetry and novels, so it is the incorrect choice. **Competency 033**

**123. A**

Creating a proportion is a common solution strategy to determine constant rate problems. In this scenario, the proportion could be $\frac{20}{30} = \frac{x}{90}$, where the numerators represent the number of pages read and the denominators are the lengths of time Vince read the said amount of pages. Notice it was important to convert 1.5 hours into 90 minutes so we are discussing the same type of units (minutes) in the proportion. Cross multiplication can be used to solve proportions, resulting in $1800 = 30x$, therefore $x = 60$ pages. A simpler solution would involve repeated addition or multiplication. Since 1.5 hours, or 90 minutes, is a multiple of 30 minutes, we could have added three sets of 20 pages or multiplied 20 pages by 3, which would equal 60 pages read in 1.5 hours. **Competency 015**

**124. D**

The instructional reading level is generally considered to be the level at which a reader can decode with 90-95% accuracy. Below 90% is the frustrational reading level and above that is the independent reading level. **Competency 004**

**125. A**

The 1901 discovery of oil at Spindletop and the subsequent oil boom led to major economic growth in Texas cities such as Houston and Dallas, so answer (A) is correct. No oil field found prior to Spindletop had ever been as productive. Although natural gas (B) was also found at Spindletop, its discovery did not produce the same level of economic growth as oil. The discovery of gold (C) produced economic growth, but primarily for cities located on the West Coast including those in California. Limestone (D) is a natural Texas resource, but it did not lead to huge economic growth there. **Competency 031**

**126. A**

A primary source is (A), a document or piece of evidence that was produced during the period of time being studied. Primary sources might include eyewitness accounts, newspaper articles, political cartoons, maps, speeches, photographs, and so forth. Choice (B) is incorrect because a historian's analysis of the past is often referred to as a secondary source. Choice (C) is incorrect because there are multiple primary sources produced during a particular period of history. Choice (D) cannot be correct because a summary about a historical figure on a website is a secondary source, unless it is an autobiographical narrative written by the actual person. **Competency 034**

**127. D**

To determine the dimensions of each smaller block, we begin by looking at each labeled dimension. The length is 15 inches and comprises 3 small boxes; $15 \div 3 = 5$, so each small box is 5 inches long. The width of the base for the rectangular prism is 4 inches and comprises 2 small boxes;

$4 \div 2 = 2$, so each small box is 2 inches wide. The height of the rectangular prism is 12 inches and comprises 3 small boxes; $12 \div 3 = 4$, so each small box is 4 inches high. Therefore, the dimensions of each small box are $5 \times 2 \times 4$, or answer (D). **Competency 017**

## 128. D

Answer choice (A), guide students toward a single perspective, is incorrect since critical thinking should involve the consideration of multiple perspectives. Because critical thinking involves making informed and reasoned decisions, answer choice (B), preventing students from practicing evidence, is also incorrect. Answer choice (C) is incorrect because helping students to memorize key facts is often important, but does not ensure students are engaging in critical thinking practices. The only choice that helps encourage students to engage in critical thinking is (D), encouraging students to apply their knowledge to the real world. **Competency 034**

## 129. A

The two angles labeled in the figure are supplementary angles, where the sum of their measures is 180°, so $x° + y° = 180°$. Since $y° = 4x°$, we can use substitution to show $x° + 4x° = 180°$ or $5x° = 180°$ and $x° = 36°$. **Competency 018**

## 130. B

Glass represents 25% of the recyclable materials and it is known to weigh approximately 40 tons. Therefore, the total weight of all recyclable materials is 4 times this amount, or 160 tons. The graph shows paper being 45% of the recyclable materials. So (B) is the correct answer since 45% of 160 tons is 72 tons. **Competency 021**

# PRACTICE TEST 2

# TExES Generalist 4-8 (111)

**Also available at the REA Study Center (*www.rea.com/studycenter*)**

This practice test is also offered online at the REA Study Center. Although the TExES Generalist 4-8 (111) exam is offered in both paper- and computer-based formats, we recommend that you take the online version of the test to receive these added benefits:

- **Timed testing conditions** – helps you gauge how much time you can spend on each question
- **Automatic scoring** – find out how you did on the test, instantly
- **On-screen detailed explanations of answers** – gives you the correct answer and explains why the other answer choices are wrong
- **Diagnostic score reports** – pinpoint where you're strongest and where you need to focus your study

# Answer Sheet

1. Ⓐ Ⓑ Ⓒ Ⓓ
2. Ⓐ Ⓑ Ⓒ Ⓓ
3. Ⓐ Ⓑ Ⓒ Ⓓ
4. Ⓐ Ⓑ Ⓒ Ⓓ
5. Ⓐ Ⓑ Ⓒ Ⓓ
6. Ⓐ Ⓑ Ⓒ Ⓓ
7. Ⓐ Ⓑ Ⓒ Ⓓ
8. Ⓐ Ⓑ Ⓒ Ⓓ
9. Ⓐ Ⓑ Ⓒ Ⓓ
10. Ⓐ Ⓑ Ⓒ Ⓓ
11. Ⓐ Ⓑ Ⓒ Ⓓ
12. Ⓐ Ⓑ Ⓒ Ⓓ
13. Ⓐ Ⓑ Ⓒ Ⓓ
14. Ⓐ Ⓑ Ⓒ Ⓓ
15. Ⓐ Ⓑ Ⓒ Ⓓ
16. Ⓐ Ⓑ Ⓒ Ⓓ
17. Ⓐ Ⓑ Ⓒ Ⓓ
18. Ⓐ Ⓑ Ⓒ Ⓓ
19. Ⓐ Ⓑ Ⓒ Ⓓ
20. Ⓐ Ⓑ Ⓒ Ⓓ
21. Ⓐ Ⓑ Ⓒ Ⓓ
22. Ⓐ Ⓑ Ⓒ Ⓓ
23. Ⓐ Ⓑ Ⓒ Ⓓ
24. Ⓐ Ⓑ Ⓒ Ⓓ
25. Ⓐ Ⓑ Ⓒ Ⓓ
26. Ⓐ Ⓑ Ⓒ Ⓓ
27. Ⓐ Ⓑ Ⓒ Ⓓ
28. Ⓐ Ⓑ Ⓒ Ⓓ
29. Ⓐ Ⓑ Ⓒ Ⓓ
30. Ⓐ Ⓑ Ⓒ Ⓓ
31. Ⓐ Ⓑ Ⓒ Ⓓ
32. Ⓐ Ⓑ Ⓒ Ⓓ
33. Ⓐ Ⓑ Ⓒ Ⓓ

34. Ⓐ Ⓑ Ⓒ Ⓓ
35. Ⓐ Ⓑ Ⓒ Ⓓ
36. Ⓐ Ⓑ Ⓒ Ⓓ
37. Ⓐ Ⓑ Ⓒ Ⓓ
38. Ⓐ Ⓑ Ⓒ Ⓓ
39. Ⓐ Ⓑ Ⓒ Ⓓ
40. Ⓐ Ⓑ Ⓒ Ⓓ
41. Ⓐ Ⓑ Ⓒ Ⓓ
42. Ⓐ Ⓑ Ⓒ Ⓓ
43. Ⓐ Ⓑ Ⓒ Ⓓ
44. Ⓐ Ⓑ Ⓒ Ⓓ
45. Ⓐ Ⓑ Ⓒ Ⓓ
46. Ⓐ Ⓑ Ⓒ Ⓓ
47. Ⓐ Ⓑ Ⓒ Ⓓ
48. Ⓐ Ⓑ Ⓒ Ⓓ
49. Ⓐ Ⓑ Ⓒ Ⓓ
50. Ⓐ Ⓑ Ⓒ Ⓓ
51. Ⓐ Ⓑ Ⓒ Ⓓ
52. Ⓐ Ⓑ Ⓒ Ⓓ
53. Ⓐ Ⓑ Ⓒ Ⓓ
54. Ⓐ Ⓑ Ⓒ Ⓓ
55. Ⓐ Ⓑ Ⓒ Ⓓ
56. Ⓐ Ⓑ Ⓒ Ⓓ
57. Ⓐ Ⓑ Ⓒ Ⓓ
58. Ⓐ Ⓑ Ⓒ Ⓓ
59. Ⓐ Ⓑ Ⓒ Ⓓ
60. Ⓐ Ⓑ Ⓒ Ⓓ
61. Ⓐ Ⓑ Ⓒ Ⓓ
62. Ⓐ Ⓑ Ⓒ Ⓓ
63. Ⓐ Ⓑ Ⓒ Ⓓ
64. Ⓐ Ⓑ Ⓒ Ⓓ
65. Ⓐ Ⓑ Ⓒ Ⓓ
66. Ⓐ Ⓑ Ⓒ Ⓓ

67. Ⓐ Ⓑ Ⓒ Ⓓ
68. Ⓐ Ⓑ Ⓒ Ⓓ
69. Ⓐ Ⓑ Ⓒ Ⓓ
70. Ⓐ Ⓑ Ⓒ Ⓓ
71. Ⓐ Ⓑ Ⓒ Ⓓ
72. Ⓐ Ⓑ Ⓒ Ⓓ
73. Ⓐ Ⓑ Ⓒ Ⓓ
74. Ⓐ Ⓑ Ⓒ Ⓓ
75. Ⓐ Ⓑ Ⓒ Ⓓ
76. Ⓐ Ⓑ Ⓒ Ⓓ
77. Ⓐ Ⓑ Ⓒ Ⓓ
78. Ⓐ Ⓑ Ⓒ Ⓓ
79. Ⓐ Ⓑ Ⓒ Ⓓ
80. Ⓐ Ⓑ Ⓒ Ⓓ
81. Ⓐ Ⓑ Ⓒ Ⓓ
82. Ⓐ Ⓑ Ⓒ Ⓓ
83. Ⓐ Ⓑ Ⓒ Ⓓ
84. Ⓐ Ⓑ Ⓒ Ⓓ
85. Ⓐ Ⓑ Ⓒ Ⓓ
86. Ⓐ Ⓑ Ⓒ Ⓓ
87. Ⓐ Ⓑ Ⓒ Ⓓ
88. Ⓐ Ⓑ Ⓒ Ⓓ
89. Ⓐ Ⓑ Ⓒ Ⓓ
90. Ⓐ Ⓑ Ⓒ Ⓓ
91. Ⓐ Ⓑ Ⓒ Ⓓ
92. Ⓐ Ⓑ Ⓒ Ⓓ
93. Ⓐ Ⓑ Ⓒ Ⓓ
94. Ⓐ Ⓑ Ⓒ Ⓓ
95. Ⓐ Ⓑ Ⓒ Ⓓ
96. Ⓐ Ⓑ Ⓒ Ⓓ
97. Ⓐ Ⓑ Ⓒ Ⓓ
98. Ⓐ Ⓑ Ⓒ Ⓓ
99. Ⓐ Ⓑ Ⓒ Ⓓ

100. Ⓐ Ⓑ Ⓒ Ⓓ
101. Ⓐ Ⓑ Ⓒ Ⓓ
102. Ⓐ Ⓑ Ⓒ Ⓓ
103. Ⓐ Ⓑ Ⓒ Ⓓ
104. Ⓐ Ⓑ Ⓒ Ⓓ
105. Ⓐ Ⓑ Ⓒ Ⓓ
106. Ⓐ Ⓑ Ⓒ Ⓓ
107. Ⓐ Ⓑ Ⓒ Ⓓ
108. Ⓐ Ⓑ Ⓒ Ⓓ
109. Ⓐ Ⓑ Ⓒ Ⓓ
110. Ⓐ Ⓑ Ⓒ Ⓓ
111. Ⓐ Ⓑ Ⓒ Ⓓ
112. Ⓐ Ⓑ Ⓒ Ⓓ
113. Ⓐ Ⓑ Ⓒ Ⓓ
114. Ⓐ Ⓑ Ⓒ Ⓓ
115. Ⓐ Ⓑ Ⓒ Ⓓ
116. Ⓐ Ⓑ Ⓒ Ⓓ
117. Ⓐ Ⓑ Ⓒ Ⓓ
118. Ⓐ Ⓑ Ⓒ Ⓓ
119. Ⓐ Ⓑ Ⓒ Ⓓ
120. Ⓐ Ⓑ Ⓒ Ⓓ
121. Ⓐ Ⓑ Ⓒ Ⓓ
122. Ⓐ Ⓑ Ⓒ Ⓓ
123. Ⓐ Ⓑ Ⓒ Ⓓ
124. Ⓐ Ⓑ Ⓒ Ⓓ
125. Ⓐ Ⓑ Ⓒ Ⓓ
126. Ⓐ Ⓑ Ⓒ Ⓓ
127. Ⓐ Ⓑ Ⓒ Ⓓ
128. Ⓐ Ⓑ Ⓒ Ⓓ
129. Ⓐ Ⓑ Ⓒ Ⓓ
130. Ⓐ Ⓑ Ⓒ Ⓓ

## Mathematics Definitions and Formulas

### CALCULUS

First Derivative: $f'(x) = \dfrac{dy}{dx}$

Second Derivative: $f''(x) = \dfrac{d^2 y}{dx^2}$

### PROBABILITY

$P(A \text{ or } B) = P(A) + P(B) - P(A \text{ and } B)$

$P(A \text{ and } B) = P(A)P(B|A) = P(B)P(A|B)$

### GEOMETRY

Congruent Angles

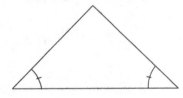

Congruent Sides

Parallel Sides

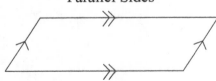

Circumference of a Circle
$C = 2\pi r$

### ALGEBRA

| | |
|---|---|
| $i$ | $i^2 = -1$ |
| $A^{-1}$ | inverse of matrix $A$ |

Compound interest: Where $A$ is the final value

$A = P\left(1 + \dfrac{r}{n}\right)^{nt}$

$P$ is the principal
$r$ is the interest rate
$t$ is the term
$n$ is the number of divisions within the term

$[x] = n$  Greatest integer function, where $n$ is the integer such that $n \le x < n + 1$

### VOLUME

| | |
|---|---|
| Cylinder: | (area of base) × height |
| Cone: | $\dfrac{1}{3}$ (area of base) × height |
| Sphere: | $\dfrac{4}{3}\pi r^3$ |
| Prism: | (area of base) × height |

### AREA

| | |
|---|---|
| Triangle: | $\dfrac{1}{2}$ (base × height) |
| Rhombus: | $\dfrac{1}{2}$ (diagonal$_1$ × diagonal$_2$) |
| Trapezoid: | $\dfrac{1}{2}$ height(base$_1$ + base$_2$) |
| Sphere: | $4\pi r^2$ |
| Circle: | $\pi r^2$ |
| Lateral surface area of a cylinder: | $2\pi rh$ |

### TRIGONOMETRY

Law of Sines: $\dfrac{\sin A}{a} = \dfrac{\sin B}{b} = \dfrac{\sin C}{c}$

Law of Cosines: $c^2 = a^2 + b^2 - 2ab \cos C$

$b^2 = a^2 + c^2 - 2ac \cos B$

$a^2 = b^2 + c^2 - 2bc \cos A$

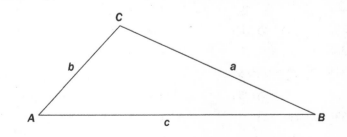

# Practice Test 2

**Time:** **5-hour time limit**
**130 questions: 30 Social Studies (23%)**
**30 Science (23%)**
**30 Math (23%)**
**40 English Language Arts (31%)**

**Directions**: Read each item and select the best response.

1. Which of the following is NOT an economic factor of production?

   A. Goods

   B. Natural resources

   C. Entrepreneurship

   D. Labor

2. The Northern Hemisphere is located between _____ and _____.

   A. The Prime Meridian; the International Date Line

   B. The Equator; the South Pole

   C. The Equator; the North Pole

   D. The Tropic of Cancer; the Tropic of Capricorn

3. Which of the following is a secondary social studies source?

   A. A diary

   B. A photograph

   C. A biography

   D. A letter

4. Mr. Stephens wants his seventh-grade language arts students to develop skills in the area of oral speech presentations. He especially wants his students to develop their use of standard, formal academic English. Which of the following tasks would best help him in reaching this learning objective with his students?

   A. Provide students with a list of commonly used academic terms and vocabulary that would be useful to incorporate into a speech

   B. Model academic speeches by experts and have students discuss what types of language would be appropriate for which audience

   C. Give students a grading rubric and discuss how they can help each other peer edit their written speeches

   D. Require students to submit their written speeches for written feedback from the teacher

5. Use the information below to answer the question that follows.

   • A swimming pool measures 50 meters by 25 meters.

   • The average depth of the deep end is about 2 meters.

   • The shallow end is about one-fourth the length of the pool.

   • The swimming pool covers about $1.25 \times 10^3$ square meters.

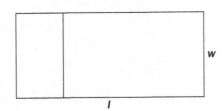

What is the volume for the deep end of the pool in cubic meters?

A. $2.5 \times 10^3$

B. $1.875 \times 10^3$

C. $6.25 \times 10^2$

D. $3.125 \times 10^2$

**Use the following passage to answer questions 6–7.**

We hold these truths to be self-evident. That all men are created equal; that they are endowed by their Creator with certain unalienable rights; that among these are life, liberty and the pursuit of happiness. That, to secure these rights, governments are instituted among men, deriving their just powers from the consent of the governed that, whenever any form of government becomes destructive of these ends, it is the right of the people to alter or to abolish it, and to institute a new government.

6. This quotation is from which of the following?

   A. Articles of Confederation
   B. U.S. Constitution
   C. Declaration of Independence
   D. Missouri Compromise

7. Who was the primary author of this document?

   A. George Washington
   B. John Marshall
   C. James Madison
   D. Thomas Jefferson

8. Given the graph of $f(x)$ below, which of the following would be true for $f'(x)$ at $x = 2$?

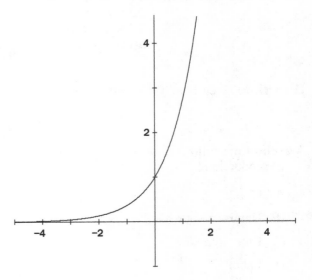

A. $f'(x)$ is constant
B. $f'(x)$ is decreasing
C. $f'(x)$ is positive
D. $f'(x)$ is negative

9. Given that $a = 15$, $x = 20$, and $y = 35$, find the measure of side $b$.

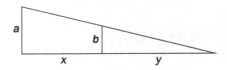

A. 9.54
B. 10.39
C. 11.25
D. 12.09

10. The total value of all goods and services produced in a country is referred to as what?

A. Capital
B. Gross domestic product (GDP)
C. Investment
D. Inflation

11. A researcher wants to test the effect of the number of hours students work during the week on their grade point average (GPA). Which of the following would be an appropriate group from which the researcher could recruit?

   A. Students in a remedial math class at a local high school

   B. Students working in local area restaurants

   C. Students from in an honors geometry course

   D. Students from all of the 12th-grade English classes at a local high school

12. The data set below represents customers who ate a meal at a hotel. What is the probability that the customer ate lunch at the hotel if we know that the customer is satisfied with the meal?

| Meal | Satisfied | Not Satisfied | Total |
|------|-----------|---------------|-------|
| Breakfast | 25 | 11 | 36 |
| Lunch | 40 | 6 | 46 |
| Dinner | 60 | 18 | 78 |
| Total | 125 | 35 | 160 |

   A. $\dfrac{8}{25}$

   B. $\dfrac{25}{32}$

   C. $\dfrac{23}{80}$

   D. $\dfrac{46}{125}$

13. Shared reading is a method that facilitates students' understanding of the text while the teacher reads aloud and students follow along with the same text. A fourth-grade teacher wants to use this technique as a small-group activity for a group of students who are reading on a first-grade reading level. What would be the teacher's reasoning for implementing shared reading as a whole class activity?

   A. Students significantly below grade level are likely not motivated to read, so the teacher can support their motivation by doing the reading for them.

   B. By reading the text aloud, the teacher can continue to model fluency, build vocabulary, and focus on comprehension strategies and active reading while accommodating for diverse reading levels.

   C. In reading aloud, the teacher is developing the listening comprehension of the students.

   D. Shared reading is an activity that easily manages student behavior because students are less likely to be off task.

14. Which of the following is an example of a writing mini-lesson that focuses on developing process skills in writing?

   A. Modeling for students how to revise a drafted piece

   B. Modeling for students how to use better adjectives

   C. Modeling for students how to write with better details

   D. Modeling for students how to use stronger verbs

15. What should be occurring in the mathematics classroom?

   I.   Paper-and-pencil busywork
   II.  Calculator use for computing answers
   III. Homework
   IV.  Discovery and inquiry learning

   A. Decrease I and increase IV

   B. Increase I and decrease III

C. Decrease II and decrease III

D. Increase I, II, III, and IV

16. The Dust Bowl created what classification of migrants?

A. Emigrants

B. Immigrants

C. Refugees

D. Internally displaced persons

17. Students who are using number lines to add numbers produce the two number lines shown below. What property of addition are they modeling?

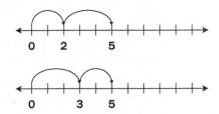

A. Additive inverse property

B. Commutative property

C. Associative property

D. Closure property

18. The PRIMARY reason "mentor texts" are useful to writing instruction is that they

A. provide material for read-aloud and fostering reader response.

B. integrate reading and writing by demonstrating exemplar texts.

C. develop fluency in the amount of writing students can produce.

D. develop awareness of comprehension strategies.

19. Where should caustic materials such as acids be stored?

A. In a locked cabinet on a high shelf out of reach of children

B. In the classroom refrigerator to maintain a constant temperature

C. In a locked cabinet on a low shelf nearest to the floor

D. Not in or near the classroom at all

20. How do topographic maps differ from other maps?

A. Topographic maps use census data to show population density.

B. Topographic maps use contour lines to show elevation change on the surface of Earth.

C. Topographic maps use latitude and longitude to show relative location.

D. Topographic maps use latitude and longitude to show absolute location.

21. Ms. Weaver knows that her fifth graders need to have a solid understanding of text structure in order to better facilitate their reading and understanding of expository text. The types of text structure can include, for instance, chronological, cause-and-effect, problem/solution, compare and contrast, and sequence. What types of instructional activity would best help develop students' understanding and recognition of these types of text structures?

A. Stock the classroom library with a wide variety of reading materials that contain these types of text structures

B. Model how to recognize the common types of text structures

C. Demonstrate and practice with students the use of graphic organizers that align with the common text structures

D. Discuss with students how text structure impacts the way the writer chose to organize the information

22. Which of the following is true regarding asexual reproduction?

    A. Asexual reproduction is the splitting of one cell, after replicating all of its genetic material, into two daughter cells, with each having genetic material identical to the parent cell.

    B. Asexual reproduction involves the joining of two cells, each consisting of half the number of chromosomes as the parent cells, with their union forming a new cell containing a mixture of genetic material from each parent cell.

    C. Asexual reproduction involves the exchange of genetic material between two organisms of the same species to produce two identical daughter cells.

    D. Asexual reproduction is a process that occurs only in specialized cells of the organism to produce four daughter cells with half the number of chromosomes as the parent cell.

23. Which of the following types of journal writing facilitates writing between the teacher and student?

    A. Reflective journals

    B. Dialogue journals

    C. Learning logs

    D. Personal journals

24. Which of the following best describes the discipline of science and the rationale for how science should be taught in the classroom?

    A. Science is a body of indisputable facts determined over time by scientists, indicating that science information should be presented by the teacher to the whole class and later discussed small groups.

    B. Science is discovering, experimenting, observing, concluding, and other processes, indicating that science should be taught as an active, inquiry process by which findings are based on observable and logic-based evidence.

    C. Science is unchangeable and authoritatively known, indicating their reading science text-

books and lectures should be the primary teaching procedures used in the classroom.

    D. Science is based upon verification of facts, indicating that students conducting laboratory investigations should first be informed of the content, procedures, and expected findings, and then carry out the experiments in the laboratory as instructed.

25. The primary purpose of semantic mapping in reading instruction is to

    A. make explicit the relationships between words and concepts.

    B. provide a way for students to draw on their understanding of the text.

    C. create an assessment tool to grade students during guided reading.

    D. help students to organize their thinking as a prewriting tool.

26. Which class of fire extinguisher is recommended for a fire involving flammable liquids such as acetone and alcohols?

    A. Class A

    B. Class B

    C. Class C

    D. Class D

27. When children begin to read, they learn that letters represent sound. Which of the following represents this concept best?

    A. Alphabetic principle

    B. Concepts about print

    C. Conventional spelling

    D. Phonological awareness

28. In the flow of energy from one organism to the next in a food chain, energy is

    A. gained by each organism in the food chain as one organism gains energy from the organism ingested.

B. lost by each organism in the food chain as one organism loses energy from the organism ingested.

C. maintained along the food chain with each organism gaining an equal amount of energy from the organism ingested.

D. not transferred along the food chain from one organism to the next; only inorganic nutrients are transferred.

29. Which of the following is NOT equivalent to 10 kilometers?

   A. 10,000 meters

   B. 1,000 decameters

   C. 100,000 centimeters

   D. 10,000,000 millimeters

30. The Thirteenth Amendment to the U.S. Constitution did what?

   A. Established a federal income tax

   B. Abolished slavery

   C. Abolished the sale and manufacture of alcohol in the United States

   D. Gave women the right to vote

31. Velocity is equal to

   A. the square root of acceleration.

   B. the change in distance per some unit of time.

   C. speed.

   D. speed with direction.

32. In evolution, the fossil record refers to which of the following?

   A. A large collection of fossils maintained by scientists for use in museums and scientific exhibitions to show the variety of species that lived on Earth long ago

   B. Evidence that layers of rock are found on Earth in sequence according to age, and we can trace fossils of organisms buried in these layers during each time period to observe how

characteristics of the same species have gradually changed over time

   C. The finding that appendages of organisms may be homologous, meaning similar in structure, between two different present-day species, such as the bones in the wing of a bat and the arm of a human

   D. The observation that some species have analogous structures, which are structures with the same function but a different evolutionary origin, such as the wing of a bird and the wing of a mosquito

33. A box contains four red balls and two green balls. Two balls are selected at random from the box. After a ball is selected, it is not replaced in the box before the next ball is selected. What is the probability of selecting two red balls?

   A. $\dfrac{2}{3}$

   B. $\dfrac{1}{3}$

   C. $\dfrac{3}{5}$

   D. $\dfrac{2}{5}$

34. An example of a chemical change in everyday life is which of the following?

   A. Burning gasoline in a car

   B. Melting ice (boiling water)

   C. Tearing paper

   D. Chopping wood

35. Assessments that provide the teacher with information about student understanding as they are learning content are called

   A. direct assessments.

   B. informal assessments.

   C. summative assessments.

   D. formative assessments.

36. Index fossils are used to determine the

    A. age of a particular layer of sediment.

    B. approximate mass of an unknown fossil.

    C. relative lengths of appendages.

    D. approximate size of an unknown fossil.

37. Which type of economic system is based on the premise that an economy can regulate itself in a freely competitive market through the relationship of supply and demand with little governmental intervention?

    A. Free enterprise

    B. Centrally planned

    C. Mixed

    D. Socialist

38. An isosceles right triangle has a hypotenuse of 12 cm. How long are each of the other two legs?

    A. 6.00 cm

    B. 8.40 cm

    C. 8.49 cm

    D. 12.00 cm

39. Mrs. Davis wants her students to read books that are memoirs. This type of book would fall into the broader genre category of which of the following?

    A. Science fiction

    B. Autobiography

    C. Traditional literature

    D. Folklore

40. Which of the following expressions would describe the number of ways that a 12-person basketball team could choose a forward, center, and point guard for the starting lineup?

    A. $_{12}P_9$

    B. $_9P_{12}$

    C. $_{12}P_3$

    D. $_3P_{12}$

41. A school board wishes to determine opinions of parents regarding the assigning of homework in mathematics classes. Which of the following procedures would be most appropriate for obtaining a statistically unbiased sample?

    A. Survey a selection of parents from the official school roster of parents

    B. Survey a selection of people whose names are randomly chosen from the telephone directory

    C. Survey a selection of people whose names are randomly chosen from a listing of parents of mathematics students

    D. Survey the first 1,000 names on an alphabetical listing of parents of mathematics students

42. Who sets monetary policy in the United States?

    A. Congress

    B. The president

    C. The U.S. Treasury

    D. The Federal Reserve

43. The graph below shows terms of a sequence. Find the limit of the sequence as $n$ approaches infinity.

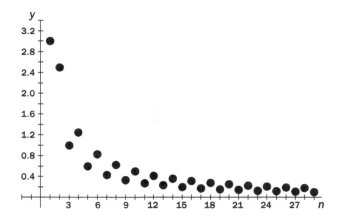

A. 27

B. 30

C. 3.0

D. 0.2

44. An example of an informal way to assess a student's written compositions and use of the writing process might include which of the following?

A. Conferring with the student individually about his or her written work

B. Grading a student's errors and assigning a percentage grade

C. Assessing a student's use of an editing checklist

D. Conducting an item analysis on scores of a released standardized test

45. Which of the following best describes the geographic focus of the social studies TEKS in grades four and seven?

A. The United States

B. The world

C. North America

D. Texas

46. Which of the following is an example of *reflection* in light energy?

A. Light passing through a glass

B. Looking in a mirror

C. Light passing through a prism

D. A rainbow in the sky

47. In teaching viewing and representing, a language arts teacher might teach students to recognize and apply visual coherence to visual representations. The best definition of *visual coherence* is which of the following?

A. The ways in which the overall design appeals to the viewer

B. The ways in which the layout and use of color appeal to the viewer

C. The ways in which the design of the visual creates a sense of unity

D. The ways in which the layout creates a unique pattern

48. The process of judicial review was established in which Supreme Court decision?

A. *Plessy v. Ferguson*

B. *Marbury v. Madison*

C. *Brown v. Board of Education of Topeka*

D. *Dred Scott v. Sandford*

49. Which of the following best describes the way in which the Farm Security Administration labor camp in Robstown, Texas, relates to the beginning teacher's knowledge of geography? The beginning teacher

A. understands the basic concepts of culture and the processes of cultural adaptation, diffusion, and exchange.

B. understands the characteristics, distribution, and migration of populations in Texas and the United States.

C. understands how people use oral tradition, stories, real and mythical heroes, music, paintings, and sculpture to create and represent culture in communities in Texas, the United States, and the world.

D. understands the physical environments of Texas.

50. The table below shows the price for a pizza with the given diameter. Which pizza should you order if you want the best price per square inch?

| Mini (6 in) | Small (10 in) | Medium (12 in) | Large (14 in) |
| --- | --- | --- | --- |
| $3.49 | $8.99 | $11.69 | $13.75 |

A. Mini

B. Small

C. Medium

D. Large

51. Mr. Johnson wants his students to use clues from the text to make predictions about what is coming up next in the story based on what they have read so far. This technique is also known as which of the following?

   A. Drawing inferences

   B. Generating questions

   C. Determining important ideas

   D. Summarizing

52. If $a < b$ and $b = c$, which statement must be true?

   A. The values of $a$, $b$, and $c$ are positive.

   B. The values of $a$, $b$, and $c$ are negative.

   C. The value of $a$ is less than the value of $c$.

   D. The value of $a$ is greater than the value of $c$.

53. In properly reading and recording the volume of water in a graduated cylinder, it is necessary to take into account which of the following to ensure accuracy?

   A. The water will arc or curve downward from the sides, forming a meniscus within the cylinder with its lowest point in the center. The bottom of this meniscus in the center of the graduated cylinder is the proper measure to read and use.

   B. The water will arc or curve upward from the sides, forming a meniscus within the cylinder with its highest point in the center. The top of this meniscus in the center of the graduated cylinder is the proper measure to read and use.

   C. The water will arc or curve downward from the sides, forming a meniscus within the cylinder with its lowest point in the center. The two sides of the meniscus where the water touches the inside walls of the graduated cylinder is the proper measure to read and use.

   D. The water will arc or curve upward from the sides, forming a meniscus within the cylinder with its highest point in the center. The two sides of the meniscus where the water touches the inside walls of the graduated cylinder is the proper measure to read and use.

54. Students who have difficulties reading typically have core deficits in phonological awareness. Which of the following instructional activities by the teacher best supports development in this area?

   A. Breaking words into phonemes, orally, and asking the students to count the number of phonemes

   B. Reading a story and having students follow along and track print while reading

   C. Pausing and having students supply the missing word while reading aloud to students

   D. Practicing sight word vocabulary with students to help their automaticity

55. When a human is exposed to cold temperatures, the blood vessels constrict, and the person experiences shivering and numbness in extremities. When exposed to warmth, the blood vessels expand or dilate, perspiration occurs, and extremities may swell. Why do these responses to cold and warm temperatures occur?

   A. The responses occur because the body is attempting to cause imbalance in the stable condition, or disrupt homeostasis.

   B. The responses occur to promote the digestion of proteins for a needed supply of energy or impede the digestion of proteins to slow metabolism.

   C. The responses occur as feedback mechanisms in response to external stimuli in the body's effort to maintain homeostasis, or an internal stable condition.

   D. The responses occur because changes in temperature and light exposure create a blood cell imbalance in the body that may interfere with feedback mechanisms and homeostatic responses.

56. The "Matthew effect" in reading explains which of the following?

   A. English language learners increase their reading comprehension by improving their academic vocabulary.

B.  Good readers, already fluent and skilled at reading text, become better readers, whereas poor readers become worse.

C.  Systematic oral language instruction better facilitates reading comprehension.

D.  Fluency is increased by practice with a wide variety of independent reading.

57.  Consider a standard deck of cards. How many ways can we choose a group of three queens at random from a deck of cards?

A.  4

B.  24

C.  22,100

D.  132,600

58.  Slavery arose in the southern colonies partly as a perceived economic means to

A.  increase slave owners' natural resources.

B.  cultivate large plantations of cotton, tobacco, rice, indigo, and other crops.

C.  provide Africans with humanitarian aid, such as health care, Christianity, and literacy.

D.  provoke war with the northern colonies.

59.  An example of an exothermic reaction is

A.  melting ice cubes.

B.  combining baking soda and vinegar.

C.  using a cold pack.

D.  burning firewood.

60.  What is the *primary* goal of sustained silent reading (SSR)?

A.  To keep students busy while the teacher is with a reading group

B.  To increase students' stamina for taking standardized tests

C.  To provide models of good writing for a writing workshop

D.  To boost reading comprehension and fluency

61.  After students concluded their inquiry lab experiments about respiration, Mr. Davis provided real-life examples of anaerobic respiration. He used the example of intensely exercising muscle cells breaking the bonds of sugar molecules to release energy without the use of oxygen (anaerobically). This energy, which is in the form of ATP energy, will be added to the ATP energy made available to the body when sugar is metabolized through aerobic respiration (with the use of oxygen). Mr. Davis described playing football, wrestling, and boxing in his examples. What is one major issue that is wrong with Mr. Davis's approach to teaching?

A.  The content of cell respiration is abstract, thus the teacher should not have used inquiry in teaching students this topic.

B.  The teacher used only male-dominated sports examples, whereas he should have given a variety of examples that would appeal to a wider range of his students' interests.

C.  The content the teacher is presenting to students is not accurate because it is not possible to carry on respiration in the absence of oxygen.

D.  The teacher should have described anaerobic respiration and provided real-life examples before the students carried out their inquiry activities.

62.  The type of writing that explains and clarifies ideas about an informational topic is also known by which other general term?

A.  Narrative writing

B.  Expository writing

C.  Persuasive writing

D.  Letter writing

63.  The phase of the moon in which about three-quarters of the moon is illuminated is known as which of the following?

A.  Crescent moon

B.  Blue moon

C.  Gibbous moon

D. New moon

64. What forces are acting upon a stationary book placed on a stationary desk?

A. Normal force

B. Gravitational force

C. Normal force and gravitational force

D. Contact force

65. Which of the following would be most useful to a seventh-grade teacher preparing class resources about how Texans have contributed to technology and society in the twenty-first century?

A. The mandated textbook

B. Various maps and other graphics to present geographic, political, historical, economic and cultural features, distributions, and relationships

C. Various primary and secondary sources, such as photographs, biographies, interviews, and artifacts

D. The local newspaper

66. A warm air mass was over the Gulf of Mexico and has moved over the state of Texas. The warm air mass has high humidity due to water evaporation while over the Gulf. A cold dry air mass moves southward to Texas from Canada. What can be expected to occur when the two air masses meet over Texas?

A. The cold, dry air mass will move under the warm, moist air mass, forcing the warm air to move upward, creating wind, thunderstorms, and precipitation.

B. The cold, dry air mass will move above the warm, moist air mass, causing thick high clouds in the atmosphere, colder temperatures, but no precipitation.

C. The two air masses will remain next to each other in a stationary front, with little movement or circulation of air between the air masses.

D. The cold, dry air mass will push the warm air mass back toward the Gulf of Mexico, causing

a hurricane over the coast, likely near Galveston.

67. If you are given the density and volume of a particular substance, then you can determine its mass by

A. taking the product of its density and volume.

B. dividing density by volume.

C. dividing volume by density.

D. it cannot be determined.

68. Ms. Ojeda wants her eighth-grade students to understand how to use visuals to communicate meaning with an audience. Which of the following activities best develops this skill in her students?

A. Provide students with a rubric detailing how they will be evaluated on their use of visuals

B. Ask students to write a paragraph describing whey they chose their visuals

C. Have students display their visual work for other students to examine silently

D. Actively question and discuss with students their visual choices and encourage them to provide reasons for their choices

69. A rectangular prism has a volume of 256 cubic feet. Which of the following could be the dimensions, in feet, of the prism?

A. $8' \times 8' \times 4'$

B. $8'' \times 8'' \times 4''$

C. $8' \times 6' \times 4'$

D. $16' \times 16'$

70. What is the only branch of government included in the Articles of Confederation?

A. Judicial

B. Legislative

C. Executive

D. Federal

71. An example of kinetic energy is which of the following?

    A. A moving car

    B. An apple hanging on a tree

    C. A ball at rest

    D. A spring that is stretched

72. A cloze passage is a passage that has about every fifth word deleted and replaced with a blank. Students read the passage and have to decide what would be the best and most appropriate word to put in the blank to complete the sentence. The purpose of using a cloze passage with students would be which of the following?

    A. To develop skills in using semantic and syntactic reading clues

    B. To develop skills in self-monitoring and using metacognition while reading

    C. To develop decoding skills at the word level

    D. To build fluency and rate of reading

73. What type of redress did the Civil Liberties Act of 1988, H.R. 442, offer to qualified Japanese Americans who were relocated and interned by the government of the United States?

    A. Payment of $20,000

    B. Guarantees of nonrepetition

    C. Restoration of victims to their original situation before the violations occurred

    D. New housing for all victims

74. The first stage of the writing process is known as:

    A. revising.

    B. editing.

    C. publishing.

    D. brainstorming.

75. Given the tables of function values shown below, which of the following could NOT be a quadratic function?

    A.

    | $x$ | $f(x)$ |
    | --- | --- |
    | 0 | 1 |
    | 1 | 2 |
    | 2 | 5 |
    | 3 | 10 |

    B.

    | $x$ | $f(x)$ |
    | --- | --- |
    | 0 | 1 |
    | 1 | 4 |
    | 2 | 7 |
    | 3 | 10 |

    C.

    | $x$ | $f(x)$ |
    | --- | --- |
    | 0 | 1 |
    | 1 | 2 |
    | 2 | 4 |
    | 3 | 7 |

    D.

    | $x$ | $f(x)$ |
    | --- | --- |
    | 0 | −4 |
    | 1 | −1 |
    | 2 | 0 |
    | 3 | −1 |

76. Which of the following is the molecular building block of proteins?

    A. Monosaccharide

    B. Glycerol

    C. Fatty acid

    D. Amino acid

77. Mr. Chan is introducing a new novel to his seventh-grade language arts class. He wants to do some effective prereading activities that will help the students activate their background knowledge about the topic of immigration. Which of the following would best support this instructional objective of activating schema and background knowledge?

    A. Review new vocabulary that is related to the topic of immigration

    B. Ask students to brainstorm about their experiences and knowledge about immigration and chart their responses as a class conversation

    C. Provide a written summary about the topic to students and explain the main ideas of the topic

    D. Watch a movie clip about immigrant experiences and have students write a summary

78. The figure below is a regular pentagon. What is the measure of $\angle AED$? Point $F$ is the center of the pentagon.

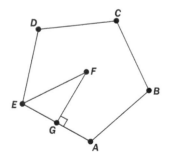

    A. 72°

    B. 108°

    C. 180°

    D. 540°

79. On February 1, 1861, the Texas legislature voted to

    A. secede from the Union and join the Confederacy.

    B. relinquish all claims to New Mexico.

    C. annex Texas to the United States.

    D. adopt the Texas Declaration of Independence.

80. Diane and Liam are college students who share a two-bedroom apartment. At their part-time jobs, Diane earns $650 a month and Liam earns $730 a month. Their rent each month is 29% of their total monthly income. What is a reasonable amount for their rent?

    A. $189

    B. $212

    C. $400

    D. $414

81. The teacher asks students to conduct an experiment in which they each fill two jars of water to the same level, marking the level of water with a piece of tape or marker. A cover is placed on jar A, and jar B is left uncovered. The two jars are placed side by side on a shelf in the classroom. Each day the students measure the height of the water in the two jars and record their data in their science journals. After several weeks, what will the students discover, and why?

    A. The water level in the two jars has remained the same due to equal humidity in the room.

    B. The water level in jar A is lower than the water level in jar B due to evaporation of water from jar A.

    C. The water level in jar A is higher than the water level in jar B due to evaporation of water from jar B.

    D. The water level in both jars is equal but lower due to evaporation taking place from both jars.

82. If a teacher is attempting to look for signs that a student might have oral language delays, which of the following might be an indicator of such a delay?

    A. The student speaks in a different dialect.

    B. The student comes from a country where there is no written language.

    C. The student's speech is characterized by false starts and hesitations.

    D. The student code-switches back and forth between two languages.

83. Mr. Thomas, a seventh-grade science teacher, wants to use formative assessment to evaluate his students' authentic understanding of the process of scientific inquiry during their lab time. Which of the following would best be suited to this?

    A. Do an item analysis of scores on the most recent science standardized test, and chart where students are making progress

    B. Evaluate the content of what students are writing in a scientific notebook by using a teacher-designed rubric

    C. Give a true/false quiz over content about of the most recent science unit, and go over the answers in class

    D. Test students on their knowledge of the vocabulary terms associated with the science unit by using a fill-in-the-blank format

84. A paleontologist unearths a fossil that possesses primarily canine and incisor teeth. The scientist infers that the organism was a meat eater. What unifying concept of science is present in this example?

    A. Form and function

    B. Models and explanation

    C. Systems and subsystems

    D. Equilibrium and disequilibrium

85. In order for the U.S. Constitution to be amended, what proportion of the U.S. Congress must propose the amendment?

    A. $\dfrac{1}{2}$

    B. $\dfrac{2}{3}$

    C. $\dfrac{3}{4}$

    D. $\dfrac{3}{5}$

86. A student who is having trouble spelling words with middle vowel sounds (e.g., words with double vowels such as *bread*) is typically in which stage of spelling?

    A. Prephonetic

    B. Phonetic

    C. Transitional

    D. Conventional

87. Which of the following graphs represents the solution to the inequality $2y + x \le 5$?

    A.
    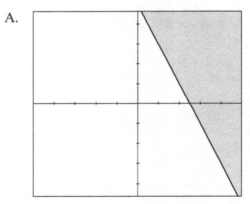

    B.
    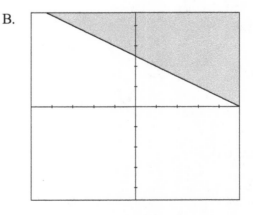

C.

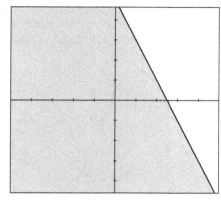

D.

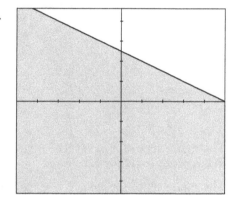

88. The purchasing power of money is most affected by what?

    A. Inflation

    B. Tax rates

    C. Interest rates

    D. Debt

89. A sequence of DNA in a specific location on a chromosome in the nucleus of cells may code for a specific hereditary trait. This DNA code is known as a

    A. nucleotide.

    B. nucleolus.

    C. gene.

    D. phenotype.

90. Which of the following best describes the way in which the U.S. Constitution assigns governmental power?

    A. It assigns it entirely to the states.

    B. It assigns it entirely to the national government.

    C. It divides it between the states and the national government.

    D. It does not divide power.

91. In the consolidated alphabetic stage of word identification, students can do which of the following?

    A. Students are beginning to learn that letters represent sounds.

    B. Students are beginning to learn sound-symbol correspondence.

    C. Students can spell words with the correct initial sounds of the words.

    D. Students can use components of words they know to decode new words.

92. An ice cream cone is similar to a hemisphere on top of a cone. If the radius of the scoop of ice cream on top is 1.5 inches, and the height of the cone is 4 inches. Find the approximate volume of ice cream (assuming the cone can be completely filled).

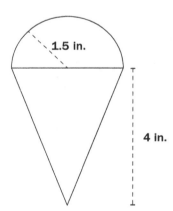

A. 9.42 cubic inches

B. 14.14 cubic inches

C. 16.49 cubic inches

D. 23.56 cubic inches

93. Ms. Jimenez uses several methods of informal assessment to track her students' progress in the area of decoding. She is working with a group of below-level readers in her fourth-grade class. She wants to use an assessment to determine the accuracy of her students' individual oral reading and wants to gain more insight into the problem-solving processes and strategies that students are using in decoding while reading aloud. Which of the following assessment tools would best support this assessment objective?

A. Timed reading

B. Written summary

C. Running record

D. Oral retelling

94. Which of the following are the best instruments to use in measuring the density of a relatively small, irregularly shaped rock?

A. A beaker of water and a metric tape measure

B. A graduated cylinder of water and a metric tape measure

C. A beaker of water and a triple beam or electronic balance

D. A graduated cylinder of water and a triple beam or electronic balance

95. Which one of the following famous Texans contributed significant medical advances in science, technology, and society?

A. Michael Dell

B. Benjy Brooks

C. Walter Cunningham

D. Howard Hughes

96. The test scores from two different classes are shown below. If the scores are normally distributed, which of the following statements is true?

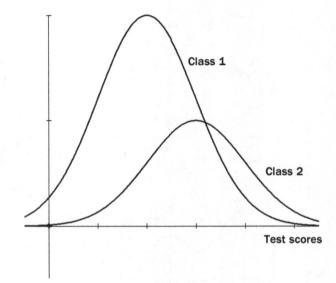

A. The mean score for class 1 is greater than the mean score for class 2.

B. The mean score for class 2 is greater than the mean score for class 1.

C. The mode for class 2 is less than the mode for class 1.

D. The standard deviations for the two classes are equal.

97. The author's mood or expression in a story is also known as

A. style.

B. tone.

C. plot.

D. setting.

98. The U.S. census is conducted every 10 years. Based on census data, which governmental entity might be affected based on population changes?

A. U.S. Senate

B. U.S. House of Representatives

C. Supreme Court justices

D. Federal Reserve Bank

99. Which of the following mini-lessons would best help a language arts teacher to implement editing checklists into the writing workshop?

    A. Conduct a mini-lesson on how to use the editing checklist by modeling how to use one with the teacher's own writing

    B. Discuss with students how they will be graded on their use of the editing checklist to motivate them to use it

    C. Suggest to students that the editing checklist is used by real writers in their daily lives

    D. Model a brainstorming activity of how to generate ideas in a writing notebook

100. To develop fluency, Mr. Madaris has his students engage in repeated readings of a text. He does this in a fun and interactive way. The technique he is using is which of the following?

    A. Reciprocal teaching

    B. Reader's theater

    C. Oral retelling

    D. Reading inventories

101. Which transformation would move the function $f(x)$ to the right 3 units?

    A. $f(x + 3)$

    B. $f(x) + 3$

    C. $f(x) - 3$

    D. $f(x - 3)$

102. If triangle A'B'C' is obtained when triangle ABC is reflected over the line $x = 1$, which of the following would be the location of point B'?

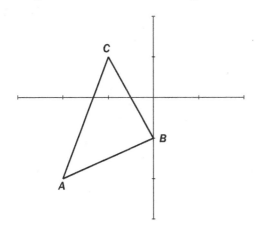

A. $(0, -1)$

B. $(1, -1)$

C. $(2, -1)$

D. $(1, 0)$

103. Mr. Hart wants his students' writing to show their own uniqueness and personal style. Mr. Hart wants his students to develop their skills in which of the following?

    A. Organization

    B. Ideas

    C. Focus

    D. Voice

104. The Indian Removal Act and the Trail of Tears were a result of whose presidency?

    A. Abraham Lincoln

    B. James Monroe

    C. Andrew Jackson

    D. James Madison

105. The box-and-whisker plot represents the heights, in feet, of a group of 11 people. Which of the following statements is NOT true?

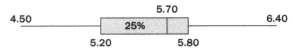

    A. The shortest person is 4.5 feet tall

    B. Half of the people are 5.7 feet tall or taller

    C. The heights of people within the 25 percentile are between 4.5 feet and 5.2 feet

    D. The interquartile range is 0.5 feet

106. In helping students to become more equipped with study skills, why might a teacher use a Venn diagram?

    A. It can help teachers to compare and contrast ideas across two different readings.

B. It can help students to outline the main ideas of a text.

C. It can help students as they make inferences about ideas.

D. It can help students to identify the text structure of the reading.

107. When reading fictional text, the teacher can focus students' attention on such aspects of the story as character, plot, setting, problem, and solution. This instructional focus is also known as

A. plot summary.

B. get the gist.

C. story grammar.

D. a directed reading-thinking activity.

108. Given that lines $\ell_1$ and $\ell_2$ are parallel, which angle is congruent to $\angle 1$.

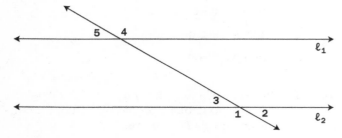

A. $\angle 2$

B. $\angle 3$

C. $\angle 4$

D. $\angle 5$

109. Which of the following would be the best strategy to teach students so they can successfully read expository text?

A. Teach them to look up all unknown words in the glossary before reading

B. Teach them to write a written summary after reading an expository text

C. Teach them to create a story grammar map during and after reading expository text

D. Teach them to read expository text more slowly than they would read narrative text

110. Which of the following best describes the way in which a beginning teacher would appropriately use technology as a tool for learning and communicating social studies concepts?

A. Information about social studies is available from the Internet; however, students need to limit technology to use only primary sources.

B. Information about social studies is available from the Internet; however, students need to evaluate the scholarship of the many sources available and use only those that align directly with the textbook.

C. Information about social studies is available from the Internet; however, students need to evaluate the scholarship of the many sources available and use only those known to be reliable.

D. Information about social studies is available from the Internet; however, students need to know that the sources available are limited to secondary sources.

111. Teaching students about morphology can help them in which of the following ways with their reading?

A. It will help students to understand the overall meaning of the entire story or text.

B. It will help students to unlock the meanings of words as they consider the meanings of prefixes, suffixes, or root words.

C. It will help students to analyze the grammatical structure at the sentence level.

D. It will help students to be able to react to the texts with a personal and interpretive response.

112. If Jacqueline can paint a wall that is 40 feet by 20 feet in 25 minutes, how many minutes will it take her to paint a wall 40 feet by 30 feet?

A. 12.5 minutes

B. 15 minutes

C. 15 minutes

D. 37.5 minutes

113. Mr. Navarro is a seventh-grade language arts teacher. He is working with a group of students who are having trouble with comprehending basic text. Which of the following is the *most* effective strategy that he can teach students to do to support their comprehension when it breaks down while reading?

    A. Rereading

    B. Evaluating

    C. Judging

    D. Inferring

114. Why are schemes such as astrology, fortune telling, and tarot cards considered to be pseudo-science (not true science)?

    A. Because there is substantial evidence to support claims that one's personality or future events can be accurately predicted

    B. Because no controlled experiments have been conducted to provide data that supports the claims made

    C. Because any procedures followed and information revealed can be replicated with repeated experiments providing the same or consistent results

    D. Because information is routinely presented to peers at professional conferences and subject to rigorous scrutiny and review before acceptance

115. The equation $3x + 2 = 2x + 6$ is modeled below. What is the value of $x$?

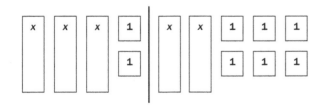

    A. 2

    B. 4

    C. 6

    D. 8

116. Which concept is NOT embodied as a right in the First Amendment to the U.S. Constitution?

    A. Peaceable assembly

    B. Freedom of speech

    C. Petition for redress of grievances

    D. Protection against unreasonable search and seizure

117. A study strategy by which the teacher helps students establish a purpose for reading and guides students to make predictions while reading is also known as which of the following?

    A. Directed reading-thinking activity

    B. KWL (know/want to know/learn)

    C. Graphophonemic awareness

    D. Phonological awareness

118. The acceleration of a given object is equal to the

    A. change of speed per some unit of time.

    B. product of the force and mass.

    C. change in velocity per some unit of time.

    D. product of force times distance.

119. A fifth-grade teacher wants students to gain skills in reading with expression. Which of the following instructional methods would *best* facilitate this?

    A. Modeling reading by the teacher of a wide genre of texts

    B. Providing comprehension activities at the computer center

    C. Requiring students to engage in silent reading during reading center time

    D. Providing access to a wide variety of texts in the classroom library

120. Where two of Earth's huge plates collide, near the edge of at least one of the plates there will typically be a

    A. large canyon, such as the Grand Canyon, as the two plates pull apart after colliding.

    B. river that was formed when the two plates collided and the water table rose to the surface.

    C. hot spot, such as the island chain that includes Hawaii.

    D. mountain range as the two plates over time push together and the earth folds upwards.

121. Which of the following best describes the historical diet of Atakapans and Karankawas American Indians who inhabited the coastal regions of present-day Texas?

    A. Atakapans and Karankawas consumed bear and deer from the land as well as alligators, oysters, clams, ducks, and turtles.

    B. Atakapans and Karankawas grew and consumed beans, squash, and sunflowers, along with eating bear, deer, and occasionally buffalo.

    C. Atakapans and Karankawas ate bison, fish, turtles, crawfish, snails, pecans, acorns, wild fruits, rattlesnakes, and rabbits.

    D. Atakapans and Karankawas gathered wild berries, plants, and other locally grown items.

122. Ms. Rodriguez presents a writing sample to the class that contains common errors and then asks the class to help provide corrective feedback about the errors. What is her purpose in this instructional activity?

    A. Students will be able to develop their skills in writing an effective composition.

    B. Students will be able to identify correct writing conventions.

    C. Students will be able to construct coherent sentences.

    D. Students will be able to write for a particular audience.

123. All investigations are guided by one or more

    A. hypotheses.

    B. questions.

    C. educated guesses.

    D. controls.

124. An example of a word that is a homonym is which of the following?

    A. Club

    B. Too

    C. Butterfly

    D. Blue

125. A company finds that the demand for its new television varies inversely with the price of the television. When the company sells the TV at a price of $2,050, the demand is for 100 televisions. Find an equation that describes the demand, $D$, for the television sold at price $p$.

    A. $D = \dfrac{205,000}{p}$

    B. $D = \dfrac{p}{205,000}$

    C. $D = \dfrac{20.5}{p}$

    D. $D = \dfrac{p}{20.5}$

126. From 1836 to 1845, Texas functioned as

    A. a slave state in the United States.

    B. a Mexican state.

    C. a Spanish territory.

    D. an independent nation.

127. Teaching students to use connecting discourse improves the overall effectiveness of their writing. The types of words that aid in this learning objective are known as

    A. morphemes.

    B. clauses.

    C. transitions.

    D. conventions.

128. Which of the following is an example of a word with a consonant digraph?

    A. Gnat

    B. Try

    C. Chair

    D. Hose

129. Mr. Whitfield has his seventh-grade students regularly engage in small group discussions following a social studies lesson in which they discuss a shared text. Using small group roles, the students take turns reading the text, pausing to discuss the text according to each student's assigned role. One student is a question generator, one is a summarizer, one is a predictor, and the fourth student is a clarifier of tricky concepts in the text. What is the name for this strategy?

    A. Thinking aloud

    B. Role play

    C. Literature circles

    D. Reciprocal teaching

130. Which female played a significant role in the Chicano civil rights movement by fighting for better working conditions and fair compensation for farm workers?

    A. Rosa Parks

    B. Martha Cotera

    C. Dolores Huerta

    D. Ida B. Wells

# Answer Key

| Question | Answer | Competency |
|----------|--------|------------|
| 1 | A | 031 |
| 2 | C | 030 |
| 3 | C | 034 |
| 4 | B | 001 |
| 5 | B | 010 |
| 6 | C | 029 |
| 7 | D | 029 |
| 8 | C | 016 |
| 9 | A | 019 |
| 10 | B | 031 |
| 11 | B | 023 |
| 12 | A | 022 |
| 13 | B | 002 |
| 14 | A | 007 |
| 15 | A | 027 |
| 16 | D | 030 |
| 17 | B | 011 |
| 18 | B | 007 |
| 19 | C | 036 |
| 20 | B | 034 |
| 21 | C | 005 |
| 22 | A | 047 |
| 23 | B | 007 |
| 24 | B | 056 |
| 25 | A | 004 |
| 26 | B | 036 |
| 27 | A | 002 |
| 28 | B | 050 |
| 29 | C | 037 |
| 30 | B | 032 |
| 31 | D | 041 |

| Question | Answer | Competency |
|----------|--------|------------|
| 32 | B | 048 |
| 33 | D | 022 |
| 34 | A | 042 |
| 35 | D | 028 |
| 36 | A | 055 |
| 37 | A | 031 |
| 38 | C | 019 |
| 39 | B | 005 |
| 40 | C | 012 |
| 41 | C | 023 |
| 42 | D | 031 |
| 43 | D | 016 |
| 44 | A | 007 |
| 45 | D | 035 |
| 46 | B | 044 |
| 47 | C | 008 |
| 48 | B | 032 |
| 49 | B | 030 |
| 50 | D | 019 |
| 51 | A | 005 |
| 52 | C | 024 |
| 53 | A | 037 |
| 54 | A | 002 |
| 55 | C | 049 |
| 56 | B | 003 |
| 57 | A | 012 |
| 58 | B | 031 |
| 59 | D | 045 |
| 60 | D | 003 |
| 61 | B | 056 |
| 62 | B | 007 |

*(continued)*

# Answer Key (continued)

| Question | Answer | Competency |
|----------|--------|------------|
| 63 | C | 054 |
| 64 | C | 041 |
| 65 | C | 034 |
| 66 | A | 053 |
| 67 | A | 042 |
| 68 | D | 008 |
| 69 | A | 017 |
| 70 | B | 029 |
| 71 | A | 044 |
| 72 | A | 004 |
| 73 | A | 033 |
| 74 | D | 007 |
| 75 | B | 013 |
| 76 | D | 046 |
| 77 | B | 004 |
| 78 | B | 020 |
| 79 | A | 029 |
| 80 | C | 025 |
| 81 | C | 052 |
| 82 | C | 001 |
| 83 | B | 058 |
| 84 | A | 040 |
| 85 | B | 032 |
| 86 | C | 006 |
| 87 | D | 014 |
| 88 | A | 031 |
| 89 | C | 047 |
| 90 | C | 032 |
| 91 | D | 002 |
| 92 | C | 017 |
| 93 | C | 002 |
| 94 | D | 057 |
| 95 | B | 033 |
| 96 | B | 021 |

| Question | Answer | Competency |
|----------|--------|------------|
| 97 | B | 005 |
| 98 | B | 032 |
| 99 | A | 006 |
| 100 | B | 003 |
| 101 | D | 015 |
| 102 | C | 020 |
| 103 | D | 007 |
| 104 | C | 029 |
| 105 | D | 021 |
| 106 | A | 009 |
| 107 | C | 004 |
| 108 | C | 018 |
| 109 | D | 005 |
| 110 | C | 034 |
| 111 | B | 003 |
| 112 | D | 015 |
| 113 | A | 005 |
| 114 | B | 039 |
| 115 | B | 026 |
| 116 | D | 032 |
| 117 | A | 009 |
| 118 | C | 041 |
| 119 | A | 003 |
| 120 | D | 051 |
| 121 | A | 033 |
| 122 | B | 006 |
| 123 | B | 038 |
| 124 | A | 003 |
| 125 | A | 015 |
| 126 | D | 032 |
| 127 | C | 006 |
| 128 | C | 002 |
| 129 | D | 005 |
| 130 | C | 029 |

# Practice Test 2 Answer Explanations

**1. A**

Economic factors of production include natural resources (B), entrepreneurship (C), labor (D), and capital. Thus, goods (A) is the only choice that is NOT an economic factor of production. Goods actually are created as a *result* of the factors of production and are not factors of production themselves. **Competency 031**

**2. C**

The Northern Hemisphere is located between the equator and the North Pole (C), encompassing everything north of the Equator. Response (A) is incorrect, because the Prime Meridian and the International Date Line divide the Eastern and Western Hemispheres. The Eastern Hemisphere is located east of the Prime Meridian and west of the International Date Line, and the Western Hemisphere is located west of the Prime Meridian and east of the International Date Line. The Southern Hemisphere is located between the equator and the South Pole, so response (B) is also incorrect. Answer choice (D) is incorrect because the equator is between the Tropic of Cancer and Tropic of Capricorn. **Competency 030**

**3. C**

A biography (C) is a secondary social studies source. A diary (A), a photograph (B), and a letter (D), are all primary social studies sources, and thus are incorrect choices. **Competency 034**

**4. B**

Answer choice (B) is correct because it provides the most demonstration and explicit instruction related to what will help students in applying academic language into their own speechmaking and speechwriting. The other answers are too teacher-centered or do not provide explicit enough instruction to be of the best use to students. **Competency 001**

**5. B**

To find the volume of the deep end of the pool, multiply the dimensions of that region. First, we need to determine the length of just the deep end. We are told the shallow end of the pool is about $\frac{1}{4}$ of the pool length, or 12.5 meters. Therefore, the length of the deep end of the pool is $50 - 12.5 = 37.5$ meters. The volume of the deep end of the pool is $37.5 \times 25 \times 2 = 1,875$ cubic meters. In scientific notation, 1,875 is $1.875 \times 10^3$, which is answer (B). **Competency 010**

**6. C**

The quotation is from the Declaration of Independence (C), written in 1776 by Thomas Jefferson. The document specifically highlights the reasons the American colonies wanted to seek independence from British rule. The Articles of Confederation (A), adopted in 1781, was an agreement among the 13 founding states that legally established the United States of America as a confederation of sovereign states and served as its first constitution. The U.S. Constitution (B), adopted in 1787, established the governmental structure we still have today. The Missouri Compromise of 1820 (D) dealt primarily with how slave and free states would be admitted to the Union. **Competency 029**

**7. D**

The primary author of the Declaration of Independence was Thomas Jefferson (D). At the time of the crafting of the Declaration, George Washington (A) was a prominent military leader who would eventually become the first president of the United States. John Marshall (B) was an influential

Supreme Court justice and leader of the Federalist party, but had nothing to do with the crafting of the Declaration of Independence. James Madison (C) is incorrect; he was the primary author of the U.S. Constitution and not the Declaration of Independence. **Competency 029**

**8. C**

The graph of $f(x)$ is some exponential function, let's say $f(x) = e^x$. So, $f'(x) = e^x$, and when we evaluate at $x = 2$, we find the associated $y$-value will be positive since $e$ raised to any positive number results in a positive number, verifying that answer (C) is correct. **Competency 016**

**9. A**

The triangles in the figure provided are similar triangles with proportional side lengths. Solving the following proportion will determine the length of $b$.

$$\frac{15}{20+35} = \frac{b}{35}$$

$$\frac{15}{55} = \frac{b}{35}$$

Answer (A) is correct as $b \approx 9.54$.

**Competency 019**

**10. B**

The total value of all goods and services produced in a country is a country's gross domestic product (GDP), choice (B). Capital (A) is incorrect because it is actually a factor of production that is used in the production of goods and services and not the total value. Although investment (C) is an important component of GDP, since it helps provide the resources needed to produce goods and services, it does not represent the total value of all goods and services. Inflation (D) is incorrect because it refers to the reduction in the purchasing power of money and decreases a country's real GDP. **Competency 031**

**11. B**

To test the effects of working while in high school, a sample would need to consist of students with a job, hence students working in local area restaurants (B). Answers (A), (C), and (D) include students, but not necessarily students who work. **Competency 023**

**12. A**

There are 40 people who had lunch and were satisfied out of a total of 125 satisfied people. The probability that a person ate lunch at the hotel, knowing they were satisfied is $\frac{40}{125} = \frac{8}{25}$. **Competency 022**

**13. B**

Shared reading is an opportunity for students to participate in the balanced reading process with support from the teacher. Answer choice (B) is correct because while the teacher is reading the shared text aloud, she or he can take the opportunity to model reading processes and skills. Since the teacher is doing the reading, students who might not be able to decode and/or read the text fluently can still have access to the text and modeling by the teacher. Choice (A) is incorrect because shared reading is not primarily intended to be just a motivational technique. Choice (C) is incorrect because students are developing both reading and listening comprehension. Choice (D) is not correct because the shared reading process may or may not manage student behavior. **Competency 002**

**14. A**

The correct answer choice is (A) because it focuses on a key aspect of the writing process itself. Students should be taught how the writing process works, including how to take a writing piece through its various stages. The other three answer choices focus more on the skills of writing with a specific craft focus, whereas (A) focuses on the writing process itself. **Competency 007**

**15. A**

In a mathematics classroom there should be ample discovery and inquiry learning and little to no busy work. Discovery and inquiry learning can occur through the use of manipulatives, problem-solving activities, partner or small group projects, and so forth. **Competency 027**

**16. D**

The Dust Bowl created people who were classified as internally displaced persons (D), or people forced to leave their home regions because of unfavorable conditions but who didn't cross any boundaries. Persons classified as emigrants, immigrants, and refugees all leave one country to reside in another. The Dust Bowl forced people from the United States to move to other geographic locations within the United States, so answer choices (A), (B), and (C) are all incorrect responses. **Competency 030**

**17. B**

The two number lines show 2 + 3 = 5 and 3 + 2 = 5. Answer (B) is correct, since the sum of two numbers, regardless of the order in which they were added, is the commutative property. **Competency 011**

**18. B**

Mentor texts are primarily used during writing workshops and writing mini-lessons to provide examples of quality writing for students to imitate or as sources of inspiration for writing. Mentor texts can provide examples of a genre, a writing trait, or a specific author's style. Mentor text lessons have a specific teaching focus, such as how to write with detail. Choice (B) best summarizes this definition of mentor text. Choices (A) and (D) are incorrect because mentor texts focus on inte-

grating reading and writing. They are not solely for the purpose of the read-aloud experience (A) or comprehension development (D). Choice (C) is incorrect because using mentor texts doesn't mean that a student's fluency will automatically increase. **Competency 007**

**19. C**

Acids should be stored in a locked cabinet on a low shelf (C) so that if it is accidentally dropped or spilled, the material is close to the ground, reducing the possibility of the acid splashing and spreading, and allowing the spill to be contained. Choice (A) is incorrect because taking materials such as acid off a high shelf would be dangerous due to the splatter if it were dropped or spilled. Choice (B) is incorrect because the refrigerator cannot typically be locked, and it is not necessary to refrigerate most chemicals used in science, including acids. Choice (D) is incorrect because many science experiments require access to acids so students can learn about pH and other important topics. Use of such caustic materials simply requires proper safety by storing them in a locked acid cabinet on a low shelf, and *always* requiring the use of safety goggles when handling them. Also note that many mild acids, such as white vinegar and lemon juice, provide good substitutions for more dangerous acids, such as hydrochloric and sulfuric acid. **Competency 036**

**20. B**

Answer (B) is correct, because it reveals the purpose behind why cartographers opt to use topographic maps. Topographic maps use contour lines to show elevation change on the surface of Earth. Even though both relative and absolute location provide information about where we are in the world, they are not what makes a topographic map special. Thus, answers (C) and (D) are incorrect. We use latitude and longitude to determine global location. Population maps show the density of humans in a given location, which means (A) is also incorrect. **Competency 034**

**21. C**

Choice (C) best promotes understanding of text structure. The types of expository text structure listed in this question are aligned with commonly used graphic organizers. The graphic organizers can help students to see how texts are typically organized. Choice (A) is too vague and doesn't provide direct instruction in identifying text structure. Similarly, choice (B) doesn't allow for student practice, so it is less effective than choice (C). Choice (D) is less direct and less explicit than choice (C). **Competency 005**

**22. A**

Asexual reproduction is accomplished through a process of binary fission, or mitosis, in which the DNA (genetic material) is first replicated, and, after a series of events, the parent cell divides into two daughter cells with genetic material that is identical to the one parent cell and to each other. Choices (B), (C), and (D) all describe sexual reproduction, where parent cells divide into four daughter cells containing half the genetic material (DNA) as the original parent. The daughter cell may be a sperm or egg cell, for example. The daughter cell of one organism joins with the daughter cell of another organism of the same species to form a new cell that has a combination of genetic material from both parent cells. **Competency 047**

**23. B**

Dialogue journals (B) are like a "pen pal" writing connection between teacher and student. In dialogue journals, the teacher and student write back and forth (in a notebook or online) in order to facilitate a meaningful dialogue around authentic writing topics. Reflective journals (A) are more broadly used to reflect on a wide variety of topics; however, they don't focus on back-and-forth writing between two people. Learning logs (C) are more for content-area subjects for the student to keep track of learning and thoughts. Simi-

larly, personal journals (D) are not interactive. **Competency 007**

**24. B**

Science is an active process characterized by words such as discovering, observing, hypothesizing, experimenting, measuring, communicating, inferring, and concluding. Scientific theory is based on evidence and is changeable in light of new evidence. Therefore, science teaching must be consistent with the discipline of science and taught as an active inquiry process. Choices (A), (C), and (D) indicate that science is a body of facts that is unchangeable, which is an inaccurate depiction of science. In addition, choice (D) presents science as the verification of information, which is contrary to scientific discovery, experimentation, and inquiry. **Competency 056**

**25. A**

Semantic mapping is a reading tool that shows the relationships between words and concepts (A). It is a visual diagram with specific links between words and concepts. By showing the ways that words and concepts relate to other words and concepts, students can understand the interrelatedness of words and ideas in a visual, concrete, and organized way as they read. Semantic maps can be used before, during, and after reading instruction. **Competency 004**

**26. B**

Fires and fire extinguishers are categorized based on the fuel's chemical properties. Choice (A) is incorrect because a Class A extinguisher should be used with ordinary combustibles such as paper. Choice (B) is correct because Class B is used for organic solvents such as acetone and alcohols. Choice (C) is incorrect because Class C is used for electrical fires, and choice (D) is incorrect because Class D is used for metals such as sodium. **Competency 036**

## 27.  A

The alphabetic principle (A) is the idea that letters represent sounds. As children develop graphophonemic awareness, they build on this principle and learn that certain letters or a group of letters can represent certain sounds. Choice (B) is incorrect because it focuses more on aspects about language, such as reading left to right, concept of a word, and so on, which is known as concepts about print. Choice (C) is incorrect because conventional spelling is generally the last state of spelling development and not one that beginning readers have grasped yet. Choice (D) is incorrect because phonological awareness is an auditory process and skill. **Competency 002**

## 28.  B

Energy is lost from one organism to the next along the food chain (B). The energy originates from the sun and is transferred to green plants in photosynthesis, where it is locked within the chemical bonds of simple sugars (glucose). Thus, green plants contain the most energy from the sun in the chemical bonds of the glucose molecules it forms. As each organism in the chain ingests an organism (sun → grass → rabbit → coyotes → decomposers), some of the original sun energy has already been lost to support the life functions of that organism, so energy content reduces as you progress along the food chain, with the most energy being supplied to the plants, followed by primary consumers, secondary consumers, and so on with the lowest levels of energy being available for decomposers. Choice (A) is incorrect because energy is lost and not gained through the food chain. Choice (C) is incorrect because energy is not maintained at the same levels since some energy is always used by the organism to carry on its own life functions. Choice (D) is incorrect because energy along with inorganic nutrients is transferred from one organism to the next in a food chain. **Competency 050**

## 29.  C

It is important for clear scientific communication that students understand the metric system, including the prefixes. Choices (A), (B), and (D) are all equivalent to 10 kilometers. Choice (C) is not equivalent because it takes 1,000,000 centimeters to equal 10 kilometers. **Competency 037**

## 30.  B

The Thirteenth Amendment to the U.S. Constitution abolished slavery (B). The Sixteenth Amendment established a federal income tax (A); the Eighteenth Amendment abolished the sale and manufacture of alcohol in the United States (C); and the Nineteenth Amendment gave women the right to vote (D). **Competency 032**

## 31.  D

Velocity is defined as the change in position and direction per some unit of time (D). Choice (A) is not correct because acceleration is defined as the change in velocity, not its square. Choices (B) and (C) are not correct because they do not refer to a direction, which is necessary because velocity is a vector. **Competency 041**

## 32.  B

The fossil record is one line of evidence for evolution, which refers to the layers of rocks that indicate periods of time throughout Earth's history (B). These layers contain fossils that show clear patterns of change in species over time. Scientists now know that these changes were due to DNA mutations that provided the organism, and subsequently the offspring, with more favorable traits for survival in that environment. Choice (A) is incorrect because it does not refer to the fossil record found in rock layers and sequencing according to geologic age. Choices (C) and (D) are incorrect in terms of the fossil record, but do represent other lines of evidence for evolution in the area of morphology, namely homologous and analogous structures, respectively. **Competency 048**

### 33. D

The probability of selecting a red ball as the first ball is $\frac{4}{6} = \frac{2}{3}$. Multiply this probability by the chance of pulling a second red ball, which is $\frac{3}{5}$ since there are only three red balls left out of five remaining balls in the box. Answer (D) is correct since $\frac{2}{3} \times \frac{3}{5} = \frac{6}{15} = \frac{2}{5}$. **Competency 022**

### 34. A

The burning of gasoline (A) is an example of a chemical change. A chemical change occurs when the substances that were combined are no longer the same molecules—they have changed to new substances. A physical change is a change in which the form of matter is altered, but one substance is not transformed into another. Therefore, answer choices (B), (C), and (D) are exmples of physical changes and are incorrect. **Competency 042**

### 35. D

Formative assessments (D) are ongoing and occur while students are learning information. These types of assessments help teachers make decisions about the how the subject is taught, and they can make adjustments as needed. Summative assessments show what students know at a particular time, such as through a unit or comprehensive end-of-term exam. **Competency 028**

### 36. A

The correct answer is (A) because index fossils are short-lived organisms whose fossil, once dated, can help determine the approximate date of a layer of sediment. Answers (B), (C), and (D) are thus incorrect by definition. **Competency 055**

### 37. A

Free enterprise (otherwise known as capitalism or market economies) is an economic system that promotes private ownership of land, capital, and business with minimal government intervention. A centrally planned economy (B) is incorrect because it relies heavily on government intervention and regulation of markets. Mixed (C) and socialist (D) economies are incorrect because these types of economic systems use a combination of government planning (usually at the upper level of the economy) and markets (usually for the prices of consumer goods and wages). **Competency 031**

### 38. C

An isosceles right triangle has two congruent legs and a hypotenuse. The Pythagorean theorem will determine the length of the legs. Let $x$ be the measure of each leg on the isosceles right triangle. Then (C) is correct because

$$x^2 + x^2 = 12^2$$
$$2x^2 = 144$$
$$x^2 = 72$$
$$x \approx 8.49.$$

**Competency 019**

### 39. B

Memoirs are a collection of stories written by the author to share aspects of her or his life. A memoir is therefore a type of autobiography. **Competency 005**

### 40. C

To answer this question correctly we need to find how many ways to fill each position. If there are 12 players on a team, then there are 12 ways to select a forward, then 11 ways to choose a center, and finally only 10 ways to choose a point guard. The notation $_{12}P_3$ means "the number of permutations of 12 team members taken 3 at a time," or $_{12}P_3 = 12 \times 11 \times 10 = 1{,}320$. **Competency 012**

## 41. C

The correct answer is (C) because the selection is random among parents who have children in mathematics. A selection of parent names from a school roster does not guarantee their children take mathematics, so (A) is incorrect. Answer (B) is incorrect because randomly selecting people from a telephone book does not necessarily mean they have children, let alone children in school who are taking mathematics. Answer (D) is incorrect because it is not random to select the first 1,000 parents based on alphabetical order. **Competency 023**

## 42. D

The Federal Reserve (D) sets monetary policy for the United States. The Federal Reserve is accountable to Congress (A), but this legislative entity does not play a role in setting monetary policy. The president (B) often plays a role in fiscal policy, but may not play a role in monetary policy. The U.S. Treasury (C) does deal with monetary issues, but it does not establish monetary policy. **Competency 031**

## 43. D

As $n$ approaches infinity, the sequence becomes a very small positive number, as the points on the graph stay above $y = 0$. The smallest value labeled on the $y$-axis is 0.4, and the points on the graph are below this value; this would allude to answer (D) to be correct, making 0.2 the limit of the sequence as $n$ approaches infinity. **Competency 016**

## 44. A

Choice (A) focuses on the informal assessment that most closely relates to the content of the students' composition process. By conferring individually with students, the teacher can make observations (and record anecdotal notes), collect work samples, and ask questions about the writing process as well as the student's strengths and any challenges the student is facing. Choices (B), (C), and (D) are incorrect because they don't give insight into a student's writing *process*. **Competency 007**

## 45. D

The geographic focus in grades four and seven is on Texas, making (D) the correct choice. Students focus on the United States in grades five and eight, making choice (A) incorrect. Grades four and seven also include North America as a more remote geographic focus. Even though Texas is in North America, it is not the focus of those grades, so (C) is also incorrect. Grade six offers a world focus, so response (B) is wrong as well. **Competency 035**

## 46. B

Reflection refers to light waves bouncing back, as when someone is looking in a mirror (B). The other answer choices are examples of refraction, or the bending of light. **Competency 044**

## 47. C

Visual coherence describes the overall unity of the way a visual representation is designed (C). The more unified it is, the more visually appealing it will be to the viewer. Choice (A) is incorrect because it describes visual impact. Choice (B) is incorrect because it is describing visual salience. Choice (D) is incorrect because it is describing organization of the design. **Competency 008**

## 48. B

*Marbury v. Madison* (B) established the process of judicial review in 1803. *Plessy v. Ferguson* (A) is incorrect because it established segregation via the separate but equal clause. The *Brown v. Board of Education of Topeka* case (C) is incorrect because it reversed the segregated conditions created by *Plessy v. Ferguson. Dred Scott v. Sandford*

(D) is incorrect because it dealt primarily with the issue of slavery and due process. **Competency 032**

### 49. B

Response (B), the beginning teacher understands the characteristics, distribution, and migration of populations in Texas and the United States, best describes the way in which the Farm Security Administration labor camp in Robstown, Texas, relates to the beginning teacher's knowledge of geography. There is no explicit detailing of culture exchange or stories, thus choices (B) and (C) are incorrect. Choice (D) is an incorrect choice because it relates primarily to physical geography and not migration patterns. **Competency 030**

### 50. D

The best price per square inch can be determined by dividing the price of each pizza by the area for each pizza. The formula for the area of a circle is $A = \pi r^2$, where $r$ is half the diameter.

| Pizza | Price per square inch |
|---|---|
| Mini | $\dfrac{\$3.49}{3^2\pi} = \$0.1234$ per square inch |
| Small | $\dfrac{\$8.99}{5^2\pi} = \$0.1145$ per square inch |
| Medium | $\dfrac{\$11.69}{6^2\pi} = \$0.1034$ per square inch |
| Large | $\dfrac{\$13.75}{7^2\pi} = \$0.0894$ per square inch |

The best price per square inch is the large pizza (D), which costs about $0.09 per square inch. **Competency 019**

### 51. A

When students make predictions, they need to use clues located and stated directly within the text, combined with their own background and prior knowledge, in order to form new ideas. Therefore, predicting and confirming those predictions is a type of inference (A) the reader makes while reading. **Competency 005**

### 52. C

Answers (A) and (B) are incorrect because no information was given about the values of any variables being positive or negative. Answer (D) is incorrect because if $a < b$ and $b = c$, then substituting $c$ for $b$ and gives $a < c$, proving the correct answer is (C). **Competency 024**

### 53. A

Water is a polar molecule; therefore, rather than having a straight surface when poured into a vessel such as a graduated cylinder, the water "adheres" to the sides, forming a downward arc or curve known as the meniscus, with the lowest point of this meniscus in the center. The lowest point of the meniscus is the proper measure of volume. It is also important to read the meniscus at eye level for accuracy. Choices (B) and (D) are incorrect because the water does not arc upward at all. Choice (C) is incorrect because only the water directly in contact with the sides clings to the walls of the graduated cylinder, and therefore is not a measure of the actual volume of water in the container. **Competency 037**

### 54. A

Choice (A) is correct because the definition of phonological awareness includes the broader auditory awareness of sound. The task of having students segment the sounds in words as an auditory task is included in the category of phonological awareness. Choice (B) is incorrect because it focuses on teaching concepts about print. Choice (C) is not correct because it is a listening comprehension task. Choice (D) is incorrect because sight vocabulary is a distinct part of the reading process separate from phonological awareness. **Competency 002**

## 55. C

The body undergoes a series of feedback mechanisms in response to cold and warm temperatures in an effort to maintain a constant internal temperature. This is critical in maintaining an internal stable condition, or homeostasis (C). These responses conserve energy when exposed to prolonged cold temperatures and release energy when exposed to prolonged warm temperatures. The mechanisms described in blood vessels constricting or dilating, the body shivering or perspiring, and numbness (indicating lack of blood flow to extremities to maintain warmth and blood flow to critical internal organs) or swelling of extremities (indicating blood going to extremities to cool critical internal organs) are responses to the body's efforts to maintain homeostasis. Choice (A) is incorrect because it describes processes that would be in opposition to maintaining homeostasis. Choice (B) is incorrect because it describes digestive processes that are not part of the scenario described in this item to maintain homeostasis. Choice (D) is incorrect because a blood cell imbalance will not cause the conditions described in the scenario. **Competency 049**

## 56. B

The "Matthew effect," a term coined by Keith Stanovich in 1986, describes how good readers who are able to process text with fluency and automaticity become better readers by virtue of these skills. In contrast, students who are already poor readers read less due to less automatic reading processes, and therefore are less likely to become better readers. **Competency 003**

## 57. A

When selecting a group of three queen cards at random from a standard deck, we are concerned only that three or four cards have been selected, and not about order. Since order does not matter in

combinations, there are clearly fewer combinations than permutations. The combinations are a subset of the permutations and are denoted by the top row of the chart below. Let $a$, $b$, $c$, and $d$ represent the four distinct queen cards.

| *abc* | *abd* | *acd* | *bcd* |
|-------|-------|-------|-------|
| *acb* | *adb* | *adc* | *bdc* |
| *bac* | *bad* | *cad* | *cbd* |
| *bca* | *bda* | *cda* | *cdb* |
| *cab* | *dab* | *dac* | *dbc* |
| *cba* | *dba* | *dca* | *dcb* |

Each column is 3! permutations of that combination, but they are all one combination because the order does not matter. Therefore, $_4C_3 = {_4}P_3 \div 3!$ or $\frac{4 \cdot 3 \cdot 2}{3 \cdot 2 \cdot 1} = 4$, or answer (A). **Competency 012**

## 58. B

Slavery arose in the southern colonies partly as an economic means to cultivate large plantations of cotton, tobacco, rice, indigo, and other crops (B). The inexpensive nature of slave labor allowed large-scale plantations to turn significant profits for agricultural production. Answer choice (A), increase slave owners' natural resources, is incorrect because slave labor was not a natural resource, but rather a labor resource. Slavery was certainly not a means to provide Africans with humanitarian aid of any sort (C). In fact, the treatment of slaves in the South was often inhumane. While the use of slave labor in the South did eventually help to provoke war with the northern colonies (D), this was certainly not the intent of southern colonists and was not an economic rationale. **Competency 031**

## 59. D

The correct answer is the burning of wood (D). When heat is given off in a chemical change, it is an exothermic reaction; conversely, when heat is absorbed in a chemical change (the combination becomes colder), it is an endothermic reaction. Examples of endothermic reactions include, for example, a cold pack or the combination of baking soda and vinegar. **Competency 045**

## 60.  D

Sustained silent reading (SSR) has a primary focus of developing comprehension and vocabulary as students are taught to self-select an appropriate text for their reading level, background knowledge, and interests. The process of wide reading promotes fluency, vocabulary, and comprehension development overall, provided the students select appropriate texts for themselves. The other answer choices, although helpful in creating successful readers, are not the *primary* goal of SSR. **Competency 003**

## 61.  B

The examples teachers provide in class should tap into the prior knowledge of students to help promote learning. In the examples given by Mr. Davis, only the prior knowledge of males in his class who have had these types of experiences was activated. Teachers must be careful not to use examples that appeal to only certain groups (e.g., gender, ethnicity), which marginalizes the rest of the students. Teachers must develop a wide range of examples to use in teaching that will address the interests of all students (B). Choices (A) and (D) address the issue of students needing hands-on, concrete, and inquiry-based experiences (rather than lecture explanations) to best learn science, so Mr. Davis is correct in using inquiry to introduce the topic. Choice (C) is incorrect because it is possible for cells to carry on certain types of respiration without the use of oxygen (e.g., anaerobic respiration and fermentation). **Competency 056**

## 62.  B

Expository text (B) is also known as informational text. It typically covers content areas such as science, social studies, math, health, and other core academic areas. Expository text is typically in the format of news stories, articles, biographies, textbooks, and magazine articles, among others, including online reading. Narrative writing (A) usually consists of story-like text, such as fiction. Choice (C) is a more specific type of expository text. Choice (D) is incorrect because it is not a broad category of informational text. **Competency 007**

## 63.  C

In a gibbous moon (C), one can see about three-fourths of the moon. A gibbous moon is typically referred to as either a waxing gibbous or a waning gibbous Moon. In a new moon phase (D), one cannot see the Moon from Earth because it is not being lit by the Sun. In a crescent moon phase (A), the shape appears to be like a banana. A blue moon (B) occurs when there are two full moons in one month. **Competency 054**

## 64.  C

The book at rest in this case has two opposite and equal forces, the normal or contact force and the force of gravity. If the other choices were true, then the book would not be at rest. **Competency 041**

## 65.  C

A seventh-grade teacher preparing class resources about how Texans have contributed to technology and society in the twenty-first century would want to use a variety of appropriate primary and secondary sources, such as photographs, biographies, interviews, and artifacts (C). When using maps, a teacher would want to include various maps and other graphics to present geographic, political, historical, economic, and cultural features, and distributions and relationships, as listed in response (B). However, maps are not the best tool for this type of investigation, so (B) is incorrect. Since textbooks are printed, they may not be up-to-date enough to include the most recent advances in science, technology, and society, so response (A) is also incorrect. Local newspapers are great resources; however, they may not cover the scope, breadth, and depth needed to research the given topic. Thus, (D) is also incorrect. **Competency 034**

## 66. A

Warm air rises, whereas cold air sinks. Therefore, warm moist air is forced upward when cold dry air mass moves into Texas. The warm, moist air quickly cools and loses its moisture in the form of precipitation. The movement of air masses often creates friction among air molecules, which results in lightning and thunder that may be severe, and may even give rise to tornadoes. Choice (B) is incorrect because cold air sinks, so it will not rise above a warm air mass. Choice (C) is incorrect because the air masses have different temperatures, water content, and, therefore, different air pressures; thus, they will not remain stationary. Choice (D) is incorrect because hurricanes originate over water, not over land. **Competency 053**

## 67. A

Choice (A) is the correct answer based on the definition of density = mass/volume (mass divided by volume). **Competency 042**

## 68. D

Choice (D) is correct because it shows the ways that a teacher can actively engage students in critical thinking about design features. Asking students to explain their thinking encourages them to externalize their thinking and also evaluate, judge, and critique their own work, drawing on higher orders of thinking. Choices (A) and (B) don't engage students in active learning and evaluation about their choices as much as choice (D) does. Choice (C) is incorrect because it doesn't focus specifically on the aspect of active discussion and higher-order thinking about design choices. **Competency 008**

## 69. A

The volume formula for any rectangular prism is $l \times w \times h$. Answer (A) is correct since 8 feet $\times$ 8 feet $\times$ 4 feet is 256 cubic feet. Answer (B) is incorrect strictly because the units are in inches and our problem specifies feet. Answer (C) is incorrect because the product of 8, 6, and 4 is not 256. Answer (D) is incorrect since there are only two equal dimensions, which would imply the figure is a square. **Competency 017**

## 70. B

The Articles of Confederation mention only the legislative branch (B) in the form of Congress. The judicial (A) and executive branches (C) were later outlined in the U.S. Constitution, but were not mentioned in the Articles of Confederation. The federal branch (D) is not a branch of government, and is thus incorrect. **Competency 029**

## 71. A

Kinetic energy refers to an object possessing energy because of its ability to move. A car that is moving (A) has kinetic energy. Choices (B), (C), and (D) are examples of potential energy, defined as energy an object has because of its position. **Competency 044**

## 72. A

By leaving strategic blanks throughout the reading passage, the reader draws upon semantic (meaning-based) and syntactic (grammar-based) clues to construct and problem solve about what the best possible choice for the missing word might be. Choice (B) is a metacognitive strategy that focuses on overall meaning, and choice (C) is focused more on individual words. Choice (D) is incorrect because the cloze passage is not intended to be a fluency-building activity. **Competency 004**

## 73. A

While the United Nations draft of Basic Principles and Guidelines on the Right to Remedy and Reparation suggested four forms of redress, including (1) restitution, (2) compensation, (3) rehabilitation, and (4) satisfaction, and guarantees of nonrepetition, the Civil Liberties Act of 1988, H.R. 442, offers only an apology and restitution. Thus, responses (B), (C), and (D) are incorrect. Answer (A), indicating a payment of $20,000, is correct. **Competency 033**

**74. D**

The writing process, although not always linear, generally is sequenced in the following steps: brainstorming, revising, editing, and publishing. Brainstorming is the beginning of the writing process. **Competency 007**

**75. B**

Investigate each table. Quadratic equations do not have a linear relationship; therefore, there is not a constant rate of change between the $y$- and $x$-values. Answer (B) is correct, because the table shows a linear relationship. The $y$-values increase by 3 units for every 1-unit increase in the $x$-values; hence, the slope of the linear equation is 3. In the table for option (A). The $y$-values increase by 1, 3 and 5; these are consecutive odd integers whose difference is 2 units. The table for answer (C) has increasing $y$-values by consecutive integers, 1, 2, and 3, which increase by 1 unit. The $y$-values for answer (D) increase by 3 then 1, then decrease by 1 unit; the difference between these differences is 2 units, so the table of values reflects quadratic function for (A), (C), and (D). **Competency 013**

**76. D**

Proteins are made of a chain of amino acid molecules (D) that are arranged in a particular order for that specific protein (for example, hormones, enzymes, hair, fingernails). There are 20 amino acids, arranged in a vast variety of sequences, with each sequence and shape that results being unique for that particular protein. Choice (A) is incorrect because a monosaccharide is the building block of

carbohydrates. Choices (B) and (C) are incorrect because these molecules are the components of lipids (fats). **Competency 046**

**77. B**

Prereading is designed to activate students' background and prior knowledge about a topic or theme(s) in a book prior to reading. Choice (B) best fosters this type of instructional goal. Through discussion, students can share background knowledge while also constructing and learning new concepts by listening to others' ideas. The teacher can support students' understanding by monitoring, facilitating, and contributing to the pre-reading conversation. Choice (A) doesn't allow students to share background knowledge in a collaborative way. Choice (C) is too teacher-centered and doesn't facilitate active learning on the part of the students surrounding schema building before reading. Choice (D) is similarly passive and doesn't activate the students' specific background knowledge and schema. **Competency 004**

**78. B**

In a regular pentagon, all interior angles are congruent. The total measure of all interior angles in a regular polygon is $(n - 2) \times 180°$. So the total for a pentagon is $3 \times 180° = 540°$, and each angle contains $540 \div 5 = 108°$. An alternative solution involves recognizing that if $F$ is the center of the pentagon, then $\angle EFG$ is 36 (one-tenth of a 360° rotation). Then, since $\angle FGE = 90°$, $\angle AEF$ is $180° - (36° + 90°) = 54°$ because the angles of $\triangle EFG$ must total 180°. Since $\overline{EF}$ must bisect $\angle AED$, $\angle AED = 2(54°). = 108°$. **Competency 020**

**79. A**

After the election of Abraham Lincoln, the Texas legislature held a special convention and voted to secede from the Union and join the Confederacy; thus, (A) is the correct response. Response (B) is incorrect because Texas relinquished all claims to New Mexico in 1850 in line with the terms of the Compromise of 1850. The annexation of Texas to the United States occurred two decades earlier in 1845, making response (C) incorrect. A delegation at Washington-on-the-Brazos adopted the Texas Declaration of Independence on March 2, 1836, creating the Republic of Texas. Thus, response (D) is also incorrect. **Competency 029**

## 80. C

Answer (C) is correct as it is 29% of the total monthly income of Diane and Liam: 0.29(650 + 730) = 400. Answer (A) is incorrect, as it reflects 29% of Diane's monthly income. Answer (B) is incorrect, as it reflects 29% of Liam's monthly income. Answer (D) is incorrect, as it reflects 30% of the total monthly income of Diane and Liam. **Competency 025**

## 81. C

The water in jar B will evaporate because it is exposed to the air, and so it will change to water vapor as a function of the water cycle. The water in jar A will remain relatively the same as when the experiment began because the water cannot escape the jar or evaporate due to the cover. So choice (C) is correct. Choice (A) is incorrect because there will be a difference in water levels in the two jars after several weeks. Choice (B) is incorrect because the water level will be higher in the covered jar, jar A, after several weeks. Choice (D) is incorrect because the water level in both jars will not be equal after several weeks of evaporation in jar B has taken place. **Competency 052**

## 82. C

The correct answer choice is (C) because hesitations and false starts may indicate stuttering and cluttering, which are speech and language issues. Choice (A) is incorrect because speaking in a different dialect is not an indication of a language deficiency. Choice (B) is incorrect be-

cause students who are native speakers from predominantly oral-based languages can still acquire English. Answer choice (D) is incorrect because code-switching between two languages can be a strength and is a normal part of the stages of second language acquisition. It is not an indication of language delay. **Competency 001**

## 83. B

Answer choice (B) is correct because it focuses on the curriculum-based content the students are performing on a regular basis. Because the science notebook contains understandings about related science content, and a rubric is used (informal assessment), it is best suited to assessing students' knowledge about scientific inquiry. For instance, students can describe what the lab process was like and what they did during the process, they can make predictions, and so forth. Answer choices (A), (C), and (D) are less authentic forms of assessment because they are based more on measuring student recall of knowledge rather than on their authentic understandings. **Competency 058**

## 84. A

Choice (A) is the correct answer because it is an example of how form (type of teeth) suggests function (meat eating). Choice (B) is not correct because, although the scientist comes with an explanation, the fossil is not a model. Choices (C) and (D) are unrelated to the concepts in the scenario. **Competency 040**

## 85. B

Article V of the Constitution outlines the procedures for amending the Constitution. First, an amendment must be proposed by a two-thirds majority of both houses of Congress (B). Then it must be passed to the state legislatures where three-quarters of the states are needed to ratify the amendment. Choices (A), (C), and (D) have no relation to the process of amending the Constitution. **Competency 032**

**86. C**

The word *bread* contains a vowel pair (vowel team) within the word. Students who are developmentally at the transitional stage of spelling (C) typically do not yet spell the within-word vowel pairs correctly. **Competency 006**

**87. D**

Rearrange the inequality into slope-intercept form, which identifies the slope of the line and the y-intercept: $2y + x \leq 5$ becomes $y \leq -\frac{1}{2}x + \frac{5}{2}$. Only the graphs for answers (B) and (D) have y-intercepts of 2.5 and slopes of $-\frac{1}{2}$; however, the shading is different among the two graphs. Answer (B) is incorrect because the shading occurs above the line of the inequality, which would imply $y \geq -\frac{1}{2}x + \frac{5}{2}$. Answer (D) is correct since the shading occurs below the line. Substituting a coordinate into the inequality can also verify how to shade the inequality. Choose a point not on the line drawn, say (0, 0). Substituting $x = 0$ and $y = 0$ into the original inequality yields $0 + 0 \leq 5$, which is a true statement, meaning the shaded region should cover the selected point. **Competency 014**

**88. A**

The purchasing power of money is most affected by inflation (A) or the general rise in the prices of goods and services. When prices rise due to inflation, the purchasing power of money decreases. Tax rates and interest rates are generally used to help correct inflation and do not directly change the amount of goods or services that can be purchased with a unit of currency, so (A) and (B) are incorrect. Choice (C) is incorrect because a person's debt does not affect the purchasing power of money, nor the goods and services

that can be purchased with one unit of currency. **Competency 031**

**89. C**

A gene (C) is the basic unit of inherited traits. Genes are made up of a particular sequence of DNA, and these genes carry out instructions to make proteins. These proteins may, for example, lay the foundation for traits such as eye color in the embryo or direct the production of enzymes (which are proteins) that digest certain foods. The basic unit of one DNA molecule—the nucleotide (A)—consists of the deoxyribose sugar, a phosphate group, and a nitrogen base. A gene is a sequence of DNA that may be between a few hundred to more than two million nucleotides long. Choice (B) is incorrect because the nucleolus is a specific region within the nucleus rather than a sequence of DNA. Choice (D) is incorrect because phenotype refers to the expressed physical characteristics of an organism as determined by genes. **Competency 047**

**90. C**

The U.S. Constitution divides power between the state and national government, (C) in what is referred to as federalism. There are powers that are specifically reserved for the federal government, powers specifically reserved for the state governments, and powers that are shared between the two. Thus, choices (A), (B), and (D) are incorrect. **Competency 032**

**91. D**

In the consolidated alphabetic stage, students understand and conceptualize that they can use parts of known words to decode unknown words (D). For instance, they can form new words by using onsets, rimes, and other letters. **Competency 002**

**92. C**

To find the total volume of a cone and a hemisphere, we need to know volume formulas for both solids. The TExES exam provides a definition and formula sheet, which is very helpful in solving this problem. The volume of a cone is $\frac{1}{3}$ (area of the base) $\times$ height. Since the cone is created by a circular base, the area of the base is $\pi r^2$; so $V = \frac{1}{3}\pi(1.5)^2 \times 4 \approx 9.42$. A hemisphere is half of a sphere. The volume formula of a sphere is $\frac{4}{3}\pi r^3$, and the volume of a hemisphere is $\frac{1}{2}\cdot\frac{4}{3}\pi r^3$; so $V = \frac{1}{2}\cdot\frac{4}{3}\pi(1.5)^3 \approx 7.07$. Next, combine the volumes from the cone and hemisphere to obtain approximately 16.49 cubic inches, or answer (C). **Competency 017**

**93. C**

A running record (C) is an informal assessment tool used to assess a student's word identification skills, accuracy, and use of problem solving in the decoding process of oral reading. In a running record, the teacher uses a blank page or a copy of the text to mark each word the child mispronounces as the teacher listens to a student read a text. A running record can give insight for the teacher into the student's problem-solving processes as the student reads aloud. The teacher can analyze and categorize the patterns in the types of miscues the student makes. Choice (A) is incorrect because it is meant to measure rate of reading, which is primarily an aspect of fluency. Choice (B) is incorrect because it primarily measures comprehension and recall. Choice (D) is incorrect because it focuses primarily on measuring comprehension. **Competency 002**

**94. D**

Density is the amount of matter (mass) packed into a given amount of space (volume), and is measured by determining the mass of a substance divided by its volume, or density = mass/volume (D = M/V). To measure the density of an irregularly shaped object such as a rock, the proper instruments are a balance to measure mass and a graduated cylinder with water to measure volume. The triple beam or electronic balance will provide the mass of the rock in grams. The volume of the irregularly shaped rock is obtained by filling a graduated cylinder one-half to two-thirds with water. The level of water in the graduated cylinder in milliliters is recorded. The rock is carefully dropped into the graduated cylinder, and the change in the level of water in milliliters is measured, or the amount of water that was "displaced" by the rock. One milliliter (liquid volume measure) is equal to one cubic centimeter (solid volume measure); thus, the change in water level after adding the rock is the volume of the rock. These values are then used in the formula (D = M/V) to determine the rock's density. Choices (A), (B), and (C) are not the proper instruments to use in determining an irregularly shaped object's density. A beaker does not provide a precise enough measure of the amount of water displaced, or the volume of the rock. A measuring tape is not accurate for determining the volume of an irregularly shaped object. The proper determination of density requires the use of instruments that will measure the volume and the mass of the object. **Competency 057**

**95. B**

All of the people featured in the answer choices are Texas leaders in science, technology, and society, but only Benjy Brooks (B) is known for her medical contributions. Brooks is known for her research on congenital defects, burn treatment, spleen reparation, and the prevention of hepatitis. Michael Dell contributed to science, technology, and society in the computer industry, which makes (A) incorrect. Walter Cunningham was NASA's second civilian astronaut, a fighter pilot, and a retired military physicist, making response (C) incorrect. Howard Hughes Sr. advanced science, technology, and society by designing a drill bit that could drill through hard rock, so answer (D) is also incorrect. **Competency 033**

## 96. B

A normal curve is symmetrical, with the line of symmetry passing through the mean, median, and mode of the data. It is easy to see that this line represents a higher test score for class 2 compared to class 1, meaning a higher mean, median, and mode, so answer (B) is correct. Answer (A) is incorrect since the line of symmetry for the normal curve of class 1 is to the left of (less than) the line of symmetry for the normal curve of class 2. Answer (C) is incorrect since the mode for class 1 is less than that for class 2. Answer (D) is incorrect since the heights and dispersion of the normal curves are different, showing the standard deviation of both data sets are not equal. **Competency 021**

## 97. B

Mood or expression is also known as tone (B). Style (A) is the author's overall word choice and personal voice used when writing. Choice (C) is incorrect because plot focuses more on an overall summary of the story's main events and ideas. Setting (D) includes the location and time era of the story. **Competency 005**

## 98. B

The number of members in the U.S. House of Representatives (B) is adjusted to reflect a proportion of the total U.S. population; thus, when there is a census, this proportion is subject to change. Choices (A), (C), and (D) are incorrect because population changes do not affect the composition of the Senate, Supreme Court, or the Federal Reserve. **Competency 032**

## 99. A

Choice (A) is correct because it directly and explicitly teaches students how to use an editing checklist by demonstrating it with an actual example of writing (e.g., the teacher's own writing). Choice (B) is incorrect because it doesn't directly teach students how to use and apply the actual editing checklist in their own practice. Choice (C) is incorrect because the suggestion that the checklist is useful doesn't offer to students advice on the procedure of *how* to use it. Choice (D) focuses more on the beginning of the composition process rather than the editing process itself. **Competency 006**

## 100. B

In reader's theater (B), students rehearse their reading part and then create a theater format to present the reading. Through repeated reading, the students are building fluency. Choice (A) is incorrect because it focuses on comprehension and not on fluency development. Choice (C) also has a strong comprehension focus. Choice (D) is an assessment tool used to measure comprehension and decoding, and is therefore incorrect. **Competency 003**

## 101. D

When a constant is added or subtracted within a function, $f(x \pm c)$, the graph is shifted horizontally. . When a value is added or subtracted outside of a function, $f(x) = x^2 \pm c$ the graph is translated vertically. When a constant is added within a function, the graph is shifted horizontally to the left, whereas when a constant is subtracted within the function, the graph is shifted horizontally to the right. Answer (D) is correct since 3 is being subtracted within the function. Answers (B) and (C) are incorrect because the new function is adding or subtracting 3 to the outside of the parent function. Answer (A) is incorrect since 3 is being added within the function. **Competency 015**

## 102. C

Reflecting triangle *ABC* across the line $x = 1$ will preserve the *y*-values of each point, but will change the *x*-values. Point *B* is at $(0, -1)$, and after the reflection across $x = 1$, $B'$ will be at (2, –1). The correct answer is (C).

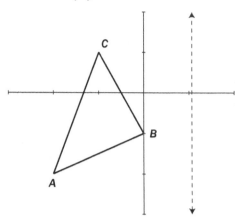

**Competency 020**

**103. D**

The writing traits each have a distinct focus in helping students to improve their composing process. The trait of voice (D) focuses on the writer's individual style and uniqueness. The other writing traits have a distinct focus other than devloping individual style. **Competency 007**

**104. C**

In 1830, just one year after taking office, Andrew Jackson (C) pushed the Indian Removal Act through both houses of Congress. This act gave the president power to negotiate removal treaties with Indian tribes living east of the Mississippi. Under these treaties, the Indians were to give up their lands east of the Mississippi in exchange for lands to the west. Those wishing to remain in the east would become citizens of their home states. The removal was supposed to be voluntary and peaceful, but for several tribes, such as the Cherokee, the removal was not peaceful and led to the Trail of Tears. Abraham Lincoln (A) is incorrect because he was president nearly 30 years after the Indian Removal Act was passed. James Monroe (B) is incorrect because he was president from 1817 to 1825 and was most well known for the Monroe Doctrine. James Madison (D) is also incorrect be-cause Madison was the fourth U.S. president, from 1809 to 1817, and was most notable for his work on the U.S. Constitution. **Competency 029**

**105. D**

Answers (A), (B), and (C) are all true statements about the box-and-whisker plot presented. The false statement with respect to the graph is answer (D), the interquartile range is 5.8 – 5.2 = 0.6 and not 0.5. The correct answer is (D). **Competency 021**

**106. A**

A Venn diagram is designed to organize ideas, words, concepts, or terms that compare and contrast (A). It is ideal for comparing ideas across two texts. The other choices do not illustrate the primary use of a Venn diagram and would be better suited to other types of graphic organizers or study aides. **Competency 009**

**107. C**

Story grammar (C) focuses on identifying and describing the common elements of fictional text, such as characters, plot, setting, problem, and solution. Teachers can develop story grammar by using graphic organizers and having students name and identify the different features of the story grammar present in the text. Choices (A), (B), and (D) focus more broadly on general comprehension development, including the main idea, whereas choice (C) focuses primarily on the structural elements specific to fictional text. **Competency 004**

**108. C**

Answer (C) is correct. The measures of $\angle 1$ and $\angle 4$ are congruent since by definition they are alternate exterior angles. The other noted angles, $\angle 2$, $\angle 3$, and $\angle 5$, are all congruent to each other and are supplementary to $\angle 1$ and $\angle 4$. **Competency 018**

**109. D**

Expository text, or informational text, often contains denser and more conceptually challenging ideas than encountered in narrative text. Therefore, students need to be taught to read this text more slowly so they can fully understand and monitor their own understanding about these denser ideas. Choice (D) has the broadest application of use to the specific reading of expository text in particular (given the text demands), whereas the other choices focus more on overall vocabulary and comprehension development. They are more instructional activities that could be used as follow-up seat work to develop comprehension. **Competency 005**

**110. C**

Information about social studies is available from the Internet; however, students need to evaluate the scholarship of the many sources available and use only those known to be reliable and credible. Thus, response (C) is correct. The Internet contains a multitude of primary and secondary sources, both of which can be appropriate for 4–8 classrooms. This makes responses (A) and (D) incorrect. Although textbooks can be excellent resources, the Internet often is used to supplement what may not be included in a textbook; thus, (B) is also incorrect. **Competency 034**

**111. B**

The study of morphology means the study of morphemes and their function in words, vocabulary, and reading. Morphemes are the smallest units of meaning in a word. Examples of morphemes include prefixes (such as *re-* or *un-*) and suffixes (such as *–ed* or *–s*) that can change the meaning of a word. By drawing students' attention to morphemes through the study of morphology, students can consider word meaning and, hence, their vocabulary. Choice (A) focuses on broader comprehension development; choice (C) focuses on grammar of the entire sentence, which is not the focus of morphology; and choice (D) has an overall comprehension focus. **Competency 003**

**112. D**

The new wall Jacqueline will paint is 10 feet wider than the wall that she could paint in 25 minutes. The area of the first wall is 800 square feet, and the area of the second wall is 1200 square feet. A proportion can be used to determine the amount of time Jacqueline will take to paint the second wall. The proportion below shows the amount of time it takes per square foot.

$$\frac{25 \text{ min}}{800 \text{ ft}^2} = \frac{x \text{ min}}{1200 \text{ ft}^2}$$

1200 square feet is 1.5 times greater than 800 square feet. Therefore, the amount of time to paint the second wall should be 1.5 times the 25 minutes to paint the first wall: $25 \times 1.5 = 37.5$ minutes. Another common way to solve a proportion is to compute cross products or cross multiplication, where we obtain $x = \left(\frac{25}{800}\right)(1200) = 3$ minutes, or answer choice (D). **Competency 015**

**113. A**

Rereading (A) is a common and widely used comprehension "fix-up" strategy that can be taught to students to help them when their comprehension is breaking down while reading. When students reread, they have another "chance" to repair or gain access to the meaning of the text. Choices (B), (C), and (D) all focus on higher-order thinking skills that first assume the reader has a good literal understanding of the text. Rereading is more effective in terms of repairing or fixing comprehension at a more basic level. **Competency 005**

**114. B**

Although some fields claim to be "scientific," they are actually pseudoscience (not authentic or sincere, in spite of appearances; not genuine). Science is based on rigorous controls of variables, repeated experimentation, and strong evidence before it is accepted by the scientific community. The areas described, including, but not limited to astrology, fortune telling, and tarot cards, do not have evidence to support claims made (B), and thus are considered pseudoscience by the scientific community. Choices (A), (C), and (D) are incorrect because the information described does not adhere to the rigor of science. **Competency 039**

## 115. B

The figure representing the equation; $3x + 2 = 2x + 6$ can be solved by crossing out like pieces from both sides of the equation, this is modeled below. The result shows $x = 4$, which is answer (B).

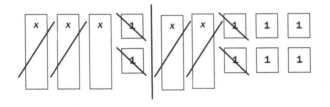

**Competency 026**

## 116. D

The First Amendment to the Constitution reads, "Congress shall make no law respecting an establishment of religion, or prohibiting the free exercise thereof; or abridging the freedom of speech [choice (B)] , or of the press; or of the right of the people to assemble peaceably [choice (A)], and to petition the government for a redress of grievances" [choice (C)]. Protection against unreasonable search and seizure (D) is a constitutional right found in the Fourth Amendment, and thus is the correct choice. **Competency 032**

## 117. A

A directed reading—thinking activity (A) is a strategy by which the teacher guides read-ing through either an expository or narrative text. Choice (B) is incorrect because KWL is primarily used as a before-during-after method to guide students through a text by connecting to background knowledge, question generation, and summarization of main ideas. Choice (C) is incorrect because it is focused on acquisition of phonics knowledge. Choice (D) is incorrect because it is focused primarily on the auditory process of hearing sounds. **Competency 009**

## 118. C

Choice (C) is the correct answer by definition. Choice (A) is missing direction, which is necessary since velocity is a vector. Choices (B) and (D) are incorrect based on Newton's second law, $F = ma$, or acceleration is equal to force divided by mass. **Competency 041**

## 119. A

Choice (A) is correct because it directly models fluent and expressive reading. Such modeling, when done well, is directly beneficial to all students. Some students may not hear fluent readers often, or they are not yet fluent readers themselves and benefit from such modeling of intonation, pitch, and expression. The other answer choices are too broad and general to have a specific focus on developing the expressive aspect of fluency development. **Competency 003**

## 120. D

Earth's surface or lithosphere consists of huge plates, like puzzle pieces, that move over the layer beneath, known as the asthenosphere, in a process known as plate tectonics. When two of Earth's giant plates collide, typically one plate rises upward and gradually forms a mountain range. An example is the Andes Mountain range along the coast of South America. Choices (A) and (B) are incorrect because the plates will not form a canyon or a river, and canyons are formed by rivers. Choice (C) is incorrect because hot spots, such as the Hawaiian Island chain, are found in the middle of a plate and not along the edge. They are caused by a break or opening in the center of the plate that allows hot magma to flow out and upwards, as in the volcano that is continuously erupting within this island chain. **Competency 051**

**121. A**

The Atakapans and Karankawas lived in the coastal areas of present-day Texas. They consumed bear and deer from the land as well as alligators, oysters, clams, ducks, and turtles (A). It was the Caddo, in present-day eastern Texas, who grew and consumed beans, squash, and sunflowers along with eating bear, deer, and occasionally buffalo, so (B) is an incorrect response. Choice (C) is also incorrect. The Tonkawas inhabited the central regions of present-day Texas and typically ate bison, fish, turtles, crawfish, snails, pecans, acorns, wild fruits, rattlesnakes, and rabbits, so (D) is also incorrect. **Competency 033**

**122. B**

A common practice to teach writing conventions in classrooms is to display or distribute sentences with errors in them. Students then fix the errors, and the corrections and reasons for making the corrections are discussed as a class. This is a teaching technique that can help students with identifying correct writing conventions (B). Choice (A) is incorrect because students don't always apply these skills to their actual compositions and this transfer can't always be assumed (as is the case with spelling instruction). Similarly, choices (C) and (D) are incorrect because, although students may be able to identify incorrect writing conventions, the answer choices incorrectly assume students will be able to transfer the knowledge of conventions to improvement in composing writing in general. **Competency 006**

**123. B**

All investigations are guided by the question asked, so (B) is the correct answer. Descriptive investigations may not have hypotheses or controls (choices (A) and (D)). And, an "educated guess" (C) leads no investigations. In fact, using this term with students diminishes the role of rational, logical thinking in scientific endeavors. **Competency 038**

**124. A**

Choice (A) is correct because homonyms are words that have the same sound and the same spelling but differ in their meaning. The word *club* can have more than one meaning, depending on the part of speech and how it is used in the context of a sentence. Choice (B) is a homophone; choice (C) is not a homonym; choice (D) is also a homophone. A homophone is a word that sounds the same as another word but is spelled differently and has a different meaning. **Competency 003**

**125. A**

Quantities vary inversely if they are associated by the relationship $y = \dfrac{k}{x}$. Another way to express that relationship is $xy = k$. We can also say, $y$ varies inversely with $x$. In this problem, the demand, $D$, is our $y$ variable, and the price $p$, is our $x$ variable. We are looking for the constant of proportionality, $k$: $D = \dfrac{k}{p}$ or $100 = \dfrac{k}{2,050}$, so $k = 205,000$, which is answer (A). **Competency 015**

**126. D**

From 1836 to 1845, Texas functioned as its own independent nation, known as the Republic of Texas (D). In 1836, following the Texas Revolution, Texas declared independence from functioning as a Mexican state (B). Prior to being a Mexican state, the territory of Texas was under Spanish control, but in 1821, Mexico won independence from Spain, so answer choice (C) a Spanish territory, is incorrect. Answer choice (A) is incorrect because Texas did not become a state in the Union until 1845. **Competency 032**

**127. C**

Transitions (C) are specific words that increase the coherence of writing and are known as *connecting discourse*. Examples include *therefore, however*, and sequence words such as *first, next,* and *then*. Choice (A) focuses on word parts (prefixes, suffixes, roots); choice (B) focuses on parts of sentences; and choice (D) focuses on the overall broader skills of using writing mechanics correctly. **Competency 006**

**128. C**

A consonant digraph is defined as a letter-sound combination where two consonant letters together represent one sound. Examples include: *ph*, *sh*, *wh*, *th*, and *ch*, as in choice (C). Choice (B) contains the consonant blend "tr"; choice (A) contains a silent consonant combination ("gn"); and choice (D) is a silent-*e* word. **Competency 002**

**129. D**

Answer (D) is correct because students who practice reciprocal teaching engage in the four "jobs," or roles, described in the test question. Answer (A) is incorrect because thinking aloud is primarily an individual, cognitive task. Answer (B), role play, is incorrect because students are not enacting a scene or scenario from the text; rather, they are discussing the content using the four roles. Answer (C) is incorrect because literature circles, while promoting group discussion about a text, are done in a wider variety of ways than described in this scenario. Literature circles also typically focus on the more open-ended responses of the reader. **Competency 005**

**130. C**

Dolores Huerta (C) is a noted labor union activist who played a significant role in the Chicano civil rights movement of the 1960s by fighting for better working conditions and fair compensation for farm workers. Rosa Parks (A) was a civil rights activist primarily known for starting the Montgomery bus boycott for refusing to give up her seat to a white man. Martha Cotera (B) is also a Chicana civil rights activist and writer, but her efforts focused primarily around organizing the 1969 Crystal City walkouts that protested the exclusion of Mexican Americans in political representation. Ida B. Wells (D), who was born into slavery, became a fierce antilynching and women's suffrage activist and established several nineteenth century women's organizations. **Competency 029**

# INDEX

# NOTES

# NOTES

# NOTES

# NOTES